P9-EKT-817

LIBRARY

# MASTERPIECES OF THE MODERN THEATRE

## A NINE VOLUME SET EDITED BY ROBERT W. CORRIGAN

**CENTRAL EUROPEAN THEATRE** / *The Game of Love* and *La Ronde* Schnitzler / *Electra* Hofmannsthal / *R.U.R.* Čapek / *The Play's the Thing* Molnár

**ENGLISH THEATRE** / *The Importance of Being Earnest* Wilde / *Major Barbara* Shaw / *Loyalties* Galsworthy / *Dear Brutus* Barrie / *Enter Solly Gold* Kops

**FRENCH THEATRE** / *The Parisian Woman* Becque / *Christopher Columbus* de Ghelderode / *Electra* Giraudoux / *Eurydice (Legend of Lovers)* Anouilh / *Queen After Death* Montherlant / *Improvisation or The Shepherd's Chameleon* Ionesco

**GERMAN THEATRE** / *Woyzeck* Buechner / *Maria Magdalena* Hebbel / *The Weavers* Hauptmann / *The Marquis of Keith* Wedekind / *The Caucasian Chalk Circle* Brecht

**IRISH THEATRE** / *The Countess Cathleen* Yeats / *The Playboy of the Western World* and *Riders to the Sea* Synge / *The Silver Tassie* and *Cock-a-Doodle Dandy* O'Casey

**ITALIAN THEATRE** / *Six Characters in Search of an Author* and *The Pleasure of Honesty* Pirandello / *Crime on Goat Island* Betti / *Filumena Marturano* Filippo / *The Academy* and *The Return* Fratti

**RUSSIAN THEATRE** / *A Month in the Country* Turgenev / *Uncle Vanya* and *The Cherry Orchard* Chekhov / *The Lower Depths* Gorky / *The Bedbug* Mayakovsky

**SCANDINAVIAN THEATRE** / *Hedda Gabler* Ibsen / *Miss Julie* and *The Ghost Sonata* Strindberg / *The Difficult Hour* Lagerkvist / *The Defeat* Grieg / *Anna Sophie Hedvig* Abell

**SPANISH THEATRE** / *The Witches' Sabbath* Benavente / *The Cradle Song* Martínez-Sierra / *The Love of Don Perlimplín and Belisa in the Garden* Lorca / *The Dream Weaver* Vallejo Buero / *Death Thrust* Sastre

LIBRARY

# MASTERPIECES OF THE MODERN ENGLISH THEATRE

+++

Edited by ROBERT W. CORRIGAN

## FIVE PLAYS

**THE IMPORTANCE OF BEING EARNEST**

**MAJOR BARBARA**

**LOYALTIES**

**DEAR BRUTUS**

**ENTER SOLLY GOLD**

COLLIER BOOKS, NEW YORK

```
LIBRARY

MAY  3 1976

UNIVERSITY OF THE PACIFIC
```

317006

COPYRIGHT © 1967 by The Macmillan Company

All rights reserved. No part of this book may be reproduced o
transmitted in any form or by any means, electronic or mechanica
including photocopying, recording or by any information storag
and retrieval system, without permission in writing from th
Publisher.

Library of Congress Catalog Card Number: 66–28635

FIRST COLLIER BOOKS EDITION 1967

*The Macmillan Company, New York*

Printed in the United States of America

CAUTION: Professionals and amateurs are hereby warned that al
the plays in this volume, being fully protected under the copyrigh
laws of the United States of America, the British Empire, includin
the Dominion of Canada, and all other countries of the Berne an
Universal Copyright Conventions, are subject to royalty. These play
are for the reading public only, and all performance rights, includin
professional, amateur, motion picture, recitation, lecturing, publi
reading, radio and television broadcasting, and the rights of transla
tion into foreign languages, are strictly reserved. Inquiries concern
ing these rights should be addressed to the author or agent name
in the acknowledgments appearing on the title page of each play
All other inquiries should be addressed to the publishers named

Grateful acknowledgment is hereby made to The Macmillan Compan
for permission to reprint material from *The Modern Theatre*, edite
by Robert W. Corrigan. Copyright © by Robert W. Corrigan, 1964

# CONTENTS

*The Modern British Theatre and the Wide Embrace*    7

*Introduction: Masters of the Modern Theatre*    11

OSCAR WILDE    33
    *"Excerpts from Oscar Wilde"*    35
    THE IMPORTANCE OF BEING EARNEST    45

GEORGE BERNARD SHAW    109
    *"Letters to Louis Calvert on Playing Undershaft"*    111
    MAJOR BARBARA    115

JOHN GALSWORTHY    211
    *"Some Platitudes Concerning Drama"*    213
    LOYALTIES    221

JAMES M. BARRIE    293
    *"To the Critics' Circle"*    295
    DEAR BRUTUS    303

BERNARD KOPS    371
    *"Letters to a Director"*    373
    ENTER SOLLY GOLD    379

*The Writers and Their Plays*    473

*Selected Bibliography*    475

# THE
## MODERN BRITISH THEATRE AND THE WIDE EMBRACE

by Robert W. Corrigan

IT IS SOMEWHAT disturbing to realize that it is possible to trace the development of the British drama in the twentieth century by dividing it into three distinct periods, and not be too guilty of either journalistic inaccuracy or pedantic over-simplification. After the bright, brief, and inimitable burst of Oscar Wilde in the nineties, the next thirty years were pretty much dominated by Shaw; the following twenty-five can only be described as a fallow period; and finally, beginning with the opening of John Osborne's *Look Back in Anger* in May of 1956, the British theatre moved into what has come to be known as the "anger" period, a time which many commentators have hailed as the renaissance of the British theatre. Of course, one no sooner sets up such tidy divisions, and all of their limitations and exceptions become immediately apparent. For instance, what about the plays of Barrie, Galsworthy, and Maugham? Can writers like Eliot, Coward, Rattigan, and Fry be glibly dismissed as so much alfalfa? Despite the critics' rage for order, no one could place playwrights as diverse in tone, style, and attitude as Osborne, Pinter, Bolt, Arden, Whiting, Wesker, Simpson, and Bernard Kops under the banner of the "angry generation." While such observations are valid, I nonetheless believe these three divisions still describe the main lines of development of the British theatre in our century.

Certainly no twentieth-century British playwright has achieved a stature comparable to Shaw's, and those writing while G.B.S. was at his dramatic best seem like midgets by comparison. The great gulf between Shaw and Barrie and Galsworthy, the other major dramatists of the first quarter of the century, becomes immediately apparent when we remember that Shaw's *Man and Superman* and Barrie's *The Admirable Crichton* were both completed in 1903, or recall that Galsworthy's *Loyalties* and Shaw's *Back to Methusaleh* were first produced in 1922, and that his *Saint Joan* came a year later.

Some people may well protest that to describe the years from 1930 to 1956 as a dormant period in the drama is to be too harsh, if not completely wrong-headed. But today, even the greatest achievements of those years seem either to have lost much of their lustre or to remain isolated monuments which were never repeated and which had little or no influence over the succeeding generation of playwrights. *Murder in the Cathedral* (1935) is a great play, but even Eliot himself considered it a museum piece, and his later plays had, at best, only partial success in the theatre, and failed to match the first in language, design, or dramatic impact. Priestley is now hopelessly out of date. We still enjoy Noel Coward's delightful, quick, almost parthenogenetic wit, but his plays are essentially a part of the century-old tradition of English drawing-room comedy. This is a noble tradition and not to be slighted, but Coward has certainly not brought anything new into the English theatre. I, for one, had great hopes that Christopher Fry would be instrumental in revitalizing the British drama. *The Lady's Not for Burning* and *A Sleep of Prisoners* have admirable qualities, and the latter still ranks as one of the most important plays written in England since the Second World War. But Fry has never been able to subordinate his undisputed lyric powers to the service of a dramatic action, and it is probably significant that in recent years he has been more successful as a translator than as a playwright in his own name. As for Terence Rattigan, there is no doubt that he is a master craftsman, and plays such as *The Winslow Boy* and *Separate Tables* were, and will continue to be, a staple in the commercial theatre. But Rattigan has not led the theatre in any new directions, nor do we expect him to. Each of these writers—not to mention others active during this period—has a record of solid achievement in the theatre but lacked the sustained creativity and vital inventiveness (characteristics which Eliot had as a poet) which make the theatre come alive and become a meaningful force in the cultural life of a nation or the world.

Then, in the mid-1950's, something new began to happen in the English theatre. Playwrights popped up everywhere, and their plays were so different in tone, theme, and form that the change could be described only as revolutionary. Interestingly enough, it was Kenneth Tynan who was to become the spokesman-critic of the new breed, who chronicled the mid-century death and rebirth of the London stage. Within the same month he reviewed the opening of Enid Bagnold's *The Chalk Garden* (which was, significantly, first produced in New York) and John Osborne's *Look Back in Anger*. Of the former, he wrote:

On Wednesday night a wonder happened: the West End theatre justified its existence. One had thought it an anachronism, wilfully preserving a formal, patrician acting style for which the modern drama had no use, a style as remote from reality as a troop of cavalry in an age of turbo-jets. One was shamefully wrong. On Wednesday night, superbly caparisoned, the cavalry went into action and gave a display of theatrical equitation which silenced all grumblers. This engagement completed, the brigade may have to be disbanded. But at least it went out with a flourish, its banners resplendent in the last rays of the sun.

Ten days later he was to write:

*Look Back in Anger* is likely to remain a minority taste. What matters, however, is the size of the minority. I estimate it at roughly 6,733,000, which is the number of people in this country between the ages of twenty and thirty. And this figure will doubtless be swelled by refugees from other age-groups who are curious to know precisely what the contemporary young pup is thinking and feeling. I doubt if I could love anyone who did not wish to see *Look Back in Anger*. It is the best young play of its decade.

As Tynan predicted, this minority was important, and within four years London had become the most vital center of the theatre in the world. There have been many attempts to explain why this radical change took place: the emergence of the lower-middle class as a political force, the changes made in British life by the postwar Labour government, the effect of national television, the rise of Joan Littlewood as a dominant force in the English theatre. All of these explanations are at least partially true, but the more important fact remains: England once again had a theatre! Osborne was soon followed by Behan (Irish, but first produced by Littlewood at the Royal Court), Delaney, Pinter, Wesker, Kops, Arden, Bolt, a new John Whiting, Simpson, and most recently Ann Jellicoe and Peter Shaffer. Now, no one will ever try to argue that all of these playwrights are alike or are members of some "new school" of the theatre. But what links writers as different as N. F. Simpson and Robert Bolt, to say nothing of John Whiting and Bernard Kops, is their willingness to try new things in the theatre. At first glance, *A Man for All Seasons* seems like a traditional British play in the heroic mode of the old dispensation. But as his Preface makes clear, Bolt is approaching his subject in a totally new way (for one thing, the influence of Brecht is readily apparent), with the result that the play's form and meaning have a quality of forcefulness which this kind of play had been lacking for so long. It is a willingness to try new things, and the insistence that the theatre must deal with new subjects if it is to be relevant to its audiences, that characterizes the drama of "Anger and After." We are still too close to this theatre to judge its accomplishments adequately, but of the fact that it is different, there can be no doubt.

It appears, then, that the traditions of the British theatre are once again enlarging. The dramas of the French court provided the impetus for the Restoration theatre. This theatre produced its first fruit with the plays of Congreve and Wycherley, and its spirit has, from that time forward, continued to assert itself in the work of playwrights so diverse as Sheridan, Wilde, Maugham, Coward, and more recently Enid Bagnold and Graham Greene. In the nineties, Shaw, under the profound influence of Ibsen, began to infuse this tradition with the qualities of social urgency and a more direct kind of moral awareness. And, now, the theatre is beginning to move in new directions—directions dictated by the emergence of the lower classes as the new leaders of Britain's theatres. But if the past means anything, we can be pretty sure that these new forces will also be assimilated into the mainstream. They may give the stream some new twists and turns, but absorbed they will be. From the days of Shakespeare's Globe, the Thames has had a wide embrace.

# MASTERS OF THE
# MODERN THEATRE

## By Robert W. Corrigan

After visiting the United States in 1835, Alexis de Tocqueville described the kind of literature he believed an industrialized democratic society would produce. "I am persuaded," he wrote in *Democracy in America,* "that in the end democracy diverts the imagination from all that is external to man and fixes it on man alone. . . . It may be foreseen in like manner that poets living in democratic times will prefer the delineation of passions and ideas to that of persons and achievements. The language, the dress, and the daily actions of men in democracies are repugnant to conceptions of the ideal. . . . This forces the poet constantly to search below the external surface which is palpable to the senses, in order to read the inner soul. . . . The destinies of mankind, man himself taken aloof from his country, and his age, and standing in the presence of Nature and of God, with his passions, his doubts, his rare prosperities and inconceivable wretchedness, will become the chief, if not the sole theme of poetry." Any examination of the arts of the past century would seem to indicate that Tocqueville's prophecy has been fulfilled, and it is certainly clear that the theatre's general pattern of development during this time can be best described as a gradual but steady shift away from universal philosophical and social concerns toward the crises and conflicts of man's inner and private life. It is possible to discover foreshadowings of this change in direction and emphasis in the plays of the early nineteenth-century romantics—Buechner, Hebbel, Kleist, Gogol, Musset—but it was not until Ibsen that the theatre's revolutionary break with the past became clearly discernible. In fact, Ibsen's career as a playwright to a large extent parallels both in form and in theme the modern drama's increasing tendency to be concerned more with the conflicts of the individual's interior world than with the significance of his public deeds.

The causes of any revolution are always as difficult to untangle as its consequences are to assess, and any attempt on the part of the critic to describe them will inevitably result in oversimplification. But it is possible to discover certain basic changes in attitude which had been evolving in Europe since the time of Luther and which had begun to crystallize in Continental thought by the second half of the nineteenth century. And the works of the revolutionary playwrights—Ibsen, Strindberg, Chekhov, Shaw, and Hauptmann —were the first to express in the theatre certain of these radical shifts in the way man had come to think of nature, society, and himself. What follows is an attempt to set forth briefly some of the more important aspects of this revolution in the drama which Ibsen referred to as "a war to the knife with the past."

One of the dominant ideas of the modern *Weltanschauung* is the belief that it is impossible to know what the world is really like. Beginning with Luther's refusal to accept that there was any intelligible relationship between faith and works, the sacramental view of experience gradually disappeared. In rejecting the phenomenal world as an outward and visible manifestation of man's spiritual condition, Luther began a revolution in thought which, because of the achievements of science and technology in the past two hundred years, now makes it impossible for man to attach any objective value to the observations of his senses. This insistence on such a clear-cut division between the physical and the spiritual aspects of reality had a profound effect on the modern dramatist. Inevitably, it made him increasingly distrustful of his sensory responses to the "outside" world, and at the same time it tended to negate whatever belief he might have had in the objective validity of his subjective feelings and sensations. The modern artist no longer holds a mirror up to nature, at least not with any confidence; he can only stare at his own image. He becomes a voyeur to his own existence.

Probably no force in the nineteenth century did more to destroy man's belief in an established norm of human nature, and hence begin this process of internalization in the theatre, than the advent of psychology as a systematized field of study. In his book *"Modernism" in The Modern Drama*, Joseph Wood Krutch argued that the basic issue confronting all the dramatists of the past hundred years was the problem of "modernism." Briefly, modernism involves both the conviction and the practice that to be modern is to be, in many important ways, different from anyone who lived before. This does not mean that man has changed; human nature is the same, but man's way of looking at himself has changed significantly. It is this new view of man that creates the problem for the dramatist.

Good examples of this changed perception can be found in Ibsen's *Hedda Gabler* (1890) and Strindberg's *Miss Julie* (1888). Hedda and Julie have the distinction of being the first fully and consciously developed neurotic heroines in dramatic literature. By neurotic we mean that they are neither logical nor insane (in the sense of being random and unaccountable) but that the aims and motives of each has a secret personal logic of their own. The significant thing about both characters is that they are motivated on the premise that there is a secret, and sometimes unconscious, world of aims and methods, a secret system of values which is more important in human experience than rational ones. This approach to character is not, however, the same as the Romantic attitude which affirms the superior validity of the nonrational. We need only read Strindberg's famous Preface to *Miss Julie* or Ibsen's working notes for *Hedda Gabler* to discover that they did not believe, as did the nineteenth-century Romantic poets, that the irrational was a supernatural and unknowable force; rather, in giving detailed account of why their heroines behaved as they did, Ibsen and Strindberg insisted that neurotic behavior and mysterious events are always explainable in terms of natural causes. The significant difference is that neither of these characters can be explained or judged by a common standard; the actions of each character (and by extension, of each human being) are explicable only in terms of that peculiar combination of forces, frustrations, and desires which is unique to himself.

For us living in the middle of the twentieth century there is nothing very new in these psychological ideas; but, coming when they did, they were quite revolutionary, and they have created problems for the playwright which have not yet been solved. By convincingly demonstrating that normal people are not as rational as they seem, and that abnormal people do not act in a random and unintelligible way, psychology has made it difficult, if not impossible, for the dramatist to present his characters in a direct way. In earlier times when it was believed that there was a sharp distinction between the sane and the insane, the irrational "aberrations" of human behavior were dramatically significant because they could be defined in terms of a commonly accepted standard of sane conduct. It seems clear, for instance, that Shakespeare believed Lear on the heath to be insane, while it is equally clear that Macbeth at the witches' cauldron was not. But for the modern dramatist deeds do not necessarily mean what they appear to mean, and in themselves they are not directly revelatory of the characters who commit them. Miss Julie, Hedda Gabler, and Kostya Treplev of Chekhov's *The Sea Gull* are all suicides; but, unlike Othello's suicide, the meaning of each of their deaths cannot be clearly ascertained from the actions that preceded it. The plight of the modern dramatist in this regard becomes apparent when we realize that without Strindberg's Preface or Ibsen's Notebook we could never know for certain what the significance of each heroine's death really was. And the ambiguity of almost every interpretation of *The Sea Gull* is largely due to the fact that Chekhov never made the meaning of Treplev's suicide explicit.

All drama of the past is based upon the axiom "By their deeds shall ye know them." The significance of the dramatic hero was revealed by his deeds, and there was a direct relationship between the hero's overt acts and his inner spiritual condition. The significance of Oedipus, for instance, is revealed by his deeds, not by some explanation that he is suffering from an Oedipus complex; and there is a direct relationship between the act of tearing out his own eyes and his solving the riddle of the Sphinx. Even when a character commits a dissembling deed, it is to deceive the other characters in the play, not the spectators. Certainly one of the chief functions of the soliloquy in Elizabethan drama was to keep the audience informed as to what was going on. Hamlet may put on an antic disposition, but not before he tells the audience he is going to do so. However, beginning in the nineteenth century, the drama began to reflect man's growing distrust in the ability of his senses to comprehend the true nature of reality. Appearances are no longer believed to be direct reflections of ideal reality, like the shadows on the wall of Plato's cave; rather they are thought of as a mask which hides or distorts reality. And by the time of Pirandello, particularly in such plays as *Right You Are, If You Think You Are* (1916), *Six Characters in Search of an Author* (1921), and *The Mock Emperor* (*Enrico IV*) (1922), appearances not only do not express reality, they contradict it, and the meaning of these plays is not to be found in appearance or reality but in the contradiction itself.

One of the great achievements of the Elizabethan dramatic form was its ability to express several levels of experience simultaneously. The world of Hamlet is both public and private, a world in which personal and familial relationships, fantasy and mystery, and political and psychological conflict co-exist in a state of constant dramatic tension. One of the main reasons why the Elizabethan dramatic form works so successfully is that appearances can be taken at face value. But when the dramatist begins to distrust the validity of his sensory perceptions, it becomes difficult, if not impossible, for him to dramatize the complex totality of experience in a single form. Reality must be broken down into its component parts, and each part can be expressed only in a form peculiar to itself. Admitting individual differences in the works of each dramatist's writing of any given period, it is nonetheless possible to describe with some accuracy the dramatic form employed by the playwrights of the fifth-century Greek theatre, the Elizabethan and Restoration theatres of England, and the French neo-classic theatre of the seventeenth century. But in discussing the modern theatre we must always speak of forms, for there is no single, dominant form in the serious theatre of the past hundred years. It is for this reason that the evolution of the drama since the time of Shakespeare has been so aptly described as a process of fragmentation.

It is likely that every serious dramatist believes it his artistic duty to be true to his presuppositions about the real nature of the world in which he lives. However, once a playwright believes that the meaning of every human action is relative and intelligible only in terms of a unique and subsurface combination of forces, the dramatic events of the plot cease to have meaning in themselves, and they take on significance only as the secret motivations of the characters who participate in them are revealed. (The technique of earlier drama is just the reverse: the motivations of the characters are revealed by the events of the plot.) But how does the dramatist objectify the hidden and unconscious, and what happens to the theatre when he feels obligated to explain and probe into his characters' hidden lives? Explanation is always a dangerous business in the theatre (since the time of the ancient Greeks, exposition has always been the dramatist's most difficult problem), but the moment a playwright assumes that if he explains his characters he has written a play, that danger becomes mortal. All too often the writers of the modern theatre have forgotten that a dramatic situation requires not that we *understand* a character but simply that we *believe* in him. Dramatic action always leads to a judgment; it requires that something shall happen to and through the characters; something that is embodied in the events of which the characters are a part. Whenever the personality of the character, rather than the action of which the character should be a part, becomes the playwright's chief concern, dramatic process dissolves into explanation, and when that occurs, the range of the theatre is drastically reduced, if not unalterably damaged.

One has only to compare the plays of the mid-twentieth century to those of Ibsen, Shaw, or Strindberg to realize just how much the scope of the theatre has been narrowed. However, early evidence of the gradual loss of belief in dramatic heroes, who needed no explaining, can be found in the sentimental bourgeois drama of the eighteenth century. For the first time a character was no longer noble, responsible, or morally significant, and therefore dramatically interesting just because of his birth, position, power, or wealth. As a result, the dramatist was obliged to justify both his choice of characters and the situations in which they are engaged. The Romantic drama of the eighteenth and nineteenth centuries resisted a break with the past and attempted unsuccessfully to perpetuate the forms and figures of earlier times. Certainly the revolt of Ibsen and his contemporaries in the last quarter of the nineteenth century was in some measure due to their conviction that the dramatic conflicts of the Romantic drama were inflated and without significance, and that the nobility of its characters was artificial and contrived. In rejecting the artificialities of Romanticism, the modernists changed the theatre in many ways; but for all their dissatisfaction with their predecessors they were unable to forestall disbelief in the possibility of heroic characters who needed no explaining.

This was largely because as a literary movement nineteenth-century naturalism was so closely related to nineteenth-century biology. Darwin's theories of evolution (*Ori-*

*gin of Species*, 1859) and the discovery of new genetic laws had convinced many writers that man's existence, including his personality, was a phenomenon that could be explained in terms of scientific laws. As a result, increasingly, man's complex biological needs rather than his capacity to make moral choices were thought to be his most significant characteristic. Once such a view was accepted, however, the exceptional man, who because of his position and power had the greatest freedom of choice, ceased to be the fullest embodiment, and therefore the best representative, of those conflicts and choices that most clearly define the human condition. Instead, the lives of the poor—where the role of natural necessity is most readily observable—became the playwright's most suitable subjects. The drama of the common man, then, did not happen by accident, nor did it evolve because some dramatist or group of dramatists wanted it to. Given the problem of creating in a world in which all human actions tend to be explained in terms of psychological or sociological cause and effect, a world in which the possibility of deliberative and moral choice is doubted if not rejected outright, it is difficult, if not impossible, for the playwright to fashion a character of traditional heroic stature.

There is an old saw about no man being a hero to his valet. Neither is he one to his psychoanalyst. Nor can he be one to a playwright who views his actions as behavioral phenomena explicable in terms of some kind of laws—scientific or otherwise. Oedipus, for example, remains a hero of great stature so long as he is not suffering from an Oedipus complex. But once we learn to explain him in terms of repressed hopes and fears, traumatic childhood experience, or a vitamin deficiency in infancy, he may remain interesting; he may in fact gain a new kind of interest, as Cocteau's *The Infernal Machine* attests, but he loses stature. Even if we are able, temporarily to accept the Elizabethan attitude toward heroes, which of us can understand a Hamlet or a Lear? And which of us can forgive an Othello or a Macbeth? But it is precisely because they seem mysteriously beyond our powers of understanding that they remain heroes for us. And it is a belief in a mysterious, unknowable quality in men that substantiates man's sense of his own importance in the universe. However, if a playwright comes to believe that all human actions are in reality predictable behavioral responses, and his moral judgments of these actions can be dissolved by psychological understanding, how can he pattern a tragedy or create characters with stature? If there can be no possibility for an appraisal of personality as such, why should Hamlet's death be any more significant than that of Rosencrantz and Guildenstern?

But the problem does not end here. For once the dramatist dismisses the possibility of passing moral judgments on his characters' actions, he comes face to face with an even more frightening spectre—guilt that has no form of expiation and thus turns into anxiety. It has long been known that art must ultimately fail in its attempt to come to grips with the facts of death. Perhaps this is also true of anxiety. How can there be drama in an Age of Anxiety? What kind of play will be produced when the central conflict is between something and nothing? Many of the arts may be able to express the condition of anxiety; but the theatre, because of the objective reality and irremovable presence of the living actor, and because the drama is essentially an embodiment of the conflict between at least two opposing recognizable and nameable forces, is incapable of dealing with anxiety, or it does so to its own great peril. Beginning with the Watchman in the opening scene of the *Orestia* right on through the ghosts of Elsinore and the tormented heroes of Schiller and Kleist, the theatre has always found a way to transform anxiety into fear; that is, give it a definite object. But when we come to such plays as Ibsen's *Ghosts* and *The Master Builder* and Strindberg's *There Are Crimes and Crimes*, and *The Ghost Sonata*, we discover that although this process of objectification is attempted, it is not totally successful. And when the transformation does not take place, the form and content of drama begin to change in uncontrollable ways, as some of the plays of Beckett and Ionesco, Pinter and Albee will attest. It is difficult enough to find a meaning for man in a world that views a return to nothingness as the ultimate reality, but it is next to impossible to create a dramatic "action" which can encompass the terror of being on the edge of the abyss. Kierkegaard, and more recently Paul Tillich, have declared that this threat of nothingness is the central anxiety of modern man. Many modern playwrights have sought to overcome the despair of this situation by maintaining that the only meaning of life is to be found in that death which is inevitable. But this is not an assertion that gives meaning to any of the particularities of life; in fact, it drains them of meaning. At best, it is a method of redeeming existence from meaningless anarchy by showing that the pattern of life is simple and imperturbable. But such a pattern, though it may appear to conquer chaos, is too abstract to live successfully in the theatre.

In life as we experience it, we are conscious of our physical natures, our social situation, and our unique psychic existence; and we live on all three of these levels simultaneously. For this reason it is impossible for us to act or make a choice without some element of human behavior—what we do out of physical necessity or because of social habit—playing a significant role in our decision. At the same time, because of the simultaneity of our being, it is impossible for us to understand completely the individuality of our actions. But in the theatre we see life as pure deed, that is, life in which the arbitrariness of human behavior has been eliminated and in which the mysterious transformations of individuality have been fixed. Thus, in contrast to a person in life, who is recognized by the continuity of his being and finally can only be known through intuition, a character in a play is an identity who is defined by the coherence of his acts. For this reason the deeds of a dramatic action are always public, and the characters best suited to drama are men and women who, either by fate or choice, lead a public life and whose deeds are of public concern. This explains why kings, princes, and nobility have traditionally been the most suitable subjects for drama. But as the increasing dominance of the machine in modern life has gradually destroyed the direct relation between a man's intention and his deeds, public figures have ceased to be our most appropriate heroes because, as W. H. Auden points out, "the good and evil they do depends less upon their characters and intentions than upon the quantity of impersonal force at their disposal."

Our world, it would seem, has become almost too big for the playwright. Power is too impersonal, great deeds are collective achievements, and the great man is one who is capable of withstanding some of the pressures of a mass society and manages, somehow, to maintain a face and stance more or less his own. Compare, for example, the achievement of a Lindbergh (our last "lone" hero) to that of a Colonel Glenn, who was interchangeable with five other astronauts. Or, how can the power of a Napoleon be envisioned today? In our times power is so enormous that it is barely visible and those who govern are little more than incidental and easily replaceable expressions of that power. Power is like an iceberg; the largest part is submerged—in abstraction, anonymity, and bureaucracy. Government, like modern physics, has lost its physical reality and can be expressed only in statistics and formulae. Indeed, the true men of action in our time, those who transform the world, are not the statesmen and politicians but the scientists. Unfortunately, their most significant actions are not suitable subjects for the theatre, because their deeds are concerned with things, not people, and are, therefore, speechless.

But what are the implications of this for the theatre? Who are the true representatives of a world whose heroes are nameless? As the Swiss playwright Duerrenmatt put it: "Any small-time crook, petty government official, or policeman better represents our world than a senator or president. Today art can only embrace victims if it can reach men at all; it can no longer come close to the mighty. Creon's secretaries close Antigone's case."

That there has been a shift in attitude toward the heroic is easily seen when we examine any one of the many modern adaptations of the Greek tragedies. For example, today most people find Anouilh's *Antigone* much more a reflection of their attitudes and thus more immediately interesting than Sophocles' tragic working of the theme. The characters and the dilemma of their situation seem more human. Antigone is not a hard and almost inhuman girl, with such a mono-maniacal fixity of purpose that she rejects all other feelings and desires. In the modern version she is, humanly, both weak and strong. She has a lover in Haemon, whom she rejects; but she is also a helpless little girl who runs to "Nanny" for comfort and strength; as she approaches death, she is afraid and seeks the consolations of even the most callous of guards. Creon is not a blind and power-mad tyrant; he is a businessman king who is caught in the complex web of compromise and expediency which will not allow abstract moral principles to upset the business of government.

However, what the play gains in humanity it loses in tragic force. The sense of Antigone's aloneness and Creon's moral blindness, and of the inevitable destruction implicit in their conflict, has been softened. Anouilh's Antigone is not alone and unloved, and his Creon is not blind. We pity their situation because they are two quite attractive people caught up in a situation which neither of them likes but which they cannot control. They are victims in a disordered world which they have not created and which they have no moral obligation to correct. As the play ends, we are left with an ambiguity that allows for no reconciliation.

One of the most important functions of the hero, both in art and life, is to supply those images, values, and ethical standards which people aspire to and which they would like, if possible, to incorporate into their own lives. It would seem, however, that increasingly our modern industrialized society not only does not need heroes, but it actually suppresses or perverts our need of them. In their important book *Industrialism and Industrial Man*, Kerr, Dunlop, Harbison, and Myers convincingly demonstrate that "like ideologies, the great personality—the one great figure around whom historians so frequently weave their story—began to seem less important. Instead of ideologies and dominant personalities, we became increasingly attentive to the inherent nature of the particular industrializing system and the basic strategy and forces at work within it." Only the system, then, is important, and it fills men's remaining need for heroes by promoting celebrities, those heroes of the surface who play well their constantly shifting roles.

Furthermore, specialization—the key operative principle of an industrial society—produces not only pluralism in our economic system but also a pluralistic deviation of heroic types. However, when there are and can be so many heroic types—one cannot even begin to count all the heroes of the popular imagination—you begin to get a leveling; and with that leveling not only is the stature of heroism diminished, but the individual's sense of his own identity is actually invalidated.

Traditionally, the hero is always best described in terms of those forces that urge him to spiritual redemption. Maxwell Anderson once wrote that "from the point of view of the playwright, the essence of a tragedy, or even a serious play, is the spiritual awakening, or regeneration, of his hero." But the one thing that characterizes the hero of surfaces—and this is certainly in large measure due to industrialization and bureaucracy—is precisely the fact that he lacks the dimensions of spiritual awareness, personal morality, and social responsibility. Paul Tillich wrote in his *The Religious*

*Situation* that "the fundamental value in ethics of a capitalistic society is economic efficiency—developed to the utmost degree of ruthless activity." Such an ethical standard is hardly conducive to the creation of great heroes in the drama.

That we live in an antiheroic age is a commonplace. Carlyle proclaimed its coming in the nineteenth century when he said: "We shall either learn to know a hero . . . when we see him, or else go on to be forever governed by the unheroic." This transformation has occurred; we have accepted it; we are even used to it. Whatever nostalgia we may still occasionally feel is more than adequately taken care of by television. In the place of the hero we have the celebrity, that triumph of the ordinary. In our time, hero worship has become horizontal; indeed, we even look down to a "man like myself."

While the advent of psychology as a systematized field of study may have been the most powerful single force to shape the modern theatre, actually the process of internalization had begun much earlier. For instance, it is clear from Hebbel's essays on the drama that the despair of old Anton's "I don't understand the world any more" in the final scene of *Maria Magdalena* is much more than an expression of the age-old frustration of the parent who does not understand the behavior of his children. It also reflects his dimly understood but tremendously painful realization that it is not longer possible for him to comprehend what the world has become or to imagine what the future will be like. Until the Industrial Revolution, patterns of life were passed on from father to son with the confidence that these patterns would satisfy the needs and desires of each new generation. Such confidence was justified, for life changed so gradually and imperceptibly that when changes did occur they were easily assimilated into the shared life of the community. But by the middle of the nineteenth century the effects of the Industrial Revolution had begun to be felt on all levels of society. Technology, with its ever increasing capacity to transform man's way of living, not only made the future so unpredictable that it soon became impossible for him to imagine what his life would be like twenty years hence, but in its singular concern with the individual's functional qualities technology tended to isolate him from his fellows and nvalidate his spiritual values and metaphysical concerns. At he same time, the discoveries of the nineteenth-century rcheologists, and the ensuing interest in anthropology, ended to break down provincial and absolutist attitudes concerning human nature. Early anthropologists like Mannardt, Robertson-Smith, Tylor, and the great James Frazer made it clear that human nature was not something fixed and unchanging but only that kind of behavior exhibited in each culture. In fact, as early as 1860 scholars were demonstrating that human nature is so plastic that it can, as Frazer was later to point out in the Preface to the first edition of *The Golden Bough* (1890), "exhibit varieties of behavior which, in the animal kingdom could only be exhibited by different species." Furthermore, by the middle of the century, democracy was finally beginning to be established both as a way of life and as a form of government. Today we tend to forget what a revolutionary idea democracy is and the shattering effects that it had upon the values of eighteenth- and nineteenth-century Europe. Alexis de Tocqueville told us long ago: "Not only does democracy make every man forget his ancestors, but it hides his descendants and separates his contemporaries from him, it throws him back forever upon himself alone and threatens in the end to confine him entirely within the solitude of his own heart." In short, by the middle of the nineteenth century every established view of God, human nature, social organization, and the physical universe was beginning to be seriously challenged if not invalidated. And this revolutionary climate had a profound effect on the theatre.

Of all the arts, theatre is the only art that has always concerned itself with human destinies. Dramatic action is historical in the sense that the perpetual present of each moment on the stage is created out of past events and is directed toward a definite, if yet unknown, future. In previous ages the destiny of any dramatic action was significant because the ever-changing events in the lives of dramatic heroes could be meaningfully related to eternity, that is, to some permanent value or idea such as Fate, the Gods, or Heaven and Hell, which transcends the human condition and which is believed in by the dramatist and/or his audience.

In the plays of Buechner and Hebbel we discover the first indications in the theatre of that sense of alienation from

both God and Society which underscores the fact that man'
belief in eternity had been shaken. And one of the mos
significant aspects of Ibsen's work (at least after *Peer Gynt*
1867) is the fact that the realm of ultimate value has eithe
disappeared or has become so mysterious that it has ceased
to have dramatic relevance. In its place we find instead a
belief in some form of social ideal or societal structure
first, as the agent of some unknown Destiny, and then as
Destiny itself. But when society begins to assume the role
of Destiny, that is, is thought of as the determining force
for good or evil in the lives of men, man cannot help but
feel eventually that the meaning of his Destiny has been
drastically reduced. For Society, as Robert Bolt writes in
the Preface to his *A Man for All Seasons*, "can only have
as much idea as we have what we are about, for it has only
our brains to think with. And the individual who tries to plot
his position by reference to our society finds no fixed points,
but only the vaunted absence of them, 'freedom' and 'opportunity'; freedom for what, opportunity to do what, is
nowhere indicated. The only positive he is given is 'get
and spend' . . . and he did not need society to tell him that.
In other words we are thrown back by our society upon
ourselves, which of course sends us flying back to society
with all the force of rebound."

Any mind capable of spiritual aspiration seeks in the
actions of the dramatic hero that which affirms the vitality
of the free will in any given situation. Man's free will may
be defeated by the forces of Destiny—in fact, the great
plays have always testified that the destroying forces of
Destiny are as much a part of the hero's character as his
free will; it may be paralyzed and thus incapable of action;
it may be submerged by the battle in such a way as to become part of that Destiny; it may even turn out to be an
illusion; but it must always be an active force if we are to
believe that we are partaking in human greatness. Such a
Destiny must be greater than an aggregate of human beings
or an expression of social patterns.

Ironically, the revolt of Ibsen and Shaw against the con-
ventional nineteenth-century drama was motivated by a desire to enlarge the range of Destiny in the theatre. In their
attempts to present men in his total historical and social
setting, they were rebelling against the narrow and private

worlds that had been dominating the stage since the Restoration. But in spite of their efforts, nothing could change the fact that in the two hundred years since Shakespeare the world of the spirit had greatly diminished. The Ekdals' attic and Mrs. Warren's drawing room were not—and never could be—the same as Elsinore or Cleopatra's barge.

Nonetheless, the pioneers of the modern drama had revitalized the theatre precisely because they believed that significant social issues should be dealt with in the theatre. Thus for nearly three decades the theatre had a vitality of spirit and a forcefulness of manner which it had lacked for more than a century for the very reason that its context had been reduced. To the playwright writing at that time the human and social problems, which were the source materials of the naturalistic play, appeared capable of solution if only man and society would learn to use their common sense; which usually meant one of two things—the acceptance of a less rigid standard of social morality or the espousal of some form of socialism. But with the collapse of the established social order in the first World War, the validity of these too-easy solutions was impugned, and beginning with the plays of the early German Expressionists (written 1912-1916) the positive optimism of the Edwardian era gave way to a sense of bewilderment, exasperation, and defeatism, only occasionally tempered by the slim hope that the war had brought man to the threshold of a "New Age." The theatre reflects these changes from confidence to doubting and despair, from complacent faith in cherished values to an anxious questioning, from a rigorous but rigid morality to the mystic evangelism, the fanatical polemics, and the frivolous apathy of a disintegrating world. These changes are most apparent in the Jekyll and Hyde theatre of the German Expressionists whose nerve-shattered playwrights alternated between a militant idealism and grotesque nightmares. But one need only compare Shaw's *Heartbreak House* to *Major Barbara*, Pirandello's *Right You Are, If You Think You Are* to *Liolá*, or Hauptmann's *Winter Ballad* to *The Weavers* to realize that the effects of the collapse of the old order were widespread and were reflected in the works of established writers as well as those of the new generation. Immediately after the war the theatre on the continent was dominated by attitudes of emotionalism and cynicism, but these gradually gave way to feelings of frustration, futility, and despair, and by the middle of the 1920's the serious drama of Europe had become almost totally introspective and psychological in its orientation.[1]

Obviously, this tendency toward paralyzing introspection has by no means been accepted by everyone writing for the theatre. In fact, a large segment of the modern theatre might be best described as a reaction against the despair and dehumanizing implications of the modernist position. These "resistance movements" have sought to discover the means, both formal and substantive, whereby the possibility and validity of selfhood and human integrity, personal responsibility, and morally significant judgments could be reasserted in the theatre. Some playwrights—especially Eliot, Fry, Betti, and Claudel—have turned to orthodox Christian belief to provide a metaphysical structure for their drama. Others, like Lorca and Synge, have written out of the traditions and value systems of premodern hieratic societies. Probably the largest group of all is composed of those dramatists who have sought to escape the deadly strictures of modernism by turning to classical mythology.

All of these writers shared one common and fundamental attitude: each of them was in some way rebelling against the conditions of the modern world. They were not only conscious of that lack of a sense of community which inevitably occurs in an increasingly democratic society; more important, they were aware of man's growing sense of his own isolation. The modern world, with its growing collectivism, paradoxically tends to throw man back upon himself, while at the same time it increasingly tends to destroy the individual's sense of his own selfhood. This creates an im-

---

[1] Because they were essentially isolated from the main currents of European history in the first two decades of the century, the Irish and American theatres were not immediately effected by the spreading paralysis which was transforming the rest of modern drama. But it is clear from O'Casey's *The Plow and the Stars* (1926) and *The Silver Tassie* (1927) that the Abbey Theatre could not withstand for long the theatre's introspective tendencies, and there was no serious American drama until O'Neill's plays were first produced right after the war. In the twenty years between O'Neill's *Beyond the Horizon* (1920) and *The Iceman Cometh* (1941) the American theatre repeated the Continental cycle in its own terms, and by the beginning of the Second World War all of the Western theatre had reached that No Man's Land between comedy and tragedy, between pathetic aspirations and ridiculous bewilderment, between never-beginning action and never-ending talk.

passe which the modern dramatist, for the most part, has been unable to overcome.

Joseph Warren Beach, in analyzing the problems of modern fiction, describes the reaction of many writers to this condition in this way: "One of the hardest things for man to bear is spiritual isolation. The sense that he stands alone in the universe goes terribly against his gregarious instincts. He has an over-powering impulse to construct a system which will enable him to feel that he does not stand alone but is intimately associated with some force or group infinitely more powerful and significant than himself." It is clearly evident in the work of all those playwrights who have rebelled against modernism that they too are seeking to construct a system that will restore meaning to life and validity to art. In the end, however, they have not been completely successful, because they have all too often had to deny the realities of the modern world in the process. Furthermore, they have not accepted the wisdom of Brecht's statement that "when one sees that our world of today no longer fits into the drama, then it is merely that the drama no longer fits into the world." By insisting upon values that we may once have cherished but which no longer in actuality exist, the playwrights of the resistance have not been able to revitalize the theatre or its audiences. And most important, they have not succeeded in stretching the imaginations of men in order that they might conquer that sense of isolation and despair that pervades the modern world. And this brings us to the playwrights of the mid-twentieth century.

In an age dominated by space orbits and telestars, the fear of nuclear war, the tension of cold war diplomacy, and the insecurity of a defense economy, our greatest uncertainty is whether or not in the midst of epochal disorder man has any good chance, to borrow Faulkner's phrase, of prevailing; and if he does, what kind of man will prevail?

This uncertainty has had a profound effect on our theatre, and if there is one thing that characterizes the work of almost all of our serious playwrights of the last two decades it is that their plays express the contemporary theatre's tremendous concern to find a metaphor for universal modern man as he lives on the brink of disaster—a metaphor that expresses the inalienable part of every man, that irreducible part of each of us that exists after all the differences have been stripped away and which is beyond and beneath all that is social, political, economic, religious, and ideological. In short, they are searching for a metaphor of man left face to face with himself.

Such an idea of the theatre has tremendous implications for the drama, and we are just now becoming aware of them. First of all, it abolishes the traditional linear plot because our contemporary playwrights are not interested in presenting an action in any Aristotelian sense but are, rather, dramatizing a condition. Whenever one asks what the central action of a Beckett, Ionesco, or Pinter play is, he comes a cropper; "action" for the contemporary playwright is an artificial concept. He is concerned with showing life as it is, and in life there is no central action, there are only people, and the only thing that is basic to each individual is the ontological solitude of his being. The dramatist's only concern is to create in his plays a situation which will reveal the private drama that each man has inside himself and which is enacted every day in the random, apparently meaningless, and undramatic events of our common routine. "History," said James Joyce's Stephen Daedalus, "is a nightmare from which I must awake." The rapidity of historical change and the apparent powerlessness of the individual to affect Collective History has led in the theatre to a retreat from history. Instead of tracing the history of an individual who is born, grows old, and dies, many modern playwrights have devoted their attention to the timeless passionate moments of life, to states of being. They want to express the paradox, the contradiction, and the incompleteness of experience. They are attempting to suggest the raggedness, the confusion, the complexity of motivation, the "discontinuous continuity," and the basic ambiguity of all human behavior. They are, in short, pursuing the premises of modernism to their fullest and most logical conclusions. The writers of the contemporary theatre are facing the "facts of life." If the dramatic meaning of their plays is that drama is no longer possible, they would contend that any other meaning would be artificial, illusory, false; if the dialogue in their plays consists of meaningless clichés and stereotyped phrases, they would insist that this is the way we talk; if their characters are constantly changing their personalities, these playwrights would point out that no one today is really consistent or truly integrated. If the people in their plays seem to be helpless puppets without any will of their own, they would argue that we are all passively at the mercy of blind fate and meaningless circumstance. They call their theatre "Anti-Theatre," and this they insist is the true theatre of our times. If they are correct, so be it! Then history has again followed its own inexorable laws. The very forces that gave life and strength to the modern theatre have caused its decline and death.

But the theatre is always dying, and with equal regularity, like the phoenix, it is resurrected. No one can say with certainty what its new form will be, but that there will be a future seems certain. First, largely because of the development of college and university theatre programs in this country and the large increase in the number of professional repertory theatres here and abroad, there are more people who have experienced good theatre than ever before. And this enlarged audience wants and needs theatre, and it will not be satisfied for long with the maimed rites of psychological and moral cliché, or impassioned jeremiads from prophets of doom, or the meandering contemplations of writers who are morbidly consumed in introspection and self-analysis. Fortunately, there are audiences who want and need the theatre, and they go to the theatre in the hopeful anticipation that the stage will be capable of accommodating all of the terrible-wonderful emotions and insoluble dilemmas of our shared life together. This insistence by audiences on a drama that deals with the significant issues and concerns of our public life will, I believe, force our playwrights to open up new frontiers in the drama and thus extend the boundaries of the theatre. The second great hope of the theatre is that, in spite of the overriding temper of despair and the dominance of antitheatricality in current drama, our playwrights still find human action significant, still find it necessary to write plays, and, in the very act of writing, attest to the miracle of life. We live in one of the most dramatic ages in the history of mankind, and if the past is any kind of reliable guide to what the future of the theatre will be, we have good reason to believe that the theatre of tomorrow can be as dramatic as the world in which we live today.

# MASTERPIECES OF THE
# MODERN ENGLISH THEATRE

# OSCAR WILDE

## 1856–1900

OSCAR WILDE, endowed with a surname appropriate to the pattern of his dissolute life, was born into a Victorian world just beginning to jell into complacency. Earlier in the century, confronted with Darwinism, German transcendentalism, and the consequences of the Industrial Revolution, people had dared to believe in a brave new world of men freed from their old fears and masters not only of their domestic fates but of their minds and souls as well. But by the time young Wilde came of age, the bright possibilities of the new discoveries had been exceedingly dulled by compromise on all sides. Wide-scale enfranchisement had left a sizable aristocracy, while producing a middle class that admired and jealously tried to imitate the respectability and manners of the wealthy.

Onto such a neo-Puritan scene as this, of unusual parents prophetic of the notoriety he was to come to, burst Oscar Wilde. An avid disciple of Walter Pater's doctrines of aestheticism, the eccentric Wilde quickly became the most decadent of the esthetes, pouring his literary energies into art-for-art's-sake essays and defenses for his licentious behavior. He turned out the horrific *Portrait of Dorian Gray,* and his drama *Salome,* banned in London, was staged in Paris by Sarah Bernhardt.

Wilde is accused, and many times justly, of hypocrisy and of opportunism because of his eclectic mixture of styles and themes popular at the time. But the latter charge lays proof, to a degree, of the versatility of the man, and to the former, Wilde might well reply, as he did in *The Importance of Being Earnest,* that nobody does anything else.

Rife with inverted clichés, terse epigrams, paradoxical characters, and sharp parody, *The Importance of Being Earnest* ranks with the great tradition of British stage wit that includes Jonson, Wycherley, and Congreve. But Wilde did not live to see the effects of the wit which he spoke so readily and wrote with facility. Having served a two-year prison sentence for immoral sexual practices, he moved to Paris, where he died in squalor.

# EXCERPTS FROM OSCAR WILDE:

## *The Decay of Lying*

PURE MODERNITY of form is always somewhat vulgarizing. It cannot help being so. The public imagine that, because they are interested in their immediate surroundings, Art should be interested in them also, and should take them as her subject-matter. But the mere fact that they are interested in these things makes them unsuitable subjects for Art. The only beautiful things, as somebody once said, are the things that do not concern us. As long as a thing is useful or necessary to us, or affects us in any way, either for pain or for pleasure, or appeals strongly to our sympathies, or is a vital part of the environment in which we live, it is outside the proper sphere of art. To art's subject-matter we should be more or less indifferent. We should, at any rate, have no preferences, no prejudices, no partisan feeling of any kind. It is exactly because Hecuba is nothing to us that her sorrows are such an admirable motive for a tragedy. . . . Believe me, my dear Cyril, modernity of form and modernity of subject-matter are entirely and absolutely wrong. We have mistaken the common livery of the age for the vesture of the Muses, and spend our days in the sordid streets and hideous suburbs of our vile cities when we should be out on the hillside with Apollo. Certainly we are a degraded race, and have sold our birthright for a mess of facts.

Take the case of the English drama. At first in the hands of the monks Dramatic Art was abstract, decorative and mythological. Then she enlisted Life in her service, and using some of life's external forms, she created an entirely new race of beings, whose sorrows were more terrible than any sorrow man has ever felt, whose joys were keener than lover's joys, who had the rage of the Titans and the calm of the gods, who had monstrous and marvellous sins, monstrous and marvellous virtues. To them she gave a language different from that of actual use, a language full of resonant music and sweet rhythm, made stately by solemm cadence, or made delicate by fanciful rhyme, jewelled with wonderful words, and enriched with lofty diction. She clothed her children in strange raiment and gave them masks, and at her bidding the antique world rose from its marble tomb. A new Caesar stalked through the streets of risen Rome, and with purple sail and flute-led oars another Cleopatra passed up the river to Antioch. Old myth and legend and dream took shape and substance. History was entirely re-written, and there was hardly one of the dramatists who did not recognize that the object of Art is not simple truth but complex beauty. In this they were perfectly right. Art itself is really a form of exaggeration; and selection, which is the very spirit of art, is nothing more than an intensified mode of overemphasis.

But Life soon shattered the perfection of the form. Even in Shakespeare we can see the beginning of the end. It shows itself by the gradual breaking-up of the blank-verse in the later plays, by the pre-dominance given to prose, and by the over-importance assigned to characterisation. The passages in Shakespeare—and they are many—where the language is uncouth, vulgar, exaggerated, fantastic, obscene even, are entirely due to Life calling for an echo of her own voice, and rejecting the intervention of beautiful style, through which alone should life be suffered to find expression. Shakespeare is not by any means a flawless artist. He is too fond of going directly to life, and borrowing life's natural utterance. He forgets that when Art surrenders her imaginative medium she surrenders everything. Goethe says, somewhere:—

*In der Beschränkung zeigt sich erst der Meister,*

It is in working within limits that the master reveals himself, and the limitation, the very condition of any art is style. However, we need not linger any longer over Shakespeare's realism. *The Tempest* is the most perfect of palinodes. All that we desired to point out was that the magnificent work of the Elizabethan and Jacobean artists contained within itself the seeds of its own dissolution, and that, if it drew some of its strength from using life as rough material, it drew all its weakness from using life as an artistic method. As the inevitable result of this substitution of an imitative for a creative medium, this surrender of an imaginative form, we have the modern English melodrama. The characters in these plays talk on the stage exactly as they would talk off it; they have neither aspirations nor aspirates; they are taken directly from life and reproduce its vulgarity down to the smallest detail; they present the gait, manner, costume and accent of real people; they would pass unnoticed in a third-class railway carriage. And yet how wearisome the plays are! They do not succeed in producing even that impression of reality at which they aim, and which is their only reason for existing. As a method, realism is a complete failure.

# EXCERPTS FROM OSCAR WILDE:

## *The Critic As Artist. I*

BUT THINK MERELY of one perfect little work of aesthetic criticism, Aristotle's *Treatise on Poetry*. It is not perfect in form, for it is badly written, consisting perhaps of notes jotted down for an art lecture, or of isolated fragments destined for some larger book, but in temper and treatment it is perfect, absolutely. The ethical effect of art, its importance to culture, and its place in the formation of character, had been done once for all by Plato; but here we have art treated, not from the moral, but from the purely aesthetic point of view. Plato had, of course, dealt with many definitely artistic subjects, such as the importance of unity in a work of art, the necessity for tone and harmony, the aesthetic value of appearances, the relation of the visible arts to the external world, and the relation of fiction to fact. He first perhaps stirred in the soul of man that desire that we have not yet satisfied, the desire to know the connection between Beauty and Truth, and the place of Beauty in the moral and intellectual order of the Kosmos. The problems of idealism and realism, as he sets them forth, may seem to many to be somewhat barren of result in the metaphysical sphere of abstract being in which he places them, but transfer them to the sphere of art, and you will find that they are still vital and full of meaning. It may be that it is as a critic of Beauty that Plato is destined to live, and that by altering the name of the sphere of his speculation we shall find a new philosophy. But Aristotle, like Goethe, deals with art primarily in its concrete manifestations, taking Tragedy, for instance, and investigating the material it uses, which is language, its subject-matter, which is life, the method by which it works, which is action, the conditions under which it reveals itself, which are those of theatric presentation, its logical structure, which is plot, and its final aesthetic appeal, which is to the sense of beauty realised through the passions of pity and awe. That purification and spiritualising of the nature which he calls Κάθαρσις is, as Goethe saw, essentially aesthetic, and is not moral, as Lessing fancied. Concerning himself primarily with the impression that the work of art produces, Aristotle sets himself to analyse that impression, to investigate its source, to see how it is engendered. As a physiologist and psychologist, he knows that the health of a function resides in energy. To have a capacity for a passion and not to realise it, is to make oneself incomplete and limited. The mimic spectacle of life that Tragedy affords cleanses the bosom of much 'perilous stuff,' and by presenting high and worthy objects for the exercise of the emotions purifies and spiritualises the man; nay, not merely does it spiritualise him, but it initiates him also into noble feelings of which he might else have known nothing, the word Κάθαρσις having, it has sometimes seemed to me, a definite allusion to the rite of initiation, if indeed that be not, as I am occasionally tempted to fancy, its true and only meaning here. This is of course a mere outline of the book. But you see what a perfect piece of aesthetic criticism it is. Who indeed but a Greek could have analysed art so well?

. . . When man acts he is a puppet. When he describes he is a poet. The whole secret lies in that. It was easy enough on the sandy plains by windy Ilion to wend the notched arrow from the painted bow, or to hurl against the shield of hide and flame-like brass the long-handled spear. It was easy for the adulterous queen to spread the Tyrian carpets for her lord, and then, as he lay couched in the marble bath, to throw over his head the purple net, and call to her smooth-faced lover to stab through the meshes at the heart that should have broken at Aulis. For Antigone even, with Death waiting for her as her bridegroom, it was easy to pass through the tainted air at noon, and climb the hill, and strew with kindly earth the wretched naked corse that had no tomb. But what of those who wrote about these things? What of those who gave them reality, and made them live for ever? Are they not greater than the men and women they sing of? 'Hector that sweet knight is dead,' and

Lucian tells us how in the dim underworld Menippus saw
the bleaching skull of Helen, and marvelled that it was for
so grim a favour that all those horned ships were launched,
those beautiful mailed men laid low, those towered cities
brought to dust. Yet, every day the swan-like daughter of
Leda comes out on the battlements, and looks down at the
tide of war. The grey-beards wonder at her loveliness, and
she stands by the side of the king. In his chamber of stained
ivory lies her leman. He is polishing his dainty armour, and
combing the scarlet plume. With squire and page, her husband passes from tent to tent. She can see his bright hair,
and hears, or fancies that she hears, that clear cold voice.
In the courtyard below, the son of Priam is buckling on his
brazen cuirass. The white arms of Andromache are around
his neck. He sets his helmet on the ground, lest their babe
should be frightened. Behind the embroidered curtains of his
pavilion sits Achilles, in perfumed raiment, while in harness
of gilt and silver the friend of his soul arrays himself to
go forth to the fight. From a curiously carven chest that his
mother Thetis had brought to his ship-side, the Lord of the
Myrmidons takes out that mystic chalice that the lip of man
had never touched, and cleanses it with brimstone, and with
fresh water cools it, and, having washed his hands, fills with
black wine its burnished hollow, and spills the thick grape-
blood upon the ground in honour of Him whom at Dodona
barefooted prophets worshipped, and prays to Him, and
knows not that he prays in vain, and that by the hands of
two knights from Troy, Panthous' son, Euphorbus, whose
love-locks were looped with gold, and the Priamid, the lion-
hearted, Patroklus, the comrade of comrades, must meet
his doom. Phantoms, are they? Heroes of mist and moun-
tain? Shadows in a song? No; they are real. Action! What
is action? It dies at the moment of its energy. It is a base
concession to fact. The world is made by the singer for the
dreamer.

# EXCERPTS FROM OSCAR WILDE:

## The Critic As Artist. II

*Gilbert.* For everything. Because Art does not hurt us. The tears that we shed at a play are a type of the exquisite sterile emotions that it is the function of Art to awaken. We weep, but we are not wounded. We grieve, but our grief is not bitter. In the actual life of man, sorrow, as Spinoza says somewhere, is a passage to a lesser perfection. But the sorrow with which Art fills us both purifies and initiates, if I may quote once more from the great art critic of the Greeks. It is through Art, and through Art only, that we can realise our perfection; through Art, and through Art only, that we can shield ourselves from the sordid perils of actual existence. This results not merely from the fact that nothing that one can imagine is worth doing, and that one can imagine everything, but from the subtle law that emotional forces, like the forces of the physical sphere, are limited in extent and energy. One can feel so much, and no more. And how can it matter with what pleasure life tries to tempt one, or with what pain it seeks to maim and mar one's soul, if in the spectacle of the lives of those who have never existed one has found the true secret of joy, and wept away one's tears over their deaths who, like Cordelia and the daughter of Brabantio, can never die?

*Ernest.* Stop a moment. It seems to me that in everything that you have said there is something radically immoral.

*Gilbert.* All art is immoral.

*Ernest.* All art?

*Gilbert.* Yes. For emotion for the sake of emotion is the aim of art, and emotion for the sake of action is the aim of life, and of that practical organization of life that we call society. Society, which is the beginning and basis of morals,

exists simply for the concentration of human energy, and i
order to ensure its own continuance and healthy stability i
demands, and no doubt rightly demands, of each of its citi
zens that he should contribute some form of productiv
labour to the common weal, and toil and travail that th
day's work may be done. Society often forgives the crim
inal; it never forgives the dreamer. The beautiful sterile
emotions that art excites in us are hateful in its eyes, and
so completely are people dominated by the tyranny of this
dreadful social ideal that they are always coming shame
lessly up to one at Private Views and other places that are
open to the general public, and saying in a loud stentorian
voice, 'What are you doing?' whereas 'What are you think
ing?' is the only question that any single civilized being
should ever be allowed to whisper to another. They mean
well, no doubt, these honest beaming folk. Perhaps that is
the reason why they are so excessively tedious. But some one
should teach them that while, in the opinion of society,
Contemplation is the gravest sin of which any citizen can
be guilty, in the opinion of the highest culture it is the
proper occupation of man.

*Gilbert.* The difference between objective and subjective
work is one of external form merely. It is accidental, not
essential. All artistic creation is absolutely subjective. The
very landscape that Corot looked at was, as he said himself,
but a mood of his own mind; and those great figures of
Greek or English drama that seem to us to possess an
actual existence of their own, apart from the poets who
shaped and fashioned them, are, in their ultimate analysis,
simply the poets themselves, not as they thought they were,
but as they thought they were not; and by such thinking
came in strange manner, though but for a moment, really
so to be. For out of ourselves we can never pass, nor can
there be in creation what in the creator was not. Nay, I
would say that the more objective a creation appears to be,
the more subjective it really is. Shakespeare might have met
Rosencrantz and Guildenstern in the white streets of London,
or seen the serving-men of rival houses bite their thumbs
at each other in the open square; but Hamlet came out of
his soul, and Romeo out of his passion. They were elements
of his nature to which he gave visible form, impulses that

stirred so strongly within him that he had, as it were per-force, to suffer them to realise their energy, not on the lower plane of actual life, where they would have been trammelled and constrained and so made imperfect, but on that imaginative plane of art where Love can indeed find in Death its rich fulfilment, where one can stab the eavesdropper behind the arras, and wrestle in a new-made grave, and make a guilty king drink his own hurt, and see one's father's spirit, beneath the glimpses of the moon, stalking in complete steel from misty wall to wall. Action being limited would have left Shakespeare unsatisfied and unexpressed; and, just as it is because he did nothing that he has been abe to achieve everything, so it is because he never speaks to us of himself in his plays that his play reveal him to us absolutely, and show us his true nature and temperament far more completely than do those strange and exquisite sonnets, even, in which he bares to crystal eyes the secret closet of his heart. Yes, the objective form is the most subjective in matter. Man is least himself when he talks in his own person. Give him a mask, and he will tell you the truth.

. . . . . . . . . . . . . . . . . . . . . . . . . . . .

. . . In every sphere of life Form is the beginning of things. The rhythmic harmonious gestures of dancing convey, Plato tells us, both rhyrhm and harmony into the mind. Forms are the food of faith, cried Newman in one of those great moments of sincerity that make us admire and know the man. He was right, though he may not have known how terribly right he was. The Creeds are believed, not because they are rational, but because they are repeated. Yes; Form is everything. It is the secret of life. Find expression for a sorrow, and it will become dear to you. Find expression for a joy, and you intensify its ecstasy. Do you wish to love? Use Love's Litany, and the words will create the yearning from which the world fancies that they spring. Have you a grief that corrodes your heart? Steep yourself in the language of grief, learn its utterance from Prince Hamlet and Queen Constance, and you will find that mere expression is a mode of consolation, and that Form, which is the birth of passion, is also the death of pain. And so, to return to the sphere of Art, it is Form that creates not merely the critical temperament, but also the aesthetic instinct, that unerring instinct that reveals to one all things under their conditions of beauty.

# THE IMPORTANCE OF

## BEING EARNEST

# THE IMPORTANCE OF BEING EARNEST

by Oscar Wilde

*1895*

# CHARACTERS

JOHN WORTHING, J.P.
ALGERNON MONCRIEFF
REV. CANON CHASUBLE, D.D.
MERRIMAN, *butler*
LANE, *manservant*
LADY BRACKNELL
HON. GWENDOLEN FAIRFAX
CECILY CARDEW
MISS PRISM, *governess*

## THE SCENES OF THE PLAY

ACT  I.   Algernon Moncrieff's Flat in Half-Moon Street, W
ACT  II.  The Garden at the Manor House, Woolton
ACT III. Drawing-Room of the Manor House, Woolton
TIME: The Present [1899]
PLACE: London

# ACT ONE

## Scene

*Morning-room in* ALGERNON'S *flat in Half-Moon Street. The room is luxuriously and artistically furnished. The sound of a piano is heard in the adjoining room.*

[LANE *is arranging afternoon tea on the table, and after the music has ceased,* ALGERNON *enters.*]

ALGERNON. Did you hear what I was playing, Lane?

LANE. I didn't think it polite to listen, sir.

ALGERNON. I'm sorry for that, for your sake. I don't play accurately—any one can play accurately—but I play with wonderful expression. As far as the piano is concerned, sentiment is my forte. I keep science for Life.

LANE. Yes, sir.

ALGERNON. And, speaking of the science of Life, have you got the cucumber sandwiches cut for Lady Bracknell?

LANE. Yes, sir. [*Hands them on a salver.*]

ALGERNON. [*Inspects them, takes two, and sits down on the sofa*]. Oh! . . . by the way, Lane, I see from your book that on Thursday night, when Lord Shoreman and Mr Worthing were dining with me, eight bottles of champagne are entered as having been consumed.

LANE. Yes sir; eight bottles and a pint.

ALGERNON. Why is it that at a bachelor's establishment the servants invariably drink the champagne? I ask merely for information.

LANE. I attribute it to the superior quality of the wine, sir. I have often observed that in married households the champagne is rarely of a first-rate brand.

ALGERNON. Good heavens! Is marriage so demoralizing as that?

LANE. I believe it *is* a very pleasant state, sir. I have had very little experience of it myself up to the present. I have only been married once. That was in consequence of a misunderstanding between myself and a young person.

ALGERNON [*languidly*]. I don't know that I am much interested in your family life, Lane.

LANE. No, sir; it is not a very interesting subject. I never think of it myself.

ALGERNON. Very natural, I am sure. That will do, Lane, thank you.

LANE. Thank you, sir.

[LANE *goes out.*]

ALGERNON. Lane's views on marriage seem somewhat lax. Really, if the lower orders don't set us a good example, what on earth is the use of them? They seem, as a class, to have absolutely no sense of moral responsibility.

[*Enter* LANE.]

LANE. Mrs. Ernest Worthing.

[*Enter* JACK. LANE *goes out.*]

ALGERNON. How are you, my dear Ernest? What brings you up to town?

JACK. Oh, pleasure, pleasure! What else should bring one anywhere? Eating as usual, I see, Algy!

ALGERNON [*stiffly*]. I believe it is customary in good society to take some slight refreshment at five o'clock. Where have you been since last Thursday?

JACK [*sitting down on the sofa*]. In the country.

ALGERNON. What on earth do you do there?

JACK [*pulling off his gloves*]. When one is in town one amuses oneself. When one is in the country one amuses other people. It is excessively boring.

ALGERNON. And who are the people you amuse?

JACK [*airly*]. Oh, neighbours, neighbours.

ALGERNON. Got nice neighbours in your part of Shropshire?

JACK. Perfectly horrid! Never speak to one of them.

ALGERNON. How immensely you must amuse them! [*Goes over and takes sandwich.*] By the way, Shropshire is your county, is it not?

JACK. Eh? Shropshire? Yes, of course. Hallo! Why all these

cups? Why cucumber sandwiches? Why such reckless extravagance in one so young? Who is coming to tea?

ALGERNON. Oh! merely Aunt Augusta and Gwendolen.

JACK. How perfectly delightful!

ALGERNON. Yes, that is all very well; but I am afraid Aunt Augusta won't quite approve of your being here.

JACK. May I ask why?

ALGERNON. My dear fellow, the way you flirt with Gwendolen is perfectly disgraceful. It is almost as bad as the way Gwendolen flirts with you.

JACK. I am in love with Gwendolen. I have come up to town expressly to propose to her.

ALGERNON. I thought you had come up for pleasure? . . . I call that business.

JACK. How utterly unromantic you are!

ALGERNON. I really don't see anything romantic in proposing. It is very romantic to be in love. But there is nothing romantic about a definite proposal. Why, one may be accepted. One usually is, I believe. Then the excitement is all over. The very essence of romance is uncertainty. If ever I get married, I'll certainly try to forget the fact.

JACK. I have no doubt about that, dear Algy. The Divorce Court was specially invented for people whose memories are so curiously constituted.

ALGERNON. Oh! there is no use speculating on that subject. Divorces are made in Heaven——[JACK *puts out his hand to take a sandwich.* ALGERNON *at once interferes.*] Please don't touch the cucumber sandwiches. They are ordered specially for Aunt Augusta. [*Takes one and eats it.*]

JACK. Well, you have been eating them all the time.

ALGERNON. That is quite a different matter. She is my aunt. [*Takes plate from below.*] Have some bread and butter. The bread and butter is for Gwendolen. Gwendolen is devoted to bread and butter.

JACK [*advancing to table and helping himself*]. And very good bread and butter it is too.

ALGERNON. Well, my dear fellow, you need not eat as if you were going to eat it all. You behave as if you were married to her already. You are not married to her already, and I don't think you ever will be.

JACK. Why on earth do you say that?

ALGERNON. Well, in the first place, girls never marry the men they flirt with. Girls don't think it right.

JACK. Oh, that is nonsense!

ALGERNON. It isn't. It is a great truth. It accounts for the extraordinary number of bachelors that one sees all over the place. In the second place, I don't give my consent.

JACK. Your consent!

ALGERNON. My dear fellow, Gwendolen is my first cousin. And before I allow you to marry her, you will have to clear up the whole question of Cecily. [*Rings bell.*]

JACK. Cecily! What on earth do you mean? What do you mean, Algy, by Cecily! I don't know any one of the name of Cecily.

[*Enter* LANE.]

ALGERNON. Bring me that cigarette case Mr Worthing left in the smoking-room the last time he dined here.

LANE. Yes, sir.

[LANE *goes out.*]

JACK. Do you mean to say you have had my cigarette case all this time? I wish to goodness you had let me know. I have been writing frantic letters to Scotland Yard about it. I was very nearly offering a large reward.

ALGERNON. Well, I wish you would offer one. I happen to be more than usually hard up.

JACK. There is no good offering a large reward now that the thing is found.

[*Enter* LANE *with the cigarette case on a salver.* ALGERNON *takes it at once.* LANE *goes out.*]

ALGERNON. I think that is rather mean of you, Ernest, I must say. [*Opens case and examines it.*] However, it makes no matter, for, now that I look at the inscription inside, I find that the thing isn't yours after all.

JACK. Of course it's mine. [*Moving to him.*] You have seen me with it a hundred times, and you have no right whatsoever to read what is written inside. It is a very ungentlemanly thing to read a private cigarette case.

ALGERNON. Oh! it is absurd to have a hard and fast rule about what one should read and what one shouldn't. More than half of modern culture depends on what one shouldn't read.

JACK. I am quite aware of the fact, and I don't propose to

discuss modern culture. It isn't the sort of thing one should talk of in private. I simply want my cigarette case back.

ALGERNON. Yes; but this isn't your cigarette case. This cigarette case is a present from someone of the name of Cecily, and you said you didn't know anyone of that name.

JACK. Well, if you want to know, Cecily happens to be my aunt.

ALGERNON. Your aunt!

JACK. Yes. Charming old lady she is, too. Lives at Tunbridge Wells. Just give it back to me, Algy.

ALGERNON [retreating to back of sofa]. But why does she call herself little Cecily if she is your aunt and lives at Tunbridge Wells? [Reading] "From little Cecily with her fondest love."

JACK [moving to sofa and kneeling upon it]. My dear fellow, what on earth is there in that? Some aunts are tall, some aunts are not tall. That is a matter that surely an aunt may be allowed to decide for herself. You seem to think that every aunt should be exactly like your aunt! That is absurd. For Heaven's sake give me back my cigarette case. [Follows ALGERNON round the room.]

ALGERNON. Yes. But why does your aunt call you her uncle? "From litle Cecily, with her fondest love to her dear Uncle Jack." There is no objection, I admit, to an aunt being a small aunt, but why an aunt, no matter what her size may be, should call her own nephew her uncle, I can't quite make out. Besides, your name isn't Jack at all; it is Ernest.

JACK. It isn't Ernest; it's Jack.

ALGERNON. You have always told me it was Ernest. I have introduced you to every one as Ernest. You answer to the name of Ernest. You look as if your name was Ernest. You are the most earnest-looking person I ever saw in my life. It is perfectly absurd your saying that your name isn't Ernest. It's on your cards. Here is one of them. [Taking it from case.] 'Mr Ernest Wothing, B.4, The Albany.' I'll keep this as a proof that your name is Ernest if ever you attempt to deny it to me, or to Gwendolen, or to any one else. [Puts the card in his pocket.]

JACK. Well, my name is Ernest in town and Jack in the country, and the cigarette case was given to me in the country.

ALGERNON. Yes, but that does not account for the fact that your small Aunt Cecily, who lives at Tunbridge Wells, calls you her dear uncle. Come, old boy, you had much better have the thing out at once.

JACK. My dear Algy, you talk exactly as if you were a dentist. It is very vulgar to talk like a dentist when one isn't a dentist. It produces a false impression.

ALGERNON. Well, that is exactly what dentists always do. Now, go on! Tell me the whole thing. I may mention that I have always suspected you of being a confirmed and secret Bunburyist; and I am quite sure of it now.

JACK. Bunburyist? What on earth do you mean by a Bunburyist?

ALGERNON. I'll reveal to you the meaning of that incomparable expression as soon as you are kind enough to inform me why you are Ernest in town and Jack in the country.

JACK. Well, produce my cigarette case first.

ALGERNON. Here it is. [*Hands cigarette case.*] Now produce your explanation, and pray make it improbable. [*Sits on sofa.*]

JACK. My dear fellow, there is nothing improbable about my explanation at all. In fact it's perfectly ordinary. Old Mr Thomas Cardew, who adopted me when I was a little boy, made me in his will guardian to his granddaughter, Miss Cecily Cardew. Cecily, who addresses me as her uncle from motives of respect that you could not possibly appreciate, lives at my place in the country under the charge of her admirable governess, Miss Prism.

ALGERNON. Where is that place in the country, by the way?

JACK. That is nothing to you, dear boy. You are not going to be invited. . . . I may tell you candidly that the place is not in Shropshire.

ALGERNON. I suspected that, my dear fellow! I have Bunburyed all over Shropshire on two separate occasions. Now, go on. Why are you Ernest in town and Jack in the country?

JACK. My dear Algy, I don't know whether you will be able to understand my real motives. You are hardly serious enough. When one is placed in the position of guardian, one has to adopt a very high moral tone on all subjects. It's one's duty to do so. And as a high moral tone can hardly be said to conduce very much to either one's health or one's happiness, in order to get up to town I have always pretended to have a younger brother of the name of Ernest, who lives in the Albany, and gets into the most dreadful scrapes. That, my dear Algy, is the whole truth pure and simple.

ALGERNON. The truth is rarely pure and never simple. Modern life would be very tedious if it were either, and modern literature a complete impossibility!

JACK. That wouldn't be at all a bad thing.

ALGERNON. Literary criticism is not your forte, my dear fellow. Don't try it. You should leave that to people who haven't been at a University. They do it so well in the daily papers. What you really are is a Bunburyist. I was quite right in saying you were a Bunburyist. You are one of the most advanced Bunburyists I know.

JACK. What on earth do you mean?

ALGERNON. You have invented a very useful younger brother called Ernest, in order that you may be able to come up to town as often as you like. I have invented an invaluable permanent invalid called Bunbury, in order that I may be able to go down into the country whenever I choose. Bunbury is perfectly invaluable. If it wasn't for Bunbury's extraordinary bad health, for instance, I wouldn't be able to dine with you at Willis's to-night, for I have been really engaged to Aunt Augusta for more than a week.

JACK. I haven't asked you to dine with me anywhere to-night.

ALGERNON. I know. You are absurdly careless about sending out invitations. It is very foolish of you. Nothing annoys people so much as not receiving invitations.

JACK. You had much better dine with your Aunt Augusta.

ALGERNON. I haven't the smallest intention of doing anything of the kind. To begin with, I dined there on Monday, and once a week is quite enough to dine with one's own relations. In the second place, whenever I do dine there I am always treated as a member of the family, and sent down with either no woman at all, or two. In the third place, I know perfectly well whom she will place me next to, to-night. She will place me next Mary Farquhar, who always flirts with her own husband across the dinner-table. That is not very pleasant. Indeed, it is not even decent . . . and that sort of thing is enormously on the increase. The amount of women in London who flirt with their own husbands is perfectly scandalous. It looks so bad. It is simply washing one's clean linen in public. Besides, now that I know you to be a confirmed Bunburyist I naturally want to talk to you about Bunburying. I want to tell you the rules.

JACK. I'm not a Bunburyist at all. If Gwendolen accepts me, I am going to kill my brother, indeed I think I'll kill him in any case. Cecily is a little too much interested in him. It is rather a bore. So I am going to get rid of Ernest. And I strongly advise you to do the same with Mr . . . with your invalid friend who has the absurd name.

ALGERNON. Nothing will induce me to part with Bunbury, and if you ever get married, which seems to me extremely problematic, you will be very glad to know Bunbury. A man who marries without knowing Bunbury has a very tedious time of it.

JACK. That is nonsense. If I marry a charming girl like Gwendolen, and she is the only girl I ever saw in my life that I would marry, I certainly won't want to know Bunbury.

ALGERNON. Then your wife will. You don't seem to realize, that in married life three is company and two is none.

JACK [*sententiously*]. That, my dear young friend, is the theory that the corrupt French Drama has been propounding for the last fifty years.

ALGERNON. Yes; and that the happy English home has proved in half the time.

JACK. For heaven's sake, don't try to be cynical. It's perfectly easy to be cynical.

ALGERNON. My dear fellow, it isn't easy to be anything nowadays. There's such a lot of beastly competition about. [*The sound of an electric bell is heard.*] Ah! that must be Aunt Augusta. Only relatives, or creditors, ever ring in that Wagnerian manner. Now, if I get her out of the way for ten minutes, so that you can have an opportunity for proposing to Gwendolen, may I dine with you to-night at Willis's?

JACK. I suppose so, if you want to.

ALGERNON. Yes, but you must be serious about it. I hate people who are not serious about meals. It is so shallow of them.

[*Enter* LANE.]

LANE. Lady Bracknell and Miss Fairfax. [ALGERNON *goes forward to meet them. Enter* LADY BRACKNELL *and* GWENDOLEN.]

LADY BRACKNELL. Good afternoon, dear Algernon, I hope you are behaving very well.

ALGERNON. I'm feeling very well, Aunt Augusta.

LADY BRACKNELL. That's not quite the same thing. In fact the two things rarely go together. [*Sees* JACK *and bows to him with icy coldness.*]

ALGERNON [*to* GWENDOLEN]. Dear me, you are smart!

GWENDOLEN. I am always smart! Am I not, Mr Worthing?

JACK. You're quite perfect, Miss Fairfax.

GWENDOLEN. Oh! I hope I am not that. It would leave no room for developments, and I intend to develop in many directions. [GWENDOLEN *and* JACK *sit down together in the corner.*]

LADY BRACKNELL. I'm sorry if we are a little late, Algernon, but I was obliged to call on dear Lady Harbury. I hadn't been there since her poor husband's death. I never saw a woman so altered; she looks quite twenty years younger. And now I'll have a cup of tea, and one of those nice cucumber sandwiches you promised me.

ALGERNON. Certainly, Aunt Augusta. [*Goes over to tea-table.*]

LADY BRACKNELL. Won't you come and sit here, Gwendolen?

GWENDOLEN. Thanks, mamma, I'm quite comfortable where I am.

ALGERNON [*picking up empty plate in horror*]. Good heavens! Lane! Why are there no cucumber sandwiches? I ordered them specially.

LANE [*gravely*]. There were no cucumbers in the market this morning, sir. I went down twice.

ALGERNON. No cucumbers!

LANE. No, sir. Not even for ready money.

ALGERNON. That will do, Lane, thank you.

LANE. Thank you, sir. [*Goes out.*]

ALGERNON. I am greatly distressed, Aunt Augusta, about there being no cucumbers, not even for ready money.

LADY BRACKNELL. It really makes no matter, Algernon. I had some crumpets with Lady Harbury, who seems to me to be living entirely for pleasure now.

ALGERNON. I hear her hair has turned quite gold from grief.

LADY BRACKNELL. It certainly has changed its colour. From what cause I, of course, cannot say. [ALGERNON *crosses and hands tea.*] Thank you. I've quite a treat for you to-night, Algernon. I am going to send you down with Mary Farquhar. She is such a nice woman, and so attentive to her husband. It's delightful to watch them.

ALGERNON. I am afraid, Aunt Augusta, I shall have to give up the pleasure of dining with you to-night after all.

LADY BRACKNELL [*frowning*]. I hope not, Algernon. It would put my table completely out. Your uncle would have to dine upstairs. Fortunately he is accustomed to that.

ALGERNON. It is a great bore, and, I need hardly say, a terrible disappointment to me, but the fact is I have just had a telegram to say that my poor friend Bunbury is very ill again. [*Exchanges glances with* JACK.] They seem to think I should be with him.

LADY BRACKNELL. It is very strange. This Mr Bunbury seems to suffer from curiously bad health.

ALGERNON. Yes; poor Bunbury is a dreadful invalid.

LADY BRACKNELL. Well, I must say, Algernon, that I think it is high time that Mr Bunbury made up his mind whether he was going to live or to die. This shilly-shallying with the question is absurd. Nor do I in any way approve of the modern sympathy with invalids. I consider it morbid. Illness of any kind is hardly a thing to be encouraged in others. Health is the primary duty of life. I am always telling that to your poor uncle, but he never seems to take much notice . . . as far as any improvement in his ailment goes. I should be much obliged if you would ask Mr Bunbury, from me, to be kind enough not to have a relapse on Saturday, for I rely on you to arrange my music for me. It is my last reception, and one wants something that will encourage conversation, particularly at the end of the season when every one has practically said whatever they had to say, which, in most cases, was probably not much.

ALGERNON. I'll speak to Bunbury, Aunt Augusta, if he is still conscious, and I think I can promise you he'll be all right by Saturday. Of course the music is a great difficulty. You see, if one plays good music, people don't listen, and if one plays bad music people don't talk. But I'll run over the programme I've drawn out, if you will kindly come into the next room for a moment.

LADY BRACKNELL. Thank you, Algernon. It is very thoughtful of you. [*Rising, and following* ALGERNON.] I'm sure the programme will be delightful, after a few expurgations. French songs I cannot possibly allow. People always seem to think that they are improper, and either look shocked, which is vulgar, or laugh, which is worse. But German sounds a thoroughly respectable language, and, indeed I believe is so. Gwendolen, you will accompany me.

GWENDOLEN. Certainly, mamma.

[LADY BRACKNELL *and* ALGERNON *go into the music-room,* GWENDOLEN *remains behind.*]

JACK. Charming day it has been, Miss Fairfax.

GWENDOLEN. Pray don't talk to me about the weather, Mr Worthing. Whenever people talk to me about the weather, I always feel quite certain that they mean something else. And that makes me so nervous.

JACK. I do mean something else.

GWENDOLEN. I thought so. In fact, I am never wrong.

JACK. And I would like to be allowed to take advantage of Lady Bracknell's temporary absence. . . .

GWENDOLEN. I would certainly advise you to do so. Mamma has a way of coming back suddenly into a room that I have often had to speak to her about.

JACK [*nervously*]. Miss Fairfax, ever since I met you I have admired you more than any girl . . . I have ever met since . . . I met you.

GWENDOLEN. Yes, I am quite well aware of the fact. And I often wish that in public, at any rate, you had been more demonstrative. For me you have always had an irresistible fascination. Even before I met you I was far from in-different to you. [JACK *looks at her in amazement.*] We live, as I hope you know, Mr Worthing, in an age if ideals. The fact is constantly mentioned in the more expensive monthly magazines, and has reached the provincial pul-pits, I am told; and my ideal has always been to love some one of the name of Ernest. There is something in that name that inspires absolute confidence. The moment Algernon first mentioned to me that he had a friend called Ernest, I knew I was destined to love you.

JACK. You really love me, Gwendolen?

GWENDOLEN. Passionately!

JACK. Darling! You don't know how happy you've made me.

GWENDOLEN. My own Ernest!

JACK. But you don't really mean to say that you couldn't love me if my name wasn't Ernest?

GWENDOLEN. But your name is Ernest.

JACK. Yes, I know it is. But supposing it was something else? Do you mean to say you couldn't love me then?

GWENDOLEN [glibly]. Ah! that is clearly a metaphysical speculation, and like most metaphysical speculations has very little reference at all to the actual facts of real life, as we know them.

JACK. Personally, darling, to speak quite candidly, I don't much care about the name of Ernest. . . . I don't think the name suits me at all.

GWENDOLEN. It suits you perfectly. It is a divine name. It has music of its own. It produces vibrations.

JACK. Well, really, Gwendolen, I must say that I think there are lots of other much nicer names. I think Jack, for instance, a charming name.

GWENDOLEN. Jack? . . . No, there is very little music in the name Jack, if any at all, indeed. It does not thrill. It produces absolutely no vibrations. . . . I have known several Jacks, and they all, without exception, were more than usually plain. Besides, Jack is a notorious domesticity for John! And I pity any woman who is married to a man called John. She would probably never be allowed to know the entrancing pleasure of a single moment's solitude. The only really safe name is Ernest.

JACK. Gwendolen, I must get christened at once—I mean we must get married at once. There is no time to be lost.

GWENDOLEN. Married, Mr Worthing?

JACK [astounded]. Well . . . surely. You know that I love you, and you led me to believe, Miss Fairfax, that you were not absolutely indifferent to me.

GWENDOLEN. I adore you. But you haven't proposed to me yet. Nothing has been said at all about marriage. The subject has not even been touched on.

JACK. Well . . . may I propose to you now?

GWENDOLEN. I think it would be an admirable opportunity. And to spare you any possible disappointment, Mr Worthing, I think it only fair to tell you quite frankly beforehand that I am fully determined to accept you.

JACK. Gwendolen!

GWENDOLEN. Yes, Mr Worthing, what have you got to say to me?

JACK. You know what I have got to say to you.

GWENDOLEN. Yes, but you don't say it.

JACK. Gwendolen, will you marry me? [*Goes on his knees.*]

GWENDOLEN. Of course I will, darling. How long you have been about it! I am afraid you have had very little experience in how to propose.

JACK. My own one, I have never loved any one in the world but you.

GWENDOLEN. Yes, but men often propose for practice. I know my brother Gerald does. All my girl-friends tell me so. What wonderfully blue eyes you have, Ernest! They are quite, quite blue. I hope you will always look at me just like that, especially when there are other people present.

[*Enter* LADY BRACKNELL.]

LADY BRACKNELL. Mr Worthing! Rise, sir, from this semi-recumbent posture. It is most indecorous.

GWENDOLEN. Mamma! [*He tries to rise; she restrains him.*] I must beg you to retire. This is no place for you. Besides, Mr Worthing has not quite finished yet.

LADY BRACKNELL. Finished what, may I ask?

GWENDOLEN. I am engaged to Mr Worthing, mamma.

[*They rise together.*]

LADY BRACKNELL. Pardon me, you are not engaged to any one. When you do become engaged to some one, I, or your father, should his health permit him, will inform you of the fact. An engagement should come on a young girl as a surprise, pleasant or unpleasant, as the case may be. It is hardly a matter that she could be allowed to arrange for herself. . . . And now I have a few questions to put to you, Mr Worthing. While I am making these inquiries, you, Gwendolen, will wait for me below in the carriage.

GWENDOLEN [*reproachfully*]. Mamma!

LADY BRACKNELL. In the carriage, Gwendolen! [GWENDOLEN *goes to the door. She and* JACK *blow kisses to each other behind* LADY BRACKNELL'S *back.* LADY BRACKNELL *looks vaguely about as if she could not understand what the noise was. Finally turns round.*] Gwendolen, the carriage!

GWENDOLEN. Yes, mamma. [*Goes out, looking back at JACK.*]

LADY BRACKNELL [*sitting down*]. You can take a seat, Mr Worthing. [*Looks in her pocket for note-book and pencil.*]

JACK. Thank you, Lady Bracknell, I prefer standing.

LADY BRACKNELL [*pencil and note-book in hand*]. I feel bound to tell you that you are not down on my list of eligible young men, although I have the same list as the dear Duchess of Bolton has. We work together, in fact. However, I am quite ready to enter your name, should your answers be what a really affectionate mother requires. Do you smoke?

JACK. Well, yes, I must admit I smoke.

LADY BRACKNELL. I am glad to hear it. A man should always have an occupation of some kind. There are far too many idle men in London as it is. How old are you?

JACK. Twenty-nine.

LADY BRACKNELL. A very good age to be married at. I have always been of opinion that a man who desires to get married should know either everything or nothing. Which do you know?

JACK [*after some hesitation*]. I know nothing, Lady Bracknell.

LADY BRACKNELL. I am pleased to hear it. I do not approve of anything that tampers with natural ignorance. Ignorance is like a delicate exotic fruit; touch it and the bloom is gone. The whole theory of modern education is radically unsound. Fortunately in England, at any rate, education produces no effect whatsoever. If it did, it would prove a serious danger to the upper classes, and probably lead to acts of violence in Grosvenor Square. What is your income?

JACK. Between seven and eight thousand a year.

LADY BRACKNELL [*makes a note in her book*]. In land, or in investments?

JACK. In investments, chiefly.

LADY BRACKNELL. That is satisfactory. What between the duties expected of one during one's lifetime, and the duties exacted from one after one's death, land has ceased to be either a profit or a pleasure. It gives one position, and prevents one from keeping it up. That's all that can be said about land.

JACK. I have a country house with some land, of course, attached to it, about fifteen hundred acres, I believe; but I don't depend on that for my real income. In fact, as far as I can make out, the poachers are the only people who make anything out of it.

LADY BRACKNELL. A country house! How many bedrooms? Well, that point can be cleared up afterwards. You have a town house, I hope? A girl with a simple, unspoiled nature, like Gwendolen, could hardly be expected to reside in the country.

JACK. Well, I own a house in Belgrave Square, but it is let by the year to Lady Bloxham. Of course, I can get it back whenever I like, at six months' notice.

LADY BRACKNELL. Lady Bloxham? I don't know her.

JACK. Oh, she goes about very little. She is a lady considerably advanced in years.

LADY BRACKNELL. Ah, nowadays that is no guarantee of respectability of character. What number in Belgrave Square?

JACK. 149.

LADY BRACKNELL [shaking her head]. The unfashionable side. I thought there was something. However, that could easily be altered.

JACK. Do you mean the fashion, or the side?

LADY BRACKNELL [sternly]. Both, if necessary, I presume. What are your politics?

JACK. Well, I am afraid I really have none. I am a Liberal Unionist.

LADY BRACKNELL. Oh, they count as Tories. They dine with us. Or come in the evening, at any rate. Now to minor matters. Are your parents living?

JACK. I have lost both my parents.

LADY BRACKNELL. To lose one parent, Mr Worthing, may be regarded as a misfortune; to lose both looks like carelessness. Who was your father? He was evidently a man of some wealth. Was he born in what the Radical papers call the purple of commerce, or did he rise from the ranks of the aristocracy?

JACK. I am afraid I really don't know. The fact is, Lady Bracknell, I said I had lost my parents. It would be nearer the truth to say that my parents seem to have lost me. . . .

I don't actually know who I am by birth. I was . . . well, I was found.

LADY BRACKNELL. Found!

JACK. The late Mr Thomas Cardew, an old gentleman of a very charitable and kindly disposition, found me, and gave me the name of Worthing, because he happened to have a first-class ticket for Worthing in his pocket at the time. Worthing is a place in Sussex. It is a seaside resort.

LADY BRACKNELL. Where did the charitable gentleman who had a first-class ticket for this seaside resort find you?

JACK [gravely]. In a hand-bag.

LADY BRACKNELL. A hand-bag?

JACK [very seriously]. Yes, Lady Bracknell. I was in a hand-bag—a somewhat large, black leather hand-bag, with handles to it—an ordinary hand-bag in fact.

LADY BRACKNELL. In what locality did this Mr James, or Thomas, Cardew come across this ordinary hand-bag?

JACK. In the cloak-room at Victoria Station. It was given to him in mistake for his own.

LADY BRACKNELL. The cloak-room at Victoria Station?

JACK. Yes. The Brighton line.

LADY BRACKNELL. The line is immaterial. Mr Worthing, I confess I feel somewhat bewildered by what you have just told me. To be born, or at any rate bred, in a hand-bag, whether it had handles or not, seems to me to display a contempt for the ordinary decencies of family life that reminds one of the worst excesses of the French Revolution. And I presume you know what that unfortunate movement led to? As for the particular locality in which the hand-bag was found, a cloak-room at a railway station might serve to conceal a social indiscretion—has probably, indeed, been used for that purpose before now—but it could hardly be regarded as an assured basis for a recognized position in good society.

JACK. May I ask you then what you would advise me to do? I need hardly say I would do anything in the world to ensure Gwendolen's happiness.

LADY BRACKNELL. I would strongly advise you, Mr Worthing, to try and acquire some relations as soon as possible, and to make a definite effort to produce at any rate one parent, of either sex, before the season is quite over.

JACK. Well, I don't see how I could possibly manage to do

that. I can produce the hand-bag at any moment. It is in my dressing-room at home. I really think that should satisfy you, Lady Bracknell.

LADY BRACKNELL. Me, sir! What has it to do with me? You can hardly imagine that I and Lord Bracknell would dream of allowing our only daughter—a girl brought up with the utmost care—to marry into a cloakroom, and form an alliance with a parcel. Good morning, Mr Worthing!

[LADY BRACKNELL *sweeps out in majestic indignation*.]

JACK. Good morning! [ALGERNON, *from the other room, strikes up the Wedding March.* JACK *looks perfectly furious, and goes to the door*.] For goodness' sake don't play the ghastly tune, Algy! How idiotic you are!

[*The music stops and* ALGERNON *enters cheerily*.]

ALGERNON. Didn't it go off all right, old boy? You don't mean to say Gwendolen refused you? I know it is a way she has. She is always refusing people. I think it is most ill-natured of her.

JACK. Oh, Gwendolen is as right as a trivet. As far as she is concerned, we are engaged. Her mother is perfectly unbearable. Never met such a Gorgon. . . . I don't really know what a Gorgon is like, but I am quite sure that Lady Bracknell is one. In any case, she is a monster, without being a myth, which is rather unfair. . . . I beg your pardon, Algy, I suppose I shouldn't talk about your own aunt in that way before you.

ALGERNON. My dear boy, I love hearing my relations abused. It is the only thing that makes me put up with them at all. Relations are simply a tedious pack of people, who haven't got the remotest knowledge of how to live, nor the smallest instinct about when to die.

JACK. Oh, that is nonsense!

ALGERNON. It isn't!

JACK. Well, I won't argue about the matter. You always want to argue about things.

ALGERNON. That is exactly what things were originally made for.

JACK. Upon my word, if I thought that, I'd shoot myself. . . .

[*A pause.*] You don't think there is any chance of Gwendolen becoming like her mother in about a hundred and fifty years, do you, Algy?

ALGERNON. All women become like their mothers. That is their tragedy. No man does. That's his.

JACK. Is that clever?

ALGERNON. It is perfectly phrased! and quite as true as any observation in civilized life should be.

JACK. I am sick to death of cleverness. Everybody is clever nowadays. You can't go anywhere without meeting clever people. The thing has become an absolute public nuisance. I wish to goodness we had a few fools left.

ALGERNON. We have.

JACK. I should extremely like to meet them. What do they talk about?

ALGERNON. The fools? Oh! about the clever people, of course.

JACK. What fools.

ALGERNON. By the way, did you tell Gwendolen the truth about your being Ernest in town, and Jack in the country?

JACK [*in a very patronizing manner*]. My dear fellow, the truth isn't quite the sort of thing one tells to a nice, sweet, refined girl. What extraordinary ideas you have about the way to behave to a woman!

ALGERNON. The only way to behave to a woman is to make love to her, if she is pretty, and to someone else, if she is plain.

JACK. Oh, that is nonsense.

ALGERNON. What about your brother? What about the profligate Ernest?

JACK. Oh, before the end of the week I shall have got rid of him. I'll say he died in Paris of apoplexy. Lots of people die of apoplexy, quite suddenly, don't they?

ALGERNON. Yes, but it's hereditary, my dear fellow. It's a sort of thing that runs in families. You had much better say a severe chill.

JACK. You are sure a severe chill isn't hereditary, or anything of that kind?

ALGERNON. Of course it isn't!

JACK. Very well, then. My poor brother Ernest is carried off suddenly, in Paris, by a severe chill. That gets rid of him.

ALGERNON. But I thought you said that . . . Miss Cardew was

a little too much interested in your poor brother Ernest? Won't she feel his loss a good deal?

ACK. Oh, that is all right. Cecily is not a silly romantic girl, I am glad to say. She has got a capital appetite, goes long walks, and pays no attention at all to her lessons.

LGERNON. I would rather like to see Cecily.

ACK. I will take very good care you never do. She is excessive pretty, and she is only just eighteen.

LGERNON. Have you told Gwendolen yet that you have an excessively pretty ward who is only just eighteen?

ACK. Oh! one doesn't blurt these things out to people. Cecily and Gwendolen are perfectly certain to be extremely great friends. I'll bet you anything you like that half an hour after they have met, they will be calling each other sister.

ALGERNON. Women only do that when they have called each other a lot of other things first. Now, my dear boy, if we want to get a good table at Willis's, we really must go and dress. Do you know it is nearly seven?

JACK [irritably]. Oh! it always is nearly seven.

ALGERNON. I'm hungry.

JACK. I never knew you when you weren't. . . .

ALGERNON. What shall we do after dinner? Go to a theatre?

JACK. Oh no! I loathe listening.

ALGERNON. Well, let us go to the Club?

JACK. Oh, no! I hate talking.

ALGERNON. Well, we might trot round to the Empire at ten?

JACK. Oh, no! I can't bear looking at things. It is so silly.

ALGERNON. Well, what shall we do?

JACK. Nothing!

ALGERNON. It is awfully hard work doing nothing. However, I don't mind hard work where there is no definite object of any kind.

[Enter LANE.]

LANE. Miss Fairfax. [Enter GWENDOLEN, LANE goes out.]

ALGERNON. Gwendolen, upon my word!

GWENDOLEN. Algy, kindly turn your back. I have something very particular to say to Mr Worthing.

ALGERNON. Really, Gwendolen, I don't think I can allow this at all.

GWENDOLEN. Algy, you always adopt a strictly immoral at-

titude towards life. You are not quite old enough to d
that.

[ALGERNON *retires to the fire-place.*]

JACK. My own darling!

GWENDOLEN. Ernest, we may never be married. From th
expression on mamma's face I fear we never shall. Fev
parents nowadays pay any regard to what their childre:
say to them. The old-fashioned respect for the young is fas
dying out. Whatever influence I ever had over mamma
I lost at the age of three. But although she may preven
us from becoming man and wife, and I may marry some
one else, and marry often, nothing that she can possibly
do can alter my eternal devotion to you.

JACK. Dear Gwendolen!

GWENDOLEN. The story of your romantic origin, as related
to me by mamma, with unpleasing comments, has nat
urally stirred the deeper fibres of my nature. Your Christian name has an irresistible fascination. The simplicity of
your character makes you exquisitely incomprehensible to
me. Your town address at the Albany I have. What is
your address in the country?

JACK. The Manor House, Woolton, Hertfordshire.

[ALGERNON, *who has been carefully listening, smiles to
himself, and writes the address on his shirt-cuff. Then picks
up the Railway Guide.*]

GWENDOLEN. There is a good postal service, I suppose? It
may be necessary to do something desperate. That of
course will require serious consideration. I will communicate with you daily.

JACK. My own one!

GWENDOLEN. How long do you remain in town?

JACK. Till Monday.

GWENDOLEN. Good! Algy, you may turn round now.

ALGERNON. Thanks, I've turned round already.

GWENDOLEN. You may also ring the bell.

JACK. You will let me see you to your carriage, my own
darling?

GWENDOLEN. Certainly.

JACK [*to* LANE, *who now enters*]. I will see Miss Fairfax
out.

LANE. Yes, sir.

[JACK *and* GWENDOLEN *go off.* LANE *presents several letters on a salver to* ALGERNON. *It is to be surmised that they are bills, as* ALGERNON, *after looking at the envelopes, tears them up.*]

ALGERNON. A glass of sherry, Lane.

LANE. Yes, sir.

ALGERNON. To-morrow, Lane, I'm going Bunburying.

LANE. Yes, sir.

ALGERNON. I shall probably not be back till Monday. You can put up my dress clothes, my smoking jacket, and all the Bunbury suits. . . .

LANE. Yes, sir. [*Handing sherry.*]

ALGERNON. I hope to-morrow will be a fine day, Lane.

LANE. It never is, sir.

ALGERNON. Lane, you're a perfect pessimist.

LANE. I do my best to give satisfaction, sir.

[*Enter* JACK. LANE *goes off.*]

JACK. There's a sensible, intellectual girl! the only girl I ever cared for in my life. [ALGERNON *is laughing immoderately.*] What on earth are you so amused at?

ALGERNON. Oh, I'm a little anxious about poor Bunbury, that is all.

JACK. If you don't take care, your friend Bunbury will get you into a serious scrape some day.

ALGERNON. I love scrapes. They are the only things that are never serious.

JACK. Oh, that's nonsense, Algy. You never talk anything but nonsense.

ALGERNON. Nobody ever does.

[JACK *looks indignantly at him, and leaves the room.* ALGERNON *lights a cigarette, reads his shirt-cuff, and smiles.*]

**CURTAIN**

# ACT TWO

SCENE. *Garden at the Manor House. A flight of grey stone steps leads up to the house. The garden, an old-fashioned one, full of roses. Time of year, July. Basket chairs, and a table covered with books, are set under a large yew-tree.*

[MISS PRISM *discovered seated at the table.* CECILY *is at the back, watering flowers.*]

MISS PRISM [*calling*]. Cecily, Cecily! Surely such a utilitarian occupation as the watering of flowers is rather Moulton's duty than yours? Especially at a moment when intellectual pleasures await you. Your German grammar is on the table. Pray open it at page fifteen. We will repeat yesterday's lesson.

CECILY [*coming over very slowly*]. But I don't like German. It isn't at all a becoming language. I know perfectly well that I look quite plain after my German lesson.

MISS PRISM. Child, you know how anxious your guardian is that you should improve yourself in every way. He laid particular stress on your German, as he was leaving for town yesterday. Indeed, he always lays stress on your German when he is leaving for town.

CECILY. Dear Uncle Jack is so very serious! Sometimes he is so serious that I think he cannot be quite well.

MISS PRISM [*drawing herself up*]. Your guardian enjoys the best of health, and his gravity of demeanour is especially to be commended in one so comparatively young as he is. I know no one who has a higher sense of duty and responsibility.

CECILY. I suppose that is why he often looks a little bored when we three are together.

MISS PRISM. Cecily! I am surprised at you. Mr Worthing has many troubles in his life. Idle merriment and triviality would be out of place in his conversation. You must remember his constant anxiety about that unfortunate youn<sub></sub> man his brother.

CECILY. I wish Uncle Jack would allow that unfortunate young man, his brother, to come down here sometimes. We might have a good influence over him, Miss Prism. I am sure you certainly would. You know German, and geology, and things of that kind influence a man very much. [CECILY *begins to write in her diary*.]

MISS PRISM [*shaking her head*]. I do not think that even I could produce any effect on a character that according to his own brother's admission is irretrievably weak and vacillating. Indeed I am not sure that I would desire to reclaim him. I am not in favour of this modern mania for turning bad people into good people at a moment's notice. As a man sows so let him reap. You must put away your diary, Cecily. I really don't see why you should keep a diary at all.

CECILY. I keep a diary in order to enter the wonderful secrets of my life. If I didn't write them down, I should probably forget all about them.

MISS PRISM. Memory, my dear Cecily, is the diary that we all carry about with us.

CECILY. Yes, but it usually chronicles the things that have never happened, and couldn't possibly have happened. I believe that Memory is responsible for nearly all the three-volume novels that Mudie sends us.

MISS PRISM. Do not speak slightingly of the three-volume novel, Cecily. I wrote one myself in earlier days.

CECILY. Did you really, Miss Prism? How wonderfully clever you are! I hope it did not end happily? I don't like novels that end happily. They depress me so much.

MISS PRISM. The good ended happily, and the bad unhappily. That is what Fiction means.

CECILY. I suppose so. But it seems very unfair. And was your novel ever published?

MISS PRISM. Alas! no. The manuscript unfortunately was abandoned. [CECILY *starts*.] I used the word in the sense of lost or mislaid. To your work, child, these speculations are profitless.

CECILY [*smiling*]. But I see dear Dr Chasuble coming up through the garden.

MISS PRISM [*rising and advancing*]. Dr Chasuble! This is indeed a pleasure.

*Enter* CANON CHASUBLE.]

CHASUBLE. And how are we this morning? Miss Prism, you are, I trust, well?

CECILY. Miss Prism has just been complaining of a slight headache. I think it would do her so much good to have a short stroll with you in the Park, Dr Chasuble.

MISS PRIM. Cecily, I have not mentioned anything about a headache.

CECILY. No, dear Miss Prism, I know that, but I felt instinctively that you had a headache. Indeed I was thinking about that, and not about my German lesson, when the rector came in.

CHASUBLE. I hope, Cecily, you are not inattentive.

CECILY. Oh, I am afraid I am.

CHASUBLE. That is strange. Were I fortunate enough to be Miss Prism's pupil, I would hang upon her lips. [MISS PRISM *glares*.] I spoke metaphorically.—My metaphor was drawn from bees. Ahem! Mr Worthing, I suppose, has not returned from town yet?

MISS PRISM. We do not expect him till Monday afternoon.

CHASUBLE. Ah yes, he usually likes to spend his Sunday in London. He is not one of those whose sole aim is enjoyment, as, by all accounts, that unfortunate young man his brother seems to be. But I must not disturb Egeria and her pupil any longer.

MISS PRISM. Egeria? My name is Laetitia, Doctor.

CHASUBLE [*bowing*]. A classical allusion merely, drawn from the Pagan authors. I shall see you both no doubt at Evensong?

MISS PRISM. I think, dear Doctor, I will have a stroll with you. I find I have a headache after all, and a walk might do it good.

CHASUBLE. With pleasure, Miss Prism, with pleasure. We might go as far as the schools and back.

MISS PRISM. That would be delightful. Cecily, you will read your Political Economy in my absence. The chapter on the Fall of the Rupee you may omit. It is somewhat too sensational. Even these metallic problems have their melodramatic side. [*Goes down the garden with* DR CHASUBLE.]

CECILY [*picks up books and throws them back on table*]. Horrid Political Economy! Horrid Geography! Horrid, horrid German!

[*Enter* MERRIMAN *with a card on a salver.*]

MERRIMAN. Mr Ernest Worthing has just driven over from the station. He has brought his luggage with him.

CECILY [*takes the card and reads it*]. 'Mr Ernest Worthing B.4, The Albany, W.' Uncle Jack's brother! Did you tell him Mr Worthing was in town?

MERRIMAN. Yes, Miss. He seemed very much disappointed. I mentioned that you and Miss Prism were in the garden. He said he was anxious to speak to you privately for a moment.

CECILY. Ask Mr Ernest Worthing to come here. I suppose you had better talk to the housekeeper about a room for him.

MERRIMAN. Yes, Miss. [MERRIMAN *goes off.*]

CECILY. I have never met any really wicked person before. I feel rather frightened. I am so afraid he will look just like every one else. [*Enter* ALGERNON, *very gay and debonair.*] He does!

ALGERNON [*raising his hat*]. You are my little cousin Cecily, I'm sure.

CECILY. You are under some strange mistake. I am not little. In fact, I believe I am more than usually tall for my age. [ALGERNON *is rather taken aback.*] But I am your cousin Cecily. You, I see from your card, are Uncle Jack's brother, my cousin Ernest, my wicked cousin Ernest.

ALGERNON. Oh! I am not really wicked at all, cousin Cecily. You mustn't think that I am wicked.

CECILY. If you are not, then you have certainly been deceiving us all in a very inexcusable manner. I hope you have not been leading a double life, pretending to be wicked and being really good all the time. That would be hypocrisy.

ALGERNON. [*looks at her in amazement*]. Oh! Of course I have been rather reckless.

CECILY. I am glad to hear it.

ALGERNON. In fact, now you mention the subject, I have been very bad in my own small way.

CECILY. I don't think you should be so proud of that, though I am sure it must have been very pleasant.

ALGERNON. It is much pleasanter being here with you.

CECILY. I can't understand how you are here at all. Uncle Jack won't be back till Monday afternoon.

ALGERNON. That is a great dissappointment. I am obliged to go up by the first train on Monday morning. I have a business appointment that I am anxious . . . to miss!

CECILY. Couldn't you miss it anywhere but in London?

ALGERNON. No: the appointment is in London.

CECILY. Well, I know, of course, how important it is not to keep a business engagement, if one wants to retain any sense of the beauty of life, but still I think you had better wait till Uncle Jack arrives. I know he wants to speak to you about your emigrating.

ALGERNON. About my what?

CECILY. Your emigrating. He has gone up to buy your outfit.

ALGERNON. I certainly wouldn't let Jack buy my outfit. He has no taste in neckties at all.

CECILY. I don't think you will require neckties. Uncle Jack is sending you to Australia.

ALGERNON. Australia! I'd sooner die.

CECILY. Well, he said at dinner on Wednesday night, that you would have to choose between this world, the next world, and Australia.

ALGERNON. Oh, well! The accounts I have received of Australia and the next world are not particularly encouraging. This world is good enough for me, cousin Cecily.

CECILY. Yes, but are you good enough for it?

ALGERNON. I'm afraid I'm not that. That is why I want you to reform me. You might make that your mission, if you don't mind, Cousin Cecily.

CECILY. I'm afraid I've no time, this afternoon.

ALGERNON. Well, would you mind my reforming myself this afternoon?

CECILY. It is rather Quixotic of you. But I think you should try.

ALGERNON. I will. I feel better already.

CECILY. You are looking a little worse.

ALGERNON. That is because I am hungry.

CECILY. How thoughtless of me. I should have remembered that when one is going to lead an entirely new life, one requires regular and wholesome meals. Won't you come in?

ALGERNON. Thank you. Might I have a buttonhole first? I have never any appetite unless I have a buttonhole first.

CECILY. A Maréchal Niel? [Picks up scissors.]

ALGERNON. No, I'd sooner have a pink rose.

CECILY. Why? [*Cuts a flower.*]

ALGERNON. Because you are like a pink rose, Cousin Cecily.

CECILY. I don't think it can be right for you to talk to me like that. Miss Prism never says such things to me.

ALGERNON. Then Miss Prism is a short-sighted old lady. [CECILY *puts the rose in his buttonhole.*] You are the prettiest girl I ever saw.

CECILY. Miss Prism says that all good looks are a snare.

ALGERNON. They are a snare that every sensible man would like to be caught in.

CECILY. Oh, I don't think I would care to catch a sensible man. I shouldn't know what to talk to him about.

[*They pass into the house.* MISS PRISM *and* DR CHASUBLE *return.*]

MISS PRISM. You are too much alone, dear Dr Chasuble. You should get married. A misanthrope I can understand—a womanthrope, never!

CHASUBLE [*with a scholar's shudder*]. Believe me, I do not deserve so neologistic a phrase. The precept as well as the practice of the Primitive Church was distinctly against matrimony.

MISS PRISM [*sententiously*]. That is obviously the reason why the Primitive Church has not lasted up to the present day. And you do not seem to realize, dear Doctor, that by persistently remaining single, a man converts himself into a permanent public temptation. Men should be more careful; this very celibacy leads weaker vessels astray.

CHASUBLE. But is a man not equally attractive when married?

MISS PRISM. No married man is ever attractive except to his wife.

CHASUBLE. And often, I've been told, not even to her.

MISS PRISM. That depends on the intellectual sympathies of the woman. Maturity can always be depended on. Ripeness can be trusted. Young women are green. [DR CHASUBLE *starts.*] I spoke horticulturally. My metaphor was drawn from fruits. But where is Cecily?

CHASUBLE. Perhaps she followed us to the schools.

[*Enter* JACK *slowly from the back of the garden. He is dressed in the deepest mourning, with crepe hatband and black gloves.*]

MISS PRISM. Mr Worthing!

CHASUBLE. Mr Worthing?

MISS PRISM. This is indeed a surprise. We did not look for you till Monday afternoon.

JACK [*shakes* MISS PRISM'S *hand in a tragic manner*]. I have returned sooner than I expected. Dr Chasuble, I hope you are well?

CHASUBLE. Dear Mr Worthing, I trust this garb of woe does not betoken some terrible calamity?

JACK. My brother.

MISS PRISM. More shameful debts and extravagance?

CHASUBLE. Still leading his life of pleasure?

JACK [*shaking his head*]. Dead!

CHASUBLE. Your brother Ernest dead?

JACK. Quite dead.

MISS PRISM. What a lesson for him! I trust he will profit by it.

CHASUBLE. Mr Worthing, I offer you my sincere condolence. You have at least the consolation of knowing that you were always the most generous and forgiving of brothers.

JACK. Poor Ernest! He had many faults, but it is a sad, sad blow.

CHASUBLE. Very sad indeed. Were you with him at the end?

JACK. No. He died abroad; in Paris, in fact. I had a telegram last night from the manager of the Grand Hotel.

CHASUBLE. Was the cause of death mentioned?

JACK. A severe chill, it seems.

MISS PRISM. As a man sows, so shall he reap.

CHASUBLE [*raising his hand*]. Charity, dear Miss Prism, charity! None of us are perfect. I myself am peculiarly susceptible to draughts. Will the interment take place here?

JACK. No. He seems to have expressed a desire to be buried in Paris.

CHASUBLE. In Paris! [*Shakes his head.*] I fear that hardly points to any very serious state of mind at the last. You would no doubt wish me to make some slight allusion to this tragic domestic affliction next Sunday. [JACK *presses his hand convulsively*.] My sermon on the meaning of the manna in the wilderness can be adapted to almost any occasion, joyful, or, as in the present case, distressing. [*All sigh.*] I have preached it at harvest celebrations, christenings, confirmations, on days of humiliation and festal days. The last time I delivered it was in the Cathedral, as a charity sermon on behalf of the Society for the Prevention of Discontent among the Upper Orders. The Bishop, who was present, was much struck by some of the analogies I drew.

JACK. Ah! that reminds me, you mentioned christenings I think, Dr Chasuble? I suppose you know how to christen all right? [DR CHASUBLE *looks astounded*.] I mean, of course, you are continually christening, aren't you?

MISS PRISM. It is, I regret to say, one of the Rector's most constant duties in this parish. I have often spoken to the poorer classes on the subject. But they don't seem to know what thrift is.

CHASUBLE. But is there any particular infant in whom you are interested, Mr Worthing? Your brother was, I believe, unmarried, was he not?

JACK. Oh yes.

MISS PRISM [*bitterly*]. People who live entirely for pleasure usually are.

JACK. But it is not for any child, dear Doctor. I am very fond of children. No! the fact is, I would like to be christened myself, this afternoon, if you have nothing better to do.

CHASUBLE. But surely, Mr Worthing, you have been christened already?

JACK. I don't remember anything about it.

CHASUBLE. But have you any grave doubts on the subject?

JACK. I certainly intend to have. Of course I don't know if the thing would bother you in any way, or if you think I am a little too old now.

CHASUBLE. Not at all. The sprinkling, and, indeed, the immersion of adults is a perfectly canonical practice.

JACK. Immersion!

CHASUBLE. You need have no apprehensions. Sprinkling is all that is necessary, or indeed I think advisable. Our weather is so changeable. At what hour would you wish the ceremony performed?

JACK. Oh, I might trot round about five if that would suit you.

CHASUBLE. Perfectly, perfectly! In fact I have two similar ceremonies to perform at that time. A case of twins that occurred recently in one of the outlying cottages on your own estate. Poor Jenkins the carter, a most hard-working man.

JACK. Oh! I don't see much fun in being christened along with other babies. It would be childish. Would half-past five do?

CHASUBLE. Admirably! Admirably! [*Takes out watch.*] And now, dear Mr Worthing, I will not intrude any longer into a house of sorrow. I would merely beg you not to be too much bowed down by grief. What seem to us bitter trials are often blessings in disguise.

MISS PRISM. This seems to me a blessing of an extremely obvious kind.

[*Enter* CECILY *from the house.*]

CECILY. Uncle Jack! Oh, I am pleased to see you back. But what horrid clothes you have got on. Do go and change them.

MISS PRISM. Cecily!

CHASUBLE. My child! my child.

[CECILY *goes toward* JACK; *he kisses her brow in a melancholy manner.*]

CECILY. What is the matter, Uncle Jack? Do look happy! You look as if you had toothache, and I have got such a surprise for you. Who do you think is in the dining-room? Your brother!

JACK. Who?

CECILY. Your brother Ernest. He arrived about half an hour ago.

JACK. What nonsense! I haven't got a brother.

CECILY. Oh, don't say that. However badly he may have behaved to you in the past he is still your brother. You couldn't be so heartless as to disown him. I'll tell him to come out. And you will shake hands with him, won't you, Uncle Jack? [*Runs back into the house.*]

CHASUBLE. These are very joyful tidings.

MISS PRISM. After we had all been resigned to his loss, his sudden return seems to me peculiarly distressing.

JACK. My brother is in the dining-room? I don't know what it all means. I think it is perfectly absurd.

[*Enter* ALGERNON *and* CECILY *hand in hand. They come slowly up to* JACK.]

JACK. Good heavens! [*Motions* ALGERNON *away*.]

ALGERNON. Brother John, I have come down from town to tell you that I am very sorry for all the trouble I have given you, and that I intend to lead a better life in the future.

[JACK *glares at him and does not take his hand.*]

CECILY. Uncle Jack, you are not going to refuse your own brother's hand?

JACK. Nothing will induce me to take his hand. I think his coming down here disgraceful. He knows perfectly well why.

CECILY. Uncle Jack, do be nice. There is some good in everyone. Ernest has just been telling me about his poor invalid friend Mr Bunbury whom he goes to visit so often. And surely there must be much good in one who is kind to an invalid, and leaves the pleasures of London to sit by a bed of pain.

JACK. Oh! he has been talking about Bunbury, has he?

CECILY. Yes, he has told me all about poor Mr Bunbury, and *his* terrible state of health.

JACK. Bunbury! Well, I won't have him talk to you about Bunbury or about anything else. It is enough to drive one perfectly frantic.

ALGERNON. Of course I admit that the faults were all on my side. But I must say that I think that Brother John's coldness to me is peculiarly painful. I expected a more enthusiastic welcome, especially considering it is the first time I have come here.

CECILY. Uncle Jack, if you don't shake hands with Ernest I will never forgive you.

JACK. Never forgive me?

CECILY. Never, never, never!

JACK. Well, this is the last time I shall ever do it. [*Shakes hands with* ALGERNON *and glares.*]

CHASUBLE. It's pleasant, is it not, to see so perfect a reconciliation? I think we might leave the two brothers together.

MISS PRISM. Cecily, you will come with us.

CECILY. Certainly, Miss Prism. My little task of reconciliation is over.

CHASUBLE. You have done a beautiful action to-day, dear child.

MISS PRISM. We must not be premature in our judgements.

CECILY. I feel very happy.

*[They all go off except JACK and ALGERNON.]*

JACK. You young scoundrel, Algy, you must get out of this place as soon as possible. I don't allow any Bunburying here.

*[Enter MERRIMAN.]*

MERRIMAN. I have put Mr Ernest's things in the room next to yours, sir. I suppose that is all right?

JACK. What?

MERRIMAN. Mr Ernest's luggage, sir. I have unpacked it and put it in the room next to your own.

JACK. His luggage?

MERRIMAN. Yes, sir. Three portmanteaus, a dressing-case, two hatboxes, and a large luncheon-basket.

ALGERNON. I am afraid I can't stay more than a week this time.

JACK. Merriman, order the dog-cart at once. Mr Ernest has been suddenly called back to town.

MERRIMAN. Yes, sir. *[Goes back into the house.]*

ALGERNON. What a fearful liar you are, Jack. I have not been called back to town at all.

JACK. Yes, you have.

ALGERNON. I haven't heard any one call me.

JACK. Your duty as a gentleman calls you back.

ALGERNON. My duty as a gentleman has never interfered with my pleasures in the smallest degree.

JACK. I can quite understand that.

ALGERNON. Well, Cecily is a darling.

JACK. You are not to talk of Miss Cardew like that. I don't like it.

ALGERNON. Well, I don't like your clothes. You look perfectly ridiculous in them. Why on earth don't you go up and change? It is perfectly childish to be in deep mourning for a man who is actually staying for a whole week with you in your house as a guest. I call it grotesque.

JACK. You are certainly not staying with me for a whole week as a guest or anything else. You have got to leave . . . by the four-five train.

ALGERNON. I certainly won't leave you so long as you are in mourning. It would be most unfriendly. If I were in mourning you would stay with me, I suppose. I should think it very unkind if you didn't.

JACK. Well, will you go if I change my clothes?

ALGERNON. Yes, if you are not too long. I never saw anybody take so long to dress, and with such little result.

JACK. Well, at any rate, that is better than being always over-dressed as you are.

ALGERNON. If I am occasionally a little over-dressed, I make up for it by being always immensely over-educated.

JACK. Your vanity is ridiculous, your conduct an outrage, and your presence in my garden utterly absurd. However, you have got to catch the four-five, and I hope you will have a pleasant journey back to town. This Bunburying, as you call it, has not been a great success for you. [*Goes into the house.*]

ALGERNON. I think it has been a great success. I'm in love with Cecily, and that is everything. [*Enter* CECILY *at the back of the garden. She picks up the can and begins to water the flowers.*] But I must see her before I go, and make arrangements for another Bunbury. Ah, there she is.

CECILY. Oh, I merely came back to water the roses. I thought you were with Uncle Jack.

ALGERNON. He's gone to order the dog-cart for me.

CECILY. Oh, is he going to take you for a nice drive?

ALGERNON. He's going to send me away.

CECILY. Then have we got to part?

ALGERNON. I am afraid so. It's a very painful parting.

CECILY. It is always painful to part from people whom one has known for a very brief space of time. The absence of old friends one can endure with equanimity. But even a momentary separation from any one to whom one has just been introduced is almost unbearable.

ALGERNON. Thank you.

[*Enter* MERRIMAN.]

MERRIMAN. The dog-cart is at the door, sir.

[ALGERNON *looks appealingly at* CECILY.]

CECILY. It can wait, Merriman . . . for . . . five minutes.

MERRIMAN. Yes, miss. [*Exit* MERRIMAN]

ALGERNON. I hope, Cecily, I shall not offend you if I state quite frankly and openly that you seem to me to be in every way the visible personification of absolute perfection.

CECILY. I think your frankness does you great credit, Ernest.

If you will allow me, I will copy your remarks into my diary. [*Goes over to table and begins writing in diary.*]

ALGERNON. Do you really keep a diary? I'd give anything to look at it. May I?

CECILY. Oh no. [*Puts her hand over it.*] You see, it is simply a very young girl's record of her own thoughts and impressions, and consequently meant for publication. When it appears in volume form I hope you will order a copy. But pray, Ernest, don't stop. I delight in taking down . from dictation. I have reached 'absolute perfection.' You can go on. I am quite ready for more.

ALGERNON [*somewhat taken aback*]. Ahem! Ahem!

CECILY. Oh, don't cough, Ernest. When one is dictating one should speak fluently and not cough. Besides, I don't know how to spell a cough. [*Writes as* ALGERNON *speaks.*]

ALGERNON [*speaking very rapidly*]. Cecily, ever since I first looked upon your wonderful and incomparable beauty, I have dared to love you wildly, passionately, devotedly, hopelessly.

CECILY. I don't think that you should tell me that you love me wildly, passionately, devotedly, hopelessly. Hopelessly doesn't seem to make much sense, does it?

ALGERNON. Cecily.

[*Enter* MERRIMAN.]

MERRIMAN. The dog-cart is waiting, sir.

ALGERNON. Tell it to come round next week, at the same hour.

MERRIMAN [*looks at* CECILY, *who makes no sign*]. Yes, sir. [MERRIMAN *retires.*]

CECILY. Uncle Jack would be very much annoyed if he knew you were staying on till next week, at the same hour.

ALGERNON. Oh, I don't care about Jack. I don't care for anybody in the whole world but you. I love you, Cecily. You will marry me, won't you?

CECILY. You silly boy! Of course. Why, we have been engaged for the last three months.

ALGERNON. For the last three months?

CECILY. Yes, it will be exactly three months on Thursday.

ALGERNON. But how did we become engaged?

CECILY. Well, ever since dear Uncle Jack first confessed to us that he had a younger brother who was very wicked and bad, you of course have formed the chief topic of conversation between myself and Miss Prism. And of course a man who is much talked about is always very attractive. One feels there must be something in him after all. I daresay it was foolish of me, but I fell in love with you, Ernest.

ALGERNON. Darling. And when was the engagement actually settled?

CECILY. On the 14th of February last. Worn out by your entire ignorance of my existence, I determined to end the matter one way or the other, and after a long struggle with myself I accepted you under this dear old tree here. The next day I bought this little ring in your name, and this is the little bangle with the true lover's knot I promised you always to wear.

ALGERNON. Did I give you this? It's very pretty, isn't it?

CECILY. Yes, you've wonderfully good taste, Ernest. It's the excuse I've always given for your leading such a bad life. And this is the box in which I keep all your dear letters. [Kneels at table, opens box, and produces letters tied up with blue ribbon.]

ALGERNON. My letters! But, my own sweet Cecily, I have never written you any letters.

CECILY. You need hardly remind me of that, Ernest. I remember only too well that I was forced to write your letters for you. I wrote always three times a week, and sometimes oftener.

ALGERNON. Oh, do let me read them, Cecily?

CECILY. Oh, I couldn't possibly. They would make you far too conceited. [Replaces box.] The three you wrote me after I had broken off the engagement are so beautiful, and so badly spelled, that even now I can hardly read them without crying a little.

ALGERNON. But was our engagement ever broken off?

CECILY. Of course it was. On the 22nd of last March. You can see the entry if you like. [Shows diary.] 'To-day I broke off my engagement with Ernest. I feel it is better to do so. The weather still continues charming.'

ALGERNON. But why on earth did you break if off? What had I done? I had done nothing at all. Cecily, I am very much hurt indeed to hear you broke it off. Particularly when the weather was so charming.

CECILY. It would hardly have been a really serious engagement if it hadn't been broken off at least once. But I forgave you before the week was out.

ALGEGNON [*crossing to her, and kneeling*]. What a perfect angel you are, Cecily.

CECILY. You dear romantic boy. [*He kisses her, she puts her fingers through his hair.*] I hope your hair curls naturally, does it?

ALGERNON. Yes, darling, with a little help from others.

CECILY. I am so glad.

ALGERNON. You'll never break off our engagement again, Cecily?

CECILY. I don't think I could break it off now that I have actually met you. Besides, of course, there is the question of your name.

ALGERNON. Yes, of course. [*Nervously.*]

CECILY. You must not laugh at me, darling, but it had always been a girlish dream of mine to love some one whose name was Ernest. [ALGERNON *rises*, CECILY *also.*] There is something in that name that seems to inspire absolute confidence. I pity any poor married woman whose husband is not called Ernest.

ALGERNON. But, my dear child, do you mean to say you could not love me if I had some other name?

CECILY. But what name?

ALGERNON. Oh, any name you like—Algernon—for instance . . .

CECILY. But I don't like the name of Algernon.

ALGERNON. Well, my own dear, sweet, loving little darling, I really can't see why you should object to the name of Algernon. It is not at all a bad name. In fact, it is rather an aristocratic name. Half of the chaps who get into the Bankruptcy Court are called Algernon. But seriously, Cecily . . . [*Moving to her.*] if my name was Algy, couldn't you love me?

CECILY [*rising*]. I might respect you, Ernest, I might admire your character, but I fear that I should not be able to give you my undivided attention.

ALGERNON. Ahem! Cecily! [*Picking up hat.*] Your Rector here is, I suppose, thoroughly experienced in the practice of all the rites and ceremonials of the Church?

CECILY. Oh, yes. Dr Chasuble is a most learned man. He

has never written a single book, so you can imagine how much he knows.

ALGERNON. I must see him at once on a most important christening—I mean on most important business.

CECILY. Oh!

ALGERNON. I shan't be away more than half an hour.

CECILY. Considering that we have been engaged since February the 14th, and that I only met you to-day for the first time, I think it is rather hard that you should leave me for so long a period as half an hour. Couldn't you make it twenty minutes?

ALGERNON. I'll be back in no time. [Kisses her and rushes down the garden.]

CECILY. What an impetuous boy he is! I like his hair so much. I must enter his proposal in my diary.

[Enter MERRIMAN.]

MERRIMAN. A Miss Fairfax has just called to see Mr Worthing. On very important business, Miss Fairfax states.

CECILY. Isn't Mr Worthing in his library?

MERRIMAN. Mr Worthing went over in the direction of the Rectory some time ago.

CECILY. Pray ask the lady to come out here; Mr Worthing is sure to be back soon. And you can bring tea.

MERRIMAN. Yes, Miss. [Goes out.]

CECILY. Miss Fairfax! I suppose one of the many good elderly women who are associated with Uncle Jack in some of his philanthropic work in London. I don't quite like women who are interested in philanthropic work. I think it is so forward of them.

[Enter MERRIMAN.]

MERRIMAN. Miss Fairfax.

[Enter GWENDOLEN. Exit MERRIMAN.]

CECILY [advancing to meet her]. Pray let me introduce myself to you. My name is Cecily Cardew.

GWENDOLEN. Cecily Cardew? [Moving to her and shaking hands.] What a very sweet name! Something tells me that we are going to be great friends. I like you already more than I can say. My first impressions of people are never wrong.

ECILY. How nice of you to like me so much after we have known each other such a comparatively short time. Pray sit down.

WENDOLEN [*still standing up*]. I may call you Cecily, may I not?

ECILY. With pleasure!

WENDOLEN. And you will always call me Gwendolen, won't you?

ECILY. If you wish.

WENDOLEN. Then that is all quite settled, is it not?

CECILY. I hope so. [*A pause. They both sit down together.*]

WENDOLEN. Perhaps this might be a favourable opportunity for my mentioning who I am. My father is Lord Bracknell. You have never heard of papa, I suppose?

CECILY. I don't think so.

GWENDOLEN. Outside the family circle, papa, I am glad to say, is entirely unknown. I think that is quite as it should be. The home seems to me to be the proper sphere for the man. And certainly once a man begins to neglect his domestic duties he becomes painfully effeminate, does he not? And I don't like that. It makes men so very attractive. Cecily, mamma, whose views on education are remarkably strict, has brought me up to be extremely shortsighted; it is part of her system; so do you mind my looking at you through my glasses?

CECILY. Oh! not at all, Gwendolen. I am very fond of being looked at.

GWENDOLEN [*after examining* CELICY *carefully through a lorgnette*]. You are here on a short visit, I suppose.

CECILY. Oh no! I live here.

GWENDOLEN [*severely*]. Really? Your mother, no doubt, or some female relative of advanced years, resides here also?

CECILY. Oh no! I have no mother, nor, in fact, any relations.

GWENDOLEN. Indeed?

CECILY. My dear guardian, with the assistance of Miss Prism, has the arduous task of looking after me.

GWENDOLEN. Your guardian?

CECILY. Yes, I am Mr Worthing's ward.

GWENDOLEN. Oh! It is strange he never mentioned to me that he had a ward. How secretive of him! He grows more interesting hourly. I am not sure, however, that the news inspires me with feelings of unmixed delight. [*Rising and going to her.*] I am very fond of you, Cecily;

I have liked you ever since I met you! But I am bound
state that now that I know that you are Mr Worthing
ward, I cannot help expressing a wish you were—wel
just a little older than you seem to be—and not quite s
very alluring in appearance. In fact, if I may spea
candidly——

CECILY. Pray do! I think that whenever one has anythir
unpleasant to say, one should always be quite candid.

GWENDOLEN. Well, to speak with perfect candour, Cecil
I wish that you were fully forty-two, and more tha
usually plain for your age. Ernest has a strong uprigl
nature. He is the very soul of truth and honour. Disloyal
would be as impossible to him as deception. But even me
of the noblest possible moral character are extremel
susceptible to the influence of the physical charms c
others. Modern, no less than Ancient History, supplies u
with many most painful examples of what I refer to. If
were not so, indeed, History would be quite unreadabl

CECILY. I beg your pardon, Gwendolen, did you say Ernest

GWENDOLEN. Yes.

CECILY. Oh, but it is not Mr Ernest Worthing who is m
guardian. It is his brother—his elder brother.

GWENDOLEN [sitting down again]. Ernest never mentione
to me that he had a brother.

CECILY. I am sorry to say they have not been on goo
terms for a long time.

GWENDOLEN. Ah! that accounts for it. And now that I thin
of it I have never heard any man mention his brother
The subject seems distasteful to most men. Cecily, yo
have lifted a load from my mind. I was growing almos
anxious. It would have been terrible if any cloud ha
come across a friendship like ours, would it not? Of cours
you are quite, quite sure that it is not Mr Ernest Worthin
who is your guardian?

CECILY. Quite sure. [A pause.] In fact, I am going to be his

GWENDOLEN [inquiringly]. I beg your pardon?

CECILY [rather shy and confidingly]. Dearest Gwendolen,
there is no reason why I should make a secret of it to you
Our little country newspaper is sure to chronicle the fac
next week. Mr Ernest Worthing and I are engaged to b
married.

GWENDOLEN [quite politely, rising]. My darling Cecily, I

think there must be some slight error. Mr Ernest Worthing is engaged to me. The announcement will appear in the *Morning Post* on Saturday at the latest.

CECILY [*very politely, rising*]. I am afraid you must be under some misconception. Ernest proposed to me exactly ten minutes ago. [*Shows diary.*]

GWENDOLEN [*examines diary through her lorgnette carefully*]. It is very curious, for he asked me to be his wife yesterday afternoon at 5.30. If you would care to verify the incident, pray do so. [*Produces diary of her own.*] I never travel without my diary. One should always have something sensational to read in the train. I am so sorry, dear Cecily, if it is any disappointment to you, but I am afraid I have the prior claim.

CECILY. It would distress me more than I can tell you, dear Gwendolen, if it caused you any mental or physical anguish, but I feel bound to point out that since Ernest proposed to you he clearly has changed his mind.

GWENDOLEN [*meditatively*]. If the poor fellow has been entrapped into any foolish promise I shall consider it my duty to rescue him at once, and with a firm hand.

CECILY [*thoughtfully and sadly*]. Whatever unfortunate entanglement my dear boy may have got into, I will never reproach him with it after we are married.

GWENDOLEN. Do you allude to me, Miss Cardew, as an entanglement? You are presumptuous. On an occasion of this kind it becomes more than a moral duty to speak one's mind. It becomes a pleasure.

CECILY. Do you suggest, Miss Fairfax, that I entrapped Ernest into an engagement? How dare you? This is no time for wearing the shallow mask of manners. When I see a spade I call it a spade.

GWENDOLEN [*satirically*]. I am glad to say that I have never seen a spade. It is obvious that our social spheres have been widely different.

[*Enter* MERRIMAN, *followed by the footman. He carries a salver, table cloth, and plate stand.* CECILY *is about to retort. The presence of the servants exercises a restraining influence, under which both girls chafe.*]

MERRIMAN. Shall I lay tea here as usual, Miss?

CECILY [*sternly, in a calm voice*]. Yes, as usual.

[MERRIMAN *begins to clear table and lay cloth. A long pause.* CECILY *and* GWENDOLEN *glare at each other.*]

GWENDOLEN. Are there many interesting walks in the vicinity, Miss Cardew?

CECILY. Oh! yes! a great many. From the top of one of the hills quite close one can see five counties.

GWENDOLEN. Five counties! I don't think I should like that. I hate crowds.

CECILY [*sweetly*]. I suppose that is why you live in town.

[GWENDOLEN *bites her lip, and beats her foot nervously with her parasol.*]

GWENDOLEN [*looking round*]. Quite a well-kept garden this is, Miss Cardew.

CECILY. So glad you like it, Miss Fairfax.

GWENDOLEN. I had no idea there were any flowers in the country.

CECILY. Oh, flowers are as common here, Miss Fairfax, as people are in London.

GWENDOLEN. Personally I cannot understand how anybody manages to exist in the country, if anybody who is anybody does. The country always bores me to death.

CECILY. Ah! This is what the newspapers call agricultural depression, is it not? I believe the aristocracy are suffering very much from it just at present. It is almost an epidemic amongst them, I have been told. May I offer you some tea, Miss Fairfax?

GWENDOLEN [*with elaborate politeness*]. Thank you. [*Aside*] Detestable girl! But I require tea!

CECILY [*sweetly*]. Sugar?

GWENDOLEN [*superciliously*]. No, thank you. Sugar is not fashionable any more.

[CECILY *looks angrily at her, takes up the tongs and puts four lumps of sugar into the cup.*]

CECILY [*severely*]. Cake or bread and butter?

GWENDOLEN [*in a bored manner*]. Bread and butter, please. Cake is rarely seen at the best houses nowadays.

CECILY [*cuts a very large slice of cake and puts it on the tray*]. Hand that to Miss Fairfax.

[MERRIMAN *does so, and goes out with footman.* GWEN-DOLEN *drinks the tea and makes a grimace. Puts down cup at once, reaches out her hand to the bread and butter, looks at it, and finds it is cake. Rises in indignation.*]

GWENDOLEN. You have filled my tea with lumps of sugar, and though I asked most distinctly for bread and butter, you have given me cake. I am known for the gentleness of my disposition, and the extraordinary sweetness of my nature, but I warn you, Miss Cardew, you may go too far.

CECILY [*rising*]. To save my poor, innocent, trusting boy from the machinations of any other girl there are no lengths to which I would not go.

GWENDOLEN. From the moment I saw you I distrusted you. I felt that you were false and deceitful. I am never deceived in such matters. My first impressions of people are invariably right.

CECILY. It seems to me, Miss Fairfax, that I am trespassing on your valuable time. No doubt you have many other calls of a similar character to make in the neighbourhood.

[*Enter* JACK.]

GWENDOLEN [*catching sight of him*]. Ernest! My own Ernest!

JACK. Gwendolen! Darling! [*Offers to kiss her.*]

GWENDOLEN [*drawing back*]. A moment! May I ask if you are engaged to be married to this young lady? [*Points to* CECILY.]

JACK [*laughing*]. To dear little Cecily! Of course not! What could have put such an idea into your pretty little head?

GWENDOLEN. Thank you. You may! [*Offers her cheek.*]

CECILY [*very sweetly*]. I knew there must be some mis-understanding, Miss Fairfax. The gentleman whose arm is at present round your waist is my guardian, Mr John Worthing.

GWENDOLEN. I beg your pardon?

CECILY. This is Uncle Jack.

GWENDOLEN [*receding*]. Jack! Oh!

[*Enter* ALGERNON.]

CECILY. Here is Ernest.

ALGERNON [*goes straight over to* CECILY *without noticing anyone else*]. My own love! [*Offers to kiss her.*]

CECILY [*drawing back*]. A moment, Ernest! May I ask you— are you engaged to be married to this young lady?

ALGERNON [*looking round*]. To what young lady? Good heavens! Gwendolen!

CECILY. Yes: to good heavens, Gwendolen, I mean to Gwendolen.

ALGERNON [*laughing*]. Of course not! What could have put such an idea into your pretty little head?

CECILY. Thank you. [*Presenting her cheek to be kissed.*] You may.

[ALGERNON *kisses her.*]

GWENDOLEN. I felt there was some slight error, Miss Cardew. The gentleman who is now embracing you is my cousin, Mr Algernon Moncrieff.

CECILY [*breaking away from* ALGERNON]. Algernon Moncrieff! Oh!

[*The two girls move towards each other and put their arms round each other's waists as if for protection.*]

CECILY. Are you called Algernon?

ALGERNON. I cannot deny it.

CECILY. Oh!

GWENDOLEN. Is your name really John?

JACK [*standing rather proudly*]. I could deny it if I liked. I could deny anything if I liked. But my name certainly is John. It has been John for years.

CECILY [*to* GWENDOLEN]. A gross deception has been practised on both of us.

GWENDOLEN. My poor wounded Cecily!

CECILY. My sweet wronged Gwendolen!

GWENDOLEN [*slowly and seriously*]. You will call me sister, will you not?

[*They embrace.* JACK *and* ALGERNON *groan and walk up and down.*]

CECILY [*rather brightly*]. There is just one question I would like to be allowed to ask my guardian.

GWENDOLEN. An admirable idea! Mr Worthing, there is just one question I would like to be permitted to put to you. Where is your brother Ernest? We are both engaged to be married to your brother Ernest, so it is a matter of some importance to us to know where your brother Ernest is at present.

JACK [*slowly and hesitatingly*]. Gwendolen—Cecily—it is very painful for me to be forced to speak the truth. It is the first time in my life that I have ever been reduced to such a painful position, and I am really quite inexperienced in doing anything of the kind. However, I will tell you quite frankly that I have no brother Ernest. I have no brother at all. I never had a brother in my life, and I certainly have not the smallest intention of ever having one in the future.

CECILY [*surprised*]. No brother at all?

JACK [*cheerily*]. None!

GWENDOLEN [*severely*]. Had you never a brother of any kind?

JACK [*pleasantly*]. Never. Not even of any kind.

GWENDOLEN. I am afraid it is quite clear, Cecily, that neither of us is engaged to be married to anyone.

CECILY. It is not a very pleasant position for a young girl suddenly to find herself in. Is it?

GWENDOLEN. Let us go into the house. They will hardly venture to come after us there.

CECILY. No, men are so cowardly, aren't they?

[*They retire into the house with scornful looks.*]

JACK. This ghastly state of things is what you call Bun-burying, I suppose?

ALGERNON. Yes, and a perfectly wonderful Bunbury it is. The most wonderful Bunbury I have ever had in my life.

JACK. Well, you've no right whatsoever to Bunbury here.

ALGERNON. That is absurd. One has a right to Bunbury any-where one chooses. Every serious Bunburyist knows that.

JACK. Serious Bunburyist? Good heavens!

ALGERNON. Well, one must be serious about something, if one wants to have any amusement in life. I happen to be serious about Bunburying. What on earth you are serious about I haven't got the remotest idea. About everything, I should fancy. You have such an absolutely trivial nature.

JACK. Well, the only small satisfaction I have in the whole of this wretched business is that your friend Bunbury is quite exploded. You won't be able to run down to the country quite so often as you used to do, dear Algy. And a very good thing too.

ALGERNON. Your brother is a little off colour, isn't he, dear Jack? You won't be able to disappear to London quite so frequently as your wicked custom was. And not a bad thing either.

JACK. As for your conduct towards Miss Cardew, I must say that your taking in a sweet, simple, innocent girl like that is quite inexcusable. To say nothing of the fact that she is my ward.

ALGERNON. I can see no possible defence at all for your deceiving a brilliant, clever, thoroughly experienced young lady like Miss Fairfax. To say nothing of the fact that she is my cousin.

JACK. I wanted to be engaged to Gwendolen, that is all. I love her.

ALGERNON. Well, I simply wanted to be engaged to Cecily. I adore her.

JACK. There is certainly no chance of your marrying Miss Cardew.

ALGERNON. I don't think there is much likelihood, Jack, of you and Miss Fairfax being united.

JACK. Well, that is no business of yours.

ALGERNON. If it was my business, I wouldn't talk about it. [Begins to eat muffins.] It is very vulgar to talk about one's business. Only people like stockbrokers do that, and then merely at dinner parties.

JACK. How you can sit there, calmly eating muffins when we are in this horrible trouble, I can't make out. You seem to me to be perfectly heartless.

ALGERNON. Well, I can't eat muffins in an agitated manner. The butter would probably get on my cuffs. One should always eat muffins quite calmly. It is the only way to eat them.

JACK. I say it's perfectly heartless your eating muffins at all, under the circumstances.

ALGERNON. When I am in trouble, eating is the only thing that consoles me. Indeed, when I am in really great trouble, as any one who knows me intimately will tell you, I refuse everything except food and drink. At the present moment I am eating muffins because I am unhappy. Besides, I am particularly fond of muffins. [Rising.]

JACK [rising]. Well, there is no reason why you should eat them all in that greedy way. [Takes muffins from ALGERNON.]

ALGERNON [*offering tea-cake*]. I wish you would have tea-cake instead. I don't like tea-cake.

JACK. Good heavens! I suppose a man may eat his own muffins in his own garden.

ALGERNON. But you have just said it was perfectly heartless to eat muffins.

JACK. I said it was perfectly heartless of you, under the circumstances. That is a very different thing.

ALGERNON. That may be. But the muffins are the same. [*He seizes the muffin-dish from* JACK.]

JACK. Algy, I wish to goodness you would go.

ALGERNON. You can't possibly ask me to go without having some dinner. It's absurd. I never go without my dinner. No one ever does, except vegetarians and people like that. Besides I have just made arrangements with Dr Chasuble to be christened at a quarter to six under the name of Ernest.

JACK. My dear fellow, the sooner you give up that nonsense the better. I made arrangements this morning with Dr Chasuble to be christened myself at 5.30, and I naturally will take the name of Ernest. Gwendolen would wish it. We can't both be christened Ernest. It's absurd. Besides, I have a perfect right to be christened if I like. There is no evidence at all that I have ever been christened by anybody. I should think it extremely probable I never was, and so does Dr Chasuble. It is entirely different in your case. You have been christened already.

ALGERNON. Yes, but I have not been christened for years.

JACK. Yes, but you have been christened. That is the important thing.

ALGERNON. Quite so. So I know my constitution can stand it. If you are not quite sure about your ever having been christened, I must say I think it rather dangerous your venturing on it now. It might make you very unwell. You can hardly have forgotten that someone very closely connected with you was very nearly carried off this week in Paris by a severe chill.

JACK. Yes, but you said yourself that a severe chill was not hereditary.

ALGERNON. It usen't to be, I know—but I daresay it is now. Science is always making wonderful improvements in things.

JACK [*picking up the muffin-dish*]. Oh, that is nonsense; you are always talking nonsense.

ALGERNON. Jack, you are at the muffins again! I wish you wouldn't. There are only two left. [*Takes them.*] I told you I was particularly fond of muffins.

JACK. But I hate tea-cake.

ALGERNON. Why on earth then do you allow tea-cake to be served up for your guests? What ideas you have of hospitality!

JACK. Algernon! I have already told you to go. I don't want you here. Why don't you go!

ALGERNON. I haven't quite finished my tea yet! and there is still one muffin left. [JACK *groans, and sinks into a chair.* ALGERNON *continues eating.*]

**CURTAIN**

# ACT THREE

SCENE: *Drawing-room at the Manor House.*

[GWENDOLEN *and* CECILY *are at the window, looking out into the garden.*]

GWENDOLEN. The fact that they did not follow us at once into the house, as any one else would have done, seems to me to show that they have some sense of shame left.

CECILY. They have been eating muffins. That looks like repentance.

GWENDOLEN [*after a pause*]. They don't seem to notice us at all. Couldn't you cough.

CECILY. But I haven't got a cough.

GWENDOLEN. They're looking at us. What effrontery!

CECILY. They're approaching. That's very forward of them.

GWENDOLEN. Let us preserve a dignified silence.

CECILY. Certainly. It's the only thing to do now.

[*Enter* JACK *followed by* ALGERNON. *They whistle some dreadful popular air from a British Opera.*]

GWENDOLEN. This dignified silence seems to produce an unpleasant effect.

CECILY. A most distasteful one.

GWENDOLEN. But we will not be the first to speak.

CECILY. Certainly not.

GWENDOLEN. Mr Worthing, I have something very particular to ask you. Much depends on your reply.

CECILY. Gwendolen, your common sense is invaluable. Mr Moncrieff, kindly answer me the following question. Why did you pretend to be my guardian's brother?

ALGERNON. In order that I might have an opportunity of meeting you.

CECILY [*to* GWENODLEN]. That certainly seems a satisfactory explanation, does it not?

[ 95 ]

GWENDOLEN. Yes, dear, if you can believe him.

CECILY. I don't. But that does not affect the wonderful beauty of his answer.

GWENDOLEN. True. In matters of grave importance, style not sincerity, is the vital thing. Mr Worthing, what explanation can you offer to me for pretending to have a brother? Was it in order that you might have an opportunity of coming up to town to see me as often as possible?

JACK. Can you doubt it, Miss Fairfax?

GWENDOLEN. I have the gravest doubts upon the subject. But I intend to crush them. This is not the moment for German scepticism. [*Moving to* CECILY.] Their explanations appear to be quite satisfactory, especially Mr Worthing's. That seems to me to have the stamp of truth upon it.

CECILY. I am more than content with what Mr Moncrieff said. His voice alone inspires one with absolute credulity.

GWENDOLEN. Then you think we should forgive them?

CECILY. Yes. I mean no.

GWENDOLEN. True! I had forgotten. There are principles at stake that one cannot surrender. Which of us should tell them? The task is not a pleasant one.

CECILY. Could we not both speak at the same time?

GWENDOLEN. An excellent idea! I nearly always speak at the same time as other people. Will you take the time from me?

CECILY. Certainly.

[GWENDOLEN *beats time with uplifted finger.*]

GWENDOLEN *and* CECILY [*speaking together*]. Your Christian name are still an insuperable barrier. That is all!

JACK *and* ALGERNON [*speaking together*]. Our Christian names! Is that all? But we are going to be christened this afternoon.

GWENDOLEN [*to* JACK]. For my sake you are prepared to do this terrible thing?

JACK. I am.

CECILY [*to* ALGERNON]. To please me you are ready to face this fearful ordeal?

ALGERNON. I am!

GWENDOLEN. How absurd to talk of the equality of the sexes! Where questions of self-sacrifice are concerned, men are infinitely beyond us.

V

ACK. We are. [*Clasps hands with* ALGERNON.]

ECILY. They have moments of physical courage of which we women know absolutely nothing.

WENDOLEN [*to* JACK]. Darling!

LGERNON [*to* CECILY]. Darling!

*They fall into each other's arms. Enter* MERRIMAN. *When  e enters he coughs loudly, seeing the situation.*]

ERRIMAN. Ahem! Ahem! Lady Bracknell.

ACK. Good heavens!

*Enter* LADY BRACKNELL. *The couples separate in alarm.  xit* MERRIMAN.]

ADY BRACKNELL. Gwendolen! What does this mean?

WENDOLEN. Merely that I am engaged to be married to Mr Worthing, mamma.

ADY BRACKNELL. Come here. Sit down. Sit down immediately. Hesitation of any kind is a sign of mental decay in the young, of physical weakness in the old. [*Turns to* JACK.] Appraised, sir, of my daughter's sudden flight by her trusty maid, whose confidence I purchased by means of a small coin, I followed her at once by a luggage train. Her unhappy father is, I am glad to say, under the impression that she is attending a more than usually lengthy lecture by the University Extension Scheme on the Influence of a permanent income on Thought. I do not propose to undeceive him. Indeed I have never undeceivd him on any question. I would consider it wrong. But of course, you will clearly understand that all communication between yourself and my daughter must cease immediately from this moment. On this point, as indeed on all points, I am firm.

JACK. I am engaged to be married to Gwendolen, Lady Bracknell!

LADY BRACKNELL. You are nothing of the kind, sir. And now as regards Algernon! . . . Algernon!

ALGERNON. Yes, Aunt Augusta.

LADY BRACKNELL. May I ask if it is in this house that your invalid friend Mr Bunbury resides?

ALGERNON [*stammering*]. Oh! No! Bunbury doesn't live here. Bunbury is somewhere else at present. In fact, Bunbury is dead.

LADY BRACKNELL. Dead! When did Mr Bunbury die? Hi
death must have been extremely sudden.

ALGERNON [*airily*]. Oh! I killed Bunbury this afternoon.
mean poor Bunbury died this afternoon.

LADY BRACKNELL. What did he die of?

ALGERNON. Bunbury? Oh, he was quite exploded.

LADY BRACKNELL. Exploded! Was he the victim of a revc
lutionary outrage? I was not aware that Mr Bunbury wa
interested in social legislation. If so, he is well punished fo
his morbidity.

ALGERNON. My dear Aunt Augusta, I mean he was foune
out! The doctors found out that Bunbury could not live
that is what I mean—so Bunbury died.

LADY BRACKNELL. He seems to have had great confidenc(
in the opinion of his physicians. I am glad, however, tha
he made up his mind at the last to some definite cours(
of action, and acted under proper medical advice. An(
now that we have finally got rid of this Mr Bunbury, may
I ask, Mr Worthing, who is that young person whose
hand my nephew Algernon is now holding in what seem:
to me a peculiarly unnecessary manner?

JACK. That lady is Miss Cecily Cardew, my ward.

[LADY BRACKNELL *bows coldly to* CECILY.]

ALGERNON. I am engaged to be married to Cecily, Aun
Augusta.

LADY BRACKNELL. I beg your pardon?

CECILY. Mr Moncrieff and I are engaged to be married,
Lady Bracknell.

LADY BRACKNELL [*with a shiver, crossing to the sofa and
sitting down*]. I do not know whether there is anything
peculiarly exciting in the air of this particular part of
Hertfordshire, but the number of engagements that go on
seems to me considerably above the proper average that
statistics have laid down for our guidance. I think some
preliminary inquiry on my part would not be out of place.
Mr Worthing, is Miss Cardew at all connected with any
of the larger railway stations in London? I merely desire
information. Until yesterday I had no idea that there
were any families or persons whose origin was a Terminus.

[JACK *looks perfectly furious, but restrains himself.*]

ᴀᴄᴋ [*in a cold, clear voice*]. Miss Cardew is the grand-daughter of the late Mr Thomas Cardew of 149 Belgrave Square, S.W.; Gervase Park, Dorking, Surrey; and the Sporan, Fifeshire, N.B.

ᴀᴅʏ BRACKNELL. That sounds not unsatisfactory. Three addresses always inspire confidence, even in tradesmen. But what proof have I of their authenticity?

ᴀᴄᴋ. I have carefully preserved the Court Guides of the period. They are open to your inspection, Lady Bracknell.

ᴀᴅʏ BRACKNELL [*grimly*]. I have known strange errors in that publication.

ᴀᴄᴋ. Miss Cardew's family solicitors are Messrs Markby, Markby, and Markby.

ᴀᴅʏ BRACKNELL. Markby, Markby, and Markby? A firm of the very highest position in their profession. Indeed I am told that one of the Mr Markby's is occasionally to be seen at dinner parties. So far I am satisfied.

ᴀᴄᴋ [*very irritably*]. How extremely kind of you, Lady Bracknell! I have also in my possession, you will be pleased to hear, certificates of Miss Cardew's birth, baptism, whooping cough, registration, vaccination, confirmation, and the measles; both the German and the English variety.

ᴀᴅʏ BRACKNELL. Ah! A life crowded with incident, I see; though perhaps somewhat too exciting for a young girl. I am not myself in favour of premature experiences. [*Rises, looks at her watch*]. Gwendolen! the time approaches for our departure. We have not a moment to lose. As a matter of form, Mr Worthing, I had better ask you if Miss Cardew has any little fortune?

ᴀᴄᴋ. Oh! about a hundred and thirty thousand pounds in the Funds. That is all. Good-bye, Lady Bracknell. So pleased to have seen you.

ᴀᴅʏ BRACKNELL [*sitting down again*]. A moment, Mr Worthing. A hundred and thirty thousand pounds! And in the Funds! Miss Cardew seems to me a most attractive young lady, now that I look at her. Few girls of the present day have any really solid qualities, any of the qualities that last, and improve with time. We live, I regret to say, in an age of surfaces. [*To* CECILY.] Come over here, dear. [CECILY *goes across*.] Pretty child! your dress is sadly simple, and your hair seems almost as Nature might have left it. But we can soon alter all that. [A] thoroughly experienced French maid produces a really marvellous result in a very brief space of time. I remember recommending one to young Lady Lancing, and after three months her own husband did not know her.

JACK. And after six months nobody knew her.

LADY BRACKNELL [glares at JACK for a few moments. Then bends, with a practised smile, to CECILY]. Kindly turn round, sweet child. [CECILY turns completely round. No, the side view is what I want. [CECILY presents her profile.] Yes, quite as I expected. There are distinct social possibilities in your profile. The two weak points in our age are its want of principle and its want of profile. The chin a little higher, dear. Style largely depends on the way the chin is worn. They are worn very high, just at present. Algernon!

ALGERNON. Yes, Aunt Augusta!

LADY BRACKNELL. There are distinct social possibilities in Miss Cardew's profile.

ALGERNON. Cecily is the sweetest, dearest, prettiest girl in the whole world. And I don't care twopence about social possibilities.

LADY BRACKNELL. Never speak disrespectfully of Society, Algernon. Only people who can't get into it do that. [To CECILY.] Dear child, of course you know that Algernon has nothing but his debts to depend upon. But I do not approve of mercenary marriages. When I married Lord Bracknell I had no fortune of any kind. But I never dreamed for a moment of allowing that to stand in my way. Well, I suppose I must give my consent.

ALGERNON. Thank you, Aunt Augusta.

LADY BRACKNELL. Cecily, you may kiss me!

CECILY [kisses her]. Thank you, Lady Bracknell.

LADY BRACKNELL. You may also address me as Aunt Augusta for the future.

CECILY. Thank you, Aunt Augusta.

LADY BRACKNELL. The marriage, I think, had better take place quite soon.

ALGERNON. Thank you, Aunt Augusta.

CECILY. Thank you, Aunt Augusta.

LADY BRACKNELL. To speak frankly, I am not in favour of long engagements. They give people the opportunity of finding out each other's character before marriage, which I think is never advisable.

CK. I beg your pardon for interrupting you, Lady Bracknell, but this engagement is quite out of the question. I am Miss Cardew's guardian, and she cannot marry without my consent until she comes of age. That consent I absolutely decline to give.

DY BRACKNELL. Upon what grounds, may I ask? Algernon is an extremely, I may almost say an ostentatiously, eligible young man. He has nothing, but he looks everything. What more can one desire?

CK. It pains me very much to have to speak frankly to you, Lady Bracknell, about your nephew, but the fact is that I do not approve at all of his moral character. I suspect him of being untruthful.

LGERNON *and* CECILY *look at him in indignant amazement.*]

ADY BRACKNELL. Untruthful! My nephew Algernon? Impossible! He is an Oxonian.

ACK. I fear there can be no possible doubt about the matter. This afternoon during my temporary absence in London on an important question of romance, he obtained admission to my house by means of the false pretence of being my brother. Under an assumed name he drank, I've just been informed by my butler, an entire pint bottle of my Perrier-Jouet, Brut, '89; wine I was specially reserving for myself. Continuing his disgraceful deception, he succeeded in the course of the afternoon in alienating the affections of my only ward. He subsequently stayed to tea, and devoured every single muffin. And what makes his conduct all the more heartless is, that he was perfectly well aware from the first that I have no brother, that I never had a brother, and that I don't intend to have a brother, not even of any kind. I distinctly told him so myself yesterday afternoon.

ADY BRACKNELL. Ahem! Mr Worthing, after careful consideration I have decided entirely to overlook my nephew's conduct to you.

ACK. That is very generous of you, Lady Bracknell. My own decision, however, is unalterable. I decline to give my consent.

LADY BRACKNELL [*to* CECILY]. Come here, sweet chil
[CECILY *goes over*.] How old are you, dear?

CECILY. Well, I am really only eighteen, but I always adm
to twenty when I go to evening parties.

LADY BRACKNELL. You are perfectly right in making som
slight alteration. Indeed, no woman should ever be qui
accurate about her age. It looks so calculating. . . . [*I*
*a meditative manner*.] Eighteen, but admitting to twent
at evening parties. Well, it will not be very long befor
you are of age and free from the restraints of tutelage. S
I don't think your guardian's consent is, after all, a matte
of any importance.

JACK. Pray excuse me, Lady Bracknell, for interrupting yo
again, but it is only fair to tell you that according to th
terms of her grandfather's will Miss Cardew does no
come legally of age till she is thirty-five.

LADY BRACKNELL. That does not seem to me to be a grav
objection. Thirty-five is a very attractive age. Londo
society is full of women of the very highest birth wh
have, of their own free choice, remained thirty-five fo
years. Lady Dumbleton is an instance in point. To my ow
knowledge she has been thirty-five ever since she arrive
at the age of forty, which was many years ago now.
see no reason why our dear Cecily should not be even sti
more attractive at the age you mention than she is a
present. There will be a large accumulation of property

CECILY. Algy, could you wait for me till I was thirty-five

ALGERNON. Of course I could, Cecily. You know I could.

CECILY. Yes, I felt it instinctively, but I couldn't wait al
that time. I hate waiting even five minutes for anybody
It always makes me rather cross. I am not punctual my
self, I know, but I do like punctuality in others, an
waiting, even to be married, is quite out of the question

ALGERNON. Then what is to be done, Cecily?

CECILY. I don't know, Mr Moncrieff.

LADY BRACKNELL. My dear Mr Worthing, as Miss Cardew
states positively that she cannot wait till she is thirty-five
—a remark which I am bound to say seems to me to
show a somewhat impatient nature—I would beg of yo
to reconsider your decision.

JACK. But my dear Lady Bracknell, the matter is entirely i
your own hands. The moment you consent to my mar

riage with Gwendolen, I will most gladly allow your
nephew to form an alliance with my ward.

LADY BRACKNELL [*rising and drawing herself up*]. You must
be quite aware that what you propose is out of the question.

JACK. Then a passionate celibacy is all that any of us can
look forward to.

LADY BRACKNELL. That is not the destiny I propose for
Gwendolen. Algernon, of course, can choose for himself.
[*Pulls out her watch.*] Come, dear, [GWENDOLEN *rises.*]
we have already missed five, if not six, trains. To miss
any more might expose us to comment on the platform.

[*Enter* DR CHASUBLE.]

CHASUBLE. Everything is quite ready for the christenings.

LADY BRACKNELL. The christenings, sir! Is not that somewhat
premature?

CHASUBLE [*looking rather puzzled, and pointing to* JACK
*and* ALGERNON]. Both these gentlemen have expressed a
desire for immediate baptism.

LADY BRACKNELL. At their age? The idea is grotesque and
irreligious! Algernon, I forbid you to be baptized. I will
not hear of such excesses. Lord Bracknell would be highly
displeased if he learned that that was the way in which
you wasted your time and money.

CHASUBLE. Am I to understand then that there are to be no
christenings at all this afternoon?

JACK. I don't think that, as things are now, it would be of
much practical value to either of us, Dr Chasuble.

CHASUBLE. I am grieved to hear such sentiments from you,
Mr Worthing. They savour of the heretical views of the
Anabaptists, views that I have completely refuted in four
of my unpublished sermons. However, as your present
mood seems to be one peculiarly secular, I will return to
the church at once. Indeed, I have just been informed by
the pew-opener that for the last hour and a half Miss
Prism has been waiting for me in the vestry.

LADY BRACKNELL [*starting*]. Miss Prism! Did I hear you
mention a Miss Prism?

CHASUBLE. Yes, Lady Bracknell. I am on my way to join her.

LADY BRACKNELL. Pray allow me to detain you for a moment. This matter may prove to be one of vital import-

ance to Lord Bracknell and myself. Is this Miss Prism female of repellent aspect, remotely connected with edu cation?

CHASUBLE [*somewhat indignantly*]. She is the most cul tivated of ladies, and the very picture of respectability.

LADY BRACKNELL. It is obviously the same person. May ask what position she holds in your household?

CHASUBLE [*severely*]. I am a celibate, madam.

JACK [*interposing*]. Miss Prism, Lady Bracknell, has been fo the last three years Miss Cardew's esteemed governess an valued companion.

LADY BRACKNELL. In spite of what I hear of her, I mus see her at once. Let her be sent for.

CHASUBLE [*looking off*]. She approaches; she is nigh.

[*Enter* MISS PRISM *hurriedly*.]

MISS PRISM. I was told you expected me in the vestry, dea Canon. I have been waiting for you there for an hour and three-quarters. [*Catches sight of* LADY BRACKNELL, *who has fixed her with a stony glare.* MISS PRISM *grows pale and quails. She looks anxiously round as if desirous to escape.*]

LADY BRACKNELL [*in a severe, judicial voice*]. Prism! [MISS PRISM *bows her head in shame.*] Come here, Prism! [MISS PRISM *approaches in a humble manner.*] Prism! Where is that baby? [*General consternation. The Canon starts back in horror.* ALGERNON *and* JACK *pretend to be anxious to shield* CECILY *and* GWENDOLEN *from hearing the the details of a terrible public scandal.*] Twenty-eight years ago, Prism, you left Lord Bracknell's house, Num ber 104, Upper Grosvenor Square, in charge of a peram bulator that contained a baby of the male sex. You never returned. A few weeks later, through the elaborate in vestigations of the Metropolitan police, the perambulator was discovered at midnight standing by itself in a remote corner of Bayswater. It contained the manuscript of a three-volume novel of more than usually revolting senti mentality. [MISS PRISM *starts in involuntary indignation.*] But the baby was not there. [*Every one looks at* MISS PRISM.] Prism! Where is that baby?

[*A pause.*]

MISS PRISM. Lady Bracknell, I admit with shame that I do not know. I only wish I did. The plain facts of the case are these. On the morning of the day you mention, a day that is for ever branded on my memory, I prepared as usual to take the baby out in its perambulator. I had also with me a somewhat old, but capacious hand-bag in which I had intended to place the manuscript of a work of fiction that I had written during my few unoccupied hours. In a moment of mental abstraction, for which I can never forgive myself, I deposited the manuscript in the bassinette and placed the baby in the hand-bag.

JACK [who has been listening attentively]. But where did you deposit the hand-bag?

MISS PRISM. Do not ask me, Mr Worthing.

JACK. Miss Prism, this is a matter of no small importance to me. I insist on knowing where you deposited the hand-bag that contained that infant.

MISS PRISM. I left it in the clock-room of one of the larger railway stations in London.

JACK. What railway station?

MISS PRISM [quite crushed]. Victoria. The Brighton line. [Sinks into a chair.]

JACK. I must retire to my room for a moment. Gwendolen, wait here for me.

GWENDOLEN. If you are not too long, I will wait here for you all my life.

[Exit JACK in great excitement.]

CHASUBLE. What do you think this means, Lady Bracknell?

LADY BRACKNELL. I dare not even suspect, Dr Chasuble. I need hardly tell you that in families of high position strange coincidences are not supposed to occur. They are hardly considered the thing.

[Noises heard overhead as if some one was throwing trunks about. Every one looks up.]

CECILY. Uncle Jack seems strangely agitated.

CHASUBLE. Your guardian has a very emotional nature.

LADY BRACKNELL. This noise is extremely unpleasant. It sounds as if he was having an argument. I dislike arguments of any kind. They are always vulgar, and often convincing.

CHASUBLE [*looking up*]. It has stopped now.

[*The noise is redoubled.*]

LADY BRACKNELL. I wish he would arrive at some conclusion.

GWENDOLEN. This suspense is terrible. I hope it will last.

[*Enter* JACK *with a hand-bag of black leather in his hand.*]

JACK. [*rushing over to* MISS PRISM]. Is this the hand-bag, Miss Prism? Examine it carefully before you speak. The happiness of more than one life depends on your answer.

MISS PRISM [*calmly*]. It seems to be mine. Yes, here is the injury it received through the upsetting of a Gower Street omnibus in younger and happier days. Here is the stain on the lining caused by the explosion of a temperance beverage, an incident that occurred at Leamington. And here, on the lock, are my initials. I had forgotten that in an extravagant mood I had had them placed there. The bag is undoubtedly mine. I am delighted to have it so unexpectedly restored to me. It has been a great inconvenience being without it all these years.

JACK [*in a pathetic voice*]. Miss Prism, more is restored to you than this hand-bag. I was the baby you placed in it.

MISS PRISM [*amazed*]. You?

JACK [*embracing her*]. Yes ... mother!

MISS PRISM [*recoiling in indignant astonishment*]. Mr Worthing. I am unmarried!

JACK. Unmarried! I do not deny that is a serious blow. But after all, who has the right to cast a stone against one who has suffered? Cannot repentance wipe out an act of folly? Why should there be one law for men, and another for women? Mother, I forgive you. [*Tries to embrace her again.*]

MISS PRISM [*still more indignant*]. Mr Worthing, there is some error. [*Pointing to* LADY BRACKNELL.] There is the lady who can tell you who you really are.

JACK [*after a pause*]. Lady Bracknell, I hate to seem inquisitive, but would you kindly inform me who I am?

LADY BRACKNELL. I am afraid that the news I have to give you will not altogether please you. You are the son of my poor sister, Mrs Moncrieff, and consequently Algernon's elder brother.

JACK. Algy's elder brother! Then I have a brother after all.

I knew I had a brother! I always said I had a brother!
Cecily—how could you have ever doubted that I had a
brother? [*Seizes hold of* ALGERNON.] Dr Chasuble, my unfortunate brother. Miss Prism, my unfortunate brother.
Gwendolen, my unfortunate brother. Algy, you young
scoundrel, you will have to treat me with more respect in
the future. You have never behaved to me like a brother in
all your life.

ALGERNON. Well, not till to-day, old boy, I admit. I did my
best, however, though I was out of practice. [*Shakes
hands.*]

GWENDOLEN [*to* JACK]. My own! But what own are you?
What is your Christian name, now that you have become
some one else?

JACK. Good heavens! . . . I had quite forgotten that point.
Your decision on the subject of my name is irrevocable,
I suppose?

GWENDOLEN. I never change, except in my affections.

CECILY. What a noble nature you have, Gwendolen!

JACK. Then the question had better be cleared up at once.
Aunt Augusta, a moment. At the time when Miss Prism
left me in the hand-bag, had I been christened already?

LADY BRACKNELL. Every luxury that money could buy, including christening, had been lavished on you by your
fond and doting parents.

JACK. Then I was christened! That is settled. Now, what
name was I given? Let me know the worst.

LADY BRACKNELL. Being the eldest son you were naturally
christened after your father.

JACK [*irritably*]. Yes, but what was my father's Christian
name?

LADY BRACKNELL [*meditatively*]. I cannot at the present
moment recall what the General's Christian name was.
But I have no doubt he had one. He was eccentric, I admit. But only in later years. And that was the result of
the Indian climate, and marriage, and indigestion, and other
things of that kind.

JACK. Algy! Can't you recollect what our father's Christian
name was?

ALGERNON. My dear boy, we were never even on speaking
terms. He died before I was a year old.

JACK. His name would appear in the Army Lists of the
period, I suppose, Aunt Augusta?

LADY BRACKNELL. The General was essentially a man of peace, except in his domestic life. But I have no doubt his name would appear in any military directory.

JACK. The Army Lists of the last forty years are here. These delightful records should have been my constant study. [*Rushes to bookcase and tears the books out.*] M. Generals . . . Mallam, Maxbohm, Magley—what ghastly names they have—Markby, Migsby, Mobbs, Moncrieff! Lieutenant 1840, Captain, Lieutenant-Colonel, Colonel, General 1869, Christian names, Ernest John. [*Puts book very quietly down and speaks quite calmly.*] I always told you, Gwendolen, my name was Ernest, didn't I? Well, it is Ernest after all. I mean it naturally is Ernest.

LADY BRACKNELL. Yes, I remember now that the General was called Ernest. I knew I had some particular reason for disliking the name.

GWENDOLEN. Ernest! My own Ernest! I felt from the first that you could have no other name!

JACK. Gwendolen, it is a terrible thing for a man to find out suddenly that all his life he has been speaking nothing but the truth. Can you forgive me?

GWENDOLEN. I can. For I feel that you are sure to change.

JACK. My own one!

CHASUBLE [*to* MISS PRISM]. Laetitia! [*Embraces her.*]

MISS PRISM [*enthusiastically*]. Frederick! At last!

ALGERNON. Cecily! [*Embraces her.*] At last!

JACK. Gwendolen! [*Embraces her.*] At last!

LADY BRACKNELL. My nephew, you seem to be displaying signs of triviality.

JACK. On the contrary, Aunt Augusta, I've now realized for the first time in my life the vital Importance of Being Ernest.

TABLEAU
CURTAIN

# *GEORGE BERNARD SHAW*

## *1856–1950*

GEORGE BERNARD SHAW needs no introduction, and it would be impossible to assess his place in the modern theatre in a single prefatory paragraph. Ludwig Lewisohn's early estimation of Shaw and his work is probably as succinct as any. In 1915 he wrote: "Mr. George Bernard Shaw is a writer of comedy with a tragic cry in his soul. In the middle ages he would have been a great saint, appalled at the gracelessness of men's hearts, militant for the Kingdom of God. Today he is a playwright, appalled at the muddle-headedness of the race, a fighter for the conquest of reason over unreason, of order over disorder, of economy over waste. The real joke, Shaw himself reminded us, is that I am earnest." But this statement does not begin to encompass the daring reach of intellect, the love of fun, and the theatrical mastery of one of the most prolific writers of the modern theatre. Shaw was a social philosopher who created the modern comedy of ideas. He was not so much an original thinker—none of the ideas expounded in his plays was radically new—as he was an articulate stage magician who inverted all accepted values and ideas in order that men might be more capable of building the good society. From his first play, *Widower's Houses* (1885), to his last, *Farfetched Fables* (1950), Shaw was concerned with ideas, and in his prodigious body of work almost every significant intellectual position of modern times was examined by his razor-sharp mind.

Readers of the plays become so involved in the intellectual intricacies and sparkling wit of Shaw's dialogue that they tend to forget that he is also a master craftsman of the theatre. No modern dramatist uses the shocking and unexpected to greater effect, and in each of his plays Shaw employs devices of sheer theatricality which may be overlooked when one reads the plays but which tend to overwhelm us when we experience them in production. Shaw wrote within the conventions of the realistic theatre of his time, but a large measure of his charm and effectiveness consists in his use of the realistic convention for ends that are radically different from those of the traditional realists. Some people complain that Shaw's characters tend to be puppets, mouthpieces for his philosophy, who have no individuality of their own. This charge may be to some degree true, but then Shaw was not interested in his characters as archetypes of human behavior. Francis Fergusson put it best when he wrote: "Shaw is never concerned with the way people do behave, but only with the way they would behave if they were characters in a Shaw play."

# LETTERS TO LOUIS CALVERT
## ON PLAYING UNDERSHAFT[1]

(From Derry Roscarberry, Ireland, July 23, 1905)

Dear Calvert—[2]

Can you play the trombone? If not, I beg you to acquire a smattering of the art during your holidays. I am getting on with the new play scrap by scrap; and the part of the millionaire cannon founder is becoming more and more formidable. Broadbent and Keegan rolled into one, with Mephistopheles thrown in; that is what it is like. Business is Business will be cheap melodrama in comparison, Irving and Tree will fade into third class when Calvert takes the stage as Andrew Undershaft. It will be TREMENDOUS, simply. But there is a great scene at the end of the second act where he buys up the Salvation Army, and has to take part in a march to a big meeting. Barker will play the drum. You will have a trombone—or a bass-horn if you prefer that instrument—and it would add greatly to the effect if you could play it prettily. Besides if you took to music you could give up those confounded cigars and save your voice and your memory (both wrecks, like Mario's,[3] from thirty-seven cigars a day) for this immense part. It is very long, speeches longer than Keegan's, and dozens of them, and infinite nuances of execution. Undershaft is diabolically subtle, gentle, self-possessed, powerful, stupendous, as well as amusing and interesting. There are the makings of ten Hamlets and six Othellos in his mere leavings. Learning it will half kill

1 *Letters to Louis Calvert on Playing Undershaft* from Bernard Shaw. Reprinted by permission of The Public Trustee and The Society of Authors, London.

2 Shaw created the role of Andrew Undershaft expressly for Calvert, who had played Broadbent in 1904. Calvert played in the original 1905 Court Theatre production of *Major Barbara*.

3 Giovanni Mario (1810–1883) was a great but erratic midcentury tenor frequently referred to in Shaw's music criticism.

you; but you can retire the next day as pre-eminent and unapproachable. That penny-plain and twopence-colored pirate Brassbound will be beneath your notice then. I have put him off for another year, as I cannot get the right Lady Cicely. ———, unluckily, has read my plays at Margate and is now full of the most insane proposals—wants Brassbound instantly. With you and Kate Rorke for one thing. But the trombone is the urgent matter of the moment.

By the way, trombone players never get cholera nor consumption—never die, in fact, until extreme old age makes them incapable of working the slide.

G. Bernard Shaw

(Letter concerning a rehearsal, November 18)

My Dear Calvert—

I hope I did not worry you too much today at rehearsal. The fact is you are ruining the end of the second act by your enormous, desolating, oblivious-to-everybody absent-mindedness. The reason I put on an understudy for Barbara was that you had driven Miss Russell almost out of her senses by letting the scene drop when she was doing her hardest to get hold of it. She did not complain; but I saw what was happening and acted on my own initiative. You see, it is all very well for you; you know that you can wake up at the last moment and do the trick; but that will not help out the unhappy victims who have to rehearse with you. And you forget your own weight. The moment you let the play go, it drops. You sit there, greatly interested (except when you are asleep) by the way to manage the play and the mistakes that all the rest are making, and trying to make out what is wrong with the whole scene. Of course, what is wrong is you. There is that frightful speech where Undershaft deliberately gives a horrible account of his business, sticking detail after detail of the horrors of war into poor bleeding Barbara to show her what Mrs Baines will stand for £5000. Cusins, who sees it all, is driven into an ecstasy of irony by it; it is sort of a fantasia played on the nerves of both him and Barbara by Machiavelli-Mephistopheles. All that is needed to produce the effect is steady concentration, magnetic intensity. Irving, who could not do lots of things that you can do, could have done this superbly. But, you are evidently thinking of Lord knows what—the returns of your Sweet Nell Companies, or how Barker always drops his voice when he ought to raise it and emphasizes the wrong word, or what a monstrous thing it is that an idiot of an author should produce a play when he doesn't know the first rudiments of his business or—then you suddenly realize that the stage has been waiting for you for ten minutes. There are moments when if we were not in a conspiracy to spoil you, we should rend you to pieces and wallow in your blood. Miss Russell has been working at the thing with the greatest enthusiasm, and when she tries to get into the rush of it, and is slacked down every time by your colossal indifference, she almost gives up in despair. If you were an insignificant actor it would not matter; they could run away from you; but they are not strong enough for this; the piece takes its time and intensity from you in spite of all they can do.

Mind, I quite appreciate your heroic study of the lines; and I don't complain of anything except the end of the second act; but for that I have no words strong enough to describe your atrocity; you will scream through endless centuries in hell for it, and implore me in vain to send you ices from heaven to cool your burning tongue. We have only one week more; and I have set my heart on your making a big success in the part. And you are taking it as easy as if Undershaft were an old uncle in a farce. Spend tomorrow in prayer. My wife was horrified at my blanched hair and lined face when I returned from rehearsal today. And I have a blinding headache and can no more.

Your unfortunate,<br>
G.B.S.

(From Adelphi Terrace, November 29, day after opening)

My Dear Calvert—

I see with disgust that the papers all say that your Undershaft was a magnificent piece of acting and Major Barbara a rottenly undramatic play, instead of pointing out that Major B is a masterpiece and that you are the most infamous amateur that ever disgraced the boards.

Do let me put——into it. A man who could let the seven deadly sins go for nothing could sit on a hat without making an audience laugh. I have taken a box for Friday and had a hundredweight of cabbages, dead cats, eggs, and gingerbeer bottles stacked in it. Every word you fluff, every speech you unact, I will shy something at you. Before you go on the stage I will insult you until your temper gets the better of your liver. You are an impostor, a sluggard, a blockhead, a shirk, a malingerer, and the worst actor that ever lived or that ever will live. I will apologize to the public for engaging you. I will tell your mother of you.[4] Barbara played you off the stage; Cremlin dwarfed you; Bill annihilated you; Clare Greet took all eyes from you. If you are too lazy to study the lines I'll coach you in them. That last act MUST be saved or I'll withdraw the play and cut you off without a shilling.

Yours,
G.B.S.

[4] Calvert's parents, Mr. and Mrs. Charles Calvert, were the proprietors and leading actors of the Queen's Theatre, Manchester, one of the finest stock theatres in late nineteenth-century England. Shaw had long admired them; he had persuaded Mrs. Calvert after her retirement to return to the stage to play Catherine Petkoff in *Arms and the Man* in 1894.

# *MAJOR BARBARA*

## by Bernard Shaw

### *1907*

# MAJOR BARBARA[5]

## CHARACTERS

STEPHEN UNDERSHAFT
LADY BRITOMART
BARBARA UNDERSHAFT
SARAH UNDERSHAFT
ANDREW UNDERSHAFT
JENNY HILL
BILL WALKER
MORRISON
ADOLPHUS CUSINS
CHARLES LOMAX
RUMMY MITCHENS
SNOBBY PRICE
PETER SHIRLEY
BILTON
MRS BAINES

*N.B.* The Euripidean verses in the second act of Major Barbara are not by me, nor even directly by Euripides. They are by Professor Gilbert Murray, whose English version of *The Bacchae* came into our dramatic literature with all the impulsive power of an original work shortly before Major Barbara was begun. The play, indeed, stands indebted to him in more ways than one.

G.B.S.

[5] *Major Barbara* by George Bernard Shaw—used by permission of The Public Trustee, The Society of Authors, and Dodd, Mead & Company, Inc. Copyright 1907, 1913, 1930, 1941 by George Bernard Shaw. Copyright 1957 by The Public Trustee as Executor of the Estate of George Bernard Shaw.

# ACT ONE

*It is after dinner in January 1906, in the library in Lady Britomart Undershaft's house in Wilton Crescent. A large and comfortable settee is in the middle of the room, upholstered in dark leather. A person sitting on it (it is vacant at present) would have, on his right, Lady Britomart's writing table, with the lady herself busy at it; a smaller writing table behind him on his left; the door behind him on Lady Britomart's side; and a window with a window seat directly on his left. Near the window is an armchair.*

LADY BRITOMART *is a woman of fifty or thereabouts, well dressed and yet careless of her dress, well bred and quite reckless of her breeding, well mannered and yet appallingly outspoken and indifferent to the opinion of her interlocutors, amiable and yet peremptory, arbitrary, and high-tempered to the last bearable degree, and withal a very typical managing matron of the upper class, treated as a naughty child until she grew into a scolding mother, and finally settling down with plenty of practical ability and worldly experience, limited in the oddest way with domestic and class limitations, conceiving the universe exactly as if it were a large house in Wilton Crescent, though handling her corner of it very effectively on that assumption, and being quite enlightened and liberal as to the books in the library, the pictures on the walls, the music in the portfolios, and the articles in the papers.*

*Her son,* STEPHEN, *comes in. He is a gravely correct young man under 25, taking himself very seriously, but still in some awe of his mother, from childish habit and bachelor shyness rather than from any weakness of character.*

STEPHEN. Whats the matter?

LADY BRITOMART. Presently, Stephen.

[STEPHEN *submissively walks to the settee and sits down. He takes up a Liberal weekly called* The Speaker.]

LADY BRITOMART. Dont begin to read, Stephen. I shall require all your attention.

STEPHEN. It was only while I was waiting—

LADY BRITOMART. Dont make excuses, Stephen. [*He puts down* The Speaker.] Now! [*She finishes her writing; rises; and comes to the settee.*] I have not kept you waiting very long, I think.

STEPHEN. Not at all, mother.

LADY BRITOMART. Bring me my cushion. [*He takes the cushion from the chair at the desk and arranges it for her as she sits down on the settee.*] Sit down. [*He sits down and fingers his tie nervously.*] Dont fiddle with your tie, Stephen: there is nothing the matter with it.

STEPHEN. I beg your pardon. [*He fiddles with his watch chain instead*].

LADY BRITOMART. Now are you attending to me, Stephen?

STEPHEN. Of course, mother.

LADY BRITOWART. No: it's not of course. I want something much more than your everyday matter-of-course attention. I am going to speak to you very seriously, Stephen. I wish you would let that chain alone.

STEPHEN [*hastily relinquishing the chain*]. Have I done anything to annoy you, mother? If so, it was quite unintentional.

LADY BRITOMART [*astonished*]. Nonsense! [*With some remorse*] My poor boy, did you think I was angry with you?

STEPHEN. What is it, then, mother? You are making me very uneasy.

LADY BRITOMART [*squaring herself at him rather aggressively*]. Stephen: may I ask how soon you intend to realize that you are a grown-up man, and that I am only a woman?

STEPHEN [*amazed*]. Only a—

LADY BRITOMART. Dont repeat my words, please: it is a most aggravating habit. You must learn to face life seriously, Stephen. I really cannot bear the whole burden of our family affairs any longer. You must advise me: you must assume the responsibility.

STEPHEN. I!

LADY BRITOMART. Yes, you, of course. You were 24 last June. Youve been at Harrow and Cambridge. Youve been to India and Japan. You must know a lot of things, now; unless you have wasted your time most scandalously. Well, advise me.

STEPHEN [*much perplexed*]. You know I have never interfered in the household—

LADY BRITOMART. No: I should think not. I dont want you to order the dinner.

STEPHEN. I mean in our family affairs.

LADY BRITOMART. Well, you must interfere now; for they are getting quite beyond me.

STEPHEN [*troubled*]. I have thought sometimes that perhaps I ought; but really, mother, I know so little about them; and what I do know is so painful! it is so impossible to mention some things to you—[*He stops, ashamed.*]

LADY BRITOMART. I suppose you mean your father.

STEPHEN [*almost inaudibly*]. Yes.

LADY BRITOMART. My dear: we cant go on all our lives not mentioning him. Of course you were quite right not to open the subject until I asked you to; but you are old enough now to be taken into my confidence, and to help me to deal with him about the girls.

STEPHEN. But the girls are all right. They are engaged.

LADY BRITOMART [*complacently*]. Yes: I have made a very good match for Sarah. Charles Lomax will be a millionaire at 35. But that is ten years ahead; and in the meantime his trustees cannot under the terms of his father's will allow him more than £800 a year.

STEPHEN. But the will says also that if he increases his income by his own exertions, they may double the increase.

LADY BRITOMART. Charles Lomax's exertions are much more likely to decrease his income than to increase it. Sarah will have to find at least another £800 a year for the next ten years; and even then they will be as poor as church mice. And what about Barbara? I thought Barbara was going to make the most brilliant career of all of you. And what does she do? Joins the Salvation Army; discharges her maid; lives on a pound a week; and walks in one evening with a professor of Greek whom she has picked up in the street, and who pretends to be a Salvationist, and

actually plays the big drum for her in public because he
has fallen head over ears in love with her.

STEPHEN. I was certainly rather taken aback when I heard
they were engaged. Cusins is a very nice fellow, certainly: nobody would ever guess that he was born in
Australia; but—

LADY BRITOMART. Oh, Adolphus Cusins will make a very
good husband. After all, nobody can say a word against
Greek: it stamps a man at once as an educated gentleman. And my family, thank Heaven, is not a pig-headed
Tory one. We are Whigs, and believe in liberty. Let snobbish people say what they please: Barbara shall marry,
not the man they like, but the man I like.

STEPHEN. Of course I was thinking only of his income. However, he is not likely to be extravagant.

LADY BRITOMART. Dont be too sure of that, Stephen. I know
your quiet, simple, refined, poetic people like Adolphus:
quite content with the best of everything! They cost more
than your extravagant people, who are always as mean as
they are second rate. No: Barbara will need at least
£2,000 a year. You see it means two additional households.
Besides, my dear, you must marry soon. I dont approve
of the present fashion of philandering bachelors and late
marriages; and I am trying to arrange something for you.

STEPHEN. It's very good of you, mother; but perhaps I had
better arrange that for myself.

LADY BRITOMART. Nonsense! you are much too young to
begin matchmaking: you would be taken in by some
pretty little nobody. Of course I dont mean that you are not
to be consulted: you know that as well as I do. [Stephen
closes his lips and is silent.] Now dont sulk, Stephen.

STEPHEN. I am not sulking, mother. What has all this got to
do with—with—with my father?

LADY BRITOMART. My dear Stephen: where is the money to
come from? It is easy enough for you and the other children to live on my income as long as we are in the same
house; but I cant keep four families in four separate
houses. You know how poor my father is: he has barely
seven thousand a year now; and really, if he were not the
Earl of Stevenage, he would have to give up society. He
can do nothing for us. He says, naturally enough, that it
is absurd that he should be asked to provide for the children of a man who is rolling in money. You see, Stephen,

your father must be fabulously wealthy, because there is always a war going on somewhere.

STEPHEN. You need not remind me of that, mother. I have hardly ever opened a newspaper in my life without seeing our name in it. The Undershaft torpedo! The Undershaft quick firers! The Undershaft ten inch! the Undershaft disappearing rampart gun! the Undershaft submarine! and now the Undershaft aerial battleship! At Harrow they called me the Woolwich Infant. At Cambridge it was the same. A little brute at King's who was always trying to get up revivals, spoilt my Bible—your first birthday present to me—by writing under my name, 'Son and heir to Undershaft and Lazarus, Death and Destruction Dealers: address Christendom and Judea.' But that was not so bad as the way I was kowtowed to everywhere because my father was making millions by selling cannons.

LADY BRITOMART. It is not only the cannons, but the war loans that Lazarus arranges under cover of giving credit for the cannons. You know, Stephen, it's perfectly scandalous. Those two men, Andrew Undershaft and Lazarus, positively have Europe under their thumbs. That is why your father is able to behave as he does. He is above the law. Do you think Bismarck or Gladstone or Disraeli could have openly defied every social and moral obligation all their lives as your father has? They simply wouldnt have dared. I asked Gladstone to take it up. I asked The Times to take it up. I asked the Lord Chamberlain to take it up. But it was just like asking them to declare war on the Sultan. They wouldnt. They said they couldnt touch him. I believe they were afraid.

STEPHEN. What could they do? He does not actually break the law.

LADY BRITOMART. Not break the law! He is always breaking the law. He broke the law when he was born: his parents were not married.

STEPHEN. Mother! Is that true?

LADY BRITOMART. Of course it's true: that was why we separated.

STEPHEN. He married without letting you know this!

LADY BRITOMART [rather taken aback by this inference]. Oh no. To do Andrew justice, that was not the sort of thing he did. Besides, you know the Undershaft motto: Unashamed. Everybody knew.

STEPHEN. But you said that was why you separated.

LADY BRITOMART. Yes, because he was not content with being a foundling himself: he wanted to disinherit you for another foundling. That was what I couldnt stand.

STEPHEN [*ashamed*]. Do you mean for—for—for—

LADY BRITOMART. Dont stammer, Stephen. Speak distinctly.

STEPHEN. But this is so frightful to me, mother. To have to speak to you about such things!

LADY BRITOMART. It's not pleasant for me, either, especially if you are still so childish that you must make it worse by a display of embarrassment. It is only in the middle classes, Stephen, that people get into a state of dumb helpless horror when they find that there are wicked people in the world. In our class, we have to decide what is to be done with wicked people; and nothing should disturb our self-possession. Now ask your question properly.

STEPHEN. Mother: have you no consideration for me? For Heaven's sake either treat me as a child, as you always do, and tell me nothing at all; or tell me everything and let me take it as best I can.

LADY BRITOMART. Treat you as a child! What do you mean? It is most unkind and ungrateful of you to say such a thing. You know I have never treated any of you as children. I have always made you my companions and friends, and allowed you perfect freedom to do and say whatever you liked, so long as you liked what I could approve of.

STEPHEN [*desperately*]. I daresay we have been the very imperfect children of a very perfect mother; but I do beg you to let me alone for once, and tell me about this horrible business of my father wanting to set me aside for another son.

LADY BRITOMART [*amazed*]. Another son! I never said anything of the kind. I never dreamt of such a thing. This is what comes of interrupting me.

STEPHEN. But you said—

LADY BRITOMART [*cutting him short*]. Now be a good boy, Stephen, and listen to me patiently. The Undershafts are descended from a foundling in the parish of St Andrew Undershaft in the city. That was long ago, in the reign of James the First. Well, this foundling was adopted by an armorer and gun-maker. In the course of time the foundling succeeded to the business; and from some notion of gratitude, or some vow or something, he adopted another

foundling, and left the business to him. And that foundling did the same. Ever since that, the cannon business has
always been left to an adopted foundling named Andrew
Undershaft.

STEPHEN. But did they never marry? Were there no legiti-
mate sons?

LADY BRITOMART. Oh yes: they married just as your father
did; and they were rich enough to buy land for their
own children and leave them well provided for. But they
always adopted and trained some foundling to succeed
them in the business; and of course they always quarrelled
with their wives furiously over it. Your father was adopted
in that way; and he pretends to consider himself bound
to keep up the tradition and adopt somebody to leave the
business to. Of course I was not going to stand that. There
may have been some reason for it when the Undershafts
could only marry women in their own class, whose sons
were not fit to govern great estates. But there could be no
excuse for passing over my son.

STEPHEN [*dubiously*]. I am afraid I should make a poor
hand of managing a cannon foundry.

LADY BRITOMART. Nonsense! you could easily get a manager
and pay him a salary.

STEPHEN. My father evidently had no great opinion of my
capacity.

LADY BRITOMART. Stuff, child! you were only a baby: it
had nothing to do with your capacity. Andrew did it on
principle, just as he did every perverse and wicked thing
on principle. When my father remonstrated, Andrew actually told him to his face that history tells us of only two
successful institutions: one the Undershaft firm, and the
other the Roman Empire under the Antonines. That was
because the Antonine emperors all adopted their succes-
sors. Such rubbish! The Stevenages are as good as the
Antonines, I hope; and you are a Stevenage. But that was
Andrew all over. There you have the man! Always clever
and unanswerable when he was defending nonsense and
wickedness: always awkward and sullen when he had to
behave sensibly and decently!

STEPHEN. Then it was on my account that your home life
was broken up, mother. I am sorry.

LADY BRITOMART. Well, dear, there were other differences.
I really cannot bear an immoral man. I am not a Phar-

isee, I hope; and I should not have minded his merely doing wrong things: we are none of us perfect. But your father didnt exactly do wrong things: he said them and thought them: that was what was so dreadful. He really had a sort of religion of wrongness. Just as one doesnt mind men practising immorality so long as they own that they are in the wrong by preaching morality; so I couldnt forgive Andrew for preaching immorality while he practised morality. You would all have grown up without principles, without any knowledge of right and wrong, if he had been in the house. You know, my dear, your father was a very attractive man in some ways. Children did not dislike him; and he took advantage of it to put the wickedest ideas into their heads, and make them quite unmanageable. I did not dislike him myself: very far from it; but nothing can bridge over moral disagreement.

STEPHEN. All this simply bewilders me, mother. People may differ about matters of opinion, or even about religion; but how can they differ about right and wrong? Right is right; and wrong is wrong; and if a man cannot distinguish them properly, he is either a fool or a rascal: thats all.

LADY BRITOMART [touched]. Thats my own boy [She pats his cheek]! Your father never could answer that: he used to laugh and get out of it under cover of some affectionate nonsense. And now that you understand the situation, what do you advise me to do?

STEPHEN. Well, what can you do?

LADY BRITOMART. I must get the money somehow.

STEPHEN. We cannot take money from him. I had rather go and live in some cheap place like Bedford Square or even Hampstead than take a farthing of his money.

LADY BRITOMART. But after all, Stephen, our present income comes from Andrew.

STEPHEN [shocked]. I never knew that.

LADY BRITOMART. Well, you surely didnt suppose your grandfather had anything to give me. The Stevenages could not do everything for you. We gave you social position. Andrew had to contribute something. He had a very good bargain, I think.

STEPHEN [bitterly]. We are utterly dependent on him and his cannons, then?

LADY BRITOMART. Certainly not: the money is settled. But he provided it. So you see it is not a question of taking money from him or not: it is simply a question of how much. I dont want any more for myself.

STEPHEN. Nor do I.

LADY BRITOMART. But Sarah does; and Barbara does. That is, Charles Lomax and Adolphus Cusins will cost them more. So I must put my pride in my pocket and ask for it, I suppose. That is your advice, Stephen, is it not?

STEPHEN. No.

LADY BRITOMART [*sharply*]. Stephen!

STEPHEN. Of course if you are determined—

LADY BRITOMART. I am not determined: I ask your advice; and I am waiting for it. I will not have all the responsibility thrown on my shoulders.

STEPHEN [*obstinately*]. I would die sooner than ask him for another penny.

LADY BRITOMART [*resignedly*]. You mean that I must ask him. Very well, Stephen: it shall be as you wish. You will be glad to know that your grandfather concurs. But he thinks I ought to ask Andrew to come here and see the girls. After all, he must have some natural affection for them.

STEPHEN. Ask him here!!!

LADY BRITOMART. Do not repeat my words, Stephen. Where else can I ask him?

STEPHEN. I never expected you to ask him at all.

LADY BRITOMART. Now dont tease, Stephen. Come! you see that it is necessary that he should pay us a visit, dont you?

STEPHEN [*reluctantly*]. I suppose so, if the girls cannot do without his money.

LADY BRITOMART. Thank you, Stephen: I knew you would give me the right advice when it was properly explained to you. I have asked your father to come this evening. [STEPHEN *bounds from his seat.*] Dont jump, Stephen: it fidgets me.

STEPHEN [*in utter consternation*]. Do you mean to say that my father is coming here tonight—that he may be here at any moment?

LADY BRITOMART [*looking at her watch*]. I said nine. [*He gasps. She rises*]. Ring the bell, please. [STEPHEN *goes to the smaller writing table; presses a button on it; and sits at it with his elbows on the table and his head in his hands, outwitted and overwhelmed*]. It is ten minutes to nine yet;

and I have to prepare the girls. I asked Charles Lomax and Adolphus to dinner on purpose that they might be here. Andrew had better see them in case he should cherish any delusions as to their being capable of supporting their wives. [*The butler enters:* LADY BRITOMART *goes behind the settee to speak to him*]. Morrison: go up to the drawing room and tell everybody to come down here at once. [MORRISON *withdraws.* LADY BRITOMART *turns to* STEPHEN]. Now remember, Stephen: I shall need all your countenance and authority. [*He rises and tries to recover some vestige of these attributes*]. Give me a chair, dear. [*He pushes a chair forward from the wall to where she stands, near the smaller writing table. She sits down; and he goes to the armchair, into which he throws himself*]. I dont know how Barbara will take it. Ever since they made her a major in the Salvation Army she has developed a propensity to have her own way and order people about which quite cows me sometimes. It's not ladylike: I'm sure I dont know where she picked it up. Anyhow, Barbara shant bully me; but still it's just as well that your father should be here before she has time to refuse to meet him or make a fuss. Dont look nervous, Stephen: it will only encourage Barbara to make difficulties. *I* am nervous enough, goodness knows; but I don't shew it.

[SARAH *and* BARBARA *come in with their respective young men,* CHARLES LOMAX *and* ADOLPHUS CUSINS. SARAH *is slender, bored, and mundane.* BARBARA *is robuster, jollier, much more energetic.* SARAH *is fashionably dressed:* BARBARA *is in Salvation Army uniform. Lomax, a young man about town, is like many other young men about town. He is afflicted with a frivolous sense of humor which plunges him at the most inopportune moments into paroxysms of imperfectly suppressed laughter.* CUSINS *is a spectacled student, slight, thin haired, and sweet voiced, with a more complex form of* LOMAX's *complaint. His sense of humor is intellectual and subtle, and is complicated by an appalling temper. The lifelong struggle of a benevolent temperament and a high conscience against impulses of inhuman ridicule and fierce impatience has set up a chronic strain which has visibly wrecked his constitution. He is a most implacable, determined, tenacious, intolerant person who by mere force of character presents himself as—and indeed actually is— consliderate, gentle, explanatory, even mild and apologetic, capable possibly of murder, but not of cruelty or coarseness. By the operation of some instinct which is not merciful enough to blind him with the illusions of love, he is obstinately bent on marrying* BARBARA. LOMAX *likes* SARAH *and thinks it will be rather a lark to marry her. Consequently he has not attempted to resist* LADY BRITOMART'S *arrangements to that end.*

*All four look as if they had been having a good deal of fun in the drawing room. The girls enter first, leaving the swains outside.* SARAH *comes to the settee.* BARBARA *comes in after her and stops at the door.*]

BARBARA. Are Cholly and Dolly to come in?

LADY BRITOMART [*forcibly*]. Barbara: I will not have Charles called Cholly: the vulgarity of it positively makes me ill.

BARBARA. It's all right, mother: Cholly is quite correct nowadays. Are they to come in?

LADY BRITOMART. Yes, if they will behave themselves.

BARBARA [*through the door*]. Come in, Dolly; and behave yourself.

[BARBARA *comes to her mother's writing table.* CUSINS *enters smiling, and wanders towards* LADY BRITOMART.]

SARAH [*calling*]. Come in, Cholly.

[LOMAX *enters, controlling his features very imperfectly, and places himself vaguely between* SARAH *and* BARBARA].

LADY BRITOMART [*peremptorily*]. Sit down, all of you. [*They sit.* CUSINS *crosses to the window and seats himself there.* LOMAX *takes a chair.* BARBARA *sits at the writing table and* SARAH *on the settee*]. I dont in the least know what you are laughing at, Adolphus. I am surprised at you, though I expected nothing better from Charles Lomax.

CUSINS [*in a remarkably gentle voice*]. Barbara has been trying to teach me the West Ham Salvation March.

LADY BRITOMART. I see nothing to laugh at in that; nor should you if you are really converted.

CUSINS [*sweetly*]. You were not present. It was really funny, I believe.

LOMAX. Ripping.

LADY BRITOMART. Be quiet, Charles. Now listen to me, children. Your father is coming here this evening.

[*General stupefaction.* LOMAX, SARAH, *and* BARBARA *rise:* SARAH *scared, and* BARBARA *amused and expectant.*]

LOMAX [*remonstrating*]. Oh I say!

LADY BRITOMART. You are not called on to say anything, Charles.

SARAH. Are you serious, mother?

LADY BRITOMART. Of course I am serious. It is on your account, Sarah, and also on Charles's. [*Silence.* SARAH *sits, with a shrug.* CHARLES *looks painfully unworthy*]. I hope you are not going to object, Barbara.

BARBARA. I! why should I? My father has a soul to be saved like anybody else. He's quite welcome as far as I am concerned. [*She sits on the table, and softly whistles 'Onward, Christian Soldiers'.*]

LOMAX [*still remonstrant*]. But really, dont you know! Oh I say!

LADY BRITOMART [*frigidly*]. What do you wish to convey, Charles?

LOMAX. Well, you must admit that this is a bit thick.

LADY BRITOMART [*turning with ominous suavity to* CUSINS]. Adolphus: you are a professor of Greek. Can you translate Charles Lomax's remarks into reputable English for us?

CUSINS [*cautiously*]. If I may say so, Lady Brit, I think Charles has rather happily expressed what we all feel. Homer, speaking of Autolycus, uses the same phrase. πυκινὸν δόμον ἐλθεῖν means a bit thick.

LOMAX [*handsomely*]. Not that I mind, you know, if Sarah don't. [*He sits*].

LADY BRITOMART [*crushingly*]. Thank you. Have I your permission, Adolphus, to invite my own husband to my own house?

CUSINS [*gallantly*]. You have my unhesitating support in everything you do.

LADY BRITOMART. Tush! Sarah: have you nothing to say?

SARAH. Do you mean that he is coming regularly to live here?

LADY BRITOMART. Certainly not. The spare room is ready for him if he likes to stay for a day or two and see a little more of you; but there are limits.

SARAH. Well, he cant eat us, I suppose. *I* dont mind.

LOMAX [*chuckling*]. I wonder how the old man will take it.

LADY BRITOMART. Much as the old woman will, no doubt, Charles.

LOMAX [*abashed*]. I didnt mean—at least—

LADY BRITOMART. You didnt think, Charles. You never do; and the result is, you never mean anything. And now please attend to me, children. Your father will be quite a stranger to us.

LOMAX. I suppose he hasnt seen Sarah since she was a little kid.

LADY BRITOMART. Not since she was a little kid, Charles, as you express it with that elegance of diction and refinement of thought that seem never to desert you. Accordingly—er—[*Impatiently*] Now I have forgotten what I was going to say. That comes of your provoking me to be sarcastic, Charles. Adolphus: will you kindly tell me where I was.

CUSINS [*sweetly*]. You were saying that as Mr Undershaft has not seen his children since they were babies, he will form his opinion of the way you have brought them up from their behavior tonight, and that therefore you wish us all to be particularly careful to conduct ourselves well, especially Charles.

LADY BRITOMART [*with emphatic approval*]. Precisely.

LOMAX. Look here, Dolly: Lady Brit didnt say that.

LADY BRITOMART [*vehemently*]. I did, Charles. Adolphus's recollection is perfectly correct. It is most important that you should be good; and I do beg you for once not to pair off into opposite corners and giggle and whisper while I am speaking to your father.

BARBARA. All right, mother. We'll do you credit. [*She comes off the table, and sits in her chair with ladylike elegance.*]

LADY BRITOMART. Remember, Charles, that Sarah will want to feel proud of you instead of ashamed of you.

LOMAX. Oh I say! theres nothing to be exactly proud of, dont you know.

LADY BRITOMART. Well, try and look as if there was.

[MORRISON, *pale and dismayed, breaks into the room in unconcealed disorder.*]

MORRISON. Might I speak a word to you, my lady?

LADY BRITOMART. Nonsense! Shew him up.

MORRISON. Yes, my lady. [*He goes.*]

LOMAX. Does Morrison know who it is?

LADY BRITOMART. Of course. Morrison has always been with us.

LOMAX. It must be a regular corker for him, dont you know.

LADY BRITOMART. Is this a moment to get on my nerves, Charles, with your outrageous expressions?

LOMAX. But this is something out of the ordinary, really——

MORRISON [*at the door*]. The——er——Mr Undershaft. [*He retreats in confusion.*]

[ANDREW UNDERSHAFT *comes in. All rise.* LADY BRITOMART *meets him in the middle of the room behind the settee.*

ANDREW *is, on the surface, a stoutish, easygoing elderly man, with kindly patient manners, and an engaging simplicity of character. But he has a watchful, deliberate, waiting, listening face, and formidable reserves of power, both bodily and mental, in his capacious chest and long head. His gentleness is partly that of a strong man who has learnt by experience that his natural grip hurts ordinary people unless he handles them very carefully, and partly the mellowness of age and success. He is also a little shy in his present very delicate situation.*]

LADY BRITOMART. Good evening, Andrew.

UNDERSHAFT. How d'ye do, my dear.

LADY BRITOMART. You look a good deal older.

UNDERSHAFT [*apologetically*]. I am somewhat older. [*Taking her hand with a touch of courtship*] Time has stood still with you.

LADY BRITOMART [*throwing away his hand*]. Rubbish! This is your family.

UNDERSHAFT [*surprised*]. Is it so large? I am sorry to say my memory is failing very badly in some things. [*He offers his hand with paternal kindness to* LOMAX.]

LOMAX [*jerkily shaking his hand*]. Ahdedoo.

UNDERSHAFT. I can see you are my eldest. I am very glad to meet you again, my boy.

LOMAX [*remonstrating*]. No, but look here dont you know ——[*Overcome*] Oh I say!

LADY BRITOMART [*recovering from momentary speechlessness*]. Andrew: do you mean to say that you dont remember how many children you have?

NDERSHAFT. Well, I am afraid I—. They have grown so much—er. Am I making any ridiculous mistake? I may as well confess: I recollect only one son. But so many things have happened since, of course—er—

ADY BRITOMART [*decisively*]. Andrew: you are talking nonsense. Of course you have only one son.

NDERSHAFT. Perhaps you will be good enough to introduce me, my dear.

ADY BRITOMART. This is Charles Lomax, who is engaged to Sarah.

NDERSHAFT. My dear sir. I beg your pardon.

OMAX. Notatall. Delighted, I assure you.

ADY BRITOMART. This is Stephen.

NDERSHAFT [*bowing*]. Happy to make your acquaintance, Mr Stephen. Then [*going to* CUSINS] you must be my son. [*Taking* CUSINS' *hands in his*] How are you, my young friend? [*To* LADY BRITOMART] He is very like you, my love.

CUSINS. You flatter me, Mr Undershaft. My name is Cusins: engaged to Barbara. [*Very explicitly*] That is Major Barbara Undershaft, of the Salvation Army. That is Sarah, your second daughter. This is Stephen Undershaft, your son.

UNDERSHAFT. My dear Stephen, I beg your pardon.

STEPHEN. Not at all.

UNDERSHAFT. Mr Cusins: I am much indebted to you for explaining so precisely. [*Turning to* SARAH] Barbara, my dear—

SARAH [*prompting him*]. Sarah.

UNDERSAHFT. Sarah, of course. [*They shake hands. He goes over to* BARBARA.] Barbara—I am right this time, I hope?

BARBARA. Quite right. [*They shake hands.*]

LADY BRITOMART [*resuming command*]. Sit down, all of you. Sit down, Andrew.

[*She comes forward and sits on the settee.* CUSINS *also brings his chair forward on her left.* BARBARA *and* STEPHEN *resume their seats.* LOMAX *gives his chair to* SARAH *and goes for another*].

UNDERSHAFT. Thank you, my love.

LOMAX [*conversationally, as he brings a chair forward between the writing table and the settee, and offers it to* UNDERSHAFT]. Takes you some time to find out exactly where you are, dont it?

UNDERSHAFT [*accepting the chair, but remaining standing*]. That is not what embarrasses me, Mr Lomax. My difficulty is that if I play the part of a father, I shall produce the effect of an intrusive stranger; and if I play the part of a discreet stranger, I may appear a callous father.

LADY BRITOMART. There is no need for you to play any part at all, Andrew. You had much better be sincere and natural.

UNDERSHAFT [*submissively*]. Yes, my dear: I dare say that will be best. [*He sits down comfortably.*] Well, here I am. Now what can I do for you all?

LADY BRITOMART. You need not do anything, Andrew. You are one of the family. You can sit with us and enjoy yourself.

[*A painfully conscious pause.* BARBARA *makes a face at* LOMAX, *whose too long suppressed mirth immediately explodes in agonized neighings.*]

LADY BRITOMART [*outraged*]. Charles Lomax: if you can behave yourself, behave yourself. If not, leave the room.

LOMAX. I'm awfully sorry, Lady Brit; but really you know, upon my soul! [*He sits on the settee between* LADY BRITOMART *and* UNDERSHAFT, *quite overcome.*]

BARBARA. Why dont you laugh if you want to, Cholly? It's good for your inside.

LADY BRITOMART. Barbara: you have had the education of a lady. Please let your father see that; and dont talk like a street girl.

UNDERSHAFT. Never mind me, my dear. As you know, I am not a gentleman; and I was never educated.

LOMAX [*encouragingly*]. Nobody'd know it, I assure you. You look all right, you know.

CUSINS. Let me advise you to study Greek, Mr Undershaft. Greek scholars are privileged men. Few of them know Greek; and none of them know anything else; but their position is unchallengeable. Other languages are the qualifications of waiters and commercial travellers: Greek is to a man of position what the hallmark is to silver.

BARBARA. Dolly: dont be insincere. Cholly: fetch your concertina and play something for us.

LOMAX [*jumps up eagerly, but checks himself to remark doubtfully to* UNDERSHAFT]. Perhaps that sort of thing isnt in your line, eh?

UNDERSAHFT. I am particularly fond of music.

LOMAX [delighted]. Are you? Then I'll get it. [He goes upstairs for the instrument.]

UNDERSHAFT. Do you play, Barbara?

BARBARA. Only the tambourine. But Cholly's teaching me the concertina.

UNDERSHAFT. Is Cholly also a member of the Salvation Army?

BARBARA. No: he says it's bad form to be a dissenter. But I dont despair of Cholly. I made him come yesterday to a meeting at the dock gates, and take the collection in his hat.

UNDERSHAFT looks whimsically at his wife!!]

LADY BRITOMART. It is not my doing, Andrew. Barbara is old enough to take her own way. She has no father to advise her.

BARBARA. Oh yes she has. There are no orphans in the Salvation Army.

UNDERSHAFT. Your father there has a great many children and plenty of experience, eh?

BARBARA [looking at him with quick interest and nodding]. Just so. How did you come to understand that?

[LOMAX is heard at the door trying the concertina.]

LADY BRITOMART. Come in, Charles. Play us something at once.

LOMAX. Righto! [He sits down in his former place, and preludes.]

UNDERSHAFT. One moment, Mr Lomax. I am rather interested in the Salvation Army. Its motto might be my own: Blood and Fire.

LOMAX [shocked]. But not your sort of blood and fire, you know.

UNDERSHAFT. My sort of blood cleanses: my sort of fire purifies.

BARBARA. So do ours. Come down tomorrow to my shelter— the West Ham shelter—and see what we're doing. We're going to march to a great meeting in the Assembly Hall at Mile End. Come and see the shelter and then march with us: it will do you a lot of good. Can you play anything?

UNDERSHAFT. In my youth I earned pennies, and even shillings occasionally, in the streets and in public house parlors by my natural talent for stepdancing. Later on, I became a member of the Undershaft orchestral society, and performed passably on the tenor trombone.

LOMAX [*scandalized—putting down the concertina*]. Oh I say!

BARBARA. Many a sinner has played himself into heaven on the trombone, thanks to the Army.

LOMAX [*to* BARBARA, *still rather shocked*]. Yes; but what about the cannon business, dont you know? [*To* UNDERSHAFT] Getting into heaven is not exactly in your line, is it?

LADY BRITOMART. Charles!!!

LOMAX. Well; but it stands to reason, dont it? The cannon business may be necessary and all that: we cant get on without cannons; but it isnt right, you know. On the other hand, there may be a certain amount of tosh about the Salvation Army—I belong to the Established Church myself—but still you cant deny that it's religion; and you cant go against religion, can you? At least unless youre downright immoral, dont you know.

UNDERSHAFT. You hardly appreciate my position, Mr Lomax—

LOMAX [*hastily*]. I'm not saying anything against you personally—

UNDERSHAFT. Quite so, quite so. But consider for a moment. Here I am, a profiteer in mutilation and murder. I find myself in a specially amiable humor just now because, this morning, down at the foundry, we blew twenty-seven dummy soldiers into fragments with a gun which formerly destroyed only thirteen.

LOMAX [*leniently*]. Well, the more destructive war becomes, the sooner it will be abolished, eh?

UNDERSHAFT. Not at all. The more destructive war becomes the more fascinating we find it. No, Mr Lomax: I am obliged to you for making the usual excuse for my trade; but I am not ashamed of it. I am not one of those men who keep their morals and their business in watertight compartments. All the spare money my trade rivals spend on hospitals, cathedrals, and other receptacles for conscience money, I devote to experiments and researches in improved methods of destroying life and property. I have always done so; and I always shall. Therefore your Christmas card moralities of peace on earth and goodwill among men are of no use to me. Your Christianity, which enjoins you to resist not evil, and to turn the other cheek, would make me a bankrupt. My morality—my religion—must have a place for cannons and torpedoes in it.

STEPHEN [coldly—almost sullenly]. You speak as if there were half a dozen moralities and religions to choose from, instead of one true morality and one true religion.

UNDERSHAFT. For me there is only one true morality; but it might not fit you, as you do not manufacture aerial battleships. There is only one true morality for every man; but every man has not the same true morality.

LOMAX [overtaxed]. Would you mind saying that again? I didnt quite follow it.

CUSINS. It's quite simple. As Euripides says, one man's meat is another man's poison morally as well as physically.

UNDERSHAFT. Precisely.

LOMAX. Oh, that! Yes, yes, yes. True. True.

STEPHEN. In other words, some men are honest and some are scoundrels.

BARBARA. Bosh! There are no scoundrels.

UNDERSHAFT. Indeed? Are there any good men?

BARBARA. No. Not one. There are neither good men nor scoundrels: there are just children of one Father; and the sooner they stop calling one another names the better. You neednt talk to me: I know them. Ive had scores of them through my hands: scoundrels, criminals, infidels, philanthropists, missionaries, county councillors, all sorts. Theyre all just the same sort of sinner; and theres the same salvation ready for them all.

UNDERSHAFT. May I ask have you ever saved a maker of cannons?

BARBARA. No. Will you let me try?

UNDERSHAFT. Well, I will make a bargain with you. If I go to see you tomorrow in your Salvation Shelter, will you come the day after to see me in my cannon works?

BARBARA. Take care. It may end in your giving up the cannons for the sake of the Salvation Army.

UNDERSHAFT. Are you sure it will not end in your giving up the Salvation Army for the sake of the cannons?

BARBARA. I will take my chance of that.

UNDERSHAFT. And I will take my chance of the other. [They shake hands on it.] Where is your shelter?

BARBARA. In West Ham. At the sign of the cross. Ask anybody in Canning Town. Where are your works?

UNDERSHAFT. In Perivale St Andrews. At the sign of the
sword. Ask anybody in Europe.

LOMAX. Hadnt I better play something?

BARBARA. Yes. Give us 'Onward, Christian Soldiers.'

LOMAX. Well, thats rather a strong order to begin with,
dont you know. Suppose I sing 'Thou'rt Passing Hence, My
Brother.' It's much the same tune.

BARBARA. It's too melancholy. You get saved, Cholly; and youll
pass hence, my brother, without making such a fuss about
it.

LADY BRITOMART. Really, Barbara, you go on as if religion
were a pleasant subject. Do have some sense of pro-
priety.

UNDERSHAFT. I do not find it an unpleasant subject, my dear.
It is the only one that capable people really care for.

LADY BRITOMART [looking at her watch]. Well, if you are
determined to have it, I insist on having it in a proper and
respectable way. Charles: ring for prayers.

[General amazement. STEPHEN rises in dismay.]

LOMAX [rising]. Oh I say!

UNDERSHAFT [rising]. I am afraid I must be going.

LADY BRITOMART. You cannot go now, Andrew: it would
be most improper. Sit down. What will the servants think?

UNDERSHAFT. My dear: I have conscientious scruples. May I
suggest a compromise? If Barbara will conduct a little
service in the drawing room, with Mr Lomax as organist,
I will attend it willingly. I will even take part, if a trombone can be procured.

LADY BRITOMART. Dont mock, Andrew.

UNDERSHAFT [shocked—to BARBARA]. You dont think I am
mocking, my love, I hope.

BARBARA. No, of course not; and it wouldnt matter if you
were: half the Army came to their first meeting for a lark.
[Rising.] Come along. [She throws her arm round her
father and sweeps him out, calling to the others from
the threshold.] Come, Dolly. Come, Cholly.

[CUSINS rises.]

LADY BRITOMART. I will not be disobeyed by everybody.
Adolphus: sit down. [He does not.] Charles: you may go.

You are not fit for prayers: you cannot keep your countenance.

LOMAX. Oh I say! [*He goes out.*]

LADY BRITOMART [*continuing*]. But you, Adolphus, can behave yourself if you choose to. I insist on your staying.

CUSINS. My dear Lady Brit: there are things in the family prayer book that I couldnt bear to hear you say.

LADY BRITOMART. What things, pray?

CUSINS. Well, you would have to say before all the servants that we have done things we ought not to have done, and left undone things we ought to have done, and that there is no health in us. I cannot bear to hear you doing yourself such an injustice, and Barbara such an injustice. As for myself, I flatly deny it: I have done my best. I shouldnt dare to marry Barbara—I couldnt look you in the face—if it were true. So I must go to the drawing room.

LADY BRITOMART [*offended*]. Well, go. [*He starts for the door.*] And remember this, Adolphus [*he turns to listen*]: I have a very strong suspicion that you went to the Salvation Army to worship Barbara and nothing else. And I quite appreciate the very clever way in which you systematically humbug me. I have found you out. Take care Barbara doesnt. Thats all.

CUSINS [*with unruffled sweetness*]. Dont tell on me. [*He steals out.*]

LADY BRITOMART. Sarah: if you want to go, go. Anything's better than to sit there as if you wished you were a thousand miles away.

SARAH [*languidly*]. Very well, mamma. [*She goes.*]

[LADY BRITOMART, *with a sudden flounce, gives way to a little gust of tears.*]

STEPHEN [*going to her*]. Mother: whats the matter?

LADY BRITOMART [*swishing away her tears with her handkerchief*]. Nothing. Foolishness. You can go with him, too, if you like, and leave me with the servants.

STEPHEN. Oh, you mustnt think that, mother. I—I dont like him.

LADY BRITOMART. The others do. That is the injustice of a woman's lot. A woman has to bring up her children; and that means to restrain them, to deny them things they want, to set them tasks, to punish them when they do wrong, to do all the unpleasant things. And then the father, who has nothing to do but pet them and spoil them, comes in when all her work is done and steals their affection from her.

STEPHEN. He has not stolen our affection from you. It is only curiosity.

LADY BRITOMART [*violently*]. I wont be consoled, Stephen. There is nothing the matter with me. [*She rises and goes towards the door.*]

STEPHEN. Where are you going, mother?

LADY BRITOMART. To the drawing room, of course. [*She goes out. 'Onward, Christian Soldiers', on the concertina, with tambourine accompaniment, is heard when the door opens*]. Are you coming, Stephen?

STEPHEN. No. Certainly not.

[*She goes. He sits down on the settee, with compressed lips and an expression of strong dislike*].

# ACT TWO

*The* yard of the West Ham shelter of the Salvation Army is
*a* cold place on a January morning. The building itself, an
*old* warehouse, is newly whitewashed. Its gabled end projects
*into* the yard in the middle, with a door on the ground
*floor,* and another in the loft above it without any balcony
*or* ladder, but with a pulley rigged over it for hoisting sacks.
*Those* who come from this central gable end into the yard
*have* the gateway leading to the street on their left, with a
*stone* horse-trough just beyond it, and, on the right, a pent-
*house* shielding a table from the weather. There are forms
*at* the table; and on them are seated a man and a woman,
*both* much down on their luck, finishing a meal of bread
*(one* thick slice each, with margarine and golden syrup) and
*diluted* milk.

*The* man, a workman out of employment, is young, agile, a
*talker,* a poser, sharp enough to be capable of anything in
*reason* except honesty or altruistic considerations of any
*kind.* The woman is a commonplace old bundle of poverty
*and* hard-worn humanity. She looks sixty and probably is
*forty-five.* If they were rich people, gloved and muffed
*and* well wrapped up in furs and overcoats, they would be
*numbed* and miserable; for it is a grindingly cold raw Janu-
*ary* day; and a glance at the background of grimy ware-
*houses* and leaden sky visible over the whitewashed walls of
*the* yard would drive any idle rich person straight to the
*Mediterranean.* But these two, being no more troubled with
*visions* of the Mediterranean than of the moon, and being
*compelled* to keep more of their clothes in the pawnship,
*and* less on their persons, in winter than in summer, are not
*depressed* by the colds: rather are they stung into vivacity, to
*which* their meal has just now given an almost jolly turn.
*The* man takes a pull at his mug, and then gets up and
*moves* about the yard with his hands deep in his pockets,
*occasionally* breaking into a stepdance.

THE WOMAN. Fee! better after your meal, sir?

THE MAN. No. Call that a meal! Good enough for yo? praps; but wot is it to me, an intelligent workin man.

THE WOMAN. Workin man! Wot are you?

THE MAN. Painter.

THE WOMAN [*sceptically*]. Yus, I dessay.

THE MAN. Yus, you dessay! I know. Every loafer that can do nothink calls isself a painter. Well, I'm a real painter: grainer, finisher, thirty-eight bob a week when I can ge? it.

THE WOMAN. Then why dont you go and get it?

THE MAN. I'll tell you why. Fust: I'm intelligent—fffff? it's rotton cold here [*he dances a step or two*]—yes? intelligent beyond the station o life into which it ha? pleased the capitalists to call me; and they dont like? man that sees through em. Second, an intelligent bei? needs a doo share of appiness; so I drink somethink crue? when I get the chawnce. Third, I stand by my class an? do as little as I can so's to leave arf the job for me fellow? workers. Fourth, I'm fly enough to know wots inside the? law and wots outside it; and inside it I do as the capital? ists do: pinch wot I can lay me ands on. In a proper state of society I am sober, industrious and honest: in Rome, s? to speak, I do as the Romans do. Wots the consequence? When trade is bad—and it's rotten bad just now—and the? employers az to sack arf their men, they generally start on me.

THE WOMAN. Whats your name?

THE MAN. Price. Bronterre O'Brien Price. Usually called? Snobby Price, for short.

THE WOMAN. Snobby's a carpenter, aint it? You said you? was a painter.

PRICE. Not that kind of snob, but the genteel sort. I'm too uppish, owing to my intelligence, and my father being a Chartist and a reading, thinking man: a stationer, too. I'm none of your common hewers of wood and drawers of water; and dont you forget it. [*He returns to his seat at the table, and takes up his mug.*] Wots your name?

THE WOMAN. Rummy Mitchens, sir.

PRICE [*quaffing the remains of his milk to her*]. Your elth, Miss Mitchens.

RUMMY [*correcting him*]. Missis Mitchens.

PRICE. Wot! Oh Rummy, Rummy! Respectable married woman, Rummy, gittin rescued by the Salvation Army by pretendin to be a bad un. Same old game!

RUMMY. What am I to do? I cant starve. Them Salvation lasses is dear good girls; but the better you are, the worse they likes to think you were before they rescued you. Why shouldnt they av a bit o credit, poor loves? theyre worn to rags by their work. And where would they get the money to rescue us if we was to let on we're no worse than other people? You know what ladies and gentlemen are.

PRICE. Thievin swine! Wish I ad their job, Rummy, all the same. Wot does Rummy stand for? Pet name praps?

RUMMY. Short for Romola.

PRICE. For wot!?

RUMMY. Romola. It was out of a new book. Somebody me mother wanted me to grow up like.

PRICE. We're companions in misfortune, Rummy. Both on us got names that nobody cawnt pronounce. Consequently I'm Snobby and youre Rummy because Bill and Sally wasnt good enough for our parents. Such is life!

RUMMY. Who saved you, Mr Price? Was it Major Barbara?

PRICE. No: I come here on my own. I'm going to be Bronterre O'Brien Price, the converted painter. I know wot they like. I'll tell em how I blasphemed and gambled and wopped my poor old mother—

RUMMY [shocked]. Used you to beat your mother?

PRICE. Not likely. She used to beat me. No matter: you come and listen to the converted painter, and youll hear how she was a pious woman that taught me me prayers at er knee, and how I used to come home drunk and drag her out o bed be er snow white airs, an lam into er with the poker.

RUMMY. Thats whats so unfair to us women. Your confessions is just as big lies as ours: you dont tell what you really done no more than us; but you men can tell your lies right out at the meetins and be made much of for it; while the sort o confessions we az to make az to be wispered to one lady at a time. It aint right, spite of all their piety.

PRICE. Right! Do you spose the Army'd be allowed if it went and did right? Not much. It combs our air and makes us good little blokes to be rc'bbed and put upon. But I'll play the game as good as any of em. I'll see somebody struck by lightnin, or hear a voice sayin 'Snobby Price: where will you spend eternity?' I'll av a time of it, I tell you.

RUMMY. You wont be let drink, though.

PRICE. I'll take it out in gorspellin, then. I dont want to drink if I can get fun enough any other way.

[JENNY HILL, *a pale, overwrought, pretty Salvation lass of 18, comes in through the yard gate, leading* PETER SHIRLEY, *a half hardened, half worn-out elderly man, weak with hunger.*]

JENNY [*supporting him*]. Come! pluck up. I'll get you something to eat. Youll be all right then.

PRICE [*rising and hurrying officiously to take the old man off* JENNY'S *hands*]. Poor old man! Cheer up, brother: youll find rest and peace and appiness ere. Hurry up with the food, miss: e's fair done. [JENNY *hurries into the shelter.*] Ere, buck up, daddy! she's fetchin y'a thick slice o breadn treacle, an a mug o skyblue. [*He seats him at the corner of the table.*]

RUMMY [*gaily*]. Keep up your old art! Never say die!

SHIRLEY. I'm not an old man. I'm ony 46. I'm as good as ever I was. The grey patch come in my hair before I was thirty. All it wants is three pennorth o hair dye: am I to be turned on the streets to starve for it? Holy God! I've worked ten to twelve hours a day since I was thirteen, and paid my way all through; and now am I to be thrown into the gutter and my job given to a young man that can do it no better than me because Ive black hair that goes white at the first change?

PRICE [*cheerfully*]. No good jawrin about it. Youre ony a jumped-up, jerked-off, orspittle-turned-out incurable of an ole workin man: who cares about you? Eh? Make the thievin swine give you a meal: theyve stole many a one from you. Get a bit o your own back. [JENNY *returns with the usual meal.*] There you are, brother. Awsk a blessin an tuck that into you.

SHIRLEY [*looking at it ravenously but not touching it, and crying like a child*]. I never took anything before.

JENNY [*petting him*]. Come, come! the Lord sends it to you: he wasnt above taking bread from his friends; and why should you be? Besides, when we find you a job you can pay us for it if you like.

HIRLEY [*eagerly*]. Yes, yes: thats true. I can pay you back: it's only a loan. [*Shivering*] Oh Lord! oh Lord! [*He turns to the table and attacks the meal ravenously.*]

JENNY. Well, Rummy, are you more comfortable now?

RUMMY. God bless you, lovey! youve fed my body and saved my soul, havent you? [JENNY, *touched, kisses her.*] Sit down and rest a bit: you must be ready to drop.

JENNY. Ive been going hard since morning. But theres more work than we can do. I mustnt stop.

RUMMY. Try a prayer for just two minutes. Youll work all the better after.

JENNY [*her eyes lighting up*]. Oh isnt it wonderful how a few minutes prayer revives you! I was quite lightheaded at twelve o'clock, I was so tired; but Major Barbara just sent me to pray for five minutes; and I was able to go on as if I had only just begun. [*To Price*] Did you have a piece of bread?

PRICE [*with unction*]. Yes, miss; but Ive got the piece that I value more; and thats the peace that passeth hall hannerstennin.

RUMMY [*fervently*]. Glory Hallelujah!

[BILL WALKER, *a rough customer of about 25, appears at the yard gate and looks malevolently at* JENNY.]

JENNY. That makes me so happy. When you say that, I feel wicked for loitering here. I must get to work again.

[*She is hurrying to the shelter, when the new-comer moves quickly up to the door and intercepts her. His manner is so threatening that she retreats as he comes at her truculently, driving her down the yard.*]

BILL. Aw knaow you. Youre the one that took awy maw girl. Youre the one that set er agen me. Well, I'm gowin to ev er aht. Not that Aw care a carse for er or you: see? Bat Aw'll let er knaow; and Aw'll let you knaow. Aw'm gowing to give her a doin thatll teach er to cat awy from me. Nah in wiv you and tell er to cam aht afore Aw cam in and kick er aht. Tell er Bill Walker wants er. She'll knaow wot thet means; and if she keeps me witin itll be worse. You stop to jawr beck at me; and Aw'll stawt on you: d'ye eah? Theres your wy. In you gow.

[*He takes her by the arm and slings her towards the door of the shelter. She falls on her hand and knee.* RUMMY *helps her up again.*]

PRICE [*rising, and venturing irresolutely towards Bill*] Easy there, mate. She aint doin you no arm.

BILL. Oo are you callin mite? [*Standing over him threateningly*] Youre gowin to stend ap for er, aw yer? Put ap your ends.

RUMMY [*running indignantly to him to scold him*]. Oh, you great brute—

[*He instantly swings his left hand back against her face. She screams and reels back to the trough, where she sits down, covering her bruised face with her hands and rocking herself and moaning with pain.*]

JENNY [*going to her*]. Oh, God forgive you! How could you strike an old woman like that?

BILL [*seizing her by the hair so violently that she also screams, and tearing her away from the old woman*]. You Gawd forgimme again an Aw'll Gawk forgive you one on the jawr thetll stop you pryin for a week. [*Holding her and turning fiercely on* PRICE] Ev you ennything to sy agen it?

PRICE [*intimidated*]. No, matey: she aint anything to do with me.

BILL. Good job for you! Aw'd pat two meals into you and fawt you with one finger arter, you stawved cur. [*To* JENNY] Nah are you gowin to fetch aht Mog Ebbijem; or em Aw to knock your fice off you and fetch her meself?

JENNY [*writing in his grasp*]. Oh please someone go in and tell Major Barbara—[*she screams again as he wrenches her head down; and* PRICE *and* RUMMY *flee into the shelter.*]

BILL. You want to gow in and tell your Mijor of me, do you?

JENNY. Oh please dont drag my hair. Let me go.

BILL. Do you or downt you? [*She stifles a scream.*] Yus or nao?

JENNY. God give me strength—

BILL [*striking her with his fist in the face*]. Gow an shaow her thet, and tell her if she wants one lawk it to cam and interfere with me. [JENNY, *crying with pain, goes into the shed. He goes to the form and addresses the old man.*] Eah: finish your mess; an git aht o maw wy.

SHIRLEY [*springing up and facing him fiercely, with the mug in his hand*]. You take a liberty with me, and I'll smash you over the face with the mug and cut your eye out. Aint you satisfied—young whelps like you—with takin the bread out o the mouths of your elders that have brought you up and slaved for you, but you must come shovin and cheekin and bullyin in here, where the bread o charity is sickenin in our stummicks?

BILL [*contemptuously, but backing a little*]. Wot good are you, you aold palsy mag? Wot good are you?

SHIRLEY. As good as you and better. I'll do a day's work agen you or any fat young soaker of your age. Go and take my job at Horrockses, where I worked for ten year. They want young men there: they cant afford to keep men over forty-five. Theyre very sorry—give you a character and happy to help you to get anything suited to your years—sure a steady man wont be long out of a job. Well, let em try you Theyll find the differ. What do you know? Not as much as how to beeyave yourself—layin your dirty fist across the mouth of a respectable woman!

BILL. Downt provowk me to ly it acrost yours: d'ye eah?

SHIRLEY [*with blighting contempt*]. Yes: you like an old man to hit, dont you, when youve finished with the women. I aint seen you hit a young one yet.

BILL [*stung*]. You loy, you aold soupkitchener, you. There was a yang menn eah. Did Aw offer to itt him or did Aw not?

SHIRLEY. Was he starvin or was he not? Was he a man or only a crosseyed thief an a loafer? Would you hit my son-in-law's brother?

BILL. Oo's ee?

SHIRLEY. Todger Fairmile o Balls Pond. Him that won £20 off the Japanese wrastler at the music hall by standin out 17 minutes 4 seconds agen him.

BILL [*sullenly*]. Aw'm nao music awl wrastler. Ken he box?

SHIRLEY. Yes: an you cant.

BILL. Wot! Aw cawnt, cawnt Aw? Wots thet you sy [*threatening him*]?

SHIRLEY [*not budging an inch*]. Will you box Todger Fairmile if I put him on to you? Say the word.

BILL [*subsiding with a slouch*]. Aw'll stend ap to enny menn
alawv, if he was ten Todger Fairmawls. But Aw dont set
ap to be a perfeshnal.

SHIRLEY [*looking down on him with unfathomable disdain*].
You box! Slap an old woman with the back o your hand!
You hadnt even the sense to hit her where a magistrate
couldnt see the mark of it, you silly young lump of conceit
and ignorance. Hit a girl in the jaw and ony make her
cry! If Todger Fairmile'd done it, she wouldnt a got up
inside o ten minutes, no more than you would if he got on
to you. Yah! I'd set about you myself if I had a week's
feedin in me instead o two months' starvation. [*He turns
his back on him and sits down moodily at the table.*]

BILL [*following him and stooping over him to drive the
taunt in*]. You loy! youve the bread and treacle in you
that you cam eah to beg.

SHIRLEY [*bursting into tears*]. Oh God! it's true: I'm only
an old pauper on the scrap heap. [*Furiously*] But youll
come to it yourself; and then youll know. Youll come to
it sooner than a teetotaller like me, fillin yourself with gin
at this hour o the mornin!

BILL. Aw'm nao gin drinker, you oald lawr; bat wen Aw
want to give my girl a bloomin good awdin Aw lawk to
ev a bit o devil in me: see? An eah Aw emm, talkin to a
rotten aold blawter like you sted o givin her wot for.
[*Working himself into a rage*] Aw'm gowin in there to
fetch her aht. [*He makes vengefully for the shelter door.*]

SHIRLEY. Youre going to the station on a stretcher, more
likely; and theyll take the gin and the devil out of you
there when they get you inside. You mind what youre
about: the major here is the Earl o Stevenage's grand-
daughter.

BILL [*checked*]. Garn!

SHIRLEY. Youll see.

BILL [*his resolution oozing*]. Well, Aw aint dan nathin to
er.

SHIRLEY. Spose she said you did! who'd believe you?

BILL [*very uneasy, skulking back to the corner of the penthouse*]. Gawd! theres no jastice in this cantry. To think
wot them people can do! Aw'm as good as er.

SHIRLEY. Tell her so. It's just what a fool like you would do.

[BARBARA, *brisk and businesslike, comes from the shelter with a note book, and addresses herself to* SHIRLEY. BILL, *cowed, sits down in the corner on a form, and turns his back on them.*]

BARBARA. Good morning.

SHIRLEY [*standing up and taking off his hat*]. Good morning, miss.

BARBARA. Sit down: make yourself at home. [*He hesitates; but she puts a friendly hand on his shoulder and makes him obey.*] Now then! since youve made friends with us, we want to know all about you. Names and addresses and trades.

SHIRLEY. Peter Shirley. Fitter. Chucked out two months ago because I was too old.

BARBARA [*not at all surprised*]. Youd pass still. Why didnt you dye your hair?

SHIRLEY. I did. Me age come out at a coroner's inquest on me daughter.

BARBARA. Steady?

SHIRLEY. Teetotaller. Never out of a job before. Good worker. And sent to the knackers like an old horse!

BARBARA. No matter: if you did your part God will do his.

SHIRLEY [*suddenly stubborn*]. My religion's no concern of anybody but myself.

BARBARA [*guessing*]. I know. Secularist?

SHIRLEY [*hotly*]. Did I offer to deny it?

BARBARA. Why should you? My own father's a Secularist, I think. Our Father—yours and mine—fulfils himself in many ways; and I daresay he knew what he was about when he made a Secularist of you. So buck up, Peter! we can always find a job for a steady man like you. [SHIRLEY, *disarmed and a little bewildered, touches his hat. She turns from him to* BILL.] Whats your name?

BILL [*insolently*]. Wots thet to you?

BARBARA [*calmly making a note*]. Afraid to give his name. Any trade?

BILL. Oo's afraid to give is nime? [*Doggledy, with a sense of heroically defying the House of Lords in the person of Lord Stevenage*] If you want to bring a chawge agen me, bring it. [*She waits, unruffled.*] Moy nime's Bill Walker.

BARBARA [*as if the name were familiar: trying to remember*

*how*]. Bill Walker? [*Recollecting*] Oh, I know: youre
the man that Jenny Hill was praying for inside just now.
[*She enters his name in her note book*.]

BILL. Oo's Jenny Ill? And wot call as she to pry for me?

BARBARA. I dont know. Perhaps it was you that cut her lip.

BILL [*defiantly*]. Yus, it was me that cat her lip. Aw aint
afride o you.

BARBARA. How could you be, since youre not afraid of God?
Youre a brave man, Mr Walker. It takes some pluck to
do our work here; but none of us dare lift our hand
against a girl like that, for fear of her father in heaven.

BILL [*sullenly*]. I want nan o your kentin jawr. I spowse
you think Aw cam eah to beg from you, like this dem-
miged lot eah. Not me. Aw downt want your bread and
scripe and ketlep. Aw dont blieve in your Gawd, no more
than you do yourself.

BARBARA [*sunnily apologetic and ladylike, as on a new foot-
ing with him*]. Oh, I beg your pardon for putting your
name down, Mr Walker. I didnt understand. I'll strike it
out.

BILL [*taking this as a slight, and deeply wounded by it*].
Eah! you let maw nime alown. Aint it good enaff to be
in your book?

BARBARA [*considering*]. Well, you see, theres no use putting
down your name unless I can do something for you, is
there? Whats your trade?

BILL [*still smarting*]. Thets nao concern o yours.

BARBARA. Just so. [*Very businesslike*] I'll put you down as
[*writing*] the man who—struck—poor little Jenny Hill—
in the mouth.

BILL [*rising threateningly*]. See eah. Awve ed enaff o this.

BARBARA [*quite sunny and fearless*]. What did you come to
us for?

BILL. Aw cam for maw gel, see? Aw cam to tike her aht o
this and to brike er jawr for er.

BARBARA [*complacently*]. You see I was right about your
trade. [BILL, *on the point of retorting furiously, finds
himself, to his great shame and terror, in danger of crying instead. He sits down again suddenly*.] Whats her
name?

BILL [*dogged*]. Er nime's Mog Ebbijem: thets wot her
nime is.

BARBARA. Mog Habbijam! Oh, she's gone to Canning Town, to our barracks there.

BILL [*fortified by his resentment of Mog's perfidy*]. Is she? [*Vindictively*] Then Aw'm gowin to Kennintahn arter her. [*He crosses to the gate; hesitates; finally comes back at* BARBARA.] Are you loyin to me to git shat o me?

BARBARA. I dont want to get shut of you. I want to keep you here and save your soul. Youd better stay: youre going to have a bad time today, Bill.

BILL. Oo's gowin to give it to me? You, preps?

BARBARA. Someone you dont believe in. But youll be glad afterwards.

BILL [*slinking off*]. Aw'll gow to Kennintahn to be aht o reach o your tangue. [*Suddenly turning on her with intense malice*] And if Aw downt fawnd Mog there, Aw'll cam beck and do two years for you, selp me Gawd if Aw downt!

BARBARA [*a shade kindlier, if possible*]. It's no use, Bill. She's got another bloke.

BILL. Wot!

BARBARA. One of her own converts. He fell in love with her when he saw her with her soul saved, and her face clean, and her hair washed.

BILL [*surprised*]. Wottud she wash it for, the carroty slat? It's red.

BARBARA. It's quite lovely now, because she wears a new look in her eyes with it. It's a pity youre too late. The new bloke has put your nose out of joint, Bill.

BILL. Aw'll put his nowse aht o joint for him. Not that Aw care a carse for er, mawnd thet. But Aw'll teach her to drop me as if Aw was dirt. And Aw'll teach him to meddle with maw judy. Wots iz bleedin nime?

BARBARA. Sergeant Todger Fairmile.

SHIRLEY [*rising with grim joy*]. I'll go with him, miss. I want to see them two meet. I'll take him to the infirmary when it's over.

BILL [*to* SHIRLEY, *with undissembled misgiving*]. Is thet im you was speakin on?

SHIRLEY. Thats him.

BILL. Im that wrastled in the music awl?

SHIRLEY. The competitions at the National Sportin Club was worth nigh a hundred a year to him. He's gev em up now for religion; so he's a bit fresh for want of the exercise he was accustomed to. He'll be glad to see you. Come along.

BILL. Wots is wight?

SHIRLEY. Thirteen four. [*Bill's last hope expires*].

BARBARA. Go and talk to him, Bill. He'll convert you.

SHIRLEY. He'll convert your head into a mashed potato.

BILL [*sullenly*]. Aw aint afride of im. Aw aint afride of ennybody. Bat e can lick me. She's dan me. [*He sits down moodily on the edge of the horse trough.*]

SHIRLEY. You aint going. I thought not. [*He resumes his seat.*]

BARBARA [*calling*]. Jenny!

JENNY [*appearing at the shelter door with a plaster on the corner of her mouth*]. Yes, Major.

BARBARA. Send Rummy Mitchens out to clear away here.

JENNY. I think she's afraid.

BARBARA [*her resemblance to her mother flashing out for a moment*]. Nonsense! she must do as she's told.

JENNY [*calling into the shelter*]. Rummy: the Major says you must come. [JENNY *comes to* BARBARA, *purposely keeping on the side next* BILL, *lest he should suppose that she shrank from him or bore malice.*]

BARBARA. Poor little Jenny! Are you tired? [*Looking at the wounded cheek*] Does it hurt?

JENNY. No: it's all right now. It was nothing.

BARBARA [*critically*]. It was as hard as he could hit, I expect. Poor Bill! You dont feel angry with him, do you?

JENNY. Oh no, no, no: indeed I dont, Major, bless his poor heart!

[BARBARA *kisses her; and she runs away merrily into the shelter.* BILL *writhes with an agonizing return of his new and alarming symptoms, but says nothing.* RUMMY MITCHENS *comes from the shelter.*]

BARBARA [*going to meet* RUMMY]. Now Rummy, bustle. Take in those mugs and plates to be washed; and throw the crumbs about for the birds.

[RUMMY *takes the three plates and mugs; but* SHIRLEY *takes back his mug from her, as there is still some milk left in it.*]

JMMY. There aint any crumbs. This aint a time to waste good bread on birds.

RICE [*appearing at the shelter door*]. Gentleman come to see the shelter, Major. Says he's your father.

ARBARA. All right. Coming. [SNOBBY *goes back into the shelter, followed by* BARBARA.]

UMMY [*stealing across to* BILL *and addressing him in a subdued voice, but with intense conviction*]. I'd av the lor of you, you flat eared pignosed potwalloper, if she'd let me. Youre no gentleman, to hit a lady in the face.

BILL, *with greater things moving in him, takes no notice.*]

HIRLEY [*following her*]. Here! in with you and dont get yourself into more trouble by talking.

RUMMY [*with hauteur*]. I aint ad the pleasure o being hintroduced to you, as I can remember. [*She goes into the shelter with the plates.*]

HIRLEY. Thats the—

BILL [*savagely*]. Downt you talk to me, d'ye eah? You lea me alown, or Aw'll do you a mischief. Aw'm not dirt under your feet, ennywy.

SHIRLEY [*calmly*]. Dont you be afeerd. You aint such prime company that you need expect to be sought after. [*He is about to go into the shelter when* BARBARA *comes out, with* UNDERSHAFT *on her right*].

BARBARA. Oh, there you are, Mr Shirley! [*Between them*] This is my father: I told you he was a Secularist, didnt I? Perhaps youll be able to comfort one another.

UNDERSHAFT [*startled*]. A Secularist! Not the least in the world: on the contrary, a confirmed mystic.

BARBARA. Sorry, I'm sure. By the way, papa, what is your religion? in case I have to introduce you again.

UNDERSHAFT. My religion? Well, my dear, I am a Millionaire. That is my religion.

BARBARA. Then I'm afraid you and Mr Shirley wont be able to comfort one another after all. Youre not a Millionaire, are you, Peter?

SHIRLEY. No; and proud of it.

UNDERSHAFT [*gravely*]. Poverty, my friend, is not a thing to be proud of.

SHIRLEY [*angrily*]. Who made your millions for you? Me

and my like. Whats kep us poor? Keepin you rich. I
wouldnt have your conscience, not for all your income.

UNDERSHAFT. I wouldnt have your income, not for all your
conscience, Mr Shirley. [*He goes to the penthouse and sits
down on a form.*]

BARBARA [*stopping* SHIRLEY *adroitly as he is about to retort*].
You wouldnt think he was my father, would you, Peter?
Will you go into the shelter and lend the lasses a hand for
a while: we're worked off our feet.

SHIRLEY [*bitterly*]. Yes: I'm in their debt for a meal, aint
I?

BARBARA. Oh, not because youre in their debt, but for love
of them, Peter, for love of them. [*He cannot understand,
and is rather scandalized.*] There! dont stare at me. In
with you; and give that conscience of yours a holiday
[*bustling him into the shelter*].

SHIRLEY [*as he goes in*]. Ah! it's a pity you never was
trained to use your reason, miss. Youd have been a very
taking lecturer on Secularism.

[BARBARA *turns to her father.*]

UNDERSHAFT. Never mind me, my dear. Go about your
work; and let me watch it for a while.

BARBARA. All right.

UNDERSHAFT. For instance, whats the matter with that
outpatient over there?

BARBARA [*looking at* BILL, *whose attitude has never changed,
and whose expression of brooding wrath has deepened*].
Oh, we shall cure him in no time. Just watch. [*She goes
over to* BILL *and waits. He glances up at her and casts
his eyes down again, uneasy, but grimmer than ever*]. It
would be nice to just stamp on Mog Habbijam's face,
wouldnt it, Bill?

BILL [*starting up from the trough in consternation*]. It's a
loy: Aw never said so. [*She shakes her head*]. Oo taold
you wot was in moy mawnd?

BARBARA. Only your new friend.

BILL. Wot new friend?

BARBARA. The devil, Bill. When he gets round people they
get miserable, just like you.

BILL [*with a heartbreaking attempt at devil-may-care cheer-
fulness*]. Aw aint miserable. [*He sits down again, and
stretches his legs in an attempt to seem indifferent.*]

BARBARA. Well, if youre happy, why dont you look happy, as we do?

BILL [*his legs curling back in spite of him*]. Aw'm eppy enaff, Aw tell you. Woy cawnt you lea me alown? Wot ev I dan to you? Aw aint smashed your fice, ev Aw?

BARBARA [*softly: wooing his soul*]. It's not me thats getting at you, Bill.

BILL. Oo else is it?

BARBARA. Somebody that doesnt intend you to smash women's faces, I suppose. Somebody or something that wants to make a man of you.

BILL [*blustering*]. Mike a menn o me! Aint Aw a menn? eh? Oo sez Aw'm not a menn?

BARBARA. Theres a man in you somewhere, I suppose. But why did he let you hit poor little Jenny Hill? That wasnt very manly of him, was it?

BILL [*tormented*]. Ev dan wiv it, Aw tell you. Chack it. Aw'm sick o your Jenny Ill and er silly little fice.

BARBARA. Then why do you keep thinking about it? Why does it keep coming up against you in your mind? Youre not getting converted, are you?

BILL [*with conviction*]. Not ME. Not lawkly.

BARBARA. Thats right, Bill. Hold out against it. Put out your strength. Dont lets get you cheap. Todger Fairmile said he wrestled for three nights against his salvation harder then he ever wrestled with the Jap at the music hall. He gave in to the Jap when his arm was going to break. But he didnt give in to his salvation until his heart was going to break. Perhaps youll escape that. You havnt any heart, have you?

BILL. Wot d'ye mean? Woy aint Aw got a awt the sime as ennybody else?

BARBARA. A man with a heart wouldnt have bashed poor little Jenny's face, would he?

BILL [*almost crying*]. Ow, will you lea me alown? Ev Aw ever offered to meddle with you, that you cam neggin and provowkin me lawk this? [*He writhes convulsively from his eyes to his toes.*]

BARBARA [*with a steady soothing hand on his arm and a gentle voice that never lets him go*]. It's your soul thats hurting you, Bill, and not me. Weve been through it all ourselves. Come with us, Bill. [*He looks wildly round.*] To brave manhood on earth and eternal glory in heaven.

[*He is on the point of breaking down.*] Come. [*A drum is heard in the shelter; and* BILL, *with a gasp, escapes from the spell as* BARBARA *turns quickly.* ADOLPHUS *enters from the shelter with a big drum.*] Oh! there you are, Dolly. Let me introduce a new friend of mine, Mr Bill Walker. This is my bloke, Bill: Mr Cusins.

[CUSINS *salutes with his drumstick.*]

BILL. Gowin to merry im?

BARBARA. Yes.

BILL [*feverently*]. Gawd elp im! Gaw-aw-aw-awd elp im!

BARBARA. Why? Do you think he wont be happy with me?

BILL. Awve aony ed to stend it for a mawnin: e'll ev to stend it for a lawftawm.

CUSINS. That is a frightful reflection, Mr Walker. But I cant tear myself away from her.

BILL. Well, Aw ken. [*To* BARBARA] Eah! do you knaow where Aw'm gowin to, and wot Aw'm gowin to do?

BARBARA. Yes: youre going to heaven; and youre coming back here before the week's out to tell me so.

BILL. You loy. Aw'm gowin to Kennintahn, to spit in Todger Fairmawl's eye. Aw beshed Jenny Ill's fice; an nar Aw'll git me aown fice beshed and cam beck and shaow it to er. Ee'll itt me ardern Aw itt her. Thatll mike us square. [*To* ADOLPHUS] Is thet fair or is it not? Youre a genlmn: you oughter knaow.

BARBARA. Two black eyes wont make one white one, Bill.

BILL. Aw didnt awst you. Cawnt you never keep your mahth shat? Oy awst the genlmn.

CUSINS [*reflectively*]. Yes: I think youre right, Mr Walker. Yes: I should do it. It's curious: it's exactly what an ancient Greek would have done.

BARBARA. But what good will it do?

CUSINS. Well, it will give Mr Fairmile some exercise; and it will satisfy Mr Walker's soul.

BILL. Rot! there aint nao sach a thing as a saoul. Ah kin you tell wevver Awve a saoul or not? You never seen it.

BARBARA. Ive seen it hurting you when you went against it.

BILL [*with compressed aggravation*]. If you was maw gel and took the word aht o me mahth lawk thet, Aw'd give you sathink youd feel urtin, Aw would. [*To* ADOLPHUS] You tike maw tip, mite. Stop er jawr; or youll doy afoah your tawm [*With intense expression*] Wore aht: thets wot youll be: wore aht. [*He goes away through the gate.*]

CUSINS [*looking after him*]. I wonder!

BARBARA. Dolly! [*indignant, in her mother's manner*].

CUSINS. Yes, my dear, it's very wearing to be in love with you. If it lasts, I quite think I shall die young.

BARBARA. Should you mind?

CUSINS. Not at all.

[*He is suddenly softened, and kisses her over the drum, evidently not for the first time, as people cannot kiss over a big drum without practice.* UNDERSHAFT *coughs.*]

BARBARA. It's all right, papa, weve not forgotten you. Dolly: explain the place to papa: I havnt time. [*She goes busily into the shelter.*]

[UNDERSHAFT *and* ADOLPHUS *now have the yard to themselves.* UNDERSHAFT, *seated on a form, and still keenly attentive, looks hard at* ADOLPHUS. ADOLPHUS *looks hard at him.*]

UNDERSHAFT. I fancy you guess something of what is in my mind, Mr Cusins. [CUSINS *flourishes his drumsticks as if in the act of beating a lively rataplan, but makes no sound.*] Exactly so. But suppose Barbara finds you out!

CUSINS. You know, I do not admit that I am imposing on Barbara. I am quite genuinely interested in the views of the Salvation Army. The fact is, I am a sort of collector of religions; and the curious thing is that I find I can believe them all. By the way, have you any religion?

UNDERSHAFT. Yes.

CUSINS. Anything out of the common?

UNDERSHAFT. Only that there are two things necessary to Salvation.

CUSINS [*disappointed, but polite*]. Ah, the Church Catechism. Charles Lomax also belongs to the Established Church.

UNDERSHAFT. The two things are—

CUSINS. Baptism and—

UNDERSHAFT. No. Money and gunpowder.

CUSINS [*surprised, but interested*]. That is the general opinion of our governing classes. The novelty is in hearing any man confess it.

UNDERSHAFT. Just so.

CUSINS. Excuse me: is there any place in your religion for honor, justice, truth, love, mercy and so forth?

UNDERSHAFT. Yes: they are the graces and luxuries of a rich, strong, and safe life.

CUSINS. Suppose one is forced to choose between them and money or gunpowder?

UNDERSHAFT. Choose money and gunpowder; for without enough of both you cannot afford the others.

CUSINS. That is your religion?

UNDERSHAFT. Yes.

[*The cadence of this reply makes a full close in the conversation,* CUSINS *twists his face dubiously and contemplates* UNDERSHAFT. UNDERSHAFT *contemplates him.*]

CUSINS. Barbara wont stand that. You will have to choose between your religion and Barbara.

UNDERSHAFT. So will you, my friend. She will find out that that drum of yours is hollow.

CUSINS. Father Undershaft: you are mistaken: I am a sincere Salvationist. You do not understand the Salvation Army. It is the army of joy, of love, of courage: it has banished the fear and remorse and despair of the old hellridden evangelical sects: it marches to fight the devil with trumpet and drum, with music and dancing, with banner and palm, as becomes a sally from heaven by its happy garrison. It picks the waster out of the public house and makes a man of him: it finds a worm wriggling in a back kitchen, and lo! a woman! Men and women of rank too, sons and daughters of the Highest. It takes the poor professor of Greek, the most artificial and self-suppressed of human creatures, from his meal of roots, and lets loose the rhapsodist in him; reveals the true worship of Dionysos to him; sends him down the public street drumming dithyrambs [*he plays a thundering flourish on the drum*].

UNDERSHAFT. You will alarm the shelter.

CUSINS. Oh, they are accustomed to these sudden ecstasies. However, if the drum worries you—[*he pockets the drumsticks; unhooks the drum; and stands it on the ground opposite the gateway*].

UNDERSHAFT. Thank you.

CUSINS. You remember what Euripides says about your money and gunpowder?

UNDERSHAFT. No.

CUSINS [*declaiming*].

> One and another
> In money and guns may outpass his brother;
> And men in their millions float and flow
> And seethe with a million hopes as leaven;
> And they win their will; or they miss their will;
> And their hopes are dead or are pined for still;
> But who'er can know
> As the long days go
> That to live is happy, has found his heaven.

My translation: what do you think of it?

UNDERSHAFT. I think, my friend, that if you wish to know, as the long days go, that to live is happy, you must first acquire money enough for a decent life, and power enough to be your own master.

CUSINS. You are damnably discouraging. [*He resumes his declamation.*]

> Is it so hard a thing to see
> That the spirit of God—whate'er it be—
> The law that abides and changes not, ages long,
> The Eternal and Nature-born: these things be strong?
> What else is Wisdom? What of Man's endeavor,
> Or God's high grace so lovely and so great?
> To stand from fear set free? to breathe and wait?
> To hold a hand uplifted over Fate?
> And shall not Barbara be loved for ever?

UNDERSHAFT. Euripides mentions Barbara, does he?

CUSINS. It is a fair translation. The word means Loveliness.

UNDERSHAFT. May I ask—as Barbara's father—how much a year she is to be loved for ever on?

CUSINS. As for Barbara's father, that is more your affair than mine. I can feed her by teaching Greek: that is about all.

UNDERSHAFT. Do you consider it a good match for her?

CUSINS [*with polite obstinacy*]. Mr Undershaft: I am in many ways a weak, timid, ineffectual person; and my health is far from satisfactory. But whenever I feel that I must have anything, I get it, sooner or later. I feel that way about Barbara. I dont like marriage: I feel intensely afraid of it; and I dont know what I shall do with Barbara or what she will do with me. But I feel that I and nobody else must marry her. Please regard that as settled.—No that I wish to be arbitrary; but why should I waste your time in discussing what is inevitable?

UNDERSHAFT. You mean that you will stick at nothing: not even the conversion of the Salvation Army to the worship of Dionysos.

CUSINS. The business of the Salvation Army is to save, not to wrangle about the name of the pathfinder. Dionysos or another: what does it matter?

UNDERSHAFT [*rising and approaching him*]. Professor Cusins: you are a young man after my own heart.

CUSINS. Mr Undershaft: you are, as far as I am able to gather, a most infernal old rascal; but you appeal very strongly to my sense of ironic humor.

[UNDERSHAFT *mutely offers his hand. They shake.*]

UNDERSHAFT [*suddenly concentrating himself*]. And now to business.

CUSINS. Pardon me. We are discussing religion. Why go back to such an uninteresting and unimportant subject as business?

UNDERSHAFT. Religion is our buiness at present, because it is through religion alone that we can win Barbara.

CUSINS. Have you, too, fallen in love with Barbara?

UNDERSHAFT. Yes, with a father's love.

CUSINS. A father's love for a grown-up daughter is the most dangerous of all infatuations. I apologize for mentioning my own pale, coy, mistrustful fancy in the same breath with it.

UNDERSHAFT. Keep to the point. We have to win her; and we are neither of us Methodists.

CUSINS. That doesnt matter. The power Barbara wields here—the power that wields Barbara herself—is not Calvinism, not Presbyterianism, not Methodism—

UNDERSHAFT. Not Greek Paganism either, eh?

CUSINS. I admit that. Barbara is quite original in her religion.

UNDERSHAFT [*triumphantly*]. Aha! Barbara Undershaft would be. Her inspiration comes from within herself.

CUSINS. How do you suppose it got there?

UNDERSHAFT [*in towering excitement*]. It is the Undershaft

inheritance. I shall hand on my torch to my daughter. She
shall make my converts and preach my gospel—

CUSINS. What! Money and gunpowder!

UNDERSHAFT. Yes, money and gunpowder. Freedom and
power. Command of life and command of death.

CUSINS [*urbanely: trying to bring him down to earth*]. This
is extremely interesting, Mr Undershaft. Of course you
know that you are mad.

UNDERSHAFT [*with redoubled force*]. And you?

CUSINS. Oh, mad as a hatter. You are welcome to my secret
since I have discovered yours. But I am astonished. Can a
madman make cannons?

UNDERSHAFT. Would anyone else than a madman make
them? And now [*with surging energy*] question for question. Can a sane man translate Euripides?

CUSINS. No.

UNDERSHAFT [*seizing him by the shoulder*]. Can a sane
woman make a man of a waster or a woman of a worm?

CUSINS [*reeling before the storm*]. Father Colossus—Mam-
moth Millionaire—

UNDERSHAFT [*pressing him*]. Are there two mad people or
three in this Salvation shelter today?

CUSINS. You mean Barbara is as mad as we are?

UNDERSHAFT [*pushing him lightly off and resuming his
equanimity suddenly and completely*]. Pooh, Professor!
let us call things by their proper names. I am a millionaire; you are a poet: Barbara is a savior of souls. What
have we three to do with the common mob of slaves and
idolators? [*He sits down again with a shrug of contempt
for the mob.*]

CUSINS. Take care! Barbara is in love with the common
people. So am I. Have you never felt the romance of that
love?

UNDERSHAFT [*cold and sardonic*]. Have you ever been in
love with Poverty, like St Francis? Have you ever been
in love with Dirt, like St Simeon? Have you ever been in
love with disease and suffering, like our nurses and philanthropists? Such passions are not virtues, but the most
unnatural of all the vices. This love of the common people
may please an earl's granddaughter and a university professor; but I have been a common man and a poor man;
and it has no romance for me. Leave it to the poor to

pretend that poverty is a blessing: leave it to the coward
to make a religion of his cowardice by preaching humil-
ity: we know better than that. We three must stand together above the common people: how else can we help
their children to climb up beside us? Barbara must belong
to us, not to the Salvation Army.

CUSINS. Well, I can only say that if you think you will get
her away from the Salvation Army by talking to her as
you have been talking to me, you dont know Barbara.

UNDERSHAFT. My friend: I never ask for what I can buy.

CUSINS [in a white fury]. Do I understand you to imply that
you can buy Barbara?

UNDERSHAFT. No; but I can buy the Salvation Army.

CUSINS. Quite impossible.

UNDERSHAFT. You shall see. All religious organizations exist
by selling themselves to the rich.

CUSINS. Not the Army. That is the Church of the poor.

UNDERSHAFT. All the more reason for buying it.

CUSINS. I dont think you quite know what the Army does
for the poor.

UNDERSHAFT. Oh yes I do. It draws their teeth: that is
enough for me as a man of business.

CUSINS. Nonsense! It makes them sober—

UNDERSHAFT. I prefer sober workmen. The profits are larger.

CUSINS. —honest—

UNDERSHAFT. Honest workmen are the most economical.

CUSINS. —attached to their homes—

UNDERSHAFT. So much the better: they will put up with
anything sooner than change their shop.

CUSISN. —happy—

UNDERSHAFT. An invaluable safeguard against revolution.

CUSINS. —unselfish—

UNDERSHAFT. Indifferent to their own interests which suits
me exactly.

CUSINS. —with their thoughts on heavenly things—

UNDERSHAFT [rising]. And not on Trade Unionism nor Socialism. Excellent.

CUSINS [revolted]. You really are an infernal old rascal.

UNDERSHAFT [indicating PETER SHIRLEY, who has just come
from the shelter and strolled dejectedly down the yard
between them]. And this is an honest man!

SHIRLEY. Yes; and what av I got by it? [He passes on bitterly
and sits on the form, in the corner of the penthouse.]

[SNOBBY PRICE, *beaming sanctimoniously*, and JENNY HILL, *with a tambourine full of coppers, come from the shelter and go to the drum, on which* JENNY *begins to count the money.*]

UNDERSHAFT [*replying to* SHIRLEY]. Oh, your employers must have got a good deal by it from first to last.

[*He sits on the table, with one foot on the side form,* CUSINS, *overwhelmed, sits down on the same form nearer the shelter.* BARBARA *comes from the shelter to the middle of the yard. She is excited and a little overwrought.*]

BARBARA. Weve just had a splendid experience meeting at the other gate in Cripps's lane. Ive hardly ever seen them so much moved as they were by your confession, Mr Price.

PRICE. I could almost be glad of my past wickedness if I could believe that it would elp to keep hathers straight.

BARBARA. So it will, Snobby. How much, Jenny?

JENNY. Four and tenpence, Major.

BARBARA. Oh Snobby, if you had given your poor mother just one more kick, we should have got the whole five shillings!

PRICE. If she heard you say that, miss, she'd be sorry I didnt. But I'm glad. Oh what a joy it will be to her when she hears I'm saved!

UNDERSHAFT. Shall I contribute the odd twopence, Barbara? The millionaire's mite, eh? [*He takes a couple of pennies from his pocket.*]

BARBARA. How did you make that twopence?

UNDERSHAFT. As usual. By selling cannons, torpedoes, submarines, and my new patent Grand Duke hand grenade.

BARBARA. Put it back in your pocket. You cant buy your salvation here for twopence: you must work it out.

UNDERSHAFT. Is twopence not enough? I can afford a little more, if you press me.

BARBARA. Two million millions would not be enough. There is bad blood on your hands; and nothing but good blood can cleanse them. Money is no use. Take it away. [*She turns to* CUSINS.] Dolly: you must write another letter for me to the papers. [*He makes a wry face.*] Yes: I know you dont like it; but it must be done. The starvation this winter is beating us: everybody is unemployed. The Gen-

eral says we must close this shelter if we cant get more
money. I force the collections at the meetings until I am
ashamed: dont I, Snobby?

PRICE. It's a fair treat to see you work it, miss. The way you
got them up from three-and-six to four-and-ten with that
hymn, penny by penny and verse by verse, was a caution.
Not a Cheap Jack on Mile End Waste could touch you at
it.

BARBARA. Yes; but I wish we could do without it. I am getting at last to think more of the collection than of the
people's souls. And what are those hatfuls of pence and
halfpence? We want thousands! tens of thousands! hundreds of thousands! I want to convert people, not to be
always begging for the Army in a way I'd die sooner than
beg for myself.

UNDERSHAFT [in profound irony]. Genuine unselfishness is
capable of anything, my dear.

BARBARA [unsuspectingly, as she turns away to take the
money from the drum and put it in a cash bag she car-
ries]. Yes, isnt it?

[UNDERSHAFT looks sardonically at CUSINS.]

CUSINS [aside to UNDERSHAFT]. Mephistopheles! Machiavelli!

BARBARA [tears coming into her eyes as she ties the bag and
pockets it]. How are we to feed them? I cant talk religion to a man with bodily hunger in his eyes. [Almost
breaking down] It's frightful.

JENNY [running to her]. Major, dear—

BARBARA [rebounding]. No: dont comfort me. It will be all
right. We shall get the money.

UNDERSHAFT. How?

JENNY. By praying for it, of course. Mrs Baines says she
prayed for it last night; and she has never prayed for it in
vain: never once. [She goes to the gate and looks out into
the street.]

BARBARA [who has dried her eyes and regained her com-
posure]. By the way, dad, Mrs Baines has come to march
with us to our big meeting this afternoon; and she is very
anxious to meet you, for some reason or other. Perhaps
she'll convert you.

UNDERSHAFT. I shall be delighted, my dear.

JENNY [*at the gate*: *excitedly*]. Major! Major! heres that man back again.

BARBARA. What man?

JENNY. The man that hit me. Oh, I hope he's coming back to join us.

[BILL WALKER, *with frost on his jacket, comes through the gate, his hands deep in his pockets and his chin sunk between his shoulders, like a cleaned-out gambler. He halts between* BARBARA *and the drum.*]

BARBARA. Hullo, Bill! Back already!

BILL [*nagging at her*]. Bin talkin ever sence, ev you?

BARBARA. Pretty nearly. Well, has Todger paid you out for poor Jenny's jaw?

BILL. Nao e aint.

BARBARA. I thought your jacket looked a bit snowy.

BILL. Sao it is snaowy. You want to knaow where the snaow cam from, downt you?

BARBARA. Yes.

BILL. Well, it cam from orf the grahnd in Pawkinses Corner in Kennintahn. It got rabbed orf be maw shaoulders: see?

BARBARA. Pity you didnt rub some off with your knees, Bill! That would have done you a lot of good.

BILL [*with sour mirthless humor*]. Aw was sivin anather menn's knees at the tawm. E was kneelin on moy ed, e was.

JENNY. Who was kneeling on your head?

BILL. Todger was. E was pryin for me: pryin camfortable wiv me as a cawpet. Sow was Mog. Sao was the aol bloomin meetin. Mog she sez 'Ow Lawd brike is stabborn sperrit; bat downt urt is dear art.' Thet was wot she said. 'Downt urt is dear art'! An er blowk—thirteen stun four! —kneelin wiv all is wight on me. Fanny, aint it?

JENNY. Oh no. We're so sorry, Mr Walker.

BARBARA [*enjoying it frankly*]. Nonsense! of course it's funny. Served you right, Bill! You must have done something to him first.

BILL [*doggedly*]. Aw did wot Aw said Aw'd do. Aw spit in is eye. E looks ap at the skoy and sez, 'Ow that Aw should be fahnd worthy to be spit upon for the gospel's sike!' e sez; an Mog sez 'Glaory Allelloolier!'; and then e called me Braddher, an dahned me as if Aw was a kid and e was me mather worshin me a Setterda nawt. Aw ednt jast nao shaow wiv im at all. Arf the street pryed; an the tather arf larfed fit to split theirselves. [*To* BAR-BARA] There! are you settisfawd nah?

BARBARA [*her eyes dancing*]. Wish I'd been there, Bill.

BILL. Yus: youd a got in a hextra bit o talk on me, wouldnt you?

JENNY. I'm so sorry, Mr Walker.

BILL [*fiercely*]. Downt you gow being sorry for me: youve no call. Listen eah. Aw browk your jawr.

JENNY. No, it didnt hurt me: indeed it didnt, except for a moment. It was only that I was frightened.

BILL. Aw downt want to be forgive be you, or be ennybody. Wot Aw did Aw'll py for. Aw trawd to gat me aown jawr browk to settisfaw you—

JENNY [*distressed*]. Oh no—

BILL [*impatiently*]. Tell y' Aw did: cawnt you listen to wots bein taold you? All Aw got be it was bein mide a sawt of in the pablic street for me pines. Well, if Aw cawnt settisfaw you one wy, Aw ken anather. Listen eah! Aw ed two quid sived agen the frost; an Awve a pahnd of it left. A mite o mawn last week ed words with the judy e's gowing to merry. E give er wot-for; an e's bin fawnd fifteen bob. E ed a rawt to itt er cause they was gowin to be merrid; but Aw ednt nao rawt to itt you; sao put anather fawv bob on an call it a pahnd's worth. [*He produces a sovereign.*] Eahs the manney. Tike it; and lets ev no more o your forgivin an prying and your Mijor jawrin me. Let wot Aw dan be dan an pide for; and let there be a end of it.

JENNY. Oh, I couldnt take it, Mr Walker. But if you would give a shilling or two to poor Rummy Mitchens! you really did hurt her; and she's old.

BILL [*contemptuously*]. Not lawkly. Aw'd give her anather as soon as look at er. Let her ev the lawr o me as she threat-ened! She aint forgiven me: not mach. Wot Aw dan to er is not on me mawnd—wot she [*indicating* BARBARA] mawt call on me conscience—no more than stickin a pig. It's this Christian gime o yours that Aw wownt ev plyed agen me: this bloomin forgivin an negging an jawrin that mikes a menn thet sore that iz lawf's a burdn to im. Aw

wownt ev it, Aw tell you; sao tike your manney and stop
thraowin your silly beshed fice hap agen me.

JENNY. Major: may I take a little of it for the Army?

BARBARA. No: the Army is not to be bought. We want your
soul, Bill; and we'll take nothing less.

BILL [*bitterly*]. Aw knaow. Me an maw few shillins is not
good enaff for you. Youre a earl's grendorter, you are.
Nathink less than a andered pahnd for you.

UNDERSHAFT. Come, Barbara! you could do a great deal of
good with a hundred pounds. If you will set this gentleman's mind at ease by taking his pound, I will give the
other ninety-nine.

[BILL, *dazed by such opulence, instinctively touches his cap*.]

BARBARA. Oh, youre too extravagant, papa. Bill offers twenty
pieces of silver. All you need offer is the other ten. That
will make the standard price to buy anybody who's for
sale. I'm not; and the Army's not. [*To* BILL] Youll never
have another quiet moment, Bill, until you come round to
us. You cant stand out against your salvation.

BILL [*sullenly*]. Aw cawnt stend aht agen music awl wras-
tlers and awtful tangued women. Awve offered to py. Aw
can do no more. Tike it or leave it. There it is. [*He
throws the sovereign on the drum, and sits down on the
horse-trough. The coin fascinates* SNOBBY PRICE, *who
takes an early opportunity of dropping his cap on it*.]

[MRS BAINES *comes from the shelter. She is dressed as a
Salvation Army Commissioner. She is an earnest looking
woman of about 40, with a caressing, urgent voice, and an
appealing manner*.]

BARBARA. This is my father, Mrs Baines. [UNDERSHAFT *comes
from the table, taking his hat off with marked civility*.]
Try what you can do with him. He wont listen to me, because he remembers what a fool I was when I was a baby.
[*She leaves them together and chats with* JENNY.]

MRS BAINES. Have you been shewn over the shelter, Mr
Undershaft? You know the work we're doing, of course.

UNDERSHAFT [*very civilly*]. The whole nation knows it, Mrs
Baines.

MRS BAINES. No, sir: the whole nation does not know it, or

we should not be crippled as we are for want of money to carry our work through the length and breadth of the land. Let me tell you that there would have been rioting this winter in London but for us.

UNDERSHAFT. You really think so?

MRS BAINES. I know it. I remember 1886, when you rich gentlemen hardened your hearts against the cry of the poor. They broke the windows of your clubs in Pall Mall.

UNDERSHAFT [*gleaming with approval of their method*]. And the Mansion House Fund went up next day from thirty thousand pounds to seventy-nine thousand! I remember quite well.

MRS BAINES. Well, wont you help me to get at the people? They wont break windows then. Come here, Price. Let me shew you to this gentleman [PRICE *comes to be inspected.*] Do you remember the window breaking?

PRICE. My ole father thought it was the revolution, maam.

MRS BAINES. Would you break windows now?

PRICE. Oh no, maam. The windows of eaven av bin opened to me. I know now that the rich man is a sinner like myself.

RUMMY [*appearing above at the loft door*]. Snobby Price!

SNOBBY. Wot is it?

RUMMY. Your mother's askin for you at the other gate in Cripps's Lane. She's heard about your confession.

[PRICE *turns pale*].

MRS BAINES. Go, Mr Price; and pray with her.

JENNY. You can go through the shelter, Snobby.

PRICE [*to* MRS BAINES]. I couldnt face her now, maam, with all the weight of my sins fresh on me. Tell her she'll find her son at ome, waitin for her in prayer. [*He skulks off through the gate, incidentally stealing the sovereign on his way out by picking up his cap from the drum.*]

MRS BAINES [*with swimming eyes*]. You see how we take the anger and the bitterness against you out of their hearts, Mr Undershaft.

UNDERSHAFT. It is certainly most convenient and gratifying to all large employers of labor, Mrs Baines.

MRS BAINES. Barbara: Jenny: I have good news: most wonderful news. [JENNY *runs to her.*] My prayers have been answered. I told you they would, Jenny, didnt I?

JENNY. Yes, yes.

BARBARA [*moving nearer to the drum*]. Have we got money enough to keep the shelter open?

MRS BAINES. I hope we shall have enough to keep all the shelters open. Lord Saxmundham has promised us five thousand pounds—

BARBARA. Hooray!

JENNY. Glory!

MRS BAINES. —if—

BARBARA. 'If!' If what?

MRS BAINES. —if five other gentlemen will give a thousand each to make it up to ten thousand.

BARBARA. Who is Lord Saxmundham? I never heard of him.

UNDERSHAFT [*who has pricked up his ears at the peer's name, and is now watching* BARBARA *curiously*]. A new creation, my dear. You have heard of Sir Horace Bodger?

BARBARA. Bodger! Do you mean the distiller? Bodger's whisky!

UNDERSHAFT. That is the man. He is one of the greatest of our public benefactors. He restored the cathedral at Hakington. They made him a baronet for that. He gave half a million to the funds of his party: they made him a baron for that.

SHIRLEY. What will they give him for the five thousand?

UNDERSHAFT. There is nothing left to give him. So the five thousand, I should think, is to save his soul.

MRS BAINES. Heaven grant it may! Oh Mr Undershaft, you have some very rich friends. Cant you help us towards the other five thousand? We are going to hold a great meeting this afternoon at the Assembly Hall in the Mile End Road. If I could only announce that one gentleman had come forward to support Lord Saxmundham, others would follow. Dont you know somebody? couldnt you? wouldnt you? [*her eyes fill with tears*] oh, think of those poor people, Mr Undershaft: think of how much it means to them, and how little to a great man like you.

UNDERSHAFT [*sardonically gallant*]. Mrs Baines: you are irresistible. I cant disappoint you; and I cant deny myself the satisfaction of making Bodger pay up. You shall have your five thousand pounds.

MRS BAINES. Thank God!

UNDERSHAFT. You dont thank me?

MRS BAINES. Oh sir, dont try to be cynical: dont be ashamed of being a good man. The Lord will bless you abundantly; and our prayers will be like a strong fortification round you all the days of your life. [*With a touch of caution*] You will let me have the cheque to shew at the meeting, wont you? Jenny: go in and fetch a pen and ink.

[JENNY *runs to the shelter door.*]

UNDERSHAFT. Do not disturb Miss Hill: I have a fountain pen [JENNY *halts. He sits at the table and writes the cheque.* CUSINS *rises to make room for him. They all watch him silently.*]

BILL [*cynically, aside to* BARBARA, *his voice and accent horribly debased*]. Wot prawce selvytion nah?

BARBARA. Stop. [UNDERSHAFT *stops writing: they all turn to her in surprise.*] Mrs Baines: are you really going to take this money?

MRS BAINES [*astonished*]. Why not, dear?

BARBARA. Why not! Do you know what my father is? Have you forgotten that Lord Saxmundham is Bodger the whisky man? Do you remember how we implored the County Council to stop him from writing Bodger's Whisky in letters of fire against the sky; so that the poor drink-ruined creatures on the Embankment could not wake up from their snatches of sleep without being reminded of their deadly thirst by that wicked sky sign? Do you know that the worst thing I have had to fight here is not the devil, but Bodger, Bodger, Bodger, with his whisky, his distilleries, and his tied houses? Are you going to make our shelter another tied house for him, and ask me to keep it?

BILL. Rotten dranken whisky it is too.

MRS BAINES. Dear Barbara: Lord Saxmundham has a soul to be saved like any of us. If heaven has found the way to make a good use of his money, are we to set ourselves up against the answer to our prayers?

BARBARA. I know he has a soul to be saved. Let him come down here; and I'll do my best to help him to his salvation. But he wants to send his cheque down to buy us, and go on being as wicked as ever.

UNDERSHAFT [*with a reasonableness which* CUSINS *alone perceives to be ironical*]. My dear Barbara: alcohol is a very necessary article. It heals the sick—

BARBARA. It does nothing of the sort.

UNDERSHAFT. Well, it assists the doctor: that is perhaps a less questionable way of putting it. It makes life bearable to millions of people who could not endure their existence if they were quite sober. It enables Parliament to do things at eleven at night that no sane person would do at eleven in the morning. Is it Bodger's fault that this inestimable gift is deplorably abused by less than one per cent of the poor? [*He turns again to the table; signs the cheque; and crosses it.*]

RS. BAINES. Barbara: will there be less drinking or more if all those poor souls we are saving come tomorrow and find the doors of our shelters shut in their faces? Lord Saxmundham gives us the money to stop drinking—to take his own business from him.

USINS [*impishly*]. Pure self-sacrifice on Bodger's part, clearly! Bless dear Bodger!

ARBARA *almost breaks down as* ADOLPHUS, *too, fails her.*]

NDERSHAFT [*tearing out the cheque and pocketing the book as he rises and goes past* CUSINS *to* MRS BAINES]. I also, Mrs Baines, may claim a little disinterestedness. Think of my business! think of the widows and orphans! the men and lads torn to pieces with shrapnel and poisoned with lyddite! [MRS BAINES *shrinks; but he goes on remorselessly*] the oceans of blood, not one drop of which is shed in a really just cause! the ravaged crops! the peaceful peasants forced, women and men, to till their fields under the fire of opposing armies on pain of starvation! the bad blood of the fierce little cowards at home who egg on others to fight for the gratification of their national vanity! All this makes money for me: I am never richer, never busier than when the papers are full of it. Well, it is your work to preach peace on earth and good will to men. [MRS BAINES'S *face lights up again.*] Every convert you make is a vote against war. [*Her lips move in prayer.*] Yet I give you this money to help you to hasten my own commercial ruin. [*He gives her the cheque.*]

USINS [*mounting the form in an ecstasy of mischief*]. The millennium will be inaugurated by the unselfishness of Undershaft and Bodger. Oh be joyful! [*He takes the drumsticks from his pocket and flourishes them.*]

MRS BAINES [*taking the cheque*]. The longer I live the more proof I see that there is an Infinite Goodness that turns everything to the work of salvation sooner or later. Who would have thought that any good could have come out of war and drink? And yet their profits are brought today to the feet of salvation to do its blessed work. [*She is* *fected to tears.*]

JENNY [*running to* MRS BAINES *and throwing her arr* *round her*]. Oh dear! how blessed, how glorious it all

CUSINS [*in a convulsion of irony*]. Let us seize this u speakable moment. Let us march to the great meeting once. Excuse me just an instant. [*He rushes into the shelte* JENNY *takes her tambourine from the drum head.*]

MRS BAINES. Mr Undershaft: have you ever seen a tho sand people fall on their knees with one impulse and pra Come with us to the meeting. Barbara shall tell them th the Army is saved, and saved through you.

CUSINS [*returning impetuously from the shelter with a fl* *and a trombone, and coming between* MRS BAINES *an* UNDERSHAFT]. You shall carry the flag down the fir street, Mrs Baines. [*He gives her the flag.*] Mr Unde shaft is a gifted trombonist: he shall intone an Olympia diapason to the West Ham Salvation March. [*Aside* UNDERSHAFT, *as he forces the trombone on him*] Blov Machiavelli, blow.

UNDERSAHFT [*aside to him, as he takes the trombone*]. Th trumpet in Zion! [CUSINS *rushes to the drum, which I* *takes up and puts on.* UNDERSHAFT *continues, aloud.*] I wi do my best. I could vamp a bass if I knew the tune.

CUSINS. It is a wedding chorus from one of Donizetti operas; but we have converted it. We convert everythin to good here, including Bodger. You remember the choru 'For thee immense rejoicing—immenso giubilo—immens giubilo.' [*With drum obbligato*] Rum tum ti tum tum tum tum ti ta—

BARBARA. Dolly: you are breaking my heart.

CUSINS. What is a broken heart more or less here? Dionyso Undershaft has descended. I am possessed.

MRS BAINES. Come, Barbara: I must have my dear Majo to carry the flag with me.

JENNY. Yes, yes, Major darling.

CUSINS [*snatches the tambourine out of* JENNY's *hand an* *mutely offers it to* BARBARA.]

BARBARA [*coming forward a little as she puts the offer be* *hind her with a shudder, whilst* CUSINS *recklessly tosses th* *tambourine back to* JENNY *and goes to the gate*]. I can come.

JENNY. Not come!

MRS BAINES [*with tears in her eyes*]. Barbara: do you think I am wrong to take the money?

BARBARA [*impulsively going to her and kissing her*]. No, no: God help you, dear, you must: you are saving the Army. Go; and may you have a great meeting!

JENNY. But arnt you coming?

BARBARA. No. [*She begins taking off the silver S brooch from her collar.*]

MRS BAINES. Barbara: what are you doing?

JENNY. Why are you taking your badge off? You cant be going to leave us, Major.

BARBARA [*quietly*]. Father: come here.

UNDERSHAFT [*coming to her*]. My dear! [*Seeing that she is going to pin the badge on his collar, he retreats to the penthouse in some alarm.*]

BARBARA [*following him*]. Dont be frightened. [*She pins the badge on and steps back towards the table, shewing him to the others.*] There! It's not much for £5000, is it?

MRS BAINES. Barbara: if you wont come and pray with us, promise me you will pray for us.

BARBARA. I cant pray now. Perhaps I shall never pray again.

MRS BAINES. Barbara!

JENNY. Major!

BARBARA [*almost delirious*]. I cant bear any more. Quick march!

CUSINS [*calling to the procession in the street outside*]. Off we go. Play up, there! Immenso giubilo. [*He gives the time with his drum; and the band strikes up the march, which rapidly becomes more distant as the procession moves briskly away.*]

MRS BAINES. I must go, dear. Youre overworked: you will be all right tomorrow. We'll never lose you. Now Jenny: step out with the old flag. Blood and Fire! [*She marches out through the gate with her flag.*]

JENNY. Glory Hallelujah! [*flourishing her tambourine and marching*].

UNDERSHAFT [*to* CUSINS, *as he marches out past him easing the slide of his trombone*]. 'My ducats and my daughter'!

CUSINS [*following him out*]. Money and gunpowder!

BARBARA. Drunkenness and Murder! My God: why hast thou forsaken me?

[*She sinks on the form with her face buried in her hand*
*The march passes away into silence.* BILL WALKER *stea*
*across to her.*]

BILL [*taunting*]. Wot prawce selvytion nah?

SHIRLEY. Dont you hit her when she's down.

BILL. She itt me wen aw wiz dahn. Waw shouldnt Aw git
bit o me aown beck?

BARBARA [*raising her head*]. I didnt take your money, Bil
[*She crosses the yard to the gate and turns her back o*
*the two men to hide her face from them.*]

BILL [*sneering after her*]. Naow, it warnt enaff for yo
[*Turning to the drum, he misses the money.*] Ellow! If yo
aint took it sammun else ez. Weres it gorn? Bly me if Jenn
Ill didnt tike it arter all!

RUMMY [*screaming at him from the loft*]. You lie, yo
dirty blackguard! Snobby Price pinched it off the drun
when he took up his cap. I was up here all the time an se
im do it.

BILL. Wot! Stowl maw manney! Waw didnt you call thie
on him, you silly aold macker you?

RUMMY. To serve you aht for ittin me acrost the fice. It'
cost y'pahnd, that az. [*Raising a pæan of squalid triumph*
I done you. I'm even with you. Uve ad it aht oy—

[BILL *snatches up* SHIRLEY's *mug and hurls it at her. Sh*
*slams the loft door and vanishes. The mug smashes against th*
*door and falls in fragments.*]

BILL [*beginning to chuckle*]. Tell us, aol menn, wot o'clock
this mawnin was it wen im as they call Snobby Prawc
was sived?

BARBARA [*turning to him more composedly, and with un-*
*spoiled sweetness*]. About half past twelve, Bill. And he
pinched your pound at a quarter to two. *I* know. Well, you
cant afford to lose it. I'll send it to you.

BILL [*his voice and accent suddenly improving*]. Not if
Aw wiz to stawve for it. Aw aint to be bought.

SHIRLEY. Aint you? Youd sell yourself to the devil for a pint
o beer; only there aint no devil to make the offer.

BILL [*unashamed*]. Sao Aw would, mite, and often ev,
cheerful. But she cawnt baw me. [*Approaching* BARBARA]
You wanted maw saoul, did you? Well, you aint got it.

BARBARA. I nearly got it, Bill. But weve sold it back to you for ten thousand pounds.

SHIRLEY. And dear at the money!

BARBARA. No, Peter: it was worth more than money.

BILL [salvationproof]. It's nao good: you cawnt get rahnd me nah. Aw downt blieve in it; and Awve seen tody that Aw was rawt. [Going] Sao long, aol soupkitchener! Ta, ta, Mijor Earl's Grendorter! [Turning at the gate] Wot prawce selvytion nah? Snobby Prawce! Ha! ha!

BARBARA [offering her hand]. Goodbye, Bill.

BILL [taken aback, half plucks his cap off; then shoves it on again defiantly]. Git aht. [BARBARA drops her hand, discouraged. He has a twinge of remorse.] But thets aw rawt, you knaow. Nathink pasnl. Naow mellice. Sao long, Judy. [He goes.]

BARBARA. No malice. So long, Bill.

SHIRLEY [shaking his head]. You make too much of him, miss, in your innocence.

BARBARA [going to him]. Peter: I'm like you now. Cleaned out, and lost my job.

SHIRLEY. Youve youth an hope. Thats two better than me.

BARBARA. I'll get you a job, Peter. Thats hope for you: the youth will have to be enough for me. [She counts her money.] I have just enough left for two teas at Lockharts, a Rowton doss for you, and my tram and bus home. [He frowns and rises with offended pride. She takes his arm.] Dont be proud, Peter: it's sharing between friends. And promise me youll talk to me and not let me cry. [She draws him towards the gate.]

SHIRLEY. Well, I'm not accustomed to talk to the like of you—

BARBARA [urgently]. Yes, yes: you must talk to me. Tell me about Tom Paine's books and Bradlaugh's lectures. Come along.

SHIRLEY. Ah, if you would only read Tom Paine in the proper spirit, miss!

[They go out through the gate together].

# ACT THREE

*Next day after lunch* LADY BRITOMART *is writing in the library in Wilton Crescent.* SARAH *is reading in the armchair near the window.* BARBARA, *in ordinary fashionable dress, pale and brooding, is on the setee.* CHARLES LOMAX *enters. He starts on seeing* BARBARA *fashionably attired and in low spirits.*

LOMAX. Youve left off your uniform!

[BARBARA *says nothing; but an expression of pain passes over her face.*]

LADY BRITOMART [*warning him in low tones to be careful*]. Charles!

LOMAX [*much concerned, coming behind the settee and bending sympathetically over* BARBARA]. I'm awfully sorry, Barbara. You know I helped you all I could with the concertina and so forth. [*Momentously*] Still, I have never shut my eyes to the fact that there is a certain amount of tosh about the Salvation Army. Now the claims of the Church of England—

LADY BRITOMART. Thats enough, Charles. Speak of something suited to your mental capacity.

LOMAX. But surely the Church of England is suited to all our capacities.

BARBARA [*pressing his hand*]. Thank you for your sympathy, Cholly. Now go and spoon with Sarah.

LOMAX [*dragging a chair from the writing table and seating himself affectionately by Sarah's side*]. How is my ownest today?

SARAH. I wish you wouldnt tell Cholly to do things, Barbara. He always comes straight and does them. Cholly: we're going to the works this afternoon.

LOMAX. What works?

[ 175 ]

SARAH. The cannon works.

LOMAX. What? your governor's shop!

SARAH. Yes.

LOMAX. Oh I say!

[CUSINS *enters in poor condition. He also starts visibly when he sees* BARBARA *without her uniform.*]

BARBARA. I expected you this morning, Dolly. Didnt you guess that?

CUSINS [*sitting down beside her*]. I'm sorry. I have only just breakfasted.

SARAH. But weve just finished lunch.

BARBARA. Have you had one of your bad nights?

CUSINS. No: I had rather a good night: in fact, one of the most remarkable nights I have ever passed.

BARBARA. The meeting?

CUSINS. No: after the meeting.

LADY BRITOMART. You should have gone to bed after the meeting. What were you doing?

CUSINS. Drinking.

LADY BRITOMART.⎫ ⎧Adolphus!
SARAH.          ⎪ ⎪Dolly!
BARBARA.        ⎬ ⎨Dolly!
LOMAX.          ⎭ ⎩Oh I say!

LADY BRITOMART. What were you drinking, may I ask?

CUSINS. A most devilish kind of Spanish burgundy, warranted free from added alcohol: a Temperance burgundy in fact. Its richness in natural alcohol made any addition superfluous.

BARBARA. Are you joking, Dolly?

CUSINS [*patiently*]. No. I have been making a night of it with the nominal head of this household: that is all.

LADY BRITOMART. Andrew made you drunk!

CUSINS. No: he only provided the wine. I think it was Dionysos who made me drunk. [*To* BARBARA] I told you I was possessed.

LADY BRITOMART. Youre not sober yet. Go home to bed at once.

CUSINS. I have never before ventured to reproach you, Lady Brit; but how could you marry the Prince of Darkness?

LADY BRITOMART. It was much more excusable to marry him than to get drunk with him. That is a new accomplishment of Andrew's, by the way. He usent to drink.

CUSINS. He doesnt now. He only sat there and completed the wreck of my moral basis, the rout of my convictions, the purchase of my soul. He cares for you, Barbara. That is what makes him so dangerous to me.

BARBARA. That has nothing to do with it, Dolly. There are larger loves and diviner dreams than the fireside ones. You know that, dont you?

CUSINS. Yes: that is our understanding. I know it. I hold to it. Unless he can win me on that holier ground he may amuse me for a while; but he can get no deeper hold, strong as he is.

BARBARA. Keep to that; and the end will be right. Now tell me what happened at the meeting?

CUSINS. It was an amazing meeting. Mrs Baines almost died of emotion. Jenny Hill simply gibbered with hysteria. The Prince of Darkness played his trombone like a madman: its brazen roarings were like the laughter of the damned. 117 conversions took place then and there. They prayed with the most touching sincerity and gratitude for Bodger, and for the anonymous donor of the £5000. Your father would not let his name be given.

LOMAX. That was rather fine of the old man, you know. Most chaps would have wanted the advertisement.

CUSINS. He said all the charitable institutions would be down on him like kites on a battle-field if he gave his name.

LADY BRITOMART. Thats Andrew all over. He never does a proper thing without giving an improper reason for it.

CUSINS. He convinced me that I have all my life been doing improper things for proper reasons.

LADY BRITOMART. Adolphus: now that Barbara has left the Salvation Army, you had better leave it too. I will not have you playing that drum in the streets.

CUSINS. Your orders are already obeyed, Lady Brit.

BARBARA. Dolly: were you ever really in earnest about it? Would you have joined if you had never seen me?

CUSINS [disingenuously]. Well—er—well, possibly, as a collector of religions—

LOMAX [cunningly]. Not as a drummer, though, you know. You are a very clearheaded brainy chap, Dolly; and it must have been apparent to you that there is a certain amount of tosh about—

LADY BRITOMART. Charles: if you must drivel, drivel like a grown-up man and not like a schoolboy.

LOMAX [*out of countenance*]. Well, drivel is drivel, dont you know, whatever a man's age.

LADY BRITOMART. In good society in England, Charles, men drivel at all ages by repeating silly formulas with an air of wisdom. Schoolboys make their own formulas out of slang, like you. When they reach your age, and get political private secretaryships and things of that sort, they drop slang and get their formulas out of the Spectator or The Times. You had better confine yourself to The Times. You will find that there is a certain amount of tosh about The Times; but at least its language is reputable.

LOMAX [*overwhelmed*]. You are so awfully strong-minded, Lady Brit—

LADY BRITOMART. Rubbish! [MORRISON *comes in.*] What is it?

MORRISON. If you please, my lady, Mr Undershaft has just drove up to the door.

LADY BRITOMART. Well, let him in. [MORRISON *hesitates.*] Whats the matter with you?

MORRISON. Shall I announce him, my lady; or is he at home here, so to speak, my lady?

LADY BRITOMART. Announce him.

MORRISON. Thank you, my lady. You wont mind my asking, I hope. The occasion is in a manner of speaking new to me.

LADY BRITOMART. Quite right. Go and let him in.

MORRISON. Thank you, my lady. [*He withdraws.*]

LADY BRITOMART. Children: go and get ready. [SARAH *and* BARBARA *go upstairs for their out-of-door wraps.*] Charles: go and tell Stephen to come down here in five minutes: you will find him in the drawing room. [CHARLES *goes.*] Adolphus: tell them to send round the carriage in about fifteen minutes. [ADOLPHUS *goes.*]

MORRISON [*at the door*]. Mr Undershaft.

[UNDERSHAFT *comes in.* MORRISON *goes out.*]

UNDERSHAFT. Alone! How fortunate!

LADY BRITOMART [*rising*]. Dont be sentimental, Andrew. Sit down. [*She sits on the settee: he sits beside her, on her left. She comes to the point before he has time to breathe.*] Sarah must have £800 a year until Charles Lomax comes into his property. Barbara will need more, and need it permanently, because Adolphus hasnt any property.

UNDERSHAFT [*resignedly*]. Yes, my dear: I will see to it. Anything else? for yourself, for instance?

LADY BRITOMART. I want to talk to you about Stephen.

UNDERSHAFT [*rather wearily*]. Dont, my dear. Stephen doesnt interest me.

LADY BRITOMART. He does interest me. He is our son.

UNDERSHAFT. Do you really think so? He has induced us to bring him into the world; but he chose his parents very incongruously, I think. I see nothing of myself in him, and less of you.

LADY BRITOMART. Andrew: Stephen is an excellent son, and a most steady, capable, highminded young man. You are simply trying to find an excuse for disinheriting him.

UNDERSHAFT. My dear Biddy: the Undershaft tradition disinherits him. It would be dishonest of me to leave the cannon foundry to my son.

LADY BRITOMART. It would be most unnatural and improper of you to leave it to anyone else, Andrew. Do you suppose this wicked and immoral tradition can be kept up for ever? Do you pretend that Stephen could not carry on the foundry just as well as all the other sons of the big business houses?

UNDERSHAFT. Yes: he could learn the office routine without understanding the business, like all the other sons; and the firm would go on by its own momentum until the real Undershaft—probably an Italian or a German—would invent a new method and cut him out.

LADY BRITOMART. There is nothing that any Italian or German could do that Stephen could not do. And Stephen at least has breeding.

UNDERSHAFT. The son of a foundling! Nonsense!

LADY BRITOMART. My son, Andrew! And even you may have good blood in your veins for all you know.

UNDERSHAFT. True. Probably I have. That is another argument in favour of a foundling.

LADY BRITOMART. Andrew: dont be aggravating. And dont be wicked. At present you are both.

UNDERSHAFT. This conversation is part of the Undershaft tradition, Biddy. Every Undershaft's wife has treated him to it ever since the house was founded. It is mere waste of breath. If the tradition be ever broken it will be for an abler man than Stephen.

LADY BRITOMART [*pouting*]. Then go away.

UNDERSHAFT [*deprecatory*]. Go away!

LADY BRITOMART. Yes: go away. If you will do nothing for Stephen, you are not wanted here. Go to your foundling, whoever he is; and look after him.

UNDERSHAFT. The fact is, Biddy—

LADY BRITOMART. Dont call me Biddy. I dont call you Andy.

UNDERSHAFT. I will not call my wife Britomart: it is not good sense. Seriously, my love, the Undershaft tradition has landed me in a difficulty. I am getting on in years; and my partner Lazarus has at last made a stand and insisted that the succession must be settled one way or the other; and of course he is quite right. You see, I havent found a fit successor yet.

LADY BRITOMART [*obstinately*]. There is Stephen.

UNDERSHAFT. Thats just it: all the foundlings I can find are exactly like Stephen.

LADY BRITOMART. Andrew!!

UNDERSHAFT. I want a man with no relations and no schooling: that is, a man who would be out of the running altogether if he were not a strong man. And I cant find him. Every blessed foundling nowadays is snapped up in his infancy by Barnardo homes, or School Board officers, or Boards of Guardians; and if he shews the least ability he is fastened on by schoolmasters; trained to win scholarships like a racehorse; crammed with secondhand ideas; drilled and disciplined in docility and what they call good taste; and lamed for life so that he is fit for nothing but teaching. If you want to keep the foundry in the family, you had better find an eligible foundling and marry him to Barbara.

LADY BRITOMART. Ah! Barbara! Your pet! You would sacrifice Stephen to Barbara.

UNDERSHAFT. Cheerfully. And you, my dear, would boil Barbara to make soup for Stephen.

LADY BRITOMART. Andrew: this is not a question of our likings and dislikings: it is a question of duty. It is your duty to make Stephen your successor.

UNDERSHAFT. Just as much as it is your duty to submit to your husband. Come, Biddy! these tricks of the governing class are of no use with me. I am one of the governing class myself; and it is waste of time giving tracts to a missionary. I have the power in this matter; and I am not to be humbugged into using it for your purposes.

LADY BRITOMART. Andrew: you can talk my head off; but you cant change wrong into right. And your tie is all on one side. Put it straight.

UNDERSHAFT [*disconcerted*]. It wont stay unless it's pinned [*he fumbles at it with childish grimaces*]—

[STEPHEN *comes in.*]

STEPHEN [*at the door*]. I beg your pardon [*about to retire*].
LADY BRITOMART. No: come in, Stephen.

[STEPHEN *comes forward to his mother's writing table.*]

UNDERSHAFT [*not very cordially*]. Good afternoon.
STEPHEN [*coldly*]. Good afternoon.
UNDERSHAFT [*to* LADY BRITOMART]. He knows all about the tradition, I suppose?
LADY BRITOMART. Yes. [*To* STEPHEN] It is what I told you last night, Stephen.
UNDERSHAFT [*sulkily*]. I understand you want to come into the cannon business.
STEPHEN. *I* go into trade! Certainly not.
UNDERSHAFT [*opening his eyes, greatly eased in mind and manner*]. Oh! in that case—
LADY BRITOMART. Cannons are not trade, Stephen. They are enterprise.
STEPHEN. I have no intention of becoming a man of business in any sense. I have no capacity for business and no taste for it. I intend to devote myself to politics.
UNDERSHAFT [*rising*]. My dear boy: this is an immense relief to me. And I trust it may prove an equally good thing for the country. I was afraid you would consider yourself disparaged and slighted. [*He moves towards* STEPHEN *as if to shake hands with him.*]
LADY BRITOMART [*rising and interposing*]. Stephen: I cannot allow you to throw away an enormous property like this.
STEPHEN [*stiffly*]. Mother: there must be an end of treating me as a child, if you please. [LADY BRITOMART *recoils, deeply wounded by his tone.*] Until last night I did not take your attitude seriously, because I did not think you meant it seri-

ously. But I find now that you left me in the dark as to matters which you should have explained to me years ago. I am extremely hurt and offended. Any further discussion of my intentions had better take place with my father, as between one man and another.

LADY BRITOMART. Stephen! [*She sits down again, her eyes filling with tears.*]

UNDERSHAFT [*with grave compassion*]. You see, my dear, it is only the big men who can be treated as children.

STEPHEN. I am sorry, mother, that you have forced me—

UNDERSHAFT [*stopping him*]. Yes, yes, yes, yes: thats all right, Stephen. She wont interfere with you any more: your independence is achieved: you have won your latchkey. Dont rub it in; and above all, dont apologize. [*He resumes his seat.*] Now what about your future, as between one man and another—I beg your pardon, Biddy: as between two men and a woman.

LADY BRITOMART [*who has pulled herself together strongly*]. I quite understand, Stephen. By all means go your own way if you feel strong enough.

[STEPHEN *sits down magisterially in the chair at the writing table with an air of affirming his majority.*]

UNDERSHAFT. It is settled that you do not ask for the succession to the cannon business.

STEPHEN. I hope it is settled that I repudiate the cannon business.

UNDERSHAFT. Come, come! dont be so devilishly sulky: it's boyish. Freedom should be generous. Besides, I owe you a fair start in life in exchange for disinheriting you. You cant become prime minister all at once. Havent you a turn for something? What about literature, art, and so forth?

STEPHEN. I have nothing of the artist about me, either in faculty or character, thank Heaven!

UNDERSHAFT. A philosopher, perhaps? Eh?

STEPHEN. I make no such ridiculous pretension.

UNDERSHAFT. Just so. Well, there is the army, the navy, the Church, the Bar. The Bar requires some ability. What about the Bar?

STEPHEN. I have not studied law. And I am afraid I have not the necessary push—I believe that is the name barristers give to their vulgarity—for success in pleading.

UNDERSHAFT. Rather a difficult case, Stephen. Hardly anything left but the stage, is there! [STEPHEN *makes an impatient movement*.] Well, come! is there anything you know or care for?

STEPHEN [*rising and looking at him steadily*]. I know the difference between right and wrong.

UNDERSHAFT [*hugely tickled*]. You dont say so! What! no capacity for business, no knowledge of law, no sympathy with art, no pretension to philosophy; only a simple knowledge of the secret that has puzzled all the philosophers, baffled all the lawyers, muddled all the men of business, and ruined most of the artists: the secret of right and wrong. Why, man, youre a genius, a master of masters, a god! At twenty-four, too!

STEPHEN [*keeping his temper with diffi*culty]. You are pleased to be facetious. I pretend to nothing more than any honorable English gentleman claims as his birthright [*he sits down angrily*].

UNDERSHAFT. Oh, thats everybody's birthright. Look at poor little Jenny Hill, the Salvation lassie! She would think you were laughing at her if you asked her to stand up in the street and teach grammar or geography or mathematics or even drawing room dancing; but it never occurs to her to doubt that she can teach morals and religion. You are all alike, you respectable people. You cant tell me the bursting strain of a ten-inch gun, which is a very simple matter; but you all think you can tell me the bursting strain of a man under temptation. You darent handle high explosives; but youre all ready to handle honesty and truth and justice and the whole duty of man, and kill one another at that game. What a country! What a world!

LADY BRITOMART [*uneasily*]. What do you think he had better do, Andrew?

UNDERSHAFT. Oh, just what he wants to do. He knows nothing and he thinks he knows everything. That points clearly to a political career. Get him a private secretaryship to someone who can get him an Under Secretaryship; and then leave him alone. He will find his natural and proper place in the end on the Treasury Bench.

STEPHEN [*springing up again*]. I am sorry, sir, that you force me to forget the respect due to you as my father. I am an Englishman and I will not hear the government of my country insulted. [*He thrusts his hands in his pockets, and walks angrily across to the window.*]

UNDERSHAFT [*with a touch of brutality*]. The government of your country! *I* am the government of your country: I, and Lazarus. Do you suppose that you and half a dozen amateurs like you, sitting in a row in that foolish gabble shop, can govern Undershaft and Lazarus? No, my friend: you will do what pays us. You will make war when it suits us, and keep peace when it doesnt. You will find out that trade requires certain measures when we have decided on those measures. When I want anything to keep my dividends up, you will discover that my want is a national need. When other people want something to keep my dividends down, you will call out the police and military. And in return you shall have the support and applause of my newspapers, and the delight of imagining that you are a great statesman. Government of your country! Be off with you, my boy, and play with your caucuses and leading articles and historic parties and great leaders and burning questions and the rest of your toys. *I* am going back to my counting-house to pay the piper and call the tune.

STEPHEN [*actually smiling, and putting his hand on his father's shoulder with indulgent patronage*]. Really, my dear father, it is impossible to be angry with you. You dont know how absurd all this sounds to me. You are very properly proud of having been industrious enough to make money; and it is greatly to your credit that you have made so much of it. But it has kept you in circles where you are valued for your money and deferred to for it, instead of in the doubtless very old-fashioned and behind-the-times public school and university where I formed my habits of mind. It is natural for you to think that money governs England; but you must allow me to think I know better.

UNDERSHAFT. And what does govern England, pray?

STEPHEN. Character, father, character.

UNDERSHAFT. Whose character? Yours or mine?

STEPHEN. Neither yours nor mine, father, but the best elements in the English national character.

UNDERSHAFT. Stephen: Ive found your profession for you. Youre a born journalist. I'll start you with a high-toned weekly review. There!

[*Before* STEPHEN *can reply* SARAH, BARBARA, LOMAX, *and* CUSINS *come in ready for walking.* BARBARA *crosses the room to the window and looks out.* CUSINS *drifts amiably* o the armchair. LOMAX *remains near the door, whilst* ARAH *comes to her mother.* STEPHEN *goes to the smaller writing table and busies himself with his letters.*]

SARAH. Go and get ready, mamma: the carriage is waiting.

LADY BRITOMART *leaves the room.*]

UNDERSHAFT [*to* SARAH]. Good day, my dear. Good afternoon, Mr Lomax.

LOMAX [*vaguely*]. Ahdedoo.

UNDERSHAFT [*to* CUSINS]. Quite well after last night, Euripides, eh?

CUSINS. As well as can be expected.

UNDERSHAFT. Thats right. [*To* BARBARA] So you are coming to see my death and devastation factory, Barbara?

BARBARA [*at the window*]. You came yesterday to see my salvation factory. I promised you a return visit.

LOMAX [*coming forward between* SARAH *and* UNDERSHAFT]. Youll find it awfully interesting. Ive been through the Woolwich Arsenal; and it gives you a ripping feeling of security, you know, to think of the lot of beggars we could kill if it came to fighting. [*To* UNDERSHAFT, *with sudden solemnity*] Still, it must be rather an awful reflection for you, from the religious point of view as it were. Youre getting on, you know, and all that.

SARAH. You dont mind Cholly's imbecility, papa, do you?

LOMAX [*much taken aback*]. Oh I say!

UNDERSHAFT. Mr Lomax looks at the matter in a very proper spirit, my dear.

LOMAX. Just so. Thats all I meant, I assure you.

SARAH. Are you coming, Stephen?

STEPHEN. Well, I am rather busy—er— [*Magnanimously*] Oh well, yes: I'll come. That is, if there is room for me.

UNDERSHAFT. I can take two with me in a little motor I am experimenting with for field use. You wont mind its being rather unfashionable. It's not painted yet; but it's bullet proof.

LOMAX [*appalled at the prospect of confronting Wilton Crescent in an unpainted motor*]. Oh I say!

SARAH. The carriage for me, thank you. Barbara doesnt mind what she's seen in.

LOMAX. I say, Dolly, old chap: do you really mind the car being a guy? Because of course if you do I'll go in it. Still—

CUSINS. I prefer it.

LOMAX. Thanks awfully, old man. Come, my ownest. [*H. hurries out to secure his seat in the carriage.* SARAH *follow. him.*]

CUSINS [*moodily walking across to* LADY BRITOMART's *writing table*]. Why are we two coming to this Works Department of Hell? that is what I ask myself.

BARBARA. I have always thought of it as a sort of pit where lost creatures with blackened faces stirred up smoky fires and were driven and tormented by my father. Is it like that, dad?

UNDERSHAFT [*scandalized*]. My dear! It is a spotlessly clean and beautiful hillside town.

CUSINS. With a Methodist chapel? Oh do say theres a Methodist chapel.

UNDERSHAFT. There are two: a Primitive one and a sophisticated one. There is even an Ethical Society; but it is not much patronized, as my men are all strongly religious. In the High Explosives Sheds they object to the presence of Agnostics as unsafe.

CUSINS. And yet they dont object to you!

BARBARA. Do they obey all your orders?

UNDERSHAFT. I never give them any orders. When I speak to one of them it is 'Well, Jones, is the baby doing well? and has Mrs Jones made a good recovery?' 'Nicely, thank you, sir.' And thats all.

CUSINS. But Jones has to be kept in order. How do you maintain discipline among your men?

UNDERSHAFT. I dont. They do. You see, the one thing Jones wont stand is any rebellion from the man under him, or any assertion of social equality between the wife of the man with 4 shillings a week less than himself, and Mrs Jones! Of course they all rebel against me, theoretically. Practically, every man of them keeps the man just below him in his place. I never meddle with them. I never bully them. I dont even bully Lazarus. I say that certain things are to be done; but I dont order anybody to do them. I dont say, mind you, that there is no ordering about and snubbing and even bullying. The men snub the boys and order them about; the carmen snub the sweepers; the artisans snub the unskilled laborers; the foremen drive and bully both the laborers and artisans; the assistant engineers find fault with the foremen; the chief engineers drop on the assistants; the departmental managers worry the chiefs; and the clerks have tall hats and hymnbooks and keep up the social tone by refusing to associate on equal terms with anybody. The result is a colossal profit, which comes to me.

CUSINS [*revolted*]. You really are a—well, what I was saying yesterday.

BARBARA. What was he saying yesterday?

UNDERSHAFT. Never mind, my dear. He thinks I have made you unhappy. Have I?

BARBARA. Do you think I can be happy in this vulgar silly dress? I! who have worn the uniform. Do you understand what you have done to me? Yesterday I had a man's soul in my hand. I set him in the way of life with his face to salvation. But when we took your money he turned back to drunkenness and derision. [*With intense conviction*] I will never forgive you that. If I had a child, and you destroyed its body with your explosives—if you murdered Dolly with your horrible guns—I could forgive you if my forgiveness would open the gates of heaven to you. But to take a human soul from me, and turn it into the soul of a wolf! that is worse than any murder.

UNDERSHAFT. Does my daughter despair so easily? Can you strike a man to the heart and leave no mark on him?

BARBARA [*her face lighting up*]. Oh, you are right: he can never be lost now: where was my faith?

CUSINS. Oh, clever clever devil!

BARBARA. You may be a devil; but God speaks through you sometimes. [*She takes her father's hands and kisses them.*] You have given me back my happiness: I feel it deep down now, though my spirit is troubled.

UNDERSHAFT. You have learnt something. That always feels at first as if you had lost something.

BARBARA. Well, take me to the factory of death; and let me learn something more. There must be some truth or other behind all this frightful irony. Come, Dolly. [*She goes out.*]

CUSINS. My guardian angel! [*To* UNDERSHAFT] Avaunt! [*He follows* BARBARA.]

STEPHEN [*quietly, at the writing table*]. You must not mind Cusins, father. He is a very amiable good fellow; but he is a Greek scholar and naturally a little eccentric.

UNDERSHAFT. Ah, quite so. Thank you, Stephen. Thank you. [*He goes out.*]

[STEPHEN *smiles patronizingly; buttons his coat responsibly; and crosses the room to the door.* LADY BRITOMART, *dressed for out-of-doors, opens it before he reaches it. She looks round for others; looks at* STEPHEN; *and turns to go without a word.*]

STEPHEN [*embarrassed*]. Mother—

LADY BRITOMART. Dont be apologetic, Stephen. And dont forget that you have outgrown your mother. [*She goes out.*]

[*Perivale St Andrews lies between two Middlesex hills, half climbing the northern one. It is an almost smokeless town of white walls, roofs of narrow green slates or red tiles, tall trees, domes, campaniles, and slender chimney shafts, beautifully situated and beautiful in itself. The best view of it is obtained from the crest of a slope about half a mile to the east, where the high explosives are dealt with. The foundry lies hidden in the depths between, the tops of its chimneys sprouting like huge skittles into the middle distance. Across the crest runs an emplacement of concrete, with a firestep, and a parapet which suggests a fortification, because there is a huge cannon of the obsolete Woolwich Infant pattern peering across it at the town. The cannon is mounted on an experimental gun carriage: possibly the original model of the Undershaft disappearing rampart gun alluded to by* STEPHEN. *The firestep, being a convenient place to sit, is furnished here and there with straw disc cushions; and at one place there is the additional luxury of a fur rug.*

BARBARA *is standing on the firestep, looking over the parapet towards the town. On her right is the cannon; on her left the end of a shed raised on piles, with a ladder of three or four steps up to the door, which opens outwards and has a little wooden landing at the threshold, with a fire bucket in the corner of the landing. Several dummy soldiers more or less mutilated, with straw protruding from their gashes, have been shoved out of the way under the landing. A few others are nearly upright against the shed; and one has fallen forward and lies, like a grotesque corpse, on the emplacement. The parapet stops short of the shed, leaving a gap which is the beginning of the path down the hill through the foundry to the town. The rug is on the firestep near this gap. Down on the emplacement behind the cannon is a trolley carrying a huge conical bombshell with a red band painted on it. Further to the right is the door of an office, which, like the sheds, is of the lightest possible construction.*

[CUSINS *arrives by the path from the town.*]

BARBARA. Well?

CUSINS. Not a ray of hope. Everything perfect! wonderful! real! It only needs a cathedral to be a heavenly city instead of a hellish one.

BARBARA. Have you found out whether they have done anything for old Peter Shirley?

CUSINS. They have found him a job as gatekeeper and timekeeper. He's frightfully miserable. He calls the time-keeping brainwork, and says he isnt used to it; and his gate lodge is so splendid that he's ashamed to use the rooms, and skulks in the scullery.

BARBARA. Poor Peter!

[STEPHEN *arrives from the town. He carries a fieldglass.*]

STEPHEN [*enthusiastically*]. Have you two seen the place? Why did you leave us?

CUSINS. I wanted to see everything I was not intended to see; and Barbara wanted to make the men talk.

STEPHEN. Have you found anything discreditable?

CUSINS. No. They call him Dandy Andy and are proud of his being a cunning old rascal; but it's all horribly, frightfully, immorally, unanswerably perfect.

[SARAH *arrives.*]

SARAH. Heavens! what a place! [*She crosses to the trolley.*] Did you see the nursing home!? [*She sits down on the shell.*]

STEPHEN. Did you see the libraries and schools!?

SARAH. Did you see the ball room and the banqueting chamber in the Town Hall!?

STEPHEN. Have you gone into the insurance fund, the pension fund, the building society, the various applications of co-operation!?

[UNDERSHAFT *comes from the office, with a sheaf of telegrams in his hand.*]

UNDERSHAFT. Well, have you seen everything? I'm sorry I was called away. [*Indicating the telegrams*] Good news from Manchuria.

STEPHEN. Another Japanese victory?

UNDERSHAFT. Oh, I dont know. Which side wins does not

concern us here. No: the good news is that the aerial battl
ship is a tremendous success. At the first trial it has wip
out a fort with three hundred soldiers in it.

CUSINS [*from the platform*]. Dummy soldiers?

UNDERSHAFT [*striding across to* STEPHEN *and kicking t*
*prostrate dummy brutally out of his way*]. No: the re
thing.

[CUSINS *and* BARBARA *exchange glances. Then* CUSINS *sits*
*the step and buries his face in his hands.* BARBARA *gravely la*
*her hand on his shoulder. He looks up at her in whimsic*
*desperation.*]

UNDERSHAFT. Well, Stephen, what do you think of the plac

STEPHEN. Oh, magnificent. A perfect triumph of modern i
dustry. Frankly, my dear father, I have been a fool: I ha
no idea of what it all meant: of the wonderful for
thought, the power of organization, the administrative c
pacity, the financial genius, the colossal capital it repr
sents. I have been repeating to myself as I came throug
your streets 'Peace hath her victories no less renowne
than War.' I have only one misgiving about it all.

UNDERSHAFT. Out with it.

STEPHEN. Well, I cannot help thinking that all this provisio
for every want of your workmen may sap their indepen
dence and weaken their sense of responsibility. And great!
as we enjoyed our tea at that splendid restaurant—how
they gave us all that luxury and cake and jam and crea
for threepence I really cannot imagine!—still you mu
remember that restaurants break up home life. Look at th
continent, for instance! Are you sure so much pamperin
is really good for the men's characters?

UNDERSHAFT. Well you see, my dear boy, when you are or
ganizing civilization you have to make up your min
whether trouble and anxiety are good things or not. If yo
decide that they are, then, I take it, you simply dont organ
ize civilization; and there you are, with trouble and anxiet
enough to make us all angels! But if you decide the othe
way, you may as well go through with it. However, Stephen
our characters are safe here. A sufficient dose of anxiety i
always provided by the fact that we may be blown to
smithereens at any moment.

SARAH. By the way, papa, where do you make the explosives

UNDERSHAFT. In separate little sheds, like that one. When on of them blows up, it costs very little; and only the people quite close to it are killed.

STEPHEN, *who is quite close to it, looks at it rather scaredly, and moves away quickly to the cannon. At the same moment the door of the shed is thrown abruptly open; and a foreman in overalls and list slippers comes out on the little landing and holds the door for* LOMAX, *who appears in the doorway.*]

LOMAX [*with studied coolness*]. My good fellow: you neednt get into a state of nerves. Nothing's going to happen to you; and I suppose it wouldnt be the end of the world if anything did. A little bit of British pluck is what you want, old chap. [*He descends and strolls across to* SARAH.]

UNDERSHAFT [*to the foreman*]. Anything wrong, Bilton?

BILTON [*with ironic calm*]. Gentleman walked into the high explosives shed and lit a cigaret, sir: thats all.

UNDERSHAFT. Ah, quite so. [*Going over to* LOMAX] Do you happen to remember what you did with the match?

LOMAX. Oh come! I'm not a fool. I took jolly good care to blow it out before I chucked it away.

BILTON. The top of it was red hot inside, sir.

LOMAX. Well, suppose it was! I didn't chuck it into any of your messes.

UNDERSHAFT. Think no more of it, Mr Lomax. By the way, would you mind lending me your matches.

LOMAX [*offering his box*]. Certainly.

UNDERSHAFT. Thanks. [*He pockets the matches.*]

LOMAX [*lecturing to the company generally*]. You know, these high explosives dont go off like gunpowder, except when theyre in a gun. When theyre spread loose, you can put a match to them without the least risk: they just burn quietly like a bit of paper. [*Warming to the scientific interest of the subject*] Did you know that, Undershaft? Have you ever tried?

UNDERSHAFT. Not on a large scale, Mr Lomax. Bilton will give you a sample of gun cotton when you are leaving if you ask him. You can experiment with it at home.

[BILTON *looks puzzled.*]

SARAH. Bilton will do nothing of the sort, papa. I suppose it's your business to blow up the Russians and Japs; but you might really stop short of blowing up poor Cholly.

[BILTON *gives it up and retires into the shed*.]

LOMAX. My ownest, there is no danger. [*He sits beside h*
*on the shell*.]

[LADY BRITOMART *arrives from the town with a bouquet*.]

LADY BRITOMART [*impetuously*]. Andrew: you shouldnt hav
let me see this place.

UNDERSHAFT. Why, my dear?

LADY BRITOMART. Never mind why: you shouldnt have: tha
all. To think of all that [*indicating the town*] being your
and that you have kept it to yourself all these years!

UNDERSHAFT. It does not belong to me. I belong to it. It
the Undershaft inheritance.

LADY BRITOMART. It is not. Your ridiculous cannons and tha
noisy banging foundry may be the Undershaft inheritanc
but all that plate and linen, all that furniture and thos
houses and orchards and gardens belong to us. They belon
to me: they are not a man's business. I wont give them u
You must be out of your senses to throw them all away
and if you persist in such folly, I will call in a doctor.

UNDERSHAFT [*stooping to smell the bouquet*]. Where did yo
get the flowers, my dear?

LADY BRITOMART. Your men presented them to me in you
William Morris Labor Church.

CUSINS. Oh! It needed only that. A Labor Church! [*H*
*mounts the firestep distractedly, and leans with his elbow*
*on the parapet, turning his back to them*.]

LADY BRITOMART. Yes, with Morris's words in mosaic letter
ten feet high round the dome. NO MAN IS GOOD ENOUGH
TO BE ANOTHER MAN'S MASTER. The cynicism of it!

UNDERSHAFT. It shocked the men at first, I am afraid. Bu
now they take no more notice of it than of the ten com
mandments in church.

LADY BRITOMART. Andrew: you are trying to put me off the
subject of the inheritance by profane jokes. Well, you shant
I dont ask it any longer for Stephen: he has inherited fa
too much of your perversity to be fit for it. But Barbara
has rights as well as Stephen. Why should not Adolphus
succeed to the inheritance? I could manage the town for
him; and he can look after the cannons, if they are really
necessary.

UNDERSHAFT. I should ask nothing better if Adolphus were a foundling. He is exactly the sort of new blood that is wanted in English business. But he's not a foundling; and theres an end of it. [*He makes for the office door.*]

CUSINS [*turning to them*]. Not quite. [*They all turn and stare at him.*] I think— Mind! I am not committing myself in any way as to my future course—but I think the foundling difficulty can be got over. [*He jumps down to the emplacement.*]

UNDERSHAFT [*coming back to him*]. What do you mean?

CUSINS. Well, I have something to say which is in the nature of a confession.

SARAH.
LADY BRITOMART.       }Confession!
BARBARA.
STEPHEN.

LOMAX. Oh I say!

CUSINS. Yes, a confession. Listen, all. Until I met Barbara I thought myself in the main an honorable, truthful man, because I wanted the approval of my conscience more than I wanted anything else. But the moment I saw Barbara, I wanted her far more than the approval of my conscience.

LADY BRITOMART. Adolphus!

CUSINS. It is true. You accused me yourself, Lady Brit, of joining the Army to worship Barbara; and so I did. She bought my soul like a flower at a street corner; but she bought it for herself.

UNDERSHAFT. What! Not for Dionysos or another?

CUSINS. Dionysos and all the others are in herself. I adored what was divine in her, and was therefore a true worshipper. But I was romantic about her too. I thought she was a woman of the people, and that a marriage with a professor of Greek would be far beyond the wildest social ambitions of her rank.

LADY BRITOMART. Adolphus! !

LOMAX. Oh I say! ! !

CUSINS. When I learnt the horrible truth—

LADY BRITOMART. What do you mean by the horrible truth, pray?

CUSINS. That she was enormously rich; that her grandfather was an earl; that her father was the Prince of Darkness—

UNDERSHAFT. Chut!

CUSINS. —and that I was only an adventurer trying to catch
a rich wife, then I stooped to deceive her about my birth

BARBARA [*rising*]. Dolly!

LADY BRITOMART. Your birth! Now Adolphus, dont dare to
make up a wicked story for the sake of these wretched
cannons. Remember: I have seen photographs of your
parents; and the Agent General for South Western Australia
knows them personally and has assured me that they are
most respectable married people.

CUSINS. So they are in Australia; but here they are outcasts.
Their marriage is legal in Australia, but not in England. My
mother is my father's deceased wife's sister; and in this
island I am consequently a foundling. [*Sensation.*]

BARBARA. Silly! [*She climbs to the cannon, and leans, listening, in the angle it makes with the parapet.*]

CUSINS. Is the subterfuge good enough, Machiavelli?

UNDERSHAFT [*thoughtfully*]. Biddy: this may be a way out of
the difficulty.

LADY BRITOMART. Stuff! A man cant make cannons any the
better for being his own cousin instead of his proper self
[*she sits down on the rug with a bounce that expresses her
downright contempt for their casuistry*].

UNDERSHAFT [*to* CUSINS] You are an educated man. That is
against the tradition.

CUSINS. Once in ten thousand times it happens that the schoolboy is a born master of what they try to teach him. Greek
has not destroyed my mind: it has nourished it. Besides,
I did not learn it at an English public school.

UNDERSHAFT. Hm! Well, I cannot afford to be too particular:
you have cornered the foundling market. Let it pass. You
are eligible, Euripides: you are eligible.

BARBARA. Dolly: yesterday morning, when Stephen told us all
about the tradition, you became very silent; and you have
been strange and excited ever since. Were you thinking of
your birth then?

CUSINS. When the finger of Destiny suddenly points at a man
in the middle of his breakfast, it makes him thoughtful.

UNDERSHAFT. Aha! You have had your eye on the business,
my young friend, have you?

CUSINS. Take care! There is an abyss of moral horror between
me and your accursed aerial battleships.

UNDERSHAFT. Never mind the abyss for the present. Let us

settle the practical details and leave your final decision open. You know that you will have to change your name. Do you object to that?

CUSINS. Would any man named Adolphus—any man called Dolly!—object to be called something else?

UNDERSHAFT. Good. Now, as to money! I propose to treat you handsomely from the beginning. You shall start at a thousand a year.

CUSINS [with sudden heat, his spectacles twinkling with mischief]. A thousand! You dare offer a miserable thousand to the son-in-law of a millionaire! No, by Heavens, Machiavelli! you shall not cheat me. You cannot do without me; and I can do without you. I must have two thousand five hundred a year for two years. At the end of that time, if I am a failure, I go. But if I am a success, and stay on, you must give me the other five thousand.

UNDERSHAFT. What other five thousand?

CUSINS. To make the two years up to five thousand a year. The two thousand five hundred is only half pay in case I should turn out a failure. The third year I must have ten per cent on the profits.

UNDERSHAFT [taken aback]. Ten per cent! Why, man, do you know what my profits are?

CUSINS. Enormous, I hope: otherwise I shall require twenty-five per cent.

UNDERSHAFT. But, Mr Cusins, this is a serious matter of business. You are not bringing any capital into the concern.

CUSINS. What! no capital! Is my mastery of Greek no capital? Is my access to the subtlest thought, the loftiest poetry yet attained by humanity, no capital? My character! my intellect! my life! my career! what Barbara calls my soul! are these no capital? Say another word; and I double my salary.

UNDERSHAFT. Be reasonable—

CUSINS [peremptorily]. Mr Undershaft: you have my terms. Take them or leave them.

UNDERSHAFT [recovering himself]. Very well. I note your terms; and I offer you half.

CUSINS [disgusted]. Half!

UNDERSHAFT [firmly]. Half.

CUSINS. You call yourself a gentleman; and you offer me half!

UNDERSHAFT. I do not call myself a gentleman; but I offer you half.

CUSINS. This to your future partner! your successor! your so
in-law!

BARBARA. You are selling your own soul, Dolly, not mir
Leave me out of the bargain, please.

UNDERSHAFT. Come! I will go a step further for Barbar:
sake. I will give you three fifths; but that is my last wor

CUSINS. Done!

LOMAX. Done in the eye! Why, *I* get only eight hundre
you know.

CUSINS. By the way, Mac, I am a classical scholar, not :
arithmetical one. Is three fifths more than half or less?

UNDERSHAFT. More, of course.

CUSINS. I would have taken two hundred and fifty. How yc
can succeed in business when you are willing to pay :
that money to a University don who is obviously not wor
a junior clerk's wages!—well! What will Lazarus say?

UNDERSHAFT. Lazarus is a gentle romantic Jew who car:
for nothing but string quartets and stalls at fashionab
theatres. He will be blamed for your rapacity in mone
matters, poor fellow! as he has hitherto been blamed f(
mine. You are a shark of the first order, Euripides. S
much the better for the firm!

BARBARA. Is the bargain closed, Dolly? Does your soul belon
to him now?

CUSINS. No: the price is settled: that is all. The real tug c
war is still to come. What about the moral question?

LADY BRITOMART. There is no moral question in the matte
at all, Adolphus. You must simply sell cannons and weap
ons to people whose cause is right and just, and refus
them to foreigners and criminals.

UNDERSHAFT [*determinedly*]. No: none of that. You mus
keep the true faith of an Armorer, or you dont come i.
here.

CUSINS. What on earth is the true faith of an Armorer?

UNDERSHAFT. To give arms to all men who offer an hones
price for them, without respect of persons or principles: t(
aristocrat and republican, to Nihilist and Tsar, to Capitalis
and Socialist, to Protestant and Catholic, to burglar an(
policeman, to black man, white man and yellow man, t(
all sorts and conditions, all nationalities, all faiths, all fol
lies, all causes and all crimes. The first Undershaft wrote u[
in his shop IF GOD GAVE THE HAND, LET NOT MAN WITH
HOLD THE SWORD. The second wrote up ALL HAVE THE

RIGHT TO FIGHT: NONE HAVE THE RIGHT TO JUDGE. The third wrote up TO MAN THE WEAPON: TO HEAVEN THE VICTORY. The fourth had no literary turn; so he did not write up anything; but he sold cannons to Napoleon under the nose of George the Third. The fifth wrote up PEACE SHALL NOT PREVAIL SAVE WITH A SWORD IN HER HAND. The sixth, my master, was the best of all. He wrote up NOTHING IS EVER DONE IN THIS WORLD UNTIL MEN ARE PREPARED TO KILL ONE ANOTHER IF IT IS NOT DONE. After that, there was nothing left for the seventh to say. So he wrote up, simply, UNASHAMED.

CUSINS. My good Machiavelli, I shall certainly write something up on the wall; only, as I shall write it in Greek, you wont be able to read it. But as to your Armorer's faith, if I take my neck out of the noose of my own morality I am not going to put it into the noose of yours. I shall sell cannons to whom I please and refuse them to whom I please. So there!

UNDERSHAFT. From the moment when you become Andrew Undershaft, you will never do as you please again. Dont come here lusting for power, young man.

CUSINS. If power were my aim I should not come here for it. You have no power.

UNDERSHAFT. None of my own, certainly.

CUSINS. I have more power than you, more will. You do not drive this place: it drives you. And what drives the place?

UNDERSHAFT [enigmatically]. A will of which I am part.

BARBARA [startled]. Father! Do you know what you are saying; or are you laying a snare for my soul?

CUSINS. Dont listen to his metaphysics, Barbara. The place is driven by the most rascally part of society, the money hunters, the pleasure hunters, the military promotion hunters; and he is their slave.

UNDERSHAFT. Not necessarily. Remember the Armorer's Faith. I will take an order from a good man as cheerfully as from a bad one. If you good people prefer preaching and shirking to buying my weapons and fighting the rascals, dont blame me. I can make cannons: I cannot make courage and conviction. Bah! you tire me, Euripides, with your morality mongering. Ask Barbara: she understands. [He suddenly reaches up and takes BARBARA'S hands, looking powerfully into her eyes.] Tell him, my love, what power really means.

BARBARA [*hypnotized*]. Before I joined the Salvation Army
I was in my own power; and the consequence was tha
I never knew what to do with myself. When I joined it,
had not time enough for all the things I had to do.

UNDERSHAFT [*approvingly*]. Just so. And why was that, do you
suppose?

BARBARA. Yesterday I should have said, because I was in the
power of God. [*She resumes her self-possession, withdraw
ing her hands from his with a power equal to his own.*] Bu
you came and shewed me that I was in the power of Bodger
and Undershaft. Today I feel—oh! how can I put it into
words? Sarah: do you remember the earthquake at Cannes
when we were little children?—how little the surprise of
the first shock mattered compared to the dread and horror
of waiting for the second? That is how I feel in this place
today. I stood on the rock I thought eternal; and without a
word of warning it reeled and crumbled under me. I was
safe with an infinite wisdom watching me, an army marching to Salvation with me; and in a moment, at a stroke of
your pen in a cheque book, I stood alone; and the heavens
were empty. That was the first shock of the earthquake: I
am waiting for the second.

UNDERSHAFT. Come, come, my daughter! dont make too much
of your little tinpot tragedy. What do we do here when
we spend years of work and thought and thousands of
pounds of solid cash on a new gun or an aerial battleship
that turns out just a hairsbreadth wrong after all? Scrap it.
Scrap it without wasting another hour or another pound on
it. Well, you have made for yourself something that you
call a morality or a religion or what not. It doesnt fit the
facts. Well, scrap it. Scrap it and get one that does fit. That
is what is wrong with the world at present. It scraps its obsolete steam engines and dynamos; but it wont scrap its old
prejudices and its old moralities and its old religions and
its old political constitutions. Whats the result? In machinery it does very well; but in morals and religion and politics
it is working at a loss that brings it nearer bankruptcy every
year. Dont persist in that folly. If your old religion broke
down yesterday, get a newer and a better one for tomorrow.

BARBARA. Oh how gladly I would take a better one to my soul!
But you offer me a worse one. [*Turning on him with sudden vehemence.*] Justify yourself: shew me some light

through the darkness of this dreadful place, with its beautifully clean workshops, and respectable workmen, and model homes.

UNDERSHAFT. Cleanliness and respectability do not need justification, Barbara: they justify themselves. I see no darkness here, no dreadfulness. In your Salvation shelter I saw poverty, misery, cold and hunger. You gave them bread and treacle and dreams of heaven. I give from thirty shillings a week to twelve thousand a year. They find their own dreams; but I look after the drainage.

BARBARA. And their souls?

UNDERSHAFT. I save their souls just as I saved yours.

BARBARA [revolted]. You saved my soul! What do you mean?

UNDERSHAFT. I fed you and clothed you and housed you. I took care that you should have money enough to live handsomely—more than enough; so that you could be wasteful, careless, generous. That saved your soul from the seven deadly sins.

BARBARA [bewildered]. The seven deadly sins!

UNDERSHAFT. Yes, the deadly seven. [Counting on his fingers] Food, clothing, firing, rent, taxes, respectability and children. Nothing can lift those seven millstones from Man's neck but money; and the spirit cannot soar until the millstones are lifted. I lifted them from your spirit. I enabled Barbara to become Major Barbara; and I saved her from the crime of poverty.

CUSINS. Do you call poverty a crime?

UNDERSHAFT. The worst of crimes. All the other crimes are virtues beside it: all the other dishonors are chivalry itself by comparison. Poverty blights whole cities; spreads horrible pestilences; strikes dead the very souls of all who come within sight, sound, or smell of it. What you call crime is nothing: a murder here and a theft there, a blow now and a curse then: what do they matter? they are only the accidents and illnesses of life: there are not fifty genuine professional criminals in London. But there are millions of poor people, abject people, dirty people, ill fed, ill clothed people. They poison us morally and physically: they kill the happiness of society: they force us to do away with our own liberties and to organize unnatural cruelties for fear they should rise against us and drag us down into their abyss. Only fools fear crime: we all fear poverty. Pah!

[*turning on* BARBARA] you talk of your half-saved ruffian i
West Ham: you accuse me of dragging his soul back to per
dition. Well, bring him to me here; and I will drag his sou
back again to salvation for you. Not by words and dream:
but by thirty-eight shillings a week, a sound house in a hand
some street, and a permanent job. In three weeks he wi
have a fancy waistcoat; in three months a tall hat and
chapel sitting; before the end of the year he will shake hand
with a duchess at a Primrose League meeting, and join th
Conservative Party.

BARBARA. And will he be the better for that?

UNDERSHAFT. You know he will. Dont be a hypocrite, Bar
bara. He will be better fed, better housed, better clothed
better behaved; and his children will be pounds heavie
and bigger. That will be better than an American clotl
mattress in a shelter, chopping firewood, eating bread and
treacle, and being forced to kneel down from time to tim
to thank heaven for it: knee drill, I think you call it. It i
cheap work converting starving men with a Bible in one
hand and a slice of bread in the other. I will undertake to
convert West Ham to Mahometanism on the same terms
Try your hand on my men: their souls are hungry because
their bodies are full.

BARBARA. And leave the east end to starve?

UNDERSHAFT [*his energetic tone dropping into one of bitter
and brooding remembrance*]. I was an east ender. I mor-
alized and starved until one day I swore that I would be a
full-fed free man at all costs; that nothing should stop me
except a bullet, neither reason nor morals nor the lives of
other men. I said 'Thou shalt starve ere I starve'; and with
that word I became free and great. I was a dangerous man
until I had my will: now I am useful, beneficent, kindly
person. That is the history of most self-made millionaires,
I fancy. When it is the history of every Englishman we shall
have an England worth living in.

LADY BRITOMART. Stop making speeches, Andrew. This is not
the place for them.

UNDERSHAFT [*punctured*]. My dear: I have no other means
of conveying my ideas.

LADY BRITOMART. Your ideas are nonsense. You got on because you were selfish and unscrupulous.

UNDERSHAFT. Not at all. I had the strongest scruples about

poverty and starvation. Your moralists are quite unscrupulous about both: they make virtues of them. I had rather be a thief than a pauper. I had rather be a murderer than a slave. I dont want to be either; but if you force the alternative on me, then, by Heaven, I'll choose the braver and more moral one. I hate poverty and slavery worse than any other crimes whatsoever. And let me tell you this. Poverty and slavery have stood up for centuries to your sermons and leading articles: they will not stand up to my machine guns. Dont preach at them: dont reason with them. Kill them.

BARBARA. Killing. Is that your remedy for everything?

UNDERSHAFT. It is the final test of conviction, the only lever strong enough to overturn a social system, the only way of saying Must. Let six hundred and seventy fools loose in the streets; and three policemen can scatter them. But huddle them together in a certain house in Westminster; and let them go through certain ceremonies and call themselves certain names until at last they get the courage to kill; and your six hundred and seventy fools become a government. Your pious mob fills up ballot papers and imagines it is governing its masters; but the ballot paper that really governs is the paper that has a bullet wrapped up in it.

CUSINS. That is perhaps why, like most intelligent people, I never vote.

UNDERSHAFT. Vote! Bah! When you vote, you only change the names of the cabinet. When you shoot, you pull down governments, inaugurate new epochs, abolish old orders and set up new. Is that historically true, Mr Learned Man, or is it not?

CUSINS. It is historically true. I loathe having to admit it. I repudiate your sentiments. I abhor your nature. I defy you in every possible way. Still, it is true. But it ought not to be true.

UNDERSHAFT. Ought! ought! ought! ought! ought! Are you going to spend your life saying ought, like the rest of our moralists? Turn your oughts into shalls, man. Come and make explosives with me. Whatever can blow men up can blow society up. The history of the world is the history of those who had courage enough to embrace this truth. Have you the courage to embrace it, Barbara?

LADY BRITOMART. Barbara: I positively forbid you to listen to your father's abominable wickedness. And you, Adolphus, ought to know better than to go about saying that wrong things are true. What does it matter whether they are true if they are wrong?

UNDERSHAFT. What does it matter whether they are wrong if they are true?

LADY BRITOMART [*rising*]. Children: come home instantly Andrew: I am exceedingly sorry I allowed you to call or us. You are wickeder than ever. Come at once.

BARBARA [*shaking her head*]. It's no use running away from wicked people, mamma.

LADY BRITOMART. It is every use. It shews your disapprobation of them.

BARBARA. It does not save them.

LADY BRITOMART. I can see that you are going to disobey me. Sarah: are you coming home or are you not?

SARAH. I daresay it's very wicked of papa to make cannons; but I dont think I shall cut him on that account.

LOMAX [*pouring oil on the troubled waters*]. The fact is, you know, there is a certain amount of tosh about this notion of wickedness. It doesnt work. You must look at facts. Not that I would say a word in favor of anything wrong; but then, you see, all sorts of chaps are always doing all sorts of things; and we have to fit them in somehow, dont you know. What I mean is that you cant go cutting everybody; and thats about what it comes to. [*Their rapt attention to his eloquence makes him nervous.*] Perhaps I dont make myself clear.

LADY BRITOMART. You are lucidity itself, Charles. Because Andrew is successful and has plenty of money to give to Sarah, you will flatter him and encourage him in his wickedness.

LOMAX [*unruffled*]. Well, where the carcase is, there will the eagles be gathered, dont you know. [*To* UNDERSHAFT] Eh? What?

UNDERSHAFT. Precisely. By the way, may I call you Charles?

LOMAX. Delighted. Cholly is the usual ticket.

UNDERSHAFT [*to* LADY BRITOMART]. Biddy—

LADY BRITOMART [*violently*]. Dont dare call me Biddy. Charles Lomax: you are a fool. Adolphus Cusins: you are a Jesuit. Stephen: you are a prig. Barbara: you are a lunatic. Andrew: you are a vulgar tradesman. Now you all know my opinion; and my conscience is clear, at all events [*she sits down with a vehemence that the rug fortunately softens*].

UNDERSHAFT. My dear: you are the incarnation of morality. [*She snorts.*] Your conscience is clear and your duty done when you have called everybody names. Come, Euripides! it is getting late; and we all want to go home. Make up your mind.

CUSINS. Understand this, you old demon—

LADY BRITOMART. Adolphus!

UNDERSHAFT. Let him alone, Biddy. Proceed, Euripides.

CUSINS. You have me in a horrible dilemma. I want Barbara.

UNDERSHAFT. Like all young men, you greatly exaggerate the difference between one young woman and another.

BARBARA. Quite true, Dolly.

CUSINS. I also want to avoid being a rascal.

UNDERSHAFT [*with biting contempt*]. You lust for personal righteousness, for self-approval, for what you call a good conscience, for what Barbara calls salvation, for what I call patronizing people who are not so lucky as yourself.

CUSINS. I do not: all the poet in me recoils from being a good man. But there are things in me that I must reckon with. Pity—

UNDERSHAFT. Pity! The scavenger of misery.

CUSINS. Well, love.

UNDERSHAFT. I know. You love the needy and the outcast: you love the oppressed races, the negro, the Indian ryot, the underdog everywhere. Do you love the Japanese? Do you love the French? Do you love the English?

CUSINS. No. Every true Englishman detests the English. We are the wickedest nation on earth; and our success is a moral horror.

UNDERSHAFT. That is what comes of your gospel of love, is it?

CUSINS. May I not love even my father-in-law?

UNDERSHAFT. Who wants your love, man? By what right do you take the liberty of offering it to me? I will have your due heed and respect, or I will kill you. But your love! Damn your impertinence!

CUSINS [*grinning*]. I may not be able to control my affections, Mac.

UNDERSHAFT. You are fencing, Euripides. You are weakening: your grip is slipping. Come! try your last weapon. Pity and love have broken in your hand: forgiveness is still left.

CUSINS. No: forgiveness is a beggar's refuge. I am with you there: we must pay our debts.

UNDERSHAFT. Well said. Come! you will suit me. Remember the words of Plato.

CUSINS [starting]. Plato! You dare quote Plato to me!

UNDERSHAFT. Plato says, my friend, that society cannot be saved until either the Professors of Greek take to making gunpowder, or else the makers of gunpowder become Professors of Greek.

CUSINS. Oh, tempter, cunning tempter!

UNDERSHAFT. Come! choose, man, choose.

CUSINS. But perhaps Barbara will not marry me if I make the wrong choice.

BARBARA. Perhaps not.

CUSINS [desperately perplexed]. You hear!

BARBARA. Father: do you love nobody?

UNDERSHAFT. I love my best friend.

LADY BRITOMART. And who is that, pray?

UNDERSHAFT. My bravest enemy. That is the man who keeps me up to the mark.

CUSINS. You know, the creature is really a sort of poet in his way. Suppose he is a great man, after all!

UNDERSHAFT. Suppose you stop talking and make up your mind, my young friend.

CUSINS. But you are driving me against my nature. I hate war.

UNDERSHAFT. Hatred is the coward's revenge for being intimidated. Dare you make war on war? Here are the means: my friend Mr Lomax is sitting on them.

LOMAX [springing up]. Oh I say! You dont mean that this thing is loaded, do you? My ownest: come off it.

SARAH [sitting placidly on the shell]. If I am to be blown up, the more thoroughly it is done the better. Dont fuss, Cholly.

LOMAX [to UNDERSHAFT, strongly remonstrant]. Your own daughter, you know!

UNDERSHAFT. So I see. [To CUSINS] Well, my friend, may we expect you here at six tomorrow morning?

CUSINS [firmly]. Not on any account. I will see the whole establishment blown up with its own dynamite before I will get up at five. My hours are healthy, rational hours: eleven to five.

UNDERSHAFT. Come when you please: before a week you will come at six and stay until I turn you out for the sake of your health. [Calling] Bilton! [He turns to LADY BRITOMART, *who rises.*] My dear: let us leave those two young people to themselves for a moment. [BILTON *comes from the shed.*] I am going to take you through the gun cotton shed.

BILTON [*barring the way*]. You cant take anything explosive in here, sir.

LADY BRITOMART. What do you mean? Are you alluding to me?

BILTON [*unmoved*]. No, maam. Mr Undershaft has the other gentleman's matches in his pocket.

LADY BRITOMART [*abruptly*]. Oh! I beg your pardon. [*She goes into the shed.*]

UNDERSHAFT. Quite right, Bilton, quite right: here you are. [*He gives* BILTON *the box of matches.*] Come, Stephen. Come, Charles. Bring Sarah. [*He passes into the shed.*]

[BILTON *opens the box and deliberately drops the matches into the fire-bucket.*]

LOMAX. Oh! I say [BILTON *stolidly hands him the empty box.*] Infernal nonsense! Pure scientific ignorance! [*He goes in.*]

SARAH. Am I all right, Bilton?

BILTON. Youll have to put on list slippers, miss: thats all. Weve got em inside. [*She goes in.*]

STEPHEN [*very seriously to* CUSINS]. Dolly, old fellow, think. Think before you decide. Do you feel that you are a sufficiently practical man? It is a huge undertaking, an enormous responsibility. All this mass of business will be Greek to you.

CUSINS. Oh, I think it will be much less difficult than Greek.

STEPHEN. Well, I just want to say this before I leave you to yourselves. Dont let anything I have said about right and wrong prejudice you against this great chance in life. I have satisfied myself that the business is one of the highest character and a credit to our country. [*Emotionally*] I am very proud of my father. I—[*Unable to proceed, he presses* CUSINS' *hand and goes hastily into the shed, followed by* BILTON.]

[BARBARA *and* CUSINS, *left alone together, look at one another silently.*]

CUSINS. Barbara: I am going to accept this offer.

BARBARA. I thought you would.

CUSINS. You understand, dont you, that I had to decide without consulting you. If I had thrown the burden of the choice on you, you would sooner or later have despised me for it

BARBARA. Yes: I did not want you to sell your soul for me any more than for this inheritance.

CUSINS. It is not the sale of my soul that troubles me: I have sold it too often to care about that. I have sold it for a professorship. I have sold it for an income. I have sold it to escape being imprisoned for refusing to pay taxes for hangmen's ropes and unjust wars and things that I abhor. What is all human conduct but the daily and hourly sale of our souls for trifles? What I am now selling it for is neither money nor position nor comfort, but for reality and for power.

BARBARA. You know that you will have no power, and that he has none.

CUSINS. I know. It is not for myself alone. I want to make power for the world.

BARBARA. I want to make power for the world too; but it must be spiritual power.

CUSINS. I think all power is spiritual: these cannons will not go off by themselves. I have tried to make spiritual power by teaching Greek. But the world can never be really touched by a dead language and a dead civilization. The people must have power; and the people cannot have Greek. Now the power that is made here can be wielded by all men.

BARBARA. Power to burn women's houses down and kill their sons and tear their husbands to pieces.

CUSINS. You cannot have power for good without having power for evil too. Even mother's milk nourishes murderers as well as heroes. This power which only tears men's bodies to pieces has never been so horribly abused as the intellectual power, the imaginative power, the poetic, religious power that can enslave men's souls. As a teacher of Greek I gave the intellectual man weapons against the common man. I now want to give the common man weapons against the intellectual man. I love the common people. I want to arm them against the lawyers, the doctors, the priests, the literary men, the professors, the artists, and the politicians, who, once in authority, are more disastrous and tyrannical than all the fools, rascals, and impostors. I want a power simple enough for common men to use, yet strong enough to force the intellectual oligarchy to use its genius for the general good.

BARBARA. Is there no higher power than that [*pointing to the shell*]?

CUSINS. Yes; but that power can destroy the higher powers just as a tiger can destroy a man: therefore Man must master that power first. I admitted this when the Turks and Greeks were last at war. My best pupil went out to fight for Hellas. My parting gift to him was not a copy of Plato's Republic, but a revolver and a hundred Undershaft cartridges. The blood of every Turk he shot—if he shot any—is on my head as well as on Undershaft's. That act committed me to this place for ever. Your father's challenge has beaten me. Dare I make war on war? I must. I will. And now, is it all over between us?

BARBARA [*touched by his evident dread of her answer*]. Silly baby Dolly! How could it be!

CUSINS [*overjoyed*]. Then you—you—you— Oh for my drum! [*He flourishes imaginary drumsticks.*]

BARBARA [*angered by his levity*]. Take care, Dolly, take care. Oh, if only I could get away from you and from father and from it all! if I could have the wings of a dove and fly away to heaven!

CUSINS. And leave me!

BARBARA. Yes, you, and all the other naughty mischievous children of men. But I cant. I was happy in the Salvation Army for a moment. I escaped from the world into a paradise of enthusiasm and prayer and soul saving; but the moment our money ran short, it all came back to Bodger: it was he who saved our people: he, and the Prince of Darkness, my papa. Undershaft and Bodger: their hands stretch everywhere: when we feed a starving fellow creature, it is with their bread, because there is no other bread; when we tend the sick, it is in the hospitals they endow; if we turn from the churches they build, we must kneel on the stones of the streets they pave. As long as that lasts, there is no getting away from them. Turning our backs on Bodger and Undershaft is turning our backs on life.

CUSINS. I thought you were determined to turn your back on the wicked side of life.

BARBARA. There is no wicked side: life is all one. And I never wanted to shirk my share in whatever evil must be endured,

whether it be sin or suffering. I wish I could cure you of
middle-class ideas, Dolly.

CUSINS [*gasping*]. Middle cl—! A snub! A social snub to me!
from the daughter of a foundling!

BARBARA. That is why I have no class, Dolly: I come straight
out of the heart of the whole people. If I were middle-class
I should turn my back on my father's business; and we
should both live in an artistic drawing room, with you reading the reviews in one corner, and I in the other at the
piano, playing Schumann: both very superior persons, and
neither of us a bit of use. Sooner than that, I would
sweep out the gun cotton shed, or be one of Bodger's bar-
maids. Do you know what would have happened if you had
refused papa's offer?

CUSINS. I wonder!

BARBARA. I should have given you up and married the man
who accepted it. After all, my dear old mother has more
sense than any of you. I felt like her when I saw this place
—felt that I must have it—that never, never, never could I
let it go; only she thought it was the houses and the kitchen
ranges and the linen and china, when it was really all the
human souls to be saved: not weak souls in starved bodies,
sobbing with gratitude for a scrap of bread and treacle, but
fullfed, quarrelsome, snobbish, uppish creatures, all standing on their little rights and dignities, and thinking that my
father ought to be greatly obliged to them for making so
much money for him—and so he ought. That is where salvation is really wanted. My father shall never throw it in
my teeth again that my converts were bribed with bread.
[*She is transfigured.*] I have got rid of the bribe of bread.
I have got rid of the bribe of heaven. Let God's work be
done for its own sake: the work he had to create us to do
because it cannot be done except by living men and women.
When I die, let him be in my debt, not I in his; and let me
forgive him as becomes a woman of my rank.

CUSINS. Then the way of life lies through the factory of
death?

BARBARA. Yes, through the raising of hell to heaven and of
man to God, through the unveiling of an eternal light in the
Valley of The Shadow. [*Seizing him with both hands*] Oh,
did you think my courage would never come back? did you
believe that I was a deserter? that I, who have stood in the
streets, and taken my people to my heart, and talked of the

holiest and greatest things with them, could ever turn back and chatter foolishly to fashionable people about nothing in a drawing room? Never, never, never, never: Major Barbara will die with the colors. Oh! and I have my dear little Dolly boy still; and he has found me my place and my work. Glory Hallelujah! [*She kisses him.*]

CUSINS. My dearest: consider my delicate health. I cannot stand as much happiness as you can.

BARBARA. Yes: it is not easy work being in love with me, is it? But it's good for you. [*She runs to the shed, and calls, childlike*] Mamma! Mamma! [BILTIN *comes out of the shed, followed by* UNDERSHAFT.] I want Mamma.

UNDERSHAFT. She is taking off her list slippers, dear. [*He passes on to* CUSINS.] Well? What does she say?

CUSINS. She has gone right up into the skies.

LADY BRITOMART [*coming from the shed and stopping on the steps, obstructing* SARAH, *who follows with* LOMAX. BARBARA *clutches like a baby at her mother's skirt*]. Barbara: when will **you** learn to be independent and to act and think for yourself? I know as well as possible what that cry of 'Mamma, Mamma,' means. Always running to me!

SARAH [*touching* LADY BRITOMART's *ribs with her finger tips and imitating a bicycle horn*]. Pip! pip!

LADY BRITOMART [*highly indignant*]. How dare you say Pip! pip! to me, Sarah? You are both very naughty children. What do you want, Barbara?

BARBARA. I want a house in the village to live in with Dolly. [*Dragging at the skirt*] Come and tell me which one to take.

UNDERSHAFT [*to* CUSINS]. Six o'clock tomorrow morning, Euripides.

THE END

kindest and sweetest things you think, come over here and
sit there quietly to listen to people about people, acting
in a dreamy mood. Don't never, never, never fall in
love like she will die within a week. Oh no! I have my ears
too. (She hey will! Oh no! It's fun me, my shoes that
by every Cheryl Hazelnut [she Elizabeth].

SARAH. My sister's another my brilliant path's a symbol
of . . . . (hesitates) . . . . .

SARAH (I'm not sure thus) oughtn't have any more . . . .
(If) but it's good for you Elly, now to decorate and eat . . .
CHECK (I'm glad) Alright! (If) it rises out mine, and
BOUGH it be (I'm sorry) . . . I'm a musician.

DR SARAH. But it isn't complicated. Isn't Shippen going who
never . . . to reason loyalty when you are say . . .
Come look too loud . . . with . . . the cup . . .

LADY EDITH (MARY leaning steadily)
says, snivelling, as one who knows with tunnels . . .
don't be like a coward. Are anyone . . . acid . . . kindred. And
will you learn to be independent and to account think, for
yourself? Known well as possible when that cry of things?

DR. Mumma can us, Always running to th . . . . . . .
SARAH Dominating (and mirrors) . . . ? All . . . . . . . .
and nothing a force. You're their parents . . . . . . .
LADY PETHERLY (firmly, indignant) How dare you say things
like to me Sarah! Oh go! high, over naughty children,
what do you want Sarah?

SARAH. I want a house in the country to live in with Cheryl.
(Dreaming of its after Cairo, and tell me which one is
one)

DRESS-SHADE (to Chloe I. St., which romantic-looking
European)

THE END

# JOHN GALSWORTHY

## 1867–1933

JOHN GALSWORTHY dedicated his life and, for the most part, his letters to the pursuit of reform in the late and post Victorian world in which he lived. A compassionate man with an acute sense of injustice, Galsworthy never ceased striving for improved social conditions and fairness to all men, communicating with Winston Churchill and other public figures in support of societal regeneration. The titles of some of his plays—*Strife, Justice, Loyalties*—indicate his generous concern. But while his personal impartiality and sincerity are unassailable, his rank as a dramatist is not; for it is impossible to succeed in the theatre without certain inequities, without cheating in the right places to create moving dramatic conflict.

Galsworthy's drama fails primarily for this reason, that it is overly balanced. With a judiciousness to be commended in his capacities as a lawyer, Galsworthy relentlessly mapped out the plots of his problem plays. The result is that in reading a play like *Loyalties* the modern reader is apt to feel a disturbing similarity to the Ellery Queen midnight movie re runs. There is some suspense, but the clues and clichés are all there for the reader-sleuth to come easily and unemotionally to the correct conclusion. On top of this, Galsworthy slips sometimes into sentimentality.

The importance of Galsworthy's work lies in the themes he treated, which were revolutionary and controversial for the theatre of his time: he dealt with the conflicts between labor and management in *Strife*; with anti-Semitism in *Loyalties*; with prisoner rehabilitation in *Justice*. In our day when civil rights issues and the inadequacies of the great society are the concern of much of our drama, it is worth remembering Galsworthy's courageous beginnings.

# SOME PLATITUDES CONCERNING DRAMA[1]
## (1909)

A DRAMA MUST BE SHAPED so as to have a spire of meaning. Every grouping of life and character has its inherent moral; and the business of the dramatist is so to pose the group as to bring that moral poignantly to the light of day. Such is the moral that exhales from plays like *Lear*, *Hamlet*, and *Macbeth*. But such is not the moral to be found in the great bulk of contemporary Drama. The moral of the average play is now, and probably has always been, the triumph at all costs of a supposed immediate ethical good over a supposed immediate ethical evil.

The vice of drawing these distorted morals has permeated the Drama to its spine; discolored its art, humanity, and significance; infected its creators, actors, audience, critics; too often turned it from a picture into a caricature. A Drama which lives under the shadow of the distorted moral forgets how to be free, fair, and fine—forgets so completely that it often prides itself on having forgotten.

Now, in writing plays, there are, in this matter of the moral, three courses open to the serious dramatist. The first is: To definitely set before the public that which it wishes to have set before it, the views and codes of life by which the public lives and in which it believes. This way is the most common, successful, and popular. It makes the dramatist's position sure, and not too obviously authoritative.

The second course is: To definitely set before the public those views and codes of life by which the dramatist himself lives, those theories in which he himself believes, the more effectively if they are the opposite of what the public wishes

1 "Some Platitudes Concerning Drama" is reprinted with the permission of Charles Scribner's Sons from *The Inn of Tranquility* by John Galsworthy. Copyright 1912 by Charles Scribner's Sons; renewal copyright 1940 Ada Galsworthy.

to have placed before it, presenting them so that the au
dience may swallow them like powder in a spoonful of jam

There is a third course: To set before the public no cu
and-dried codes, but the phenomena of life and characte
selected and combined, *but not distorted,* by the dramatist
outlook, set down without fear, favor, or prejudice, leavin
the public to draw such poor moral as nature may afford
This third method requires a certain detachment; it requires
sympathy with, a love of, and a curiosity as to, things for the
own sake; it requires a far view, together with patient indus
try, for no immediately practical result.

It was once said of Shakespeare that he had never done an
good to anyone, and never would. This, unfortunately, coul
not, in the sense in which the word "good" was then mean
be said of most modern dramatists. In truth, the good tha
Shakespeare did to humanity was of a remote, and, shall w
say, eternal nature; something of the good that men get from
having the sky and the sea to look at. And this partly becaus
he was, in his greater plays at all events, free from the habi
of drawing a distorted moral. Now, the playwright who sup
plies to the public the facts of life distorted by the mora
which it expects, does so that he may do the public what he
considers an immediate good, by fortifying its prejudices
and the dramatist who supplies to the public facts distorted
by his own advanced morality, does so because he consider
that he will at once benefit the public by substituting for
its worn-out ethics, his own. In both cases the advantage the
dramatist hopes to confer on the public is immediate and
practical.

But matters change, and morals change; men remain—and
to set men, and the facts about them, down faithfully, so tha
they draw for us the moral of their natural actions, may also
possibly be of benefit to the community. It is, at all events,
harder then to set men and facts down, as they ought, or
ought not to be. This, however, is not to say that a dramatist
should, or indeed can, keep himself and his temperamental
philosophy out of his work. As a man lives and thinks, so
will he write. But it is certain, that to the making of good
drama, as to the practice of every other art, there must be
brought an almost passionate love of discipline, a white heat
of self-respect, a desire to make the truest, fairest, best thing
in one's power; and that to these must be added an eye

that does not flinch. Such qualities alone will bring to a drama
the selfless character which soaks it with inevitability.

The word "pessimist" is frequently applied to the few
dramatists who have been content to work in this way. It has
been applied, among others, to Euripides, to Shakespeare, to
Ibsen; it will be applied to many in the future. Nothing, however, is more dubious than the way in which these two words
"pessimist" and "optimist" are used; for the optimist appears
to be he who cannot bear the world as it is, and is forced by
his nature to picture it as it ought to be, and the pessimist
one who cannot only bear the world as it is, but loves it
well enough to draw it faithfully. The true lover of the human
race is surely he who can put up with it in all its forms, in
vice as well as in virtue, in defeat no less than in victory; the
true seer is he who sees not only joy but sorrow, the true
painter of human life one who blinks at nothing. It may be
that he is also, incidentally, its true benefactor.

In the whole range of the social fabric there are only two
impartial persons, the scientist and the artist, and under the
latter heading such dramatists as desire to write not only for
today, but for tomorrow, must strive to come.

But dramatists being as they are made—past remedy—
it is perhaps more profitable to examine the various points at
which their qualities and defects are shown.

The plot! A good plot is that sure edifice which slowly rises
out of the interplay of circumstance on temperament, and
temperament on circumstance, within the enclosing atmosphere of an idea. A human being is the best plot there is; it
may be impossible to see why he is a good plot, because the
idea within which he was brought forth cannot be fully
grasped; but it is plain that *he is a good plot*. He is organic.
And so it must be with a good play. Reason alone produces
no good plots; they come by original sin, sure conception,
and instinctive after-power of selecting what benefits the
germ. A bad plot, on the other hand, is simply a row of
stakes, with a character impaled on each—characters who
would have liked to live, but came to untimely grief; who
started bravely, but fell on these stakes, placed beforehand
in a row, and were transfixed one by one, while their ghosts
stride on, squeaking and gibbering, through the play. Whether
these stakes are made of facts or of ideas, according to the
nature of the dramatist who planted them, their effect on the

unfortunate characters is the same; the creatures were bego
ten to be staked, and staked they are! The demand for
good plot, not unfrequently heard, commonly signifies
"Tickle my sensations by stuffing the play with arbitrary ac
ventures, so that I need not be troubled to take the character
seriously. Set the persons of the play to action, regardless c
time, sequence, atmosphere, and probability!"

Now, true dramatic action is what characters do, at onc
contrary, as it were, to expectation, and yet because the
have already done other things. No dramatist should let hi
audience know what is coming; but neither should he suffe
his characters to act without making his audience feel tha
those actions are in harmony with temperament, and aris
from previous known actions, together with the tempera
ments and previous known actions of the other characters i
the play. The dramatist who hangs his characters to his plo
instead of hanging his plot to his characters, is guilty o
cardinal sin.

The dialogue! Good dialogue again is character, marshale
so as continually to stimulate interest or excitement. Th
reason good dialogue is seldom found in plays is merely tha
it is hard to write, for it requires not only a knowledge of wha
interests or excites, but such a feeling for character as bring
misery to the dramatist's heart when his creations speak a
they should not speak—ashes to his mouth when they sa
things for the sake of saying them—disgust when they ar
"smart."

The art of writing true dramatic dialogue is an auster
art, denying itself all license, grudging every sentence devote
to the mere machinery of the play, suppressing all jokes an
epigrams severed from character, relying for fun and patho
on the fun and tears of life. From start to finish good dialogu
is handmade, like good lace; clear, of fine texture, furtherin
with each thread the harmony and strength of a design t
which all must be subordinated.

But good dialogue is also spiritual action. In so far as th
dramatist divorces his dialogue from spiritual action—that i
to say, from progress of events, or toward events which ar
significant of character—he is stultifying $\tau o$ $\delta\rho\alpha\mu\alpha$ the thing
done; he may make pleasing disquisitions, he is not making
drama. And in so far as he twists character to suit his mora
or his plot, he is neglecting a first principle, that truth t
Nature which alone invests art with handmade quality.

The dramatist's license, in fact, ends with his design. In conception alone he is free. He may take what character or group of characters he chooses, see them with what eyes, knit them with what idea, within the limits of his temperament; but once taken, seen, and knitted, he is bound to treat them like a gentleman, with the tenderest consideration of their mainsprings. Take care of character; action and dialogue will take care of themselves! The true dramatist gives full rein to his temperament in the scope and nature of his subject; having once selected subject and characters, he is just, gentle, restrained, neither gratifying his lust for praise at the expense of his offspring, nor using them as puppets to flout his audience. Being himself the nature that brought them forth, he guides them in the course predestined at their conception. So only have they a chance of defying Time, which is always lying in wait to destroy the false, topical, or fashionable, all —in a word—that is not based on the permanent elements of human nature. The perfect dramatist rounds up his characters and facts within the ring-fence of a dominant idea which fulfills the craving of his spirit; having got them there, he suffers them to live their own lives.

Plot, action, character, dialogue! But there is yet another subject for a platitude. Flavor! An impalpable quality, less easily captured than the scent of a flower, the peculiar and most essential attribute of any work of art! It is the thin, poignant spirit which hovers up out of a play, and is as much its differentiating essence as is caffeine of coffee. Flavor, in fine, is the spirit of the dramatist projected into his work in a state of volatility, so that no one can exactly lay hands on it, here, there, or anywhere. This distinctive essence of a play, marking its brand, is the one thing at which the dramatist cannot work, for it is outside his consciousness. A man may have many moods, he has but one spirit; and this spirit he communicates in some subtle, unconscious way to all his work. It waxes and wanes with the currents of his vitality, but no more alters than a chestnut changes into an oak.

For, in truth, dramas are very like unto trees, springing from seedlings, shaping themselves inevitably in accordance with the laws fast hidden within themselves, drinking sustenance from the earth and air, and in conflict with the natural forces round them. So they slowly come to full growth, until warped, stunted, or risen to fair and gracious height, they stand open to all the winds. And the trees that spring from each dramatist are of different race; he is the spirit of his own sacred grove, into which no stray tree can by any chance enter.

One more platitude. It is not unfashionable to pit one form of drama against another—holding up the naturalistic to the disadvantage of the epic; the epic to the belittlement of the fantastic; the fantastic to the detriment of the naturalistic. Little purpose is thus served. The essential meaning, truth, beauty, and irony of things may be revealed under all these forms. Vision over life and human nature can be as keen and just, the revelation as true, inspiring, delight-giving, and thought-provoking, whatever fashion be employed—it is simply a question of doing it well enough to uncover the kernel of the nut. Whether the violet come from Russia, from Parma, or from England, matters little. Close by the Greek temples at Paestum there are violets that seem redder, and sweeter, than any ever seen—as though they have sprung up out of the footprints of some old pagan goddess; but under the April sun, in a Devonshire lane, the little blue scentless violets capture every bit as much of the spring. And so it is with drama—no matter what its form—it need only be the "real thing," need only have caught some of the precious fluids, revelation, or delight, and imprisoned them within a chalice to which we may put our lips and continually drink.

And yet, starting from this last platitude, one may perhaps be suffered to speculate as to the particular forms that our renascent drama is likely to assume. For our drama is renascent, and nothing will stop its growth. It is not renascent because this or that man is writing, but because of a new spirit. A spirit that is no doubt in part the gradual outcome of the impact on our home-grown art of Russian, French, and Scandinavian influences, but which in the main rises from an awakened humanity in the conscience of our time.

What, then, are to be the main channels down which the renascent English drama will float in the coming years? It is more than possible that these main channels will come to be two in number and situate far apart.

The one will be the broad and clear-cut channel of naturalism, down which will course a drama poignantly shaped, and inspired with high intention, but faithful to the seething and multiple life around us, drama such as some are inclined to term photographic, deceived by a seeming simplicity into orgetfulness of the old proverb, *"Ars est celare artem,"* and oblivious of the fact that, to be vital, to grip, such drama is in every respect as dependent on imagination, construction, selection, and elimination—the main laws of artistry—as ever was the romantic or rhapsodic play. The question of naturalistic technique will bear, indeed, much more study than has yet been given to it. The aim of the dramatist employing it is obviously to create such an illusion of actual life passing on the stage as to compel the spectator to pass through an experience of his own, to think, and talk, and move with the people he sees thinking, talking, and moving in front of him. A false phrase, a single word out of tune or time, will destroy that illusion and spoil the surface as surely as a stone heaved into a still pool shatters the image seen there. But this is only the beginning of the reason why the naturalistic is the most exacting and difficult of all techniques. It is easy enough to *reproduce* the exact conversation and movements of persons, in a room; it is desperately hard to *produce* the perfectly natural conversion and movements of those persons when each natural phrase spoken and each natural movement made has not only to contribute toward the growth and perfection of a drama's soul, but also to be a revelation, phrase by phrase, movement by movement, of essential traits of character. To put it another way, naturalistic art, when alive, indeed to be alive at all, is simply the art of manipulating a procession of most delicate symbols. Its service is the swaying and focusing of men's feelings and thought in the various departments of human life. It will be like a steady lamp, held up from time to time, in whose light things will be seen for a space clearly and in due proportion, freed from the mists of prejudice and partisanship.

And the other of these two main channels will, I think, be a twisting and delicious stream, which will bear on its breast new barques of poetry, shaped, it may be, like prose, but a prose incarnating through its fantasy and symbolism all the deeper aspirations, yearning, doubts, and mysterious stirrings of the human spirit; a poetic prose drama, emotionalizing us by its diversity and purity of form and invention, and whose province will be to disclose the elemental soul of man and the forces of Nature, not perhaps as the old tragedies disclosed them, not necessarily in the epic mood, but always with beauty and in the spirit of discovery.

Such will, I think, be the two vital forms of our drama in

the coming generation. And between these two forms there must be no crude unions; they are too far apart, the cross is too violent. For, where there is a seeming blend of lyricism and naturalism, it will on examination be found, I think, to exist only in plays whose subjects or settings—as in Synge's *Playboy of the Western World*, or in Mr. Masefield's *Nan*— are so removed from our ken that we cannot really tell, and therefore do not care, whether an absolute illusion is maintained. The poetry which may and should exist in naturalistic drama, can only be that of perfect rightness of proportion, rhythm, shape—the poetry, in fact, that lies in all vital things. It is the ill-mating of forms that has killed a thousand plays. We want no more bastard drama; no more attempts to dress out the simple dignity of everyday life in the peacock's feathers of false lyricism; no more straw-stuffed heroes or heroines; no more rabbits and goldfish from the conjurer's pockets, nor any limelight. Let us have starlight, moonlight, sunlight, and the light of our own self-respects.

# *L O Y A L T I E S*

## by John Galsworthy

### *1 9 2 2*

# LOYALTIES[1]

## CHARACTERS

CHARLES WINSOR, *owner of Meldon Court, near Newmarket*
LADY ADELA, *his wife*
FERDINAND DE LEVIS, *young, rich, and new*
TREISURE, *Winsor's butler*
GENERAL CANYNGE, *a racing oracle*
MARGARET ORME, *a society girl*
CAPTAIN RONALD DANCY, D.S.O., *retired*
MABEL, *his wife*
INSPECTOR DEDE, *of the County Constabulary*
ROBERT, *Winsor's footman*
CONSTABLE, *attendant on Dede*
AUGUSTUS BORRING, *a clubman*
LORD ST ERTH, *a peer of the realm*
A FOOTMAN, *of the club*
MAJOR COLFORD, *a brother officer of Dancy's*
EDWARD GRAVITER, *a solicitor*
A YOUNG CLERK, *of Twisden & Graviter's*
GILMAN, *a large grocer*
JACOB TWISDEN, *senior partner of Twisden & Graviter's*
RICARDOS, *an Italian, in wine*

[1] *Loyalties* is reprinted with the permission of Charles Scribner's Son's. (Copyright 1922 Charles Scribner's Sons; renewal copyright 1950 Ada Galsworthy.)

## ACT ONE

*Scene 1.* CHARLES WINSOR's dressing-room at Meldon Court, near Newmarket, of a night in early October.

*Scene 2.* DE LEVIS's bedroom at Meldon Court, a few minutes later.

## ACT TWO

*Scene 1.* The card room of a London club between four and five in the afternoon, three weeks later.

*Scene 2.* The sitting-room of the DANCYS' flat, the following morning.

## ACT THREE

*Scene 1.* Old MR JACOB TWISDEN's room at Twisden & Graviter's in Lincoln's Inn Fields, at four in the afternoon, three months later.

*Scene 2.* The same, next morning at half-past ten.

*Scene 3.* The sitting-room of the DANCYS' flat, an hour later.

# ACT ONE

## Scene 1

*The dressing-room of* CHARLES WINSOR, *owner of Meldon Court, near Newmarket; about eleven-thirty at night. The room has pale grey walls, unadorned; the curtains are drawn over a window Back Left Centre. A bed lies along the wall, Left. An open door, Right Back, leads into* LADY ADELA'S *bedroom; a door, Right Forward, into a long corridor, on to which abut rooms in a row, the whole length of the house's left wing.* WINSOR'S *dressing-table, with a light over it, is Stage Right of the curtained window. Pyjamas are laid out on the bed, which is turned back. Slippers are handy, and all the usual gear of a well-appointed bed-dressing-room.* CHARLES WINSOR, *a tall, fair, good-looking man about thirty-eight, is taking off a smoking jacket.*

WINSOR. Hallo! Adela!

VOICE OF LADY ADELA [*from her bedroom*]. Hallo!

WINSOR. In bed?

VOICE OF LADY ADELA. No. [*She appears in the doorway in under-garment and a wrapper. She, too, is fair, about thirty-five, rather delicious, and suggestive of porcelain.*]

WINSOR. Win at Bridge?

LADY ADELA. No fear.

WINSOR. Who did?

LADY ADELA. Lord St Erth and Ferdy De Levis.

WINSOR. That young man has too much luck—the young bounder won two races to-day; and he's as rich as Crœsus.

LADY ADELA. Oh! Charlie, he did look so exactly as if he'd sold me a carpet when I was paying him.

WINSOR. [*changing into slippers*]. His father did sell carpets, wholesale, in the City.

[ 225 ]

LADY ADELA. Really? And you say I haven't intuition! [*With a finger on her lips*] Morison's in there.

WINSOR. [*motioning towards the door, which she shuts*]. Ronny Dancy took a tenner off him, anyway, before dinner.

LADY ADELA. No! How?

WINSOR. Standing jump on to a bookcase four feet high. De Levis had to pay up, and sneered at him for making money by parlour tricks. That young Jew gets himself disliked.

LADY ADELA. Aren't you rather prejudiced?

WINSOR. Not a bit. I like Jews. That's not against him—rather the contrary these days. But he pushes himself. The General tells me he's deathly keen to get into the Jockey Club. [*Taking off his tie*] It's amusing to see him trying to get round old St Erth.

LADY ADELA. If Lord St Erth and General Canynge backed him he'd get in if he *did* sell carpets!

WINSOR. He's got some pretty good horses. [*Taking off his waistcoat*] Ronny Dancy's on his bones again, I'm afraid. He had a bad day. When a chap takes to doing parlour stunts for a bet—it's a sure sign. What made him chuck the Army?

LADY ADELA. He says it's too dull, now there's no fighting.

WINSOR. Well, he can't exist on backing losers.

LADY ADELA. Isn't it just like him to get married now? He really is the most reckless person.

WINSOR. Yes. He's a queer chap. I've always liked him, but I've never quite made him out. What do you think of his wife?

LADY ADELA. Nice child; awfully gone on him.

WINSOR. Is *he*?

LADY ADELA. Quite indecently—both of them. [*Nodding towards the wall, Left*] They're next door.

WINSOR. Who's beyond them?

LADY ADELA. De Levis; and Margaret Orme at the end. Charlie, do you realise that the bathroom out there has to wash those four?

WINSOR. I know.

LADY ADELA. Your grandfather was crazy when he built this wing; six rooms in a row with balconies like an hotel, and only one bath—if we hadn't put ours in.

WINSOR. [*looking at his watch*]. Half-past eleven. [*Yawns.*] Newmarket always makes me sleepy. You're keeping Mori-

son up. [LADY ADELA *goes to the door, blowing a kiss.*
CHARLES *goes up to his dressing-table and begins to brush
his hair, sprinkling on essence. There is a knock on the
corridor door.*] Come in. [DE LEVIS *enters, clad in pyjamas
and flowered dressing-gown. He is a dark, good-looking,
rather Eastern young man. His face is long and disturbed.*]
Hallo! De Levis! Anything I can do for you?

DE LEVIS [*in a voice whose faint exoticism is broken by a
vexed excitement*]. I say, I'm awfully sorry, Winsor, but I
thought I'd better tell you at once. I've just had—er—
rather a lot of money stolen.

WINSOR. What! [*There is something of outrage in his tone
and glance, as who should say*: "*In my house?*"] How
do you mean *stolen?*

DE LEVIS. I put it under my pillow and went to have a bath;
when I came back it was gone.

WINSOR. Good Lord! How much?

DE LEVIS. Nearly a thousand—nine hundred and seventy, I
think.

WINSOR. Phew! [*Again the faint tone of outrage, that a man
should have so much money about him.*]

DE LEVIS. I sold my Rosemary filly to-day on the course to
Kentman the bookie, and he paid me in notes.

WINSOR. What? That weed Dancy gave you in the Spring?

DE LEVIS. Yes. But I tried her pretty high the other day; and
she's in the Cambridgeshire. I was only out of my room a
quarter of an hour, and I locked my door.

WINSOR [*again outraged*]. You *locked*——

DE LEVIS. [*not seeing the fine shade*]. Yes, and had the key
here. [*He taps his pocket.*] Look here! [*He holds out a
pocket-book.*] It's been stuffed with my shaving papers.

WINSOR [*between feeling that such things don't happen, and
a sense that he will have to clear it up*]. This is damned
awkward, De Levis.

DE LEVIS. [*with steel in his voice*]. Yes. I should like it back.

WINSOR. Have you got the numbers of the notes?

DE LEVIS. No.

WINSOR. What were they?

DE LEVIS. One hundred, three fifties, and the rest tens and
fives.

WINSOR. What d'you want me to do?

DE LEVIS. Unless there's anybody you think——

WINSOR [*eyeing him*]. Is it likely?

DE LEVIS. Then I think the police ought to see my room. It's a lot of money.

WINSOR. Good Lord! We're not in Town; there'll be nobody nearer than Newmarket at this time of night—four miles.

[*The door from the bedroom is suddenly opened and* LADY ADELA *appears. She has on a lace cap over her finished hair, and the wrapper.*]

LADY ADELA [*closing the door*]. What is it? Are you ill, Mr De Levis?

WINSOR. Worse; he's had a lot of money stolen. Nearly a thousand pounds.

LADY ADELA. Gracious! Where?

DE LEVIS. From under my pillow, Lady Adela—my door was locked—I was in the bathroom.

LADY ADELA. But how fearfully thrilling!

WINSOR. Thrilling! What's to be done? He wants it back.

LADY ADELA. Of course! [*With sudden realisation*] Oh! But — Oh! it's quite too unpleasant!

WINSOR. Yes! What am I to do? Fetch the servants out of their rooms? Search the grounds? It'll make the devil of a scandal.

DE LEVIS. Who's next to me?

LADY ADELA [*coldly*]. Oh! Mr De Levis!

WINSOR. Next to you? The Dancys on this side, and Miss Orme on the other. What's that to do with it?

DE LEVIS. They may have heard something.

WINSOR. Let's get them. But Dancy was downstairs when I came up. Get Morison, Adela! No, look here! When *was* this exactly? Let's have as many alibis as we can.

DE LEVIS. Within the last twenty minutes, certainly.

WINSOR. How long has Morison been up with you?

LADY ADELA. I came up at eleven, and rang for her at once.

WINSOR [*looking at his watch*]. Half an hour. Then she's all right. Send her for Margaret and the Dancys—there's nobody else in this wing. No; send her to bed. We don't want gossip. D'you mind going yourself, Adela?

LADY ADELA. Consult General Canynge, Charlie.

WINSOR. Right. Could you get him too? D'you really want the police, De Levis?

DE LEVIS [*stung by the faint contempt in his tone of voice*]. Yes, I do.

WINSOR. Then, look here, dear! Slip into my study and telephone to the police at Newmarket. There'll be somebody there; they're sure to have drunks. I'll have Treasure up, and speak to him. [*He rings the bell.*]

[LADY ADELA *goes out into her room and closes the door.*]

WINSOR. Look here, De Levis! This isn't an hotel. It's the sort of thing that doesn't happen in a decent house. Are you sure you're not mistaken, and didn't have them stolen on the course?

DE LEVIS. Absolutely. I counted them just before putting them under my pillow; then I locked the door and had the key here. There's only one door, you know.

WINSOR. How was your window?

DE LEVIS. Open.

WINSOR [*drawing back the curtains of his own window*]. You've got a balcony like this. Any sign of a ladder or anything?

DE LEVIS. No.

WINSOR. It must have been done from the window, unless someone had a skeleton key. Who knew you'd got that money? Where did Kentman pay you?

DE LEVIS. Just round the corner in the further paddock.

WINSOR. Anybody about?

DE LEVIS. Oh, yes!

WINSOR. Suspicious?

DE LEVIS. I didn't notice anything.

WINSOR. You must have been marked down and followed here.

DE LEVIS. How would they know my room?

WINSOR. Might have got it somehow. [*A knock from the corridor.*] Come in.

[TREASURE, *the butler, appears, a silent, grave man of almost supernatural conformity.* DE LEVIS *gives him a quick, hard look, noted and resented by* WINSOR.]

TREASURE [*to* WINSOR]. Yes, sir?

WINSOR. Who valets Mr De Levis?

TRESISURE. Robert, sir.

WINSOR. When was he up last?

TREASURE. In the ordinary course of things, about ten o'clock, sir.

WINSOR. When did he go to bed?

TREISURE. I dismissed at eleven.

WINSOR. But did he go?

TREISURE. To the best of my knowledge. Is there anything *I* can do, sir?

WINSOR [*disregarding a sign from* DE LEVIS]. Look here, Treisure, Mr De Levis has had a large sum of money taken from his bedroom within the last half hour.

TREISURE. Indeed, sir!

WINSOR. Robert's quite all right, isn't he?

TREISURE. He is, sir.

DE LEVIS. How do you know?

[TREISURE'S *eyes rest on* DE LEVIS.]

TREISURE. I am a pretty good judge of character, sir, if you'll excuse me.

WINSOR. Look here, De Levis, eighty or ninety notes must have been pretty bulky. You didn't have them on you at dinner?

DE LEVIS. No.

WINSOR. Where did you put them?

DE LEVIS. In a boot, and the boot in my suitcase, and locked it.

[TREISURE *smiles faintly*.]

WINSOR [*again slightly outraged by such precautions in his house*]. And you found it locked—and took them from there to put under your pillow?

DE LEVIS. Yes.

WINSOR. Run your mind over things, Treisure—has any stranger been about?

TREISURE. No, sir.

WINSOR. This seems to have happened between 11.15 and 11.30. Is that right? [DE LEVIS *nods*.] Any noise—anything outside—anything suspicious anywhere?

TREISURE [*running his mind—very still*]. No, sir.

WINSOR. What time did you shut up?

TREISURE. I should say about eleven-fifteen, sir. As soon as Major Colford and Captain Dancy had finished billiards. What was Mr De Levis doing out of his room, if I may ask, sir?

WINSOR. Having a bath; with his room locked and the key in his pocket.

TREISURE. Thank you, sir.

DE LEVIS [*conscious of indefinable suspicion*]. Damn it! What do you mean? I *was*.

TREISURE. I beg your pardon, sir.

WINSOR [*concealing a smile*]. Look here, Treisure, it's infernally awkward for everybody.

TREISURE. It is, sir.

WINSOR. What do you suggest?

TREISURE. The proper thing, sir, I suppose, would be a cordon and a complete search—in our interests.

WINSOR. I entirely refuse to suspect anybody.

TREISURE. But if Mr De Levis feels otherwise, sir?

DE LEVIS [*stammering*]. I? All I know is—the money was there, and it's gone.

WINSOR [*compunctious*]. Quite! It's pretty sickening for you. But so it is for anybody else. However, we must do our best to get it back for you.

[*A knock on the door.*]

WINSOR. Hallo! [TREISURE *opens the door, and* GENERAL CANYNGE *enters.*] Oh! It's you, General. Come in. Adela's told you?

[GENERAL CANYNGE *nods. He is a slim man of about sixty, very well preserved, intensely neat and self-contained, and still in evening dress. His eyelids droop slightly, but his eyes are keen and his expression astute.*]

WINSOR. Well, General, what's the first move?

CANYNGE [*lifting his eyebrows*]. Mr De Levis presses the matter?

DE LEVIS [*flicked again*]. Unless you think it's too plebeian of me, General Canynge—a thousand pounds.

CANYNGE [*drily*]. Just so! Then we must wait for the police, Winsor. Lady Adela has got through to them. What height are these rooms from the ground, Treisure?

TREISURE. Twenty-three feet from the terrace, sir.

CANYNGE. Any ladders near?

TREISURE. One in the stables, sir, very heavy. No others within three hundred yards.

CANYNGE. Just slip down, and see whether that's been moved.

TREISURE. Very good, General. [*He goes out.*]

DE LEVIS [*uneasily*]. Of course, he—I suppose you——

WINSOR. We do.

CANYNGE. You had better leave this in our hands, De Levis.

DE LEVIS. Certainly; only, the way he——

WINSOR [*curtly*]. Treisure has been here since he was a boy. I should as soon suspect myself.

DE LEVIS [*looking from one to the other—with sudden anger*]. You seem to think——! What was I to do? Take it lying down and let whoever it is get clear off? I suppose it's natural to want my money back?

[CANYNGE *looks at his nails;* WINSOR *out of the window.*]

WINSOR [*turning*]. Of course, De Levis!

DE LEVIS [*sullenly*]. Well, I'll go to my room. When the police come, perhaps you'll let me know. [*He goes out.*]

WINSOR. Phew! Did you ever see such a dressing-gown?

[*The door is opened.* LADY ADELA *and* MARGARET ORME *come in. The latter is a vivid young lady of about twenty-five in a vivid wrapper; she is smoking a cigarette.*]

LADY ADELA. I've told the Dancys—she was in bed. And I got through to Newmarket, Charles, and Inspector Dede is coming like the wind on a motor cycle.

MARGARET. Did he say "like the wind," Adela? He must have imagination. Isn't this gorgeous? Poor little Ferdy!

WINSOR [*vexed*]. You might take it seriously, Margaret; it's pretty beastly for us all. What time did *you* come up?

MARGARET. I came up with Adela. Am I suspected, Charles? How thrilling!

WINSOR. Did you hear anything?

MARGARET. Only little Ferdy splashing.

WINSOR. And saw nothing?

MARGARET. Not even that, alas!

LADY ADELA [*with a finger held up*]. Leste! Un peu leste! Oh! Here are the Dancys. Come in, you two!

[MABLE *and* RONALD DANCY *enter. She is a pretty young woman with bobbed hair, fortunately, for she has just got out of bed, and is in her nightgown and a wrapper.* DANCY *is in his smoking jacket. He has a pale, determined face with high cheekbones, small, deep-set dark eyes, reddish crisp hair, and looks like a horseman.*]

WINSOR. Awfully sorry to disturb you, Mrs Dancy; but I suppose you and Ronny haven't heard anything. De Levis's room is just beyond Ronny's dressing-room, you know.

MABEL. I've been asleep nearly half an hour, and Ronny's only just come up.

CANYNGE. Did you happen to look out of your window, Mrs Dancy?

MABEL. Yes. I stood there quite five minutes.

CANYNGE. When?

MABEL. Just about eleven, I should think. It was raining hard then.

CANYNGE. Yes, it's just stopped. You saw nothing?

MABEL. No.

DANCY. What time does he say the money was taken?

WINSOR. Between the quarter and half past. He'd locked his door and had the key with him.

MARGARET. How quaint! Just like an hotel. Does he put his boots out?

LADY ADELA. Don't be so naughty, Meg.

CANYNGE. When exactly did *you* come up, Dancy?

DANCY. About ten minutes ago. I'd only just got into my dressing-room before Lady Adela came. I've been writing letters in the hall since Colford and I finished billiards.

CANYNGE. You weren't up for anything in between?

DANCY. No.

MARGARET. The mystery of the grey room.

DANCY. Oughtn't the grounds to be searched for footmarks?

CANYNGE. That's for the police.

DANCY. The deuce! Are they coming?

CANYNGE. Directly. [*A knock*] Yes? [TREASURE *enters.*] Well?

TREASURE. The ladder has not been moved, General. There isn't a sign.

WINSOR. All right. Get Robert up, but don't say anything to him. By the way, we're expecting the police.

TREASURE. I trust they will not find a mare's nest, sir, if I may say so. [*He goes.*]

WINSOR. De Levis has got wrong with Treasure. [*Suddenly*] But, I say, what would any of us have done if *we'd* been in his shoes?

MARGARET. A thousand pounds? I can't even conceive having it.

DANCY. We probably shouldn't have found it out.

LADY ADELA. No—but if we had.

DANCY. Come to you—as he did.

WINSOR. Yes; but there's a way of doing things.

CANYNGE. We shouldn't have wanted the police.

MARGARET. No. That's it. The hotel touch.

LADY ADELA. Poor young man; I think we're rather hard on him.

WINSOR. He sold that weed you gave him, Dancy, to Kentman, the bookie, and these were the proceeds.

DANCY. Oh!

WINSOR. He'd tried her high, he said.

DANCY [*grimly*]. He would.

MABEL. Oh! Ronny, what bad luck!

WINSOR. He must have been followed here. [*At the window*] After rain like that, there ought to be footmarks.

[*The splutter of a motor cycle is heard.*]

MARGARET. Here's the wind!

WINSOR. What's the move now, General?

CANYNGE. You and I had better see the Inspector in De Levis's room, Winsor. [*To the others*] If you'll all be handy, in case he wants to put questions for himself.

MARGARET. I hope he'll want me; it's just too thrilling.

DANCY. I hope he won't want me; I'm dog-tired. Come on, Mabel. [*He puts his arm in his wife's.*]

CANYNGE. Just a minute, Charles.

[*He draws close to* WINSOR *as the others are departing to their rooms.*]

WINSOR. Yes, General?

CANYNGE. We must be careful with this Inspector fellow. If he pitches hastily on somebody in the house it'll be very disagreeable.

WINSOR. By Jove! It *will*.

CANYNGE. We don't want to rouse any ridiculous suspicion.

WINSOR. Quite. [*A knock*] Come in!

[TREISURE *enters.*]

TREISURE. Inspector Dede, sir.

WINSOR. Show him in.

TREISURE. Robert is in readiness, sir; but I could swear he knows nothing about it.

WINSOR. All right.

TREISURE *reopens the door, and says:* "Come in, please." [*The* INSPECTOR *enters, blue, formal, moustachioed, with a peaked cap in his hand.*]

WINSOR. Good-evening, Inspector. Sorry to have brought you
   out at this time of night.

INSPECTOR. Good evenin', sir. Mr Winsor? You're the owner
   here, I think?

WISNOR. Yes. General Canynge.

INSPECTOR. Good evenin', General. I understand, a large sum
   of money?

WINSOR. Yes. Shall we go straight to the room it was taken
   from? One of my guests, Mr De Levis. It's the third room
   on the left.

CANYNGE. We've not been in there yet, Inspector; in fact,
   we've done nothing, except to find out that the stable
   ladder has not been moved. We haven't even searched the
   grounds.

INSPECTOR. Right, sir; I've brought a man with me.

[*They go out.*]

CURTAIN. *Interval of a Minute.*


## Scene 2[2]

*The bedroom of* DE LEVIS *is the same in shape as* WINSOR'S
*dressing-room, except that there is only one door—to the
corridor. The furniture, however, is differently arranged; a
small four-poster bedstead stands against the wall, Right
Back, jutting into the room. A chair, on which* DE LEVIS'S
*clothes are thrown, stands at its foot. There is a dressing-
table against the wall to the left of the open windows, where
the curtains are drawn back and a stone balcony is seen.
Against the wall to the right of the window is a chest of
drawers, and a washstand is against the wall, Left. On a
small table to the right of the bed an electric reading lamp
is turned up, and there is a light over the dressing-table.
The* INSPECTOR *is standing plumb centre looking at the bed,
and* DE LEVIS *by the back of the chair at the foot of the
bed.* WINSOR *and* CANYNGE *are close to the door, Right Forward.*

   [2] The same set is used for this scene, with the different arrangement
of furniture, as specified.

INSPECTOR [*finishing a note*]. Now, sir, if this is the room as you left if for your bath, just show us exactly what you did after takin' the pocket-book from the suit case. Where was that, by the way?

DE LEVIS [*pointing*]. Where it is now—under the dressing-table. [*He comes forward to the front of the chair, opens the pocket-book, goes through the pretence of counting his shaving papers, closes the pocket-book, takes it to the head of the bed and slips it under the pillow. Makes the motion of taking up his pyjamas, crosses below the* INSPECTOR *to the washstand, takes up a bath sponge, crosses to the door, takes out the key, opens the door.*]

INSPECTOR [*writing*]. We now have the room as it was when the theft was committed. Reconstruct accordin' to 'uman nature, gentlemen—assumin' the thief to be in the room, what would he try first?—the clothes, the dressin'-table, the suit case, the chest of drawers, and last the bed. [*He moves accordingly, examining the glass on the dressing-table, the surface of the suit cases, and the handles of the drawers, with a spy-glass, for finger-marks.*]

CANYNGE [*sotto voce to* WINSOR]. The order would have been just the other way.

[*The* INSPECTOR *goes on hands and knees and examines the carpet between the window and the bed.*]

DE LEVIS. Can I come in again?

INSPECTOR [*standing up*]. Did you open the window, sir, or was it open when you first came in?

DE LEVIS. I opened it.

INSPECTOR. Drawin' the curtains back first?

DE LEVIS. Yes.

INSPECTOR [*sharply*]. Are you sure there was nobody in the room already?

DE LEVIS [*taken aback*]. I don't know. I never thought. I didn't look under the bed, if you mean that.

INSPECTOR [*jotting*]. Did not look under bed. Did you look under it after the theft?

DE LEVIS. No. I didn't.

INSPECTOR. Ah! Now, what *did* you do after you came back from your bath? Just give us that precisely.

DE LEVIS. Locked the door and left the key in. Put back my sponge, and took off my dressing-gown and put it there.

[*He points to the footrails of the bed.*] Then I drew the curtains, again.

INSPECTOR. Shutting the window?

DE LEVIS. No. I got into bed, felt for my watch to see the time. My hand struck the pocket-book, and somehow it felt thinner. I took it out, looked into it, and found the notes gone, and these shaving papers instead.

INSPECTOR. Let me have a look at those, sir. [*He applies the spy-glasses.*] And then?

DE LEVIS. I think I just sat on the bed.

INSPECTOR. Thinkin' and cursin' a bit, I suppose. Ye-es?

DE LEVIS. Then I put on my dressing-gown and went straight to Mr Winsor.

INSPECTOR. Not lockin' the door?

DE LEVIS. No.

INSPECTOR. Exactly. [*With a certain finality*] Now, sir, what time did you come up?

DE LEVIS. About eleven.

INSPECTOR. Precise, if you can give it me.

DE LEVIS. Well, I *know* it was eleven-fifteen when I put my watch under my pillow, before I went to the bath, and I suppose I'd been about a quarter of an hour undressing. I should say after eleven, if anything.

INSPECTOR. Just undressin'? Didn't look over your bettin' book?

DE LEVIS. No.

INSPECTOR. No prayers or anything?

DE LEVIS. No.

INSPECTOR. Pretty slippy with your undressin' as a rule?

DE LEVIS. Yes. Say five past eleven.

INSPECTOR. Mr Winsor, what time did the gentleman come to you?

WINSOR. Half-past eleven.

INSPECTOR. How do you fix that, sir?

WINSOR. I'd just looked at the time, and told my wife to send her maid off.

INSPECTOR. Then we've got it fixed between 11.15 and 11.30. [*Jots*] Now, sir, before we go further I'd like to see your butler and the footman that valets this gentleman.

WINSOR [*with distaste*]. Very well, Inspector; only—my butler has been with us from a boy.

INSPECTOR. Quite so. This is just clearing the ground, sir.

WINSOR. General, d'you mind touching that bell?

[CANYNGE *rings a bell by the bed*.]

INSPECTOR. Well, gentlemen, there are four possibilities. Either the thief was here all the time, waiting under the bed, and slipped out after this gentleman had gone to Mr Winsor. Or he came in with a key that fits the lock; and I'll want to see all the keys in the house. Or he came in with a skeleton key and out by the window, probably droppin' from the balcony. Or he came in by the window with a rope or ladder and out the same way. [*Pointing*] There's a footmark here from a big boot which has been out of doors since it rained.

CANYNGE. Inspector—you er—walked up to the window when you first came into the room.

INSPECTOR [*stiffly*]. I had not overlooked that, General.

CANYNGE. Of course.

[*A knock on the door relieves a certain tension*.]

WINSOR. Come in.

[*The footman* ROBERT, *a fresh-faced young man, enters, followed by* TREISURE.]

INSPECTOR. You valet Mr—Mr De Levis, I think?

ROBERT. Yes, sir.

INSPECTOR. At what time did you take his clothes and boots?

ROBERT. Ten o'clock, sir.

INSPECTOR [*with a pounce*]. Did you happen to look under his bed?

ROBERT. No, sir.

INSPECTOR. Did you come up again, to bring the clothes back?

ROBERT. No, sir; they're still downstairs.

INSPECTOR. Did you come up again for anything?

ROBERT. No, sir.

INSPECTOR. What time did you go to bed?

ROBERT. Just after eleven, sir.

INSPECTOR [*scrutinising him*]. Now, be careful. Did you go to bed at all?

ROBERT. No, sir.

INSPECTOR. Then why did you say you did? There's been a

theft here, and anything you say may be used against you.

ROBERT. Yes, sir. I meant, I went to my room.

INSPECTOR. Where is your room?

ROBERT. On the ground floor, at the other end of the right wing, sir.

WINSOR. It's the extreme end of the house from this, Inspector. He's with the other two footmen.

INSPECTOR. Were you there alone?

ROBERT. No, sir. Thomas and Frederick was there too.

TREISURE. That's right; I've seen them.

INSPECTOR [holding up his hand for silence]. Were you out of the room again after you went in?

ROBERT. No, sir.

INSPECTOR. What were you doing, if you didn't go to bed?

ROBERT [to WINSOR]. Beggin' your pardon, sir, we were playin' Bridge.

INSPECTOR. Very good. You can go. I'll see them later on.

ROBERT. Yes, sir. They'll say the same as me. [He goes out, leaving a smile on the face of all except the INSPECTOR and DE LEVIS.]

INSPECTOR [sharply]. Call him back.

[TREISURE calls "Robert," and the FOOTMAN re-enters.]

ROBERT. Yes, sir?

INSPECTOR. Did you notice anything particular about Mr De Levis's clothes?

ROBERT. Only that they were very good, sir.

INSPECTOR. I mean—anything peculiar?

ROBERT [after reflection]. Yes, sir.

INSPECTOR. Well?

ROBERT. A pair of his boots this evenin' was reduced to one, sir.

INSPECTOR. What did you make of that?

ROBERT. I thought he might have thrown the other at a cat or something.

INSPECTOR. Did you look for it?

ROBERT. No, sir; I meant to draw his attention to it in the morning.

INSPECTOR. Very good.

ROBERT. Yes, sir. [He goes again.]

INSPECTOR [*looking at* DE LEVIS]. Well, sir, there *your* story corroborated.

DE LEVIS [*stiffly*]. I don't know why it should need corroboration, Inspector.

INSPECTOR. In my experience, you can never have too much of that. [*To* WINSOR] I understand there's a lady in the room on this side [*pointing Left*] and a gentleman on this [*pointing Right*]. Were they in their rooms?

WINSOR. Miss Orme was; Captain Dancy not.

INSPECTOR. Do they know of the affair?

WINSOR. Yes.

INSPECTOR. Well, I'd just like the keys of their doors for a minute. My man will get them. [*He goes to the door, opens it, and speaks to a constable in the corridor. [To* TREISURE] You can go with him. [TREISURE *goes out.*] In the meantime I'll just examine the balcony. [*He goes out on the balcony, followed by* DE LEVIS.]

WINSOR [*to* CANYNGE]. Damn De Levis and his money! It's deuced invidious, all this, General.

CANYNGE. The Inspector's no earthly.

[*There is a simultaneous re-entry of the* INSPECTOR *from the balcony and of* TREISURE *and the* CONSTABLE *from the corridor.*]

CONSTABLE [*handing key*]. Room on the left, sir. [*Handing key*] Room on the right, sir.

[*The* INSPECTOR *tries the keys in the door, watched with tension by the others. The keys fail.*]

INSPECTOR. Put them back. [*Hands keys to* CONSTABLE, *who goes out, followed by* TREISURE.] I'll have to try every key in the house, sir.

WINSOR. Inspector, do you really think it necessary to disturb the whole house and knock up all my guests? It's most disagreeable, all this, you know. The loss of the money is not such a great matter. Mr De Levis has a very large income.

CANYNGE. You could get the numbers of the notes from Kentman the bookmaker, Inspector; he'll probably have the big ones, anyway.

INSPECTOR [*shaking his head*]. A bookie. I don't suppose he will, sir. It's come and go with them, all the time.

WINSOR. We don't want a Meldon Court scandal, Inspector.

INSPECTOR. Well, Mr Winsor, I've formed my theory. [*As he speaks,* DE LEVIS *comes in from the balcony.*] And I don't say to try the keys is necessary to it; but strictly, I ought to exhaust the possibilities.

WINSOR. What do you say, De Levis? D'you want everybody in the house knocked up so that their keys can be tried?

DE LEVIS [*whose face, since his return, expresses a curious excitement*]. No, I don't.

INSPECTOR. Very well, gentlemen. In my opinion the thief walked in before the door was locked, probably during dinner; and was under the bed. He escaped by dropping from the balcony—the creeper at that corner [*he points stage Left*] has been violently wrenched. I'll go down now, and examine the grounds, and I'll see you again, sir. [*He makes another entry in his note-book.*] Good-night then, gentlemen!

CANYNGE. Good-night!

WINSOR [*with relief*]. I'll come with you, Inspector. [*He escorts him to the door, and they go out.*]

DE LEVIS [*suddenly*]. General, I know who took them.

CANYNGE. The deuce you do! Are you following the Inspector's theory?

DE LEVIS [*contemptuously*]. That ass! [*Pulling the shaving papers out of the case*] No! The man who put those there was clever and cool enough to wrench that creeper off the balcony, as a blind. Come and look here, General. [*He goes to the window; the* GENERAL *follows.* DE LEVIS *points stage Right.*] See the rail of my balcony, and the rail of the next? [*He holds up the cord of his dressing-gown, stretching his arms out.*] I've measured it with this. Just over seven feet, that's all! If a man can take a standing jump on to a narrow bookcase four feet high and balance there, he'd make nothing of that. And, look here! [*He goes out on the balcony and returns with a bit of broken creeper in his hand, and holds it out into the light.*] Someone's stood on that—the stalk's crushed—the inner corner too, where he'd naturally stand when he took his jump back.

CANYNGE [*after examining it—stiffly*]. That other balcony is young Dancy's, Mr De Levis; a soldier and a gentleman. This is an extraordinary insinuation.

DE LEVIS. Accusation.

CANYNGE. What!

DE LEVIS. I have intuitions, General; it's in my blood. I see the whole thing. Dancy came up, watched me into the bathroom, tried my door, slipped back into his dressing-room, saw my window was open, took that jump, sneaked the notes, filled the case up with these, wrenched the creeper there [*He points stage Left.*] for a blind, jumped back, and slipped downstairs again. It didn't take him four minutes altogether.

CANYNGE [*very gravely*]. This is outrageous, De Levis. Dancy says he was downstairs all the time. You must either withdraw unreservedly, or I must confront you with him.

DE LEVIS. If he'll return the notes and apologise, I'll do nothing—except cut him in future. He gave me that filly, you know, as a hopeless weed, and he's been pretty sick ever since, that he was such a flat as not to see how good she was. Besides, he's hard up, I know.

CANYNGE [*after a vexed turn up and down the room*]. It's mad, sir, to jump to conclusions like this.

DE LEVIS. Not so mad as the conclusion Dancy jumped to when he lighted on my balcony.

CANYNGE. Nobody could have taken this money who did not know you had it.

DE LEVIS. How do you know that he didn't?

CANYNGE. Do you know that he did?

DE LEVIS. I haven't the least doubt of it.

CANYNGE. Without any proof. This is very ugly, De Levis. I must tell Winsor.

DE LEVIS [*angrily*]. Tell the whole blooming lot. You think I've no feelers, but I've felt the atmosphere here, I can tell you, General. If I were in Dancy's shoes and he in mine, your tone to me would be very different.

CANYNGE [*suavely frigid*]. I'm not aware of using any tone, as you call it. But this is a private house, Mr De Levis, and something is due to our host and to the *esprit de corps* that exists among gentlemen.

DE LEVIS. Since when is a thief a gentleman? Thick as thieves —a good motto, isn't it?

CANYNGE. That's enough! [*He goes to the door, but stops before opening it.*] Now, look here! I have some knowledge of the world. Once an accusation like this passes beyond these walls no one can foresee the consequences. Captain Dancy is a gallant fellow, with a fine record as a soldier;

and only just married. If he's as innocent as—Christ—mud will stick to him, unless the real thief is found. In the old days of swords, either you or he would not have gone out of this room alive. If you persist in this absurd accusation, you will *both* of you go out of this room dead in the eyes of Society: you for bringing it, he for being the object of it.

DE LEVIS. Society! Do you think I don't know that I'm only tolerated for my money? Society can't add injury to insult and have my money as well, that's all. If the notes are restored I'll keep my mouth shut; if they're not, I shan't. I'm certain I'm right. I ask nothing better than to be confronted with Dancy; but, if you prefer it, deal with him in your own way—for the sake of your *esprit de corps*.

CANYNGE. 'Pon my soul, Mr De Levis, you go too far.

DE LEVIS. Not so far as I shall go, General Canynge, if those notes aren't given back.

[WINSOR *comes in.*]

WINSOR. Well, De Levis, I'm afraid that's all we can do for the present. So very sorry this should have happened in my house.

CANYNGE [*after a silence*]. There's a development, Winsor. Mr De Levis accuses one of your guests.

WINSOR. What?

CANYNGE. Of jumping from his balcony to this, taking the notes, and jumping back. I've done my best to dissuade him from indulging the fancy—without success. Dancy must be told.

DE LEVIS. You can deal with Dancy in your own way. All I want is the money back.

CANYNGE [*drily*]. Mr De Levis feels that he is only valued for his money, so that it is essential for him to have it back.

WINSOR. Damn it! This is monstrous, De Levis. I've known Ronald Dancy since he was a boy.

CANYNGE. You talk about adding injury to insult, De Levis. What do you call such treatment of a man who gave you the mare out of which you made this thousand pounds?

DE LEVIS. I didn't want the mare; I took her as a favour.

CANYNGE. With an eye to possibilities, I venture to think—the principle guides a good many transactions.

DE LEVIS [*as if flicked on a raw spot*]. In my race, do you mean?

CANYNGE [coldly]. I said nothing of the sort.

DE LEVIS. No; you don't *say* these things, any of you.

CANYNGE. Nor did I think it.

DE LEVIS. Dancy does.

WINSOR. Really, De Levis, if this is the way you repa[y] hospitality——

DE LEVIS. Hospitality that skins my feelings and costs me [a] thousand pounds!

CANYNGE. Go and get Dancy, Winsor; but don't say anythin[g] to him.

[WINSOR *goes out.*]

CANYNGE. Perhaps you will kindly control yourself, and leav[e] this to me.

[DE LEVIS *turns to the window and lights a cigarette.* WINSOR *comes back, followed by* DANCY.]

CANYNGE. For Winsor's sake, Dancy, we don't want any scandal or fuss about this affair. We've tried to make the police understand that. To my mind the whole thing turns on our finding who knew that De Levis had this money. It's about that that we want to consult you.

WINSOR. Kentman paid De Levis round the corner in the further paddock, he says.

[DE LEVIS *turns round from the window, so that he and* DANCY *are staring at each other.*]

CANYNGE. Did you hear anything that throws light, Dancy? As it was your filly originally, we thought perhaps you might.

DANCY. I? No.

CANYNGE. Didn't hear of the sale on the course at all?

DANCY. No.

CANYNGE. Then you can't suggest anyone who could have known? Nothing else was taken, you see.

DANCY. De Levis is known to be rolling, as I am known to be stony.

CANYNGE. There are a good many people still rolling, besides Mr De Levis, but not many people with so large a sum in their pocket-books.

DANCY. He won two races.

E LEVIS. Do you suggest that I bet in ready money?

ANCY. I don't know how you bet, and I don't care.

ANYNGE. You can't help us, then?

ANCY. No, I can't. Anything else? [*He looks fixedly at* DE LEVIS.]

ANYNGE [*putting his hand on* DANCY'S *arm*]. Nothing else, thank you, Dancy.

[DANCY *goes.* CANYNGE *puts his hand up to his face. A moment's silence.*]

WINSOR. You see, De Levis? He didn't even know you'd got the money.

DE LEVIS. Very conclusive.

WINSOR. Well! You *are*——!

[*There is a knock on the door, and the* INSPECTOR *enters.*]

INSPECTOR. I'm just going, gentlemen. The grounds, I'm sorry to say, have yielded nothing. It's a bit of a puzzle.

CANYNGE. You've searched thoroughly?

INSPECTOR. We have, General. I can pick up nothing near the terrace.

WINSOR [*after a look at* DE LEVIS, *whose face expresses too much*]. H'm! You'll take it up from the other end, then, Inspector?

INSPECTOR. Well, we'll see that we can do with the bookmakers about the numbers, sir. Before I go, gentlemen—you've had time to think it over—there's no one you suspect in the house, I suppose?

[DE LEVIS'S *face is alive and uncertain.* CANYNGE *is staring at him very fixedly.*]

WINSOR [*emphatically*]. No.

[DE LEVIS *turns and goes out on to the balcony.*]

INSPECTOR. If you're coming in to the racing to-morrow, sir, you might give us a call. I'll have seen Kentman by then.

WINSOR. Right you are, Inspector. Good-night, and many thanks.

INSPECTOR. You're welcome, sir. [*He goes out.*]

WINSOR. Gosh! I thought that chap [*With a nod towards the balcony*] was going to——! Look here, General, we *must* stop his tongue. Imagine it going the rounds. They may never find the real thief, you know. It's the very devil for Dancy.

CANYNGE. Winsor! Dancy's sleeve was damp.

WINSOR. How d'you mean?

CANYNGE. Quite damp. It's been raining.

[*The two look at each other.*]

WINSOR. I—I don't follow—— [*His voice is hesitative and lower, showing that he does.*]

CANYNGE. It was coming down hard; a minute out in it would have been enough—— [*He motions with his chin towards the balcony.*]

WINSOR [*hastily*]. He must have been out on his balcony since.

CANYNGE. It stopped before I came up, half an hour ago.

WINSOR. He's been leaning on the wet stone, then.

CANYNGE. With the outside of the *upper* part of the arm?

WINSOR. Against the wall, perhaps. There may be a dozen explanations. [*Very low and with great concentration*] I entirely and absolutely refuse to believe anything of the sort against Ronald Dancy—in my house. Dash it, General, we must do as we'd be done by. It hits us all—it hits us all. The thing's intolerable.

CANYNGE. I agree. Intolerable. [*Raising his voice*] Mr De Levis!

[DE LEVIS *returns into view, in the centre of the open window.*]

CANYNGE [*with cold decision*]. Young Dancy was an officer and is a gentleman; this insinuation is pure supposition, and you must not make it. Do you understand me?

DE LEVIS. My tongue is still mine, General, if my money isn't!

CANYNGE [*unmoved*]. Must not. You're a member of three Clubs, you want to be member of a fourth. No one who makes such an insinuation against a fellow-guest in a country house, except on absolute proof, can do so without complete ostracism. Have we your word to say nothing?

DE LEVIS. Social blackmail? H'm!

CANYNGE. Not at all—simple warning. If you consider it necessary in your interests to start this scandal—no matter how, we shall consider it necessary in ours to dissociate

ourselves completely from one who so recklessly disre-
gards the unwritten code.

DE LEVIS. Do you think your code applies to me? Do you,
General?

CANYNGE. To anyone who aspires to be a gentleman, sir.

DE LEVIS. Ah! But you haven't known *me* since I was a boy.

CANYNGE. Make up your mind.

[*A pause.*]

DE LEVIS. I'm not a fool, General. I know perfectly well that
you can get me outed.

CANYNGE [*icily*]. Well?

DE LEVIS [*sullenly*]. I'll say nothing about it, unless I get
more proof.

CANYNGE. Good! We have implicit faith in Dancy.

[*There is a moment's encounter of eyes; the* GENERAL'S
*steady, shrewd, impassive;* WINSOR'S *angry and defiant;* DE
LEVIS'S *mocking, a little triumphant, malicious. Then*
CANYNGE *and* WINSOR *go to the door, and pass out.*]

DE LEVIS [*to himself*]. Rats!

CURTAIN

# ACT TWO

## Scene 1

*Afternoon, three weeks later, in the card room of a London Club. A fire is burning, Left. A door, Right, leads to the billiard-room. Rather Left of Centre, at a card table,* LORD ST ERTH, *an old John Bull, sits facing the audience; to his right is* GENERAL CANYNGE, *to his left* AUGUSTUS BORRING, *an essential Clubman, about thirty-five years old, with a very slight and rather becoming stammer or click in his speech. The fourth Bridge player,* CHARLES WINSOR, *stands with his back to the fire.*

BORRING. And the r-rub.

WINSOR. By George! You do hold cards, Borring.

ST ERTH [*who has lost*]. Not a patch on the old whist—this game. Don't know why I play it—never did.

CANYNGE. St Erth, shall we raise the flag for whist again?

WINSOR. No go, General. You can't go back on pace. No getting a man to walk when he knows he can fly. The young men won't look at it.

BORRING. Better develop it so that t-two can sit out, General.

ST ERTH. We ought to have stuck to the old game. Wish I'd gone to Newmarket, Canynge, in spite of the weather.

CANYNGE [*looking at his watch*]. Let's hear what's won the Cambridgeshire. Ring, won't you, Winsor?

[WINSOR *rings.*]

ST ERTH. By the way, Canynge, young De Levis was black-balled.

CANYNGE. What!

ST ERTH. I looked in on my way down.

[ 249 ]

[CANYNGE *sits very still, and* WINSOR *utters a disturbe* *sound.*]

BORRING. But of c-course he was, General. What did yo expect?

[*A* FOOTMAN *enters.*]

FOOTMAN. Yes, my lord?

ST ERTH. What won the Cambridgeshire?

FOOTMAN. Rosemary, my lord. Sherbet second; Barbizo third. Nine to one the winner.

WINSOR. Thank you. That's all.

[FOOTMAN *goes.*]

BORRING. Rosemary! And De Levis sold her! But he got good p-price, I suppose.

[*The other three look at him.*]

ST ERTH. Many a slip between price and pocket, young man

CANYNGE. Cut!

[*They cut*].

CANYNGE. Cut! [*They cut*].

BORRING. I say, is that the yarn that's going round about his having had a lot of m-money stolen in a country house? By Jove! He'll be pretty s-sick.

WINSOR. You and I, Borring. [*He sits down in* CANYNGE'S *chair, and the* GENERAL *takes his place by the fire.*]

BORRING. Phew! Won't Dancy be mad! He gave that filly away to save her keep. He was rather pleased to find somebody who'd take her. Kentman must have won a p-pot. She was at thirty-threes a fortnight ago.

ST ERTH. All the money goes to fellows who don't know a horse from a haystack.

CANYNGE [*profoundly*]. And care less. Yes! We want men racing to whom a horse means something.

BORRING. I thought the horse m-meant the same to every-one, General—chance to get the b-better of one's neigh-bour.

CANYNGE [*with feeling*]. The horse is a noble animal, sir, as you'd know if you'd owed your life to them as often as I have.

ORRING. They always try to *take* mine, General. I shall never belong to the noble f-fellowship of the horse.

T ERTH [*drily*]. Evidently. Deal!

*As* BORRING *begins to deal the door is opened and* MAJOR OLFORD *appears—a lean and moustached cavalryman.*]

ORRING. Hallo, C-Colford.

OLFORD. General!

*Something in the tone of his voice brings them all to a* standstill.]

OLFORD. I want your advice. Young De Levis in there [*he points to the billiard-room from which he has just come*] has started a blasphemous story——

ANYNGE. One moment. Mr Borring, d'you mind——

OLFORD. It makes no odds, General. Four of us in there heard him. He's saying it was Ronald Dancy robbed him down at Winsor's. The fellow's mad over losing the price of that filly now she's won the Cambridgeshire.

ORRING [*all ears*]. Dancy! Great S-Scott!

OLFORD. Dancy's in the Club. If he hadn't been I'd have taken it on myself to wring the bounder's neck.

WINSOR *and* BORRING *have risen.* ST ERTH *alone remains* eated.]

ANYNGE [*after consulting* ST ERTH *with a look*]. Ask De Levis to be good enough to come in here. Borring, you might see that Dancy doesn't leave the Club. We shall want him. Don't say anything to him, and use your tact to keep people off.

[BORRING *goes out, followed by* COLFORD.]

WINSOR. Result of hearing he was blackballed—pretty slippy.

ANYNGE. St Erth, I told you there was good reason when I asked you to back young De Levis. Winsor and I knew of this insinuation; I wanted to keep his tongue quiet. It's just wild assertion; to have it bandied about was unfair to Dancy. The duel used to keep people's tongues in order.

ST ERTH. H'm! It never settled anything, except who could shoot straightest.

COLFORD [*reappearing*]. De Levis says he's nothing to add to what he said to you before, on the subject.

CANYNGE. Kindly tell him that if he wishes to remain member of this Club he must account to the Committe for such a charge against a fellow-member. Four of are here, and form a quorum.

[COLFORD *goes out again.*]

ST ERTH. Did Kentman ever give the police the numbers those notes, Winsor?

WINSOR. He only had the numbers of two—the hundre and one of the fifties.

ST ERTH. And they haven't traced 'em?

WINSOR. Not yet.

[*As he speaks,* DE LEVIS *comes in. He is in a highly-coloured not to say excited state.* COLFORD *follows him.*]

DE LEVIS. Well, General Canynge! It's a little too strong a this—a little too strong. [*Under emotion his voice i slightly more exotic.*]

CANYNGE [*calmly*]. It is obvious, Mr De Levis, that you and Captain Dancy can't both remain members of this Club We ask you for an explanation before requesting one res ignation or the other.

DE LEVIS. You've let me down.

CANYNGE. What!

DE LEVIS. Well, I shall tell people that you and Lord St Erth backed me up for one Club, and asked me to resign from another.

CANYNGE. It's a matter of indifference to me, sir, what you tell people.

ST ERTH [*drily*]. You seem a venomous young man.

DE LEVIS. I'll tell you what seems to me venomous, my lord—chasing a man like a pack of hounds because he isn't your breed.

CANYNGE. You appear to have your breed on the brain, sir. Nobody else does, so far as I know.

DE LEVIS. Suppose I had robbed Dancy, would you chase him out for complaining of it?

COLFORD. My God! If you repeat that——

CANYNGE. Steady, Colford!

WINSOR. You make this accusation that Dancy stole your money in my house on no proof—no proof; and you

expect Dancy's friends to treat you as if you were a gentleman! That's too strong, if you like!

DE LEVIS. No proof? Kentman told me at Newmarket yesterday that Dancy *did* know of the sale. He told Goole,
and Goole says that he himself spoke of it to Dancy.

WINSOR. Well—if he did?

DE LEVIS. Dancy told you he *didn't* know of it in General
Canynge's presence, and mine. [*To* CANYNGE] You can't
deny that, if you want to.

CANYNGE. Choose your expressions more nicely, please!

DE LEVIS. Proof! Did they find any footmarks in the grounds
below that torn creeper? Not a sign! You saw how he can
jump; he won ten pounds from me that same evening bet-
ting on what he knew was a certainty. That's your Dancy
—a common sharper!

CANYNGE [*nodding towards the billiard-room*]. Are those
fellows still in there, Colford?

COLFORD. Yes.

CANYNGE. Then bring Dancy up, will you? But don't say
anything to him.

COLFORD [*to* DE LEVIS]. You may think yourself damned
lucky if he doesn't break your neck.

[*He goes out. The three who are left with* DE LEVIS *avert
their eyes from him.*]

DE LEVIS [*smouldering*]. I have a memory, and a sting too.
Yes, my lord—since you are good enough to call me
venomous. [*To* CANYNGE] I quite understand—I'm
marked for Coventry now, whatever happens. Well, I'll
take Dancy with me.

ST ERTH [*to himself*]. This Club has always had a decent,
quiet name.

WINSOR. Are you going to retract, and apologise in front of
Dancy and the members who heard you?

DE LEVIS. No fear!

ST ERTH. You must be a very rich man, sir. A jury is likely
to take the view that money can hardly compensate for
an accusation of that sort.

[DE LEVIS *stands silent.*]

CANYNGE. Courts of law require proof.

ST ERTH. He can make it a criminal action.

WINSOR. Unless you stop this at once, you may find yourself in prison. *If* you can stop it, that is.

ST ERTH. If I were young Dancy, nothing should induce me

DE LEVIS. But you didn't steal my money, Lord St Erth.

ST ERTH. You're deuced positive, sir. So far as I could understand it, there were a dozen ways you could have been robbed. It seems to me you value other men's reputations very lightly.

DE LEVIS. Confront me with Dancy and give me fair play.

WINSOR [*aside to* CANYNGE]. Is it fair to Dancy not to let him know?

CANYNGE. Our duty is to the Club now, Winsor. We must have this cleared up.

[COLFORD *comes in, followed by* BORRING *and* DANCY.]

ST ERTH. Captain Dancy, a serious accusation has been made against you by this gentleman in the presence of several members of the Club.

DANCY. What is it?

ST ERTH. That you robbed him of that money at Winsor's.

DANCY [*hard and tense*]. Indeed! On what grounds is he good enough to say that?

DE LEVIS [*tense too*]. You gave me that filly to save yourself her keep, and you've been mad about it ever since; you knew from Goole that I had sold her to Kentman and been paid in cash, yet I heard you myself deny that you knew it. You had the next room to me, and you can jump like a cat, as we saw that evening; I found some creepers crushed by a weight on my balcony on that side. When I went to the bath your door was open, and when I came back it was shut.

CANYNGE. That's the first we have heard about the door.

DE LEVIS. I remembered it afterwards.

ST ERTH. Well, Dancy?

DANCY [*with intense deliberation*] I'll settle this matter with any weapons, when and where he likes.

ST ERTH [*drily*]. It can't be settled that way—you know very well. You must take it to the Courts, unless he retracts.

DANCY. Will you retract?

DE LEVIS. Why did you tell General Canynge you didn't know Kentman had paid me in cash?

DANCY. Because I didn't.

DE LEVIS. Then Kentman and Goole lied—for no reason?

DANCY. That's nothing to do with me.

DE LEVIS. If you were downstairs all the time, as you say, why was your door first open and then shut?

DANCY. Being downstairs, how should I know? The wind, probably.

DE LEVIS. I should like to hear what your wife says about *it*.

DANCY. Leave my wife alone, you damned Jew!

ST ERTH. Captain Dancy!

DE LEVIS [*white with rage*]. Thief!

DANCY. Will you fight?

DE LEVIS. You're very smart—dead men tell no tales. No! Bring your action, and we shall see.

DANCY *takes a step towards him, but* CANYNGE *and* WINSOR *interpose.*]

ST ERTH. That'll do, Mr De Levis; we won't keep you. [*He looks round.*] Kindly consider your membership suspended till this matter has been threshed out.

DE LEVIS [*tremulous with anger*]. Don't trouble yourselves about my membership. I resign it. [*To* DANCY] You called me a damned Jew. My race was old when you were all savages. I am proud to be a Jew. *Au revoir*, in the Courts.

*He goes out, and silence follows his departure.*]

ST ERTH. Well, Captain Dancy?

DANCY. If the brute won't fight, what am I to do, sir?

ST ERTH. We've told you—take action, to clear your name.

DANCY. Colford, you saw me in the hall writing letters after our game.

COLFORD. Certainly I did; you were there when I went to the smoking-room.

CANYNGE. How long after you left the billiard-room?

COLFORD. About five minutes.

DANCY. It's impossible for me to prove that I was there all the time.

CANYNGE. It's for De Levis to prove what he asserts. You heard what he said about Goole?

DANCY. If he told me, I didn't take it in.

ST ERTH. This concerns the honour of the Club. Are you going to take action?

DANCY [*slowly*]. That is a very expensive business, Lord St Erth, and I'm hard up. I must think it over. [*He looks round from face to face.]* Am I to take it that there is doubt in your minds, gentlemen?

COLFORD [*emphatically*]. No.

CANYNGE. That's not the question, Dancy. This accusatio was overheard by various members, and we represent th Club. If you don't take action, judgment will naturally g by default.

DANCY. I might prefer to look on the whole thing as beneath contempt.

[*He turns and goes out. When he is gone there is an eve. longer silence than after* DE LEVIS'S *departure.*]

ST ERTH [*abruptly*]. I don't like it.

WINSOR. I've known him all his life.

COLFORD. You may have my head if he did it, Lord St Erth He and I have been in too many holes together. By Gad My toe itches for that fellow's butt end.

BORRING. I'm sorry; but has he t-taken it in quite the righ way? I should have thought—hearing it s-suddenly——

COLFORD. Bosh!

WINSOR. It's perfectly damnable for him.

ST ERTH. More damnable if he did it, Winsor.

BORRING. The Courts are b-beastly distrustful, don't you know.

COLFORD. His word's good enough for me.

CANYNGE. We're as anxious to believe Dancy as you, Colford, for the honour of the Army and the Club.

WINSOR. Of course, he'll bring a case, when he's thought i over.

ST ERTH. What are we to do in the meantime?

COLFORD. If Dancy's asked to resign, you may take my resignation too.

BORRING. I thought his wanting to f-fight him a bit screeny.

COLFORD. Wouldn't you have wanted a shot at the brute? A law court? Pah!

WINSOR. Yes. What'll be his position even if he wins?

BORRING. Damages, and a stain on his c-character.

WINSOR. Quite so, unless they find the real thief. People always believe the worst.

COLFORD [*glaring at* BORRING]. They do.

CANYNGE. There *is* no decent way out of a thing of this sort.

ST ERTH. No. [*Rising*] It leaves a bad taste. I'm sorry for young Mrs Dancy—poor woman!

BORRING. Are you going to play any more?

ST ERTH [*abruptly*]. No, sir. Good night to you. Canynge, can I give you a lift?

[*He goes out, followed by* CANYNGE.]

BORRING [*after a slight pause*]. Well, I shall go and take the t-temperature of the Club. [*He goes out.*]

COLFORD. Damn that effeminate stammering chap! What can we do for Dancy, Winsor?

WINSOR. Colford! [*A slight pause*] The General felt his coat sleeve that night, and it was wet.

COLFORD. Well! What proof's that? No, by George! An old school-fellow, a brother officer, and a pal.

WINSOR. If he did do it——

COLFORD. He didn't. But if he did, I stick to him, and see him through it, if I could.

[WINSOR *walks over to the fire, stares into it, turns round and stares at* COLFORD, *who is standing motionless.*]

COLFORD. Yes, by God!

CURTAIN

## Scene 2[3]

*Morning of the following day. The* DANCY'S *flat. In the sitting-room of this small abode* MABEL DANCY *and* MARGARET ORME *are sitting full face to the audience, on a couch in the centre of the room, in front of the imaginary window. There is a fireplace, Left, with fire burning; a door below it, Left; and a door on the Right, facing the audience, leads to a corridor and the outer door of the flat, which is visible. Their voices are heard in rapid exchange; then as the curtain rises, so does* MABEL.

MABEL. But it's monstrous!

MARGARET. Of course! [*She lights a cigarette and hands the case to* MABEL, *who, however, sees nothing but her own*

---

[3] This should be a small set capable of being set quickly within that of the previous scene.

*thoughts.*] De Levis might just as well have pitched on me, except that I can't jump more than six inches in these skirts.

MABEL. It's wicked! Yesterday afternoon at the Club, did you say? Ronny hasn't said a word to me. Why?

MARGARET [*with a long puff of smoke*]. Doesn't want you bothered.

MABEL. But——Good heavens——! Me!

MARGARET. Haven't you found out, Mabel, that he isn't exactly communicative? No desperate character is.

MABEL. Ronny?

MARGARET. Gracious! Wives are at a disadvantage, especially early on. You've never hunted with him, my dear. I have. He takes more sudden decisions than any man I ever knew. He's taking one now, I'll bet.

MABEL. That beast, De Levis! I was in our room next door all the time.

MARGARET. Was the door into Ronny's dressing-room open?

MABEL. I don't know; I—I think it was.

MARGARET. Well, you can say so in Court anyway. Not that it matters. Wives are liars by law.

MABEL [*staring down at her*]. What do you mean—Court?

MARGARET. My dear, he'll have to bring an action for defamation of character, or whatever they call it.

MABEL. Were they talking of this last night at the Winsors'?

MARGARET. Well, you know a dinner-table, Mabel— Scandal is heaven-sent at this time of year.

MABEL. It's terrible, such a thing—terrible!

MARGARET [*gloomily*]. If only Ronny weren't known to be so broke.

MABEL [*with her hands to her forehead*]. I can't realise—I simply can't. If there's a case would it be all right afterwards?

MARGARET. Do you remember St Offert—cards? No, you wouldn't—you were in high frocks. Well, St Offert got damages, but he also got the hoof, underneath. He lives in Ireland. There isn't the slightest connection, so far as I can see, Mabel, between innocence and reputation. Look at me!

MABEL. We'll fight it tooth and nail!

MARGARET. Mabel, you're pure wool, right through; everybody's sorry for you.

MABEL. It's for *him* they ought——

MARGARET [*again handing the cigarette-case*]. Do smoke, old thing. [MABEL *takes a cigarette this time, but does not light it.*] It isn't altogether simple. General Canynge was there last night. You don't mind my being beastly frank, do you?

MABEL. No. I want it.

MARGARET. Well, he's all for *esprit de corps* and that. But he was awfully silent.

MABEL. I hate half-hearted friends. Loyalty comes before everything.

MARGARET. Ye-es; but loyalties cut up against each other sometimes, you know.

MABEL. I *must* see Ronny. D'you mind if I go and try to get him on the telephone?

MARGARET. Rather not. [MABEL *goes out by the door Left.*] Poor kid! [*She curls herself into a corner of the sofa, as if trying to get away from life. The bell rings.* MARGARET *stirs, gets up, and goes out into the corridor, where she opens the door to* LADY ADELA WINSOR, *whom she precedes into the sitting-room.*] Enter the second murderer! D'you know that child knew nothing?

LADY ADELA. Where is she?

MARGARET. Telephoning. Adela, if there's going to be an action, we shall be witnesses. I shall wear black georgette with an écru hat. Have you ever given evidence?

LADY ADELA. Never.

MARGARET. It must be too frightfully thrilling.

LADY ADELA. Oh! Why did I ever ask that wretch De Levis? I used to think him pathetic. Meg—did you know—— Ronald Dancy's coat was wet? The General happened to feel it.

MARGARET. So that's why he was so silent.

LADY ADELA. Yes; and after the scene in the Club yesterday he went to see those bookmakers, and Goole—what a name!—is sure he told Dancy about the sale.

MARGARET [*suddenly*]. I don't care. He's my third cousin. Don't you feel you *couldn't*, Adela?

LADY ADELA. Couldn't—what?

MARGARET. Stand for De Levis against one of ourselves?

LADY ADELA. Tha's very narrow, Meg.

MARGARET. Oh! I know lots of splendid Jews, and I rather

liked little Ferdy; but when it comes to the point——
*They* all stick together; why shouldn't we? It's in the blood
Open your jugular, and see if you haven't got it.

LADY ADELA. My dear, my great grandmother was a Jewess
I am very proud of her.

MARGARET. Inoculated. [*Stretching herself*] Prejudices, Adela
—or are they loyalties—I don't know—criss-cross—we
all cut each other's throats from the best of motives.

LADY ADELA. Oh! I shall remember that. Delightful! [*Holding
up a finger*] You got it from Bergson, Meg. Isn't he wonderful?

MARGARET. Yes; have you ever read him?

LADY ADELA. Well—no. [*Looking at the bedroom door*]
That poor child! I quite agree. I shall tell everybody it's
ridiculous. You don't really think Ronald Dancy——?

MARGARET. I don't know, Adela. There are people who simply
can't live without danger. I'm rather like that myself.
They're all right when they're getting the D.S.O. or shooting man-eaters; but if there's no excitement going, they'll
make it—out of sheer craving. I've seen Ronny Dancy
do the maddest things for no mortal reason except the risk.
He's had a past, you know.

LADY ADELA. Oh! Do tell!

MARGARET. He did splendidly in the war, of course, because
it suited him; but—just before—don't you remember—a
very queer bit of riding?

LADY ADELA. No.

MARGARET. Most dare-devil thing—but not quite. You must
remember—it was awfully talked about. And then, of
course, right up to his marriage—— [*She lights a cigarette.*]

LADY ADELA. Meg, you're very tantalising!

MARGARET. A foreign-looking girl—most plummy. Oh!
Ronny's got charm—this Mabel child doesn't know in the
least what she's got hold of!

LADY ADELA. But they're so fond of each other!

MARGARET. That's the mistake. The General isn't mentioning
the coat, is he?

LADY ADELA. Oh, no! It was only to Charles.

[MABEL *returns.*]

MARGARET. Did you get him?

MABEL. No; he's not at Tattersall's, nor at the Club.

[LADY ADELA *rises and greets her with an air which suggests bereavement.*]

LADY ADELA. Nobody's going to believe this, my dear.

MABEL [*looking straight at her*]. Nobody who does need come here, or trouble to speak to *us* again.

LADY ADELA. That's what I was afraid of; you're going to be defiant. Now don't! Just be perfectly natural.

MABEL. So easy, isn't it? I could kill anybody who believes such a thing.

MARGARET. You'll want a solicitor, Mabel. Go to old Mr Jacob Twisden.

LADY ADELA. Yes; he's so comforting.

MARGARET. He got my pearls back once—without loss of life. A frightfully good fireside manner. Do get him here, Mabel, and have a heart-to-heart talk, all three of you!

MABEL [*suddenly*]. Listen! There's Ronny!

[DANCY *comes in.*]

DANCY [*with a smile*]. Very good of you to have come.

MARGARET. Yes. We're just going. Oh! Ronny, this is quite too—— [*But his face dries her up; and sidling past, she goes.*]

LADY ADELA. Charles sent his—love—— [*Her voice dwindles on the word, and she, too, goes.*]

DANCY [*crossing to his wife*]. What have they been saying?

MABEL. Ronny! Why didn't you tell me?

DANCY. I wanted to see De Levis again first.

MABEL. That wretch! How dare he? Darling! [*She suddenly clasps and kisses him. He does not return the kiss, but remains rigid in her arms, so that she draws away and looks at him.*] It's hurt you awfully, I know.

DANCY. Look here, Mabel! Apart from that muck—this is a ghastly tame-cat sort of life. Let's cut it and get out to Nairobi. I can scare up the money for that.

MABEL [*aghast*]. But how can we? Everybody would say——

DANCY. Let them! We shan't be here.

MABEL. I couldn't bear people to think——

DANCY. I don't care a damn what people think—monkeys and cats. I never could stand their rotten menagerie. Be-

sides, what does it matter how I act; if I bring an actio
and get damages—if I pound him to a jelly—it's all n
good! I can't *prove* it. There'll be plenty of people unco
vinced.

MABEL. But they'll find the real thief.

DANCY [*with a queer little smile*]. Will staying here hel
them to do that?

MABEL [*in a sort of agony*]. Oh! I couldn't—it looks lik
running away. We *must* stay and fight it!

DANCY. Suppose I didn't get a verdict—you never can tel

MABEL. But you must—I was there all the time, with th
door open.

DANCY. Was it?

MABEL. I'm almost sure.

DANCY. Yes. But you're my wife.

MABEL [*bewildered*]. Ronny, I don't understand—suppos
I'd been accused of stealing pearls!

DANCY [*wincing*]. I can't.

MABEL. But I might—just as easily. What would you think o
me if I ran away from it?

DANCY. I see. [*A pause*] All right! You shall have a run fo
your money. I'll go and see old Twisden.

MABEL. Let me come! [DANCY *shakes his head.*] Why not?
can't be happy a moment unless I'm fighting this.

[DANCY *puts out his hand suddenly and grips hers.*]

DANCY. You *are* a little brick!

MABEL [*pressing his hand to her breast and looking into hi
face*]. Do you know what Margaret called you?

RONNY. No.

MABEL. A desperate character.

DANCY. Ha! I'm not a tame cat, any more than she.

[*The bell rings.* MABEL *goes out to the door and her voice i
heard saying coldly.*]

MABEL. Will you wait a minute, please? [*Returning.*] It'
De Levis—to see you. [*In a low voice*] Let me see hin
alone first. Just for a minute! Do!

DANCY [*after a moment's silence*]. Go ahead! [*He goes ou
into the bedroom.*]

MABEL [*going to the door, Right*]. Come in. [DE LEVI
*comes in, and stands embarrassed.*] Yes?

DE LEVIS [*with a slight bow.*] Your husband, Mrs Dancy?

MABEL. He is in. Why do you want to see him?

DE LEVIS. He came round to my rooms just now, when I was out. He threatened me yesterday. I don't choose him to suppose I'm afraid of him.

MABEL [*with a great and manifest effort at self-control*]. Mr De Levis, you are robbing my husband of his good name.

DE LEVIS [*sincerely*]. I admire your trustfulness, Mrs Dancy.

MABEL [*staring at him*]. How can you do it? What do you want? What's your motive? You can't possibly believe that my husband is a *thief!*

DE LEVIS. Unfortunately.

MABEL. How dare you? How dare you? Don't you know that I was in our bedroom all the time with the door open? Do you accuse me too?

DE LEVIS. No, Mrs Dancy.

MABEL. But you do. I must have seen, I must have heard.

DE LEVIS. A wife's memory is not very good when her husband is in danger.

MABEL. In other words, I'm lying.

DE LEVIS. No. Your wish is mother to your thought, that's all.

MABEL [*after staring again with a sort of horror, turns to get control of herself. Then turning back to him*]. Mr De Levis, I appeal to you as a gentleman to behave to us as you would we should behave to you. Withdraw this wicked charge, and write an apology that Ronald can show.

DE LEVIS. Mrs Dancy, I am not a gentleman, I am only a— damned Jew. Yesterday I might possibly have withdrawn to spare you. But when my race is insulted I have nothing to say to your husband, but as he wishes to see me, I've come. Please let him know.

MABEL [*regarding him again with that look of horror— slowly*]. I think what you are doing is too horrible for words.

[DE LEVIS *gives her a slight bow, and as he does so* DANCY *comes quickly in, Left. The two men stand with the length of the sofa between them.* MABEL, *behind the sofa, turns her eyes on her husband, who has a paper in his right hand.*]

DE LEVIS. You came to see me.

DANCY. Yes. I want you to sign this.

DE LEVIS. I will sign nothing.

DANCY. Let me read it: "I apologise to Captain Dancy fo
the reckless and monstrous charge I made against him, an
I retract every word of it."

DE LEVIS. Not much!

DANCY. You will sign.

DE LEVIS. I tell you this is useless. I will sign nothing. Th
charge is true; you wouldn't be playing this game if
weren't. I'm going. You'll hardly try violence in the pre
ence of your wife; and if you try it anywhere else—loo
out for yourself.

DANCY. Mabel, I want to speak to him alone.

MABEL. No, no!

DE LEVIS. Quite right, Mrs Dancy. Black and tan swash
buckling will only make things worse for him.

DANCY. So you shelter behind a woman, do you, you skulkin
cur!

[DE LEVIS takes a step, with fists clenched and eyes blazing
DANCY, too, stands ready to spring—the moment is cut shor
by MABEL going quickly to her husband.]

MABEL. Don't, Ronny. It's undignified! He isn't worth it.

[DANCY suddenly tears the paper in two, and flings it int
the fire.]

DANCY. Get out of here, you swine!

[DE LEVIS stands a moment irresolute, then, turning to th
door, he opens it, stands again for a moment with a smile or
his face, then goes. MABEL crosses swiftly to the door, and
shuts it as the outer door closes. Then she stands quite still,
looking at her husband—her face expressing a sort of startlec
suspense.]

DANCY [turning and looking at her]. Well! Do you agree with
him?

MABEL. What do you mean?

DANCY. That I wouldn't be playing this game unless——

MABEL. Don't! You hurt me!

DANCY. Yes. You don't know much of me, Mabel.

MABEL. Ronny!

DANCY. What did you say to that swine?

MABEL [her face averted]. That he was robbing us. [Turn-

*ing to him suddenly*] Ronny—you—didn't? I'd rather
know.

DANCY. Ha! I thought that was coming.

MABEL [*covering her face*]. Oh! How horrible of me—how
horrible!

DANCY. Not at all. The thing looks bad.

MABEL [*dropping her hands*]. If *I* can't believe in you, who
can? [*Going to him, throwing her arms round him, and
looking up into his face.*] Ronny! If all the world—*I'd*
believe in you. You know I would.

DANCY. That's all right, Mabs! That's all right! [*His face,
above her head, is contorted for a moment, then hardens
into a mask.*] Well, what shall we do?

MABEL. Oh! Let's go to that lawyer—let's go at once!

DANCY. All right. Get your hat on.

MABEL *passes him, and goes into the bedroom, Left.* DANCY,
*left alone, stands quite still, staring before him. With a sud-
den shrug of his shoulders he moves quickly to his hat and
takes it up just as* MABEL *returns, ready to go out. He opens
the door; and crossing him, she stops in the doorway, looking up with a clear and trustful gaze as*

THE CURTAIN FALLS

# ACT THREE

## Scene 1

*Three months later. Old* MR JACOB TWISDEN'S *Room, at the offices of Twisden & Graviter, in Lincoln's Inn Fields, is spacious, with two large windows at back, a fine old fire-place, Right, a door below it, and two doors, Left. Between the windows is a large table sideways to the window wall, with a chair in the middle on the right-hand side, a chair against the wall, and a client's chair on the left-hand side.*

GRAVITER, TWISDEN'S *much younger partner, is standing in front of the right-hand window looking out on to the Fields, where the lamps are being lighted, and a taxi's engine is running down below. He turns his sanguine, shrewd face from the window towards a grandfather clock, between the doors, Left, which is striking "four." The door, Left Forward, is opened.*

YOUNG CLERK [*entering*]. A Mr Gilman, sir, to see Mr Twisden.

GRAVITER. By appointment?

YOUNG CLERK. No, sir. But important, he says.

GRAVITER. I'll see him.

[*The* CLERK *goes.* GRAVITER *sits right of table. The* CLERK *returns, ushering in an oldish* MAN, *who looks what he is, the proprietor of a large modern grocery store. He wears a dark overcoat and carries a pot hat. His gingery-grey moustache and mutton-chop whiskers give him the expression of a cat.*]

GRAVITER [*sizing up his social standing*]. Mr Gilman? Yes.

GILMAN [*doubtfully*]. Mr Jacob Twisden?

GRAVITER [*smiling*]. His partner. Graviter my name is.

[ 267 ]

GILMAN. Mr Twisden's not in, then?

GRAVITER. No. He's at the Courts. They're just up; he should be in directly. But he'll be busy.

GILMAN. Old Mr Jacob Twisden—I've heard of him.

GRAVITER. Most people have.

[*A pause.*]

GILMAN. It's this Dancy De Levis case that's keepin' him at the Courts, I suppose? [GRAVITER *nods.*] Won't be finished for a day or two? [GRAVITER *shakes his head.*] No. Astonishin' the interest taken in it.

GRAVITER. As you say.

GILMAN. The Smart Set, eh? This Captain Dancy got the D.S.O., didn't he? [GRAVITER *nods.*] Sad to have a thing like that said about you. I thought he gave his evidence well; and his wife too. Looks as if this De Levis had got some private spite. *Searchy la femme,* I said to Mrs Gilman only this morning, before I——

GRAVITER. By the way, sir, what is your business?

GILMAN. Well, my business here—— No, if you'll excuse me, I'd rather wait and see old Mr Jacob Twisden. It's delicate, and I'd like his experience.

GRAVITER [*with a shrug*]. Very well; then, perhaps, you'll go in there. [*He moves towards the door, Left Back.*]

GILMAN. Thank you. [*Following*] You see, I've never been mixed up with the law——

GRAVITER [*opening the door*]. No?

GILMAN. And I don't want to begin. When you do, you don't know where you'll stop, do you? You see, I've only come from a sense of duty; and—other reasons.

GRAVITER. Not uncommon.

GILMAN [*producing card*]. This is my card. Gilman's—several branches, but this is the 'ead.

GRAVITER [*scrutinising card*]. Exactly.

GILMAN. Grocery—I daresay you know me; or your wife does. They say old Mr Jacob Twisden refused a knighthood. If it's not a rude question, why was that?

GRAVITER. Ask him, sir; ask him.

GILMAN. I said to my wife at the time, "He's holdin' out for a baronetcy."

[GRAVITER *closes the door with an exasperated smile.*]

YOUNG CLERK [*opening the door, Left Forward*]. Mr. Winsor, sir, and Miss Orme.

[*They enter, and the* CLERK *withdraws.*]

GRAVITER. How d'you do, Miss Orme? How do you do, Winsor?

WINSOR. Twisden not back, Graviter?

GRAVITER. Not yet.

WINSOR. Well, they've got through De Levis's witnesses. Sir Frederic was at the very top of his form. It's looking quite well. But I hear they've just subpœnæd Canynge after all. His evidence is to be taken to-morrow.

GRAVITER. Oho!

WINSOR. I said Dancy ought to have called him.

GRAVITER. We considered it. Sir Frederic decided that he could use him better in cross-examination.

WINSOR. Well! I don't know that. Can I go and see him before he gives evidence to-morrow?

GRAVITER. I should like to hear Mr Jacob on that, Winsor. He'll be in directly.

WINSOR. They had Kentman, and Goole, the Inspector, the other bobby, my footman, Dancy's banker, and his tailor.

GRAVITER. Did we shake Kentman or Goole?

WINSOR. Very little. Oh! by the way, the numbers of those two notes were given, and I see they're published in the evening papers. I suppose the police wanted that. I tell you what I find, Graviter—a general feeling that there's something behind it all that doesn't come out.

GRAVITER. The public wants its money's worth—always does in these Society cases; they brew so long beforehand, you see.

WINSOR. They're looking for something lurid.

MARGARET. When I was in the box, I thought they were looking for me. [*Taking out her cigarette case*] I suppose I mustn't smoke, Mr Graviter?

GRAVITER. Do!

MARGARET. Won't Mr Jacob have a fit?

GRAVITER. Yes but not till you've gone.

MARGARET. Just a whiff. [*She lights a cigarette.*]

WINSOR [*suddenly.*] It's becoming a sort of Dreyfus case—people taking sides quite outside the evidence.

MARGARET. There are more of the chosen in Court every

day. Mr Graviter, have you noticed the two on the jury?

GRAVITER [*with a smile*]. No; I can't say——

MARGARET. Oh! but quite distinctly. Don't you think they ought to have been challenged?

GRAVITER. De Levis might have challenged the other ten, Miss Orme.

MARGARET. Dear me, now! I never thought of that.

[*As she speaks, the door Left Forward is opened and old* MR JACOB TWISDEN *comes in. He is tallish and narrow, sixty-eight years old, grey, with narrow little whiskers curling round his narrow ears, and a narrow bow ribbon curling round his collar. He wears a long, narrow-tailed coat, and strapped trousers on his narrow legs. His nose and face are narrow, shrewd, and kindly. He has a way of narrowing his shrewd and kindly eyes. His nose is seen to twitch and sniff.*]

TWISDEN. Ah! How are you, Charles? How do you do, my dear?

MARGARET. Dear Mr Jacob, I'm smoking. Isn't it disgusting? But they don't allow it in Court, you know. Such a pity! The Judge might have a hookah. Oh! wouldn't he look sweet—the darling!

TWISDEN [*with a little, old-fashioned bow*]. It does not become everybody as it becomes you, Margaret.

MARGARET. Mr Jacob, how charming! [*With a slight grimace she puts out her cigarette.*]

GRAVITER. Man called Gilman waiting in there to see you specially.

TWISDEN. Directly. Turn up the light, would you, Graviter?

GRAVITER [*turning up the light*]. Excuse me. [*He goes.*]

WINSOR. Look here, Mr Twisden——

TWISDEN. Sit down; sit down, my dear. [*And he himself sits behind the table, as a cup of tea is brought in to him by the* YOUNG CLERK, *with two Marie biscuits in the saucer.*] Will you have some, Margaret?

MARGARET. No, dear Mr Jacob.

TWISDEN. Charles?

WINSOR. No, thanks.

[*The door is closed.*]

TWISDEN [*dipping a biscuit in the tea*]. Now, then?

WINSOR. The General knows something which on the face of

it looks rather queer. Now that he's going to be called, oughtn't Dancy to be told of it, so that he may be ready with his explanation, in case it comes out?

TWISDEN [*pouring some tea into the saucer*]. Without knowing, I can't tell you.

[WINSOR *and* MARGARET *exchange looks, and* TWISDEN *drinks from the saucer*.]

MARGARET. Tell him, Charles.

WINSOR. Well! It rained that evening at Meldon. The General happened to put his hand on Dancy's shoulder, and it was damp.

[TWISDEN *puts the saucer down and replaces the cup in it. They both look intently at him*.]

TWISDEN. I take it that General Canynge won't say anything he's not compelled to say.

MARGARET. No, of course; but, Mr Jacob, they might ask; they know it rained. And he is such a George Washington.

TWISDEN [*toying with a pair of tortoise-shell glasses*]. They didn't ask either of *you*. Still—no harm in your telling Dancy.

WINSOR. I'd rather *you* did it, Margaret.

MARGARET. I daresay. [*She mechanically takes out her cigarette-case, catches the lift of* TWISDEN'S *eyebrows, and puts it back*.]

WINSOR. Well, we'll go together. I don't want Mrs Dancy to hear.

MARGARET. Do tell me, Mr Jacob; is he going to win?

TWISDEN. I think so, Margaret; I think so.

MARGARET. It'll be too frightful if he doesn't get a verdict, after all this. But I don't know what we shall do when it's over. I've been sitting in that Court all these three days, watching, and it's made me feel there's nothing we like better than seeing people skinned. Well, bye-bye, bless you!

[TWISDEN *rises and pats her hand*.]

WINSOR. Half a second, Margaret. Wait for me. [*She nods and goes out*.] Mr Twisden, what do you really think?

TWISDEN. I am Dancy's lawyer, my dear Charles, as well as yours.

WINSOR. Well, can I go and see Canynge?

TWISDEN. Better not.

WINSOR. If they get that out of him, and recall me, am I to say he told me of it at the time?

TWISDEN. You didn't feel the coat yourself? And Dancy wasn't present? Then what Canynge told you is not evidence. *We'll* stop your being asked.

WINSOR. Thank goodness. Good-bye! [WINSOR *goes out.*]

[TWISDEN, *behind his table, motionless, taps his teeth with the eyeglasses in his narrow, well-kept hand. After a long shake of his head and a shrug of his rather high shoulders he sniffs, goes to the window and opens it. Then crossing to the door, Left Back, he throws it open and says:*]

TWISDEN. At your service, sir. [GILMAN *comes forth, nursing his pot hat.*] Be seated. [TWISDEN *closes the window behind him, and takes his seat.*]

GILMAN [*taking the client's chair, to the left of the table*]. Mr Twisden, I believe? My name's Gilman, head of Gilman's Department Stores. You have my card.

TWISDEN [*looking at the card*]. Yes. What can we do for you?

GILMAN. Well, I've come to you from a sense of duty, sir, and also a feelin' of embarrassment. [*He takes from his breast pocket an evening paper.*] You see, I've been followin' this Dancy case—it's a good deal talked of in Putney—and I read this at half-past two this afternoon. To be precise, at 2.25. [*He rises and hands the paper to* TWISDEN, *and with a thick gloved forefinger indicates a passage.*] When I read these numbers, I 'appened to remember givin' change for a fifty-pound note—don't often 'ave one in, you know—so I went to the cash-box out of curiosity, to see that I 'adn't got it. Well, I 'ad; and here it is. [*He draws out from his breast pocket and lays before* TWISDEN *a fifty-pound banknote.*] It was brought in to change by a customer of mine three days ago, and he got value for it. Now, that's a stolen note, it seems, and you'd like to know what I did. Mind you, that customer of mine I've known 'im—well—eight or nine years; an Italian he is—wine salesman, and so far's I know, a respectable man—foreign-lookin', but nothin' more. Now, this was at 'alf-past two, and I was at my head branch at Putney, where I live. I want you to mark the time, so as you'll see I 'aven't wasted a minute. I took a cab and I drove straight to my customer's private residence in Putney, where he lives with his daughter—Ricardos his name is, Paolio Ricardos. They tell me there that he's at his business shop in the City. So off I go in the cab again, and there I find him. Well, sir, I showed this paper to him and I produced the note. "Here," I said, "you brought this to me and you got value for it." Well, that man was taken aback. If I'm a judge, Mr Twisden, he was taken aback, not to speak in a guilty way, but he was, as you might say, flummoxed. "Now," I said to him, "where did you get it—that's the point?" He took his time to answer, and then he said: "Well, Mr Gilman," he said, "you know me; I am an honourable man. I can't tell you offhand, but I am above the board." He's foreign, you know, in his expressions. "Yes," I said, "that's all very well," I said, "but here I've got a stolen note and you've got the value for it. Now I tell you," I said, "what I'm going to do; I'm going straight with this note to Mr Jacob Twisden, who's got this Dancy De Levis case in 'and. He's a well-known Society lawyer," I said, "of great experience." "Oh!" he said, "that is what you do?"—funny the way he speaks! "Then I come with you!"—And I've got him in the cab below. I want to tell you everything before he comes up. On the way I tried to get something out of him, but I couldn't—I could *not*. "This is very awkward," I said at last. "It is, Mr Gilman," was his reply; and he began to talk about his Sicilian claret—a very good wine, mind you; but under the circumstances it seemed to me uncalled for. Have I made it clear to you?

TWISDEN [*who has listened with extreme attention*]. Perfectly, Mr Gilman. I'll send down for him. [*He touches a hand-bell. The* YOUNG CLERK *appears at the door, Left Forward.*] A gentleman in a taxi—waiting. Ask him to be so good as to step up. Oh! and send Mr Graviter here again.

[*The* YOUNG CLERK *goes out.*]

GILMAN. As I told you, sir, I've been followin' this case. It's what you might call piquant. And I should be very glad if it came about that this helped Captain Dancy. I take an interest, because, to tell you the truth [*confidentially*] I don't like—well, not to put too fine a point upon it—

'Ebrews. They work harder; they're more sober; they'r
honest; and they're everywhere. I've nothing against them
but the fact is—they get *on* so.

TWISDEN [*cocking an eye*]. A thorn in the flesh, Mr Gilman

GILMAN. Well, I prefer my own countrymen, and that's th
truth of it.

[*As he speaks,* GRAVITER *comes in by the door Left For
ward.*]

TWISDEN [*pointing to the newspaper and the note*]. M
Gilman has brought this, of which he is holder for value
His customer, who changed it three days ago, is coming
up.

GRAVITER. The fifty-pounder. I see. [*His face is long and
reflective.*]

YOUNG CLERK [*entering*]. Mr Ricardos, sir. [*He goes out.*]

[RICARDOS *is a personable, Italian-looking man in a frock
coat, with a dark moustachioed face and dark hair a little
grizzled. He looks anxious, and bows.*]

TWISDEN. Mr Ricardos? My name is Jacob Twisden. My
partner. [*Holding up a finger, as* RICARDOS *would speak*]
Mr Gilman has told us about this note. You took it to
him, he says, three days ago; that is, on Monday, and
received cash for it?

RICARDOS. Yes, sare.

TWISDEN. You were *not* aware that it was stolen?

RICARDOS [*with his hand to his breast*]. Oh! no, sare.

TWISDEN. You received it from——?

RICARDOS. A minute, sare; I would weesh to explain— [*with
an expressive shrug*] in private.

TWISDEN [*nodding*]. Mr Gilman, your conduct has been
most prompt. You may safely leave the matter in our
hands, now. Kindly let us retain this note; and ask for my
cashier as you go out and give him [*he writes*] this. He
will reimburse you. We will take any necessary steps ourselves.

GILMAN [*in slight surprise, with modest pride*]. Well, sir,
I'm in your 'ands. I must be guided by you, with your
experience. I'm glad you think I acted rightly.

TWISDEN. Very rightly, Mr Gilman—very rightly. [*Rising*]
Good-afternoon!

GILMAN. Good-afternoon, sir. Good-afternoon, gentlemen! [*To* TWISDEN] I'm sure I'm very 'appy to have made your acquaintance, sir. It's a well-known name.

TWISDEN. Thank you.

GILMAN *retreats, glances at* RICARDOS, *and turns again.*]

GILMAN. I suppose there's nothing else I ought to do, in the interests of the law? I'm a careful man.

TWISDEN. If there is, Mr Gilman, we will let you know. We have your address. You may make your mind easy; but don't speak of this. It might interfere with Justice.

GILMAN Oh! I shouldn't dream of it. I've no wish to be mixed up in anything conspicuous. That's not my principle at all. Good-day, gentlemen. [*He goes.*]

TWISDEN [*seating himself*]. Now, sir, will you sit down. [*But* RICARDOS *does not sit; he stands looking uneasily across the table at* GRAVITER.] You may speak out.

RICARDOS. Well, Mr Tweesden and sare, this matter is very serious for me, and very delicate—it concairns my honour. I am in a great difficulty.

TWISDEN. When in difficulty—complete frankness, sir.

RICARDOS. It is a family matter, sare, I——

TWISDEN. Let me be frank with you. [*Telling his points off on his fingers*] We have your admission that you changed this stopped note for value. It will be our duty to inform the Bank of England that it has been traced to you. You will have to account to them for your possession of it. I suggest to you that it will be far better to account frankly to us.

RICARDOS [*taking out a handkerchief and quite openly wiping his hands and forehead*]. I received this note, sare, with others, from a gentleman, sare, in settlement of a debt of honour, and I know nothing of where he got them.

TWISDEN. H'm! that is very vague. If that is all you can tell us, I'm afraid——

RICARDOS. Gentlemen, this is very painful for me. It is my daughter's good name—— [*He again wipes his brow.*]

TWISDEN. Come, sir, speak out!

RICARDOS [*desperately*]. The notes were a settlement to her from this gentleman, of whom she was a great friend.

TWISDEN [*suddenly*]. I am afraid we must press you for the name of the gentleman.

RICARDOS. Sare, if I give it to you, and it does 'im 'arm, what

will my daughter say? This is a bad matter for me. I
behaved well to her; and she is attached to him sti...
sometimes she is crying yet because she lost him. Ar
now we betray him, perhaps, who knows? This is very u...
pleasant for me. [*Taking up the paper*] Here it gives t...
number of another note—a 'undred-pound note. I 'av...
that too. [*He takes a note from his breast pocket.*]

GRAVITER. How much did he give you in all?

RICARDOS. For my daughter's settlement one thousan...
pounds. I understand he did not wish to give a chequ...
because of his marriage. So I did not think anything abo...
it being in notes, you see.

TWISDEN. When did he give you this money?

RICARDOS. The middle of Octobare last.

TWISDEN [*suddenly looking up*]. Mr Ricardos, was it Cap...
tain Dancy?

RICARDOS [*again wiping his forehead*]. Gentlemen, I am s...
fond of my daughter. I have only the one, and no wife...

TWISDEN [*with an effort*]. Yes, yes; but I must know.

RICARDOS. Sare, if I tell you, will you give me your goo...
word that my daughter shall not hear of it?

TWISDEN. So far as we are able to prevent it—certainly.

RICARDOS. Sare, I trust you.—It was Captain Dancy.

[*A long pause.*]

GRAVITER [*suddenly*]. Were you blackmailing him?

TWISDEN [*holding up his hand*]. My partner means, did yo...
press him for this settlement?

RICARDOS. I did think it my duty to my daughter to ask tha...
he make compensation to her.

TWISDEN. With threats that you would tell his wife?

RICARDOS [*with a shrug*]. Captain Dancy was a man o...
honour. He said: "Of course I will do this." I trusted him.
And a month later I did remind him, and he gave me this
money for her. I do not know where he got it—I do not
know. Gentlemen, I have invested it all on her—every
penny—except this note, for which I had the purpose to
buy her a necklace. That is the swearéd truth.

TWISDEN. I must keep this note. [*He touches the hundred-
pound note.*] You will not speak of this to anyone. ...
may recognise that you were a holder for value received
—others might take a different view. Good-day, sir. ...
Graviter, see Mr Ricardos out, and take his address.

RICARDOS [*pressing his hands over the breast of his frock coat—with a sigh*]. Gentlemen, I beg you—remember what I said. [*With a roll of his eyes*] My daughter—I am not happee. Good-day.

[*He turns and goes out slowly, Left Forward, followed by RAVITER.*]

WISDEN [*to himself*]. Young Dancy! [*He pins the two notes together and places them in an envelope, then stands motionless except for his eyes and hands, which restlessly express the disturbance within him.* GRAVITER *returns, carefully shuts the door, and going up to him, hands him* RICARDOS' *card. Looking at the card*] Villa Benvenuto. This will have to be verified, but I'm afraid it's true. That man was not acting.

RAVITER. What's to be done about Dancy?

WISDEN. Can you understand a gentleman——?

RAVITER. I don't know, sir. The war loosened "form" all over the place. I saw plenty of that myself. And some men have no moral sense. From the first I've had doubts.

WISDEN. We can't go on with the case.

RAVITER. Phew! . . . [*A moment's silence*] Gosh! It's an awful thing for his wife.

WISDEN. Yes.

RAVITER [*touching the envelope*]. Chance brought this here, sir. That man won't talk—he's too scared.

WISDEN. Gilman.

RAVITER. Too respectable. If De Levis got those notes back, and the rest of the money, anonymously?

WISDEN. But the case, Graviter; the case.

RAVITER. I don't believe this alters what I've been thinking.

WISDEN. Thought is one thing—knowledge another. There's duty to our profession. Ours is a fine calling. On the good faith of solicitors a very great deal hangs. [*He crosses to the hearth as if warmth would help him.*]

RAVITER. It'll let him in for a prosecution. He came to us in confidence.

WISDEN. Not as against the law.

RAVITER. No. I suppose not. [*A pause*] By Jove, I don't like losing this case. I don't like the admission we backed such a wrong 'un.

WISDEN. Impossible to go on. Apart from ourselves, there's Sir Frederic. We must disclose to him—can't let him go

on in the dark. Complete confidence between solicitor a
counsel is the essence of professional honour.

GRAVITER. What are you going to do then, sir?

TWISDEN. See Dancy at once. Get him on the 'phone.

GRAVITER [*taking up the telephone*]. Get me Captain Dancy
flat. . . . What? . . . [*To* TWISDEN] Mrs Dancy is her
That's à propos with a vengeance. Are you going to s
her, sir?

TWISDEN [*after a moment's painful hesitation*]. I must.

GRAVITER [*telephoning*]. Bring Mrs Dancy up. [*He turns
the window.*]

[MABEL DANCY *is shown in, looking very pale.* TWISDE
*advances from the fire, and takes her hand.*]

MABEL. Major Colford's taken Ronny off in his car for th
night. I thought it would do him good. I said I'd con
round in case there was anything you wanted to say be
fore to-morrow.

TWISDEN [*taken aback*]. Where have they gone?

MABEL. I don't know, but he'll be home before ten o'cloc
to-morrow. Is there anything?

TWISDEN. Well, I'd like to see him before the Court sit
Send him on here as soon as he comes.

MABEL [*with her hand to her forehead*]. Oh! Mr Twisder
when will it be over? My head's getting awful sitting i
that Court.

TWISDEN. My dear Mrs Dancy, there's no need at all for yo
to come down to-morrow; take a rest and nurse your head

MABEL. Really and truly?

TWISDEN. Yes; it's the very best thing you can do.

[GRAVITER *turns his head, and looks at them unobserved.*

MABEL. How do you think it's going?

TWISDEN. It went very well to-day; very well indeed.

MABEL. You must be awfully fed up with us.

TWISDEN. My dear young lady, that's our business. [*He
takes her hand.* MABEL'S *face suddenly quivers. Sh
draws her hand away, and covers her lips with it.*] There
there! You want a day off badly.

MABEL. I'm so tired of——! Thank you so much for al
you're doing. Good night! Good night, Mr Graviter!

GRAVITER. Good night, Mrs Dancy.

MABEL goes.]

GRAVITER. D'you know, I believe she knows.

TWISDEN. No, no! She believes in him implicitly. A staunch little woman. Poor thing!

GRAVITER. Hasn't that shaken you, sir? It has me.

TWISDEN. No, no! I—I can't go on with the case. It's breaking faith. Get Sir Frederic's chambers.

GRAVITER [telephoning, and getting a reply, looks round at TWISDEN]. Yes?

TWISDEN. Ask if I can come round and see him.

GRAVITER [telephoning]. Can Sir Frederic spare Mr Twisden a few minutes now if he comes round? [Receiving reply] He's gone down to Brighton for the night.

TWISDEN. H'm! What hotel?

GRAVITER [telephoning]. What's his address? What . . .? [To TWISDEN] The Bedford.

TWISDEN. I'll go down.

GRAVITER [telephoning]. Thank you. All right. [He rings off].

TWISDEN. Just look out the trains down and up early to-morrow.

GRAVITER takes up an A B C, and TWISDEN takes up the Ricardos card.]

TWISDEN. Send to this address in Putney, verify the fact that Ricardos has a daughter, and give me a trunk call to Brighton. Better go yourself, Graviter. If you see her, don't say anything, of course—invent some excuse. [GRAVITER nods.] I'll be up in time to see Dancy.

GRAVITER. By George! I feel bad about this.

TWISDEN. Yes. But professional honour comes first. What time is that train? [He bends over the A B C.]

CURTAIN

## Scene 2

The same room on the following morning at ten-twenty-five, by the Grandfather clock.

The YOUNG CLERK is ushering in DANCY, whose face is per-

*ceptibly harder than it was three months ago, like that of*
*man who has lived under great restraint.*

DANCY. He wanted to see me before the Court sat.

YOUNG CLERK. Yes, sir. Mr Twisden will see you in one mi
ute. He had to go out of town last night. [*He prepares
open the waiting-room door.*]

DANCY. Were *you* in the war?

YOUNG CLERK. Yes.

DANCY. How can you stick this?

YOUNG CLERK [*with a smile*]. My trouble was to stick tha
sir.

DANCY. But you get no excitement from year's end to year
end. It'd drive me mad.

YOUNG CLERK [*shyly*]. A case like this is pretty excitin
I'd give a lot to see us win it.

DANCY [*staring at him*]. Why? What is it to you?

YOUNG CLERK. I don't know, sir. It's—it's like football—yo
want your side to win. [*He opens the waiting-room doo
Expanding*] You see some rum starts, too, in a lawyer
office in a quiet way.

[DANCY *enters the waiting-room, and the* YOUNG CLERK, *shu
ting the door, meets* TWISDEN *as he comes in, Left Forwar
and takes from him overcoat, top hat, and a small bag*

YOUNG CLERK. Captain Dancy's waiting, sir. [*He indicate
the waiting-room.*]

TWISDEN [*narrowing his lips*]. Very well. Mr Graviter gon
to the Courts?

YOUNG CLERK. Yes, sir.

TWISDEN. Did he leave anything for me?

YOUNG CLERK. On the table, sir.

TWISDEN [*taking up an envelope*]. Thank you.

[*The* CLERK *goes.*]

TWISDEN [*opening the envelope and reading*]. "All corrobo
rates." H'm! [*He puts it in his pocket and takes out o
an envelope the two notes, lays them on the table, an
covers them with a sheet of blotting-paper; stands a mo
ment preparing himself, then goes to the door of the waiting-room, opens it, and says:*] Now, Captain Dancy. Sorr
to have kept you waiting.

DANCY [*entering*]. Winsor came to me yesterday about General Canynge's evidence. Is that what you wanted to speak to me about?

TWISDEN. No. It isn't that.

DANCY [*looking at his wrist watch*]. By me it's just on the half-hour, sir.

TWISDEN. Yes. I don't want you to go to the Court.

DANCY. Not?

TWISDEN. I have very serious news for you.

DANCY [*wincing and collecting himself*]. Oh!

TWISDEN. These two notes. [*He uncovers the notes*] After the Court rose yesterday we had a man called Ricardos here. [*A pause*] Is there any need for me to say more?

DANCY [*unflinching*]. No. What now?

TWISDEN. Our duty was plain; we could not go on with the case. I have consulted Sir Frederic. He felt—he felt that he must throw up his brief, and he will do that the moment the Court sits. Now I want to talk to you about what you're going to do.

DANCY. That's very good of you, considering.

TWISDEN. I don't pretend to understand, but I imagine you may have done this in a moment of reckless bravado, feeling, perhaps, that as you gave the mare to De Levis, the money was by rights as much yours as his. [*Stopping DANCY, who is about to speak, with a gesture.*] To satisfy a debt of honour to this—lady; and, no doubt, to save your wife from hearing of it from the man Ricardos. Is that so?

DANCY. To the life.

TWISDEN. It was mad, Captain Dancy, mad!—But the question now is: What do you owe to your wife? She doesn't dream—I suppose?

DANCY [*with a twitching face*]. No.

TWISDEN. We can't tell what the result of this collapse will be. The police have the theft in hand. They may issue a warrant. The money could be refunded, and the costs paid—somehow that can all be managed. But it may not help. In any case, what end is served by your staying in the country? You can't save your honour—that's gone. You can't save your wife's peace of mind. If she sticks to you—do you think she will?

DANCY. Not if she's wise.

TWISDEN. Better go! There's a war in Morocco.

DANCY [*with a bitter smile*]. Good old Morocco!

TWISDEN. Will you go, then, at once, and leave me to break it to your wife?

DANCY. I don't know yet.

TWISDEN. You must decide quickly, to catch a boat train. Many a man has made good. You're a fine soldier.

DANCY. There are alternatives.

TWISDEN. Now, go straight from this office. You've a passport, I suppose: you won't need a *visa* for France, and from there you can find means to slip over. Have you got money on you? [DANCY *nods.*] We will see what we can do to stop or delay proceedings.

DANCY. It's all damned kind of you. [*With difficulty*] But I must think of my wife. Give me a few minutes.

TWISDEN. Yes, yes; go in there and think it out.

[*He goes to the door, Right, and opens it.* DANCY *passes him and goes out.* TWISDEN *rings a bell and stands waiting.*]

CLERK [*entering*]. Yes, sir?

TWISDEN. Tell them to call a taxi.

CLERK [*who has a startled look*]. Yes, sir. Mr Graviter has come in, sir, with General Canynge. Are you disengaged?

TWISDEN. Yes. [*The* CLERK *goes out, and almost immediately* GRAVITER *and* CANYNGE *enter.*] Good-morning, General. [*To* GRAVITER] Well?

GRAVITER. Sir Frederic got up at once and said that since the publication of the numbers of those notes, information had reached him which forced him to withdraw from the case. Great sensation, of course. I left Bromley in charge. There'll be a formal verdict for the defendant, with costs. Have you told Dancy?

TWISDEN. Yes. He's in there deciding what he'll do.

CANYNGE [*grave and vexed*]. This is a dreadful thing, Twisden. I've been afraid of it all along. A soldier! A gallant fellow, too. What on earth got into him?

TWISDEN. There's no end to human nature, General.

GRAVITER. You can see queerer things in the papers, any day.

CANYNGE. That poor young wife of his! Winsor gave me a message for you, Twisden. If money's wanted quickly to save proceedings, draw on him. Is there anything *I* can do?

TWISDEN. I've advised him to go straight off to Morocco.

CANYNGE. I don't know that an asylum isn't the place for him.

He must be off his head at moments. That jump—crazy!
He'd have got a verdict on that alone—if they'd seen those
balconies. I was looking at them when I was down there
last Sunday. Daring thing, Twisden. Very few men, on a
dark night— He risked his life twice. That's a shrewd
fellow—young De Lewis. He spotted Dancy's nature.

[*The* YOUNG CLERK *enters.*]

CLERK. The taxi's here, sir. Will you see Major Colford and
Miss Orme?

TWISDEN. Graviter— No; show them in.

[*The* YOUNG CLERK *goes.*]

CANYNGE. Colford's badly cut up.

[MARGARET ORME *and* COLFORD *enter.*]

COLFORD [*striding forward*]. There must be some mistake
about this, Mr Twisden.

TWISDEN. Hssh! Dancy's in there. He's admitted it.

[*Voices are subdued at once.*]

COLFORD. What? [*With emotion*] If it were my own brother,
I couldn't feel it more. But—damn it! What right had that
fellow to chuck up the case—without letting him know,
too. I came down with Dancy this morning, and he knew
nothing about it.

TWISDEN [*coldly*]. That was unfortunately unavoidable.

COLFORD. Guilty or not, you ought to have stuck to him—
it's not playing the game, Mr Twisden.

TWISDEN. You must allow me to judge where my duty lay, in
a very hard case.

COLFORD. I thought a man was safe with his solicitor.

CANYNGE. Colford, you don't understand professional etiquette.

COLFORD. No, thank God!

TWISDEN. When you have been as long in your profession as
I have been in mine, Major Colford, you will know that
duty to your calling outweighs duty to friend or client.

COLFORD. But I serve the Country.

TWISDEN. And I serve the Law, sir.

CANYNGE. Graviter, give me a sheet of paper. I'll write a
letter for him.

MARGARET [*going up to* TWISDEN]. Dear Mr Jacob—pay De

Levis. You know my pearls—put them up the spout again
　　Don't let Ronny be—

TWISDEN. Money isn't the point, Margaret.

MARGARET. It's ghastly! It really is.

COLFORD. I'm going in to shake hands with him. [*He start*
*to cross the room*].

TWISDEN. Wait! We want him to go straight off to Morocco
　　Don't upset him. [*To* COLFORD *and* MARGARET] I think
　　you had better go. If, a little later, Margaret, you could g
　　round to Mrs Dancy——

COLFORD. Poor little Mabel Dancy! It's perfect hell for her

[*They have not seen that* DANCY *has opened the door behind*
*them.*]

DANCY. It is!

[*They all turn round in consternation.*]

COLFORD [*with a convulsive movement*]. Old boy!

DANCY. No good, Colford. [*Gazing round at them*] Oh!
　　clear out. I can't stand commiseration—and let me have
　　some air.

TWISDEN *motions to* COLFORD *and* MARGARET *to go; and as*
*he turns to* DANCY, *they go out.* GRAVITER *also moves to-*
*wards the door. The* GENERAL *sits motionless.* GRAVITER *goes*
*out.*]

TWISDEN. Well?

DANCY. I'm going home, to clear up things with my wife.
　　General Canynge, I don't quite know why I did the damned
　　thing. But I did, and there's an end of it.

CANYNGE. Dancy, for the honour of the Army, avoid further
　　scandal if you can. I've written a letter to a friend of mine
　　in the Spanish War Office. It will get you a job in their
　　war. [CANYNGE *closes the envelope.*]

DANCY. Very good of you. I don't know if I can make use of
　　it.

[CANYNGE *stretches out the letter, which* TWISDEN *hands*
*to* DANCY, *who takes it.* GRAVITER *re-opens the door.*]

TWISDEN. What is it?

GRAVITER. De Levis is here.

TWISDEN. De Levis? Can't see him.

DANCY. Let him in!

[*After a moment's hesitation* TWISDEN *nods, and* GRAVITER *goes out. The three wait in silence with their eyes fixed on the door, the* GENERAL *sitting at the table,* TWISDEN *by his chair,* DANCY *between him and the door Right.* DE LEVIS *comes in and shuts the door. He is advancing towards* TWISDEN *when his eyes fall on* DANCY, *and he stops.*]

TWISDEN. You wanted to see me?

DE LEVIS [*moistening his lips*]. Yes. I came to say that—that I overheard—I am afraid a warrant is to be issued. I wanted you to realise—it's not *my* doing. I'll give it no support. I'm content. I don't want my money. I don't even want costs. Dancy, do you understand?

[DANCY *does not answer, but looks at him with nothing alive in his face but his eyes.*]

TWISDEN. We are obliged to you, sir. It was good of you to come.

DE LEVIS [*with a sort of darting pride*]. Don't mistake me. I didn't come because I feel Christian; I am a Jew. I will take no money—not even that which was stolen. Give it to a charity. I'm proved right. And now I'm done with the damned thing. Good-morning!

[*He makes a little bow to* CANYNGE *and* TWISDEN, *and turns to face* DANCY, *who has never moved. The two stand motionless, looking at each other, then* DE LEVIS *shrugs his shoulders and walks out. When he is gone there is a silence.*]

CANYNGE [*suddenly*]. You heard what he said, Dancy. You have no time to lose.

[*But* DANCY *does not stir.*]

TWISDEN. Captain Dancy?

[*Slowly, without turning his head, rather like a man in a dream,* DANCY *walks across the room, and goes out.*]

CURTAIN

## Scene 3

*The* DANCYS' *sitting-room, a few minutes later.* MABEL DANCY
*is sitting alone on the sofa with a newspaper on her lap; she
is only just up, and has a bottle of smelling-salts in her hand.
Two or three other newspapers are dumped on the arm of
the sofa. She topples the one off her lap and takes up another
as if she couldn't keep away from them; drops it in turn
and sits staring before her, sniffing at the salts. The door
Right, is opened and* DANCY *comes in.*

MABEL [*utterly surprised*]. Ronny! Do they want me in
   Court?

DANCY. No.

MABEL. What is it, then? Why are you back?

DANCY. Spun.

MABEL [*blank*]. Spun? What do you mean? What's spun?

DANCY. The case. They've found out through those notes.

MABEL. Oh! [*Staring at his face*] Who?

DANCY. Me!

MABEL [*after a moment of horrified stillness*]. Don't, Ronny!
   Oh! No! Don't! [*She buries her face in the pillows of the
   sofa.*]

[DANCY *stands looking down at her.*]

DANCY. Pity you wouldn't come to Africa three months ago.

MABEL. Why didn't you tell me then? I would have gone.

DANCY. You wanted this case. Well, it's fallen down.

MABEL. Oh! Why didn't I face it? But I couldn't—I *had* to
   believe.

DANCY. And now you can't. It's the end, Mabel.

MABEL [*looking up at him*]. No.

[DANCY *goes suddenly on his knees and seizes her hand.*]

DANCY. Forgive me!

MABEL [*putting her hand on his head*]. Yes; oh, yes! I
   think I've known a long time, really. Only—why? What
   made you?

DANCY [*getting up and speaking in jerks*]. It was a crazy
   thing to do; but, damn it, I was only looting a looter. The

money was as much mine as his. A decent chap would have offered me half. You didn't see the brute look at me that night at dinner as much as to say: "You blasted fool!" It made me mad. That wasn't a bad jump—twice over. Nothing in the war took quite such nerve. [*Grimly*] I rather enjoyed that evening.

MABEL. But—money! To keep it!

DANCY [*sullenly*]. Yes, but I had a debt to pay.

MABEL. To a woman?

DANCY. A debt of honour—it wouldn't wait.

MABEL. It was—it was to a woman. Ronny, don't lie any more.

DANCY [*grimly*]. Well! I wanted to save your knowing. I'd promised a thousand. I had a letter from her father that morning, threatening to tell you. All the same, if that tyke hadn't jeered at me for parlour tricks!—But what's the good of all this now? [*Sullenly*] Well—it may cure you of loving me. Get over that, Mab; I never was worth it—and I'm done for!

MABEL. The woman—have you—since——?

DANCY [*energetically*]. No! You supplanted her. But if you'd known I was leaving a woman for you, you'd never have married me. [*He walks over to the hearth.*]

[MABEL *too gets up. She presses her hands to her forehead, then walks blindly round to behind the sofa and stands looking straight in front of her.*]

MABEL [*coldly*]. What has happened, exactly?

DANCY. Sir Frederic chucked up the case. I've seen Twisden; they want me to run for it to Morocco.

MABEL. To the war there?

DANCY. Yes. There's to be a warrant out.

MABEL. A prosecution? Prison? Oh, go! Don't wait a minute! Go!

DANCY. Blast them!

MABEL. Oh, Ronny! Please! Please! Think what you'll want. I'll pack. Quick! No! Don't wait to take things. Have you got money?

DANCY [*nodding*]. This'll be good-bye, then!

MABEL [*after a moment's struggle*]. Oh! No! No, no! I'll follow—I'll come out to you there.

DANCY. D'you mean you'll stick to me?

MABEL. Of course I'll stick to you.

[DANCY *seizes her hand and puts it to his lips. The bell rings*

MABEL [*in terror*]. Who's that? [*The bell rings again.* DANC
moves towards the door.] No! Let *me*!

[*She passes him and steals out to the outer door of the fla.
where she stands listening. The bell rings again. She look
through the slit of the letter-box. While she is gone* DANCY
*stands quite still, till she comes back.*]

MABEL. Through the letter-box—I can see— It's—it's police
Oh! God! . . . Ronny! I can't bear it.
DANCY. Heads up, Mab! Don't show the brutes!
MABEL. Whatever happens, I'll go on loving you. If it'
prison—*I'll wait.* Do you understand? I don't care wha
you did—I don't *care!* I'm just the same. I will be jus
the same when you come back to me.
DANCY [*slowly*]. That's not in human nature.
MABEL. It is. It's in *me*.
DANCY. I've crocked up your life.
MABEL. No, no! Kiss me!

[*A long kiss, till the bell again startles them apart, and there
is a loud knock.*]

DANCY. They'll break the door in. It's no good—we must
open. Hold them in check a little. I want a minute or two.
MABEL [*clasping him*]. Ronny! Oh, Ronny! It won't be for
long—I'll be waiting! I'll be waiting—I swear it.
DANCY. Steady, Mab! [*Putting her back from him*] Now!

[*He opens the bedroom door, Left, and stands waiting for
her to go. Summoning up her courage, she goes to open the
outer door. A sudden change comes over* DANCY'S *face;
from being stony it grows almost maniacal.*]

DANCY [*under his breath*]. No! No! By God! No! [*He goes
out into the bedroom, closing the door behind him.*]

[MABEL *has now opened the outer door, and disclosed*
INSPECTOR DEDE *and the* YOUNG CONSTABLE *who were sum-
moned to Meldon Court on the night of the theft, and have
been witnesses in the case. Their voices are heard.*]

MABEL. Yes?

INSPECTOR. Captain Dancy in, madam?

MABEL. I am not quite sure—I don't think so.

INSPECTOR. I wish to speak to him a minute. Stay here, Grover. Now, madam!

MABEL. Will you come in while I see?

*She comes in, followed by the* INSPECTOR.]

INSPECTOR. I should think you must be sure, madam. This is not a big place.

MABEL. He was changing his clothes to go out. I think he has gone.

INSPECTOR. What's that door?

MABEL. To our bedroom.

INSPECTOR [*moving towards it*]. He'll be in there, then.

MABEL. What do you want, Inspector?

INSPECTOR [*melting*]. Well, madam, it's no use disguising it. I'm exceedingly sorry, but I've a warrant for his arrest.

MABEL. Inspector!

INSPECTOR. I'm sure I've every sympathy for you, madam; but I must carry out my instructions.

MABEL. And break my heart?

INSPECTOR. Well, madam, we're—we're not allowed to take that into consideration. The Law's the Law.

MABEL. Are you married?

INSPECTOR. I am.

MABEL. If you—your wife——[*The* INSPECTOR *raises his hand, deprecating. Speaking low*]. Just half an hour! Couldn't you? It's two lives—two whole lives! We've only been married four months. Come back in half an hour. It's such a little thing—nobody will know. Nobody. Won't you?

INSPECTOR. Now, madam—you must know my duty.

MABEL. Inspector, I beseech you—just half an hour.

INSPECTOR. No, no—don't you try to undermine me—I'm sorry for you; but don't you try it! [*He tries the handle, then knocks at the door.*]

DANCY'S VOICE. One minute!

INSPECTOR. It's locked. [*Sharply*] Is there another door to that room? Come, now! [*The bell rings. Moving towards the door, Left; to the* CONSTABLE] Who's that out there?

CONSTABLE. A lady and gentleman, sir.

INSPECTOR. What lady and— Stand by, Grover!
DANCY'S VOICE. All right! You can come in *now*.

[*There is the noise of a lock being turned. And almost im
mediately the sound of a pistol shot in the bedroom.* MABE
*rushes to the door, tears it open, and disappears within, fol
lowed by the* INSPECTOR, *just as* MARGARET ORME *an*
COLFORD *come in from the passage, pursued by the* CON
STABLE. *They, too, all hurry to the bedroom door and dis
appear for a moment; then* COLFORD *and* MARGARET *reappear
supporting* MABEL, *who faints as they lay her on the sofa*
COLFORD *takes from her hand an envelope, and tears it open.*]

COLFORD. It's addressed to *me*. [*He reads it aloud to*
MARGARET *in a low voice.*] "DEAR COLFORD,—This is th
only decent thing I can do. It's too damned unfair to her
It's only another jump. A pistol keeps faith. Look after
her. Colford—my love to her, and you."

[MARGARET *gives a sort of choking sob, then, seeing th
smelling bottle, she snatches it up, and turns to reviv*
MABEL.]

COLFORD. Leave her! The longer she's unconscious, the better
INSPECTOR [*re-entering*]. This is a very serious business
sir.
COLFORD [*sternly*]. Yes, Inspector; you've done for my best
friend.
INSPECTOR. I, sir? He shot himself.
COLFORD. Hari-kari.
INSPECTOR. Beg pardon?
COLFORD [*he points with the letter to* MABEL]. For her
sake, and his own.
INSPECTOR [*putting out his hand*]. I'll want that, sir.
COLFORD [*grimly*]. You shall have it read at the inquest. Till
then—it's addressed to me, and I stick to it.
INSPECTOR. Very well, sir. Do you want to have a look at
him?

[COLFORD *passes quickly into the bedroom, followed by the*
INSPECTOR. MARGARET *remains kneeling beside* MABEL.
COLFORD *comes quickly back.* MARGARET *looks up at him. He
stands very still.*]

OLFORD. Neatly—through the heart.

MARGARET [*wildly*]. Keeps faith! We've all done that. It's not enough.

OLFORD. [*looking down at* MABEL]. All right, old boy!

**THE CURTAIN FALLS**

# JAMES M. BARRIE

## 1860–1937

SIR JAMES MATTHEW BARRIE is a name that recalls to most minds the pretty fantasy of *Peter Pan*—a play which, while being a delight to children, hardly seems of the stuff to be remarked in a history of the British theatre. *Peter Pan,* however, does demonstrate Barrie's use of the dreamlike, mythical situation that characterizes most of his plays, including the one in this volume, *Dear Brutus.*

*Dear Brutus* is the story of a group of people thrown together to have a "second chance" at life through the eerie medium of a gnome-like man on Midsummer's Eve. Weaving the realistic with the fantastic in a comic manner, Barrie, always dreading the unhappy ending, succeeded masterfully in conveying a truth first told us by Shakespeare: that the fault is in ourselves, that we are underlings.

The message of *Dear Brutus* (written at the conclusion of World War I) hints at a pessimistic strain that we may find somewhat surprising in a playwright who continually spun frothy tall tales and insisted upon belief: "I fancy," he wrote in a letter to Arthur Quiller-Couch, "I try to create an artificial world to myself because the one I really inhabit . . . becomes too sombre." Barrie, unlike Galsworthy, trusted in the magic of the theatre to create his imaginary universe. Still, the mythical world of *Dear Brutus* abounds in irony, sarcasm, and the sense of a kind of tragic paradox in which time destroys our innocence, yet leaves us, somehow, responsible for our insufficiencies.

Barrie, in his lifelong concern with the dream drama, is out of the mainstream of his contemporaries whose plays plead openly for social reform. His subdued sense of disillusionment shows that he shared their sentiments. But Barrie was busy reiterating a faith in the poetic power of the stage that stands airily, importantly apart in a time heavy with prosaic problem plays.

# *TO THE CRITICS' CIRCLE*[1]

## Savoy Hotel—May 26, 1922

M R. A. B. WALKLEY, President of the Circle, was in the Chair. Proposing a toast of 'The Drama and Barrie,' he said:—

I fear I am going to disappoint most of you at the outset, though I hope to bring unlooked-for relief to our honoured guest, Sir James Barrie. I am not going to address him as M'Connachie. Since you raised that Frankenstein's Monster, sir, at St. Andrews—you were once a journalist yourself, and will not have forgotten those journalistic favourites, Frankenstein and his Monster—since you raised that monster, you have been powerless to lay it. You have been M'Connachie here and M'Connachied there; M'Connachied with damnable iteration. Sir, let us drop it to-night. It is not, for one thing, the easiest of after-dinner words. And then, I fancy, it was an article intended for local consumption, for the people of Fife and Forfar. You told them in Fife how some of their queer words amazed you people in Forfarshire. Well, sir, we are Southrons and are apt to be—I won't say amazed—but rather puzzled by the queer words of both Fife and Forfarshire. We are like Mr. Micawber, when he quoted Burns about the 'gowans'—'I don't know exactly what gowans may be,' said Mr. Micawber.

So I will not address you as M'Connachie but simply as Sir James Barrie—and say that we have welcomed you to our board to-night as the best beloved of our dramatists. I avoid the word 'great,' still more the word 'greatest,' because those are idle words, characterizing nothing. Also, I am

[1] James M. Barrie's "Speech to The Critics' Circle," (1922) is reprinted with the permission of Charles Scribner's Sons from *M'Connachie and J.M.B.* Speeches by J. M. Barrie. Copyright 1938, 1939 Charles Scribner's Sons.

warned by a story I lately came across about Mr. Booke
Washington, the great negro philanthropist. A Southern ge
tleman of the old school met Mr. Washington and said t
him—'Well, sir, I guess you must be the greatest man i
these United States.' Mr. Washington modestly thought ther
must be some greater man, and instanced President Roose
velt. 'No, sir,' said the Southerner, 'I did think he was a grea
man, until he asked *you* to dinner.' Well, sir, after that, a
we have asked you to dinner, I feel that to use the wor
greatest would be an ambiguous compliment both to you an
to ourselves.

It is peculiarly pleasant to me to have this privilege o
toasting you as a dramatist, because I carry my mind bac
many, many years—let us say to a moment in the reign o
Queen Victoria—when you walked with me through a littl
Surrey pine-wood (I remember it was a pine-wood, becaus
you told me the fir-cones were called 'needles' in Scotland
and you confided to me how very much you wanted to writ
for the stage. Well, sir, you have had your heart's desire
Heaven forbid that I should attempt at this moment to appre
ciate, even in a bird's-eye view, the work you have done fo
our stage. This is not, I am sure you will all agree with me
an occasion for dramatic criticism; we have enough of tha
on other nights in the week; this is an off-night. Yet it woul
perhaps be just a little paradoxical if, in proposing the toas
of 'The Drama and Barrie,' I should be entirely silent abou
the relation between the two. One word, then, on that rela
tion I must say.

You seem to me, sir, to have *transfigured* our drama. I
mean that, under the most familiar and homely features
you have revealed to us unsuspected shapes of beauty. I
am not thinking of your lighter moods, when 'Queen Mab
hath been with you,' your fun and whim and quaint impish
fancies, your 'Barrieisms,' as we have to call them, because
they are unlike anything else. I am thinking of your graver
moods. But I do not forget that this is a festive occasion
and I must not be out of harmony with it. You remember
Dickens's story of Cruikshank at the funeral. He was on his
knees, when the parson said something that annoyed him,
and he whispered to his neighbour, 'If this weren't a funeral
I'd punch his head.' If this weren't a festive occasion, sir, I
would say that you have wrung our hearts, almost beyond
pardon. If this weren't a festive occasion, I would say that

you have given us glimpses into the mysteries of life and death and time that have sent us away strangely taken, almost beside ourselves. There, I think, is your magic, your fascination. It *is* a fascination. Our oldest veteran of the stage—he was with you at St. Andrews—told me he had been some dozen times to 'Mary Rose'; he simply couldn't tear himself away.

Sir James Barrie said in reply:—

Scum! Critics to right of him, critics to left of him, critics upper entrance at back leading to conservatory, critics down stage centre—into that Circle some one has blundered. How I wish I could keep it up, dealing blows all around in this author's well-known sledge-hammer style. 'Barrie gives them Beans'—*Evening News*. 'A Roland for an Oliver'—*Daily Chronicle*. 'Swashbuckler Barrie swashes on his Buckler'—*Mail*. 'Barrie spells Walkley with a small 'w'—*Morning Post*. That is the kind I should like to give you. But, alas! in the words of the poet Pewelli of the blessed isle, so familiar to you all, Poga, *mema allalula,* which means that your chairman has spiked my guns. . . .

I remember once going the length of very nearly telling a critic that quite possibly he was mistaken. It was many years ago, before I had written any plays, when red blood boiled in my veins. It is not a bad story, though unfortunately the critic comes rather well out of it, indeed I would not repeat it here except that I come rather well out of it also. It marks the night when I decided upon a rule of conduct with regard to you gentlemen, which, so far as I can remember, I have never broken. A historic occasion for me, therefore, and I am sorry I cannot remember what the weather was like. The criticized was one of my first books, a Scotch novel, and the critic was a man to whom I suppose every one here would take off his hat in homage and in proud memory—Andrew Lang. He not only slaughtered my book, but attacked my Scotch and picked out one word in particular as not being Scotch at all. To be as particular as that is perhaps always a mistake in criticism, and I thought I had him. I wrote a brief letter to that paper saying that this word was not only good Scotch but was in frequent use in the Waverley novels, that I could tell Mr. Lang in which, but that as he was at present editing them he would find them all worth reading. I then put the letter in my desk and went exultantly to bed. But there was something wrong about it and I could not sleep, and somewhere in the early hours I made up my mind to tear up that letter and never in my life to answer criticism. These two vows I have kept, and in both cases with a happy result. A few days afterwards Mr. Lang wrote in that same paper—and you are good men if you can do what Lang did—saying that he was rather unhappy about his review because he considered, on reflection, that he had not been quite fair to the book. Well, that led to a friendship much valued by me, though the word was never, never referred to between us. As for the other half of my vow, I like to think it is part of the reason why you have done me the honour of asking me here tonight.

Not, of course, that there is anything objectionable in our arguing with one another, but the other way seems to suit me best. Sometimes I must admit it has been rather a close thing. Several times I have indited a reply saying 'Oh indeed!' or something stinging like that; but my post-box is at the far end of the street and there is also time for reflection when one is putting on one's muffler. So the retort is never sent, though if the post-box were nearer or the muffler were not one of those that goes round twice, there is no telling. I have never even answered Mr. Shaw, though in the days when he was a critic he began an article on a play of mine with some such words as these, 'This is worse than Shakespeare.' I admit that this rankled. I wish I could think, gentlemen, that my forbearance towards you is owing to deeply artistic reasons; but no, it is merely because I for ever see the fates hanging over you and about to stretch forth a claw. However you may ram it in—I refer to the rapier— I have a fear that something disastrous is about to happen to you in the so much more important part of your life that has nothing to do with the pen—bad news, ill health, sudden loss; and so I forgive you and tear up. I am even letting you off cheaply to-night in case one of you is run over on the way home, as I have a presentiment is going to happen. How easy it would be for some incensed author to follow a critic or two to their office on a first night and give them a sudden push as a bus came along. But I dare say you are all rather nippy at the curbstones.

So you see it is no use my attempting to talk to you about the drama of to-morrow. That secret lies with the young, and

I beg of you not to turn away from them impatiently because of their 'knowingness,' as Mr. Hardy calls it in his new book. The young writers know as much about nothing as we know about everything. Yet they suffer much from the abominable conditions of the stage. Through them only shall its salvation come. Give them every friendly consideration, if only because they belong to the diminishing handful which does not call a play a show. 'Have you seen our show?'—'I call that a nice little show.' Heigho! Has the time come, gentlemen, for us all to pack up and depart? No, no, the drama will bloom again, though it will not be in that garden. Mr. Milne is a very fine tulip already, and there are others for you to water. Miss Dane has proved that the ladies have arrived. For my part, anything I can suggest for the drama's betterment is so simple that I am sure it must be wrong. I feel we have all become too self-conscious about the little parts we play—they are little parts even in our own little lives. If we talked less about how things should be done there might be more time for doing them. Suppose we were to have a close season, in which we confined ourselves to trying to write our plays better, act them better, produce them better, criticize them better. But it can't be so simple as that.

I wish I could write mine better, and I presume I am revealing no secret when I tell you that the only reason I don't is because I can't. If there were any other reason I should deserve the contempt of every one of you. I remember my earliest lesson in that.

For several days after my first book was published I carried it about in my pocket, and took surreptitious peeps at it to make sure that the ink had not faded. I watched a bookshop where it was exposed on a shelf outside the window, and one day a lady—most attractive—picked up my book and read whole paragraphs, laid it down, went away, came back, read more paragraphs, laid it down, went away, came back, read more paragraphs, felt for her purse, but finally went away without buying. I have always thought that if my book had been a little bit better she would have bought it. 'The little more and how much it is.' In that case a shilling. But what should be written up behind the scenes is 'The little less and how much it is.'

You have all in the course of earning your livelihood applied adjectives to me, but the only criticism that makes me writhe is that observation of Mr. Shaw's which I have already quoted. I wonder if he has changed his mind. He has changed all sorts of things. Here I must begin to be gloomy. None of your adjectives gets to the mark as much as one I have found for myself—'Inoffensive Barrie.' I see how much it at once strikes you all. A bitter pill; but it looks as if on one subject I were the best critic in the room.

Your word for me would probably be fantastic. I was quite prepared to hear it from your chairman, because I felt he could not be so shabby as to say whimsical, and that he might forget to say elusive. If you knew how dejected those terms have often made me. I am quite serious. I never believed I was any of those things until you dinned them into me. Few have tried harder to be simple and direct. I have also always thought that I was rather realistic. In this matter, gentlemen, if I may say it without any ill-feeling, as indeed I do, you have damped me a good deal, and sometimes put out the light altogether. It is a terrible business if one is to have no sense at all about his own work. Wandering in darkness.

To return to cheerier topics. I don't often go to the theatre though I always go to Mr. Shaw's plays, not so much for the ordinary reasons as to see whether I can find an explanation for that extraordinary remark of his. But I will tell you what I think is the best play written in my time. My reason for considering it the best is that it is the one I have thought most about since; not perhaps a bad test. I mean Pinero's 'Iris.' One more confession—I will tell you what has pleased me most about any play of mine. It is that everything included and the dresses coming from the theatre wardrobe, the production of one of them, a little one, is true, 'The Twelve Pound Look,' cost just under £5.

My not going often to the theatre is not because I don't like it, but because the things I like best about it can be seen without actually going in. I like to gaze at the actors, not when dressed for their parts, but as they emerge by the stage-door. I have never got past the satisfaction of this and it is heightened when the play is my own. The stage door-keeper is still to me the most romantic figure in any theatre, and I hope he is the best paid. I have even tried to dart past him, but he never knows me, and I am promptly turned back. I wait, though, in the crowd, which usually consists of about four or six persons, not of the élite, and when the star comes out they cheer and I hiss. I mean just the same as they do, but I hiss. This sometimes leads to momentary trouble with the other loiterers, but in the end we adjourn inoffensively to a coffee stall, where I stand treat, and where we were caught by a cinema machine a few months ago.

You may sometimes wonder why I write so much about islands, and indeed I have noticed a certain restiveness in some of you on the subject. There are more islands in my plays than any of you are aware of. I have the cunning to call them by other names. There is one thing I am really good at, and that is at slipping in an island. I dare say it is those islands that make you misunderstand me. I would feel as if I had left off clothing if I were to write without an island. Now could there be a more realistic statement than that. At present I am residing on an island. It is called Typee, and so you will not be surprised to hear that my companion's name is Fyaway. She is a dusky maid, composed of abstractions but not in the least elusive. She is just little bits of the golden girls who have acted for me and saved my plays. There is not one of them whom I have not watched for at the stage-door and hissed ecstatically. She moves about my coral isle with the swallow-flights of Ellen Terry, and melts into the incomparable Maude Adams. She has Irene Vanbrugh's eyes to light the beacons to scare the ships away; and there are bits in her of many other dear sirens who, little aware of what I have plucked, think that they are appearing complete to-night in London.

> With here and there a Peter Pan
> And here and there Fay Compton
> And everywhere Trevelyan.

Forbes Robertson retired so that he could lend to us, on the island, his silver voice, and du Maurier pulls in with Bancroft to make sure that we are not acting. There is no theatre as yet, but Charles Frohman is looking for a site. For the dead are here also, and you can hardly distinguish them from the living. The laughing Irving boys arrive in a skiff, trying to capsize each other; and on magic nights there is Sir Henry himself pacing along the beach, a solitary figure. If Shakespeare were to touch upon our shores he would offer to sell us Fame at a penny the yard—no bidders. Sometimes a play is written and put into a bottle and cast into the sea. I expect it never reaches you; at any rate if it is whimsical that is not it. Fyaway has a native name for me which means 'The Inoffensive One.'

Come to our island when you feel you have been sufficiently mauled by the rocks of life, and we will give you grassy huts. You can still write your criticisms. Bring your bottles. As I may not pass this way again, I may say that A. B. W.'s hut stands waiting him, a specially attractive one with palms and a running stream. We had a long discussion about Mr. Shaw, but we have decided to let him land.

I thank you heartily, gentlemen, for the high honour you have done me. Mutual respect is, I am sure, all we ask of each other. Ii must be obvious to you that in making such a long speech I had two main objects, to try a new title on you—'The Inoffensive Gentleman'; and to watch whether I thought you could stand one more island.

# DEAR BRUTUS

A Comedy in Three Acts

by James M. Barrie

*1923*

# DEAR BRUTUS[1]

## CHARACTERS

MRS. COADE
ALICE DEARTH
MABEL PURDIE
JOANNA TROUT
LADY CAROLINE LANEY
JAMES MATEY
LOB
MR. COADE
JACK PURDIE
WILL DEARTH
MARGARET DEARTH

---

[1] *Dear Brutus* is reprinted with the permission of Charles Scribner's Sons. (Copyright 1922 J. M. Barrie; renewal copyright 1950 Lady Cynthia Asquith, Peter Llewelyn Davies, Barclay's Bank).

# ACT ONE

*The scene is a darkened room, which the curtain reveals so stealthily that if there was a mouse on the stage it is there still. Our object is to catch our two chief characters unawares; they are Darkness and Light.*

*The room is so obscure as to be invisible, but at the back of the obscurity are French windows, through which is seen Lob's garden bathed in moonshine. The Darkness and Light, which this room and garden represent, are very still, but we should feel that it is only the pause in which old enemies regard each other before they come to the grip. The moonshine stealing about among the flowers, to give them their last instructions, has left a smile upon them, but it is a smile with a menace in it for the dwellers in darkness. What we expect to see next is the moonshine slowly pushing the windows open, so that it may whisper to a confederate in the house, whose name is Lob. But though we may be sure that this was about to happen it does not happen; a stir among the dwellers in darkness prevents it.*

*These unsuspecting ones are in the dining-room, and as a communicating door opens we hear them at play. Several tenebrious shades appear in the lighted doorway and hesitate on the two steps that lead down into the unlit room. The fanciful among us may conceive a rustle at the same moment among the flowers. The engagement has begun, though not in the way we had intended.*

VOICES.—
  'Go on, Coady: lead the way.'
  'Oh dear, I don't see why I should go first.'
  'The nicest always goes first.'
  'It is a strange house if I am the nicest.'
  'It is a strange house.'

[ 305 ]

*'Don't close the door; I can't see where the switch is.'*
*'Over here.'*

They have been groping their way forward, blissfully un-
aware of how they shall be groping there again more terribly before the night is out. Someone finds a switch, and the
room is illumined, with the effect that the garden seems to
have drawn back a step as if worsted in the first encounter.
But it is only waiting.

The apparently inoffensive chamber thus suddenly revealed
is, for a bachelor's home, creditably like a charming country
house drawing-room and abounds in the little feminine
touches that are so often best applied by the hand of man.
There is nothing in the room inimical to the ladies, unless it
be the cut flowers which are from the garden and possibly in
collusion with it. The fireplace may also be a little dubious.
It has been hacked out of a thick wall which may have been
there when the other walls were not, and is presumably the
cavern where Lob, when alone, sits chatting to himself among
the blue smoke. He is as much at home by this fire as any
gnome that may be hiding among its shadows; but he is less
familiar with the rest of the room, and when he sees it, as
for instance on his lonely way to bed, he often stares long
and hard at it before chuckling uncomfortably.

There are five ladies, and one only of them is elderly, the
MRS. COADE whom a voice in the darkness has already proclaimed the nicest. She is the nicest, though the voice was no
good judge. COADY, as she is familiarly called and as her
husband also is called, each having for many years been
able to answer for the other, is a rounded old lady with a
beaming smile that has accompanied her from childhood.
If she lives to be a hundred she will pretend to the census
man that she is only ninety-nine. She has no other vice that
has not been smoothed out of existence by her placid life,
and she has but one complaint against the male COADY, the
rather odd one that he has long forgotten his first wife. Our
MRS. COADE never knew the first one, but it is she alone who
sometimes looks at the portrait of her and preserves in their
home certain mementoes of her, such as a lock of brown
hair, which the equally gentle male COADY must have treas-
ured once but has now forgotten. The first wife had been
slightly lame, and in their brief married life he had carried
solicitously a rest for her foot, had got so accustomed to

doing this, that after a quarter of a century with our MRS. COADE he still finds footstools for her as if she were lame also. She has ceased to pucker her face over this, taking it as a kind little thoughtless attention, and indeed with the years has developed a friendly limp.

Of the other four ladies, all young and physically fair, two are married. MRS. DEARTH is tall, of smouldering eye and fierce desires, murky beasts lie in ambush in the labyrinths of her mind, she is a white-faced gypsy with a husky voice, most beautiful when she is sullen, and therefore frequently at her best. The other ladies when in conclave refer to her as THE DEARTH. MRS. PURDIE is a safer companion for the toddling kind of man. She is soft and pleading, and would seek what she wants by laying her head on the loved one's shoulder, while THE DEARTH might attain it with a pistol. A brighter spirit than either is JOANNA TROUT who, when her affections are not engaged, has a merry face and figure, but can dismiss them both at the important moment, which is at the word 'love.' Then JOANNA quivers, her sense of humour ceases to beat and the dullest man may go ahead. There remains LADY CAROLINE LANEY of the disdainful poise, lately from the enormously select school where they are taught to pronounce their R's as W's; nothing else seems to be taught, but for matrimonial success nothing else is necessary. Every woman who pronounces R as W will find a mate; it appeals to all that is chivalrous in man.

An old-fashioned gallantry induces us to accept from each of these ladies her own estimate of herself, and fortunately it is favourable in every case. This refers to their estimate of themselves up to the hour of ten on the evening on which we first meet them; the estimate may have changed temporarily by the time we part from them on the following morning. What their mirrors say to each of them is, A dear face, not classically perfect but abounding in that changing charm which is the best type of English womanhood; here is a woman who has seen and felt far more than her reticent nature readily betrays; she sometimes smiles, but behind that concession, controlling it in a manner hardly less than adorable, lurks the sigh called Knowledge; a strangely interesting face, mysterious; a line for her tombstone might be 'If I had been a man what adventures I could have had with her who lies here.'

Are these ladies then so very alike? They would all deny

*it, so we must take our own soundings. At this moment o*
*their appearance in the drawing-room at least they are alik*
*in having a common interest. No sooner has the dining*
*room door closed than purpose leaps to their eyes; oddl*
*enough, the men having been got rid of, the drama begins*

ALICE DEARTH [*the darkest spirit but the bravest*]. We mus
not waste a second. Our minds are made up, I think?

JOANNA. Now is the time.

MRS. COADE [*at once delighted and appalled*]. Yes, now i
at all; but should we?

ALICE. Certainly; and before the men come in.

MABEL PURDIE. You don't think we should wait for the men'
They are as much in it as we are.

LADY CAROLINE [*unlucky, as her opening remark is withou*
*a single* R]. Lob would be with them. If the thing is to be
done at all it should be done now.

MRS. COADE. Is it quite fair to Lob? After all, he is our host

JOANNA. Of course it isn't fair to him, but let's do it, Coady

MRS. COADE. Yes, let's do it!

MABEL. Mrs. Dearth *is* doing it.

ALICE [*who is writing out a telegram*]. Of course I am.
The men are not coming, are they?

JOANNA [*reconnoitring*]. No; your husband is having another
glass of port.

ALICE. I am sure he is. One of you ring, please.

[*The bold* JOANNA *rings.*]

MRS. COADE. Poor Matey!

LADY CAROLINE. He wichly desewves what he is about to
get.

JOANNA. He is coming! Don't all stand huddled together like
conspirators.

MRS. COADE. It is what we are!

[*Swiftly they find seats, and are sunk thereon like ladies*
*waiting languidly for their lords, when the doomed butler*
*appears. He is a man of brawn, who would cast any one of*
*them forth for a wager; but we are about to connive at the*
*triumph of mind over matter.*]

ALICE [*always at her best before "the bright face of*
*danger"*]. Ah, Matey, I wish this telegram sent.

MATEY [*a general favourite*]. Very good, ma'am. The village

post office closed at eight, but if your message is important——

ᴸICE. It is; and you are so clever, Matey, I am sure that
you can persuade them to oblige you.

ᴹATEY [*taking the telegram*]. I will see to it myself, ma'am;
you can depend on its going.

*There comes a little gasp from* COADY, *which is the equiva-
ent to dropping a stitch in needle-work.*]

ᴸICE [*who is* THE DEARTH *now*]. Thank you. Better read
the telegram Matey, to be sure that you can make it
out. [MATEY *reads it to himself, and he has never quite
the same faith in woman again.* THE DEARTH *continues in
a purring voice.*] Read it aloud, Matey.

ᴹATEY. Oh, ma'am!

ᴸICE [*without the purr*]. Aloud.

*Thus encouraged, he reads the fatal missive.*]

ᴹATEY. 'To Police Station, Great Cumney. Send officer first
thing to-morrow morning to arrest Matey, butler, for theft
of rings.'

ᴸICE. Yes, that is quite right.

ᴹATEY. Ma'am! [*But seeing that she has taken up a book,
he turns to* LADY CAROLINE.] My lady!

ᴸADY CAROLINE [*whose voice strikes colder than* THE
ᴰEARTH'S]. Should we not say how many rings?

ᴸICE. Yes, put in the number of rings, Matey.

[MATEY *does not put in the number, but he produces three
ᵣings from unostentatious parts of his person and returns
ᵗhem without noticeable dignity to their various owners.*]

ᴹATEY [*hopeful that the incident is now closed*]. May I
tear up the telegram, ma'am?

ᴸICE. Certainly not.

ᴸADY CAROLINE. I always said that this man was the culpwit.
I am nevaw mistaken in faces, and I see bwoad awwows
all over youws, Matey.

[*He might reply that he sees* W's *all over hers, but it is no
ᵐoment for repartee.*]

ᴹATEY. It is deeply regretted.

ALICE [*darkly*]. I am sure it is.

JOANNA [*who has seldom remained silent for so long*]. W
may as well tell him now that it is not our rings we a
worrying about. They have just been a means to an en
Matey.

[*The stir among the ladies shows that they have arrived
the more interesting point*.]

ALICE. Precisely. In other words that telegram is sent u
less——

[MATEY'S *head rises*.]

JOANNA. Unless you can tell us instantly what peculiarity
is that all we ladies have in common.

MABEL. Not only the ladies; all the guests in this house.

ALICE. We have been here a week, and we find that whe
Lob invited us he knew us all so little that we begin
wonder why he asked us. And now from words he ha
let drop we know that we were invited because of some
thing he thinks we have in common.

MABEL. But he won't say what it is.

LADY CAROLINE [*drawing back a little from* JOANNA]. On
knows that no people could be more unlike.

JOANNA [*thankfully*]. One does.

MRS. COADE. And we can't sleep at night, Matey, for won
dering what this something is.

JOANNA [*summing up*]. But we are sure you know, and i
you don't tell us—quod.

MATEY [*with growing uneasiness*]. I don't know what yo
mean, ladies.

ALICE. Oh yes, you do.

MRS. COADE. You must admit that your master is a ver
strange person.

MATEY [*wriggling*]. He is a little odd, ma'am. That is wh
every one calls him Lob; not Mr. Lob.

JOANNA. He is so odd that it has got on my nerves that w
have been invited here for some sort of horrid experiment
[MATEY *shivers*.] You look as if you thought so too!

MATEY. Oh no, miss, I—he—[*The words he would kee
back elude him*]. You shouldn't have come, ladies; yo
didn't ought to have come. [*For the moment he is sorrie
for them than for himself*.]

ADY CAROLINE. Shouldn't have come! Now, my man, what do you mean by that?

MATEY. Nothing, my lady: I—I just mean, why did you come if you are the kind he thinks?

MABEL. The kind he thinks?

LICE. What kind does he think? Now we are getting at it.

MATEY [*guardedly*]. I haven't a notion, ma'am.

ADY CAROLINE [*whose w's must henceforth be supplied by the judicious reader*]. Then it is not necessarily our virtue that makes Lob interested in us?

MATEY [*thoughtlessly*]. No, my lady; oh no, my lady. [*This makes an unfavourable impression.*]

MRS. COADE. And yet, you know, he is rather lovable.

MATEY [*carried away*]. He is, ma'am. He is the most lovable old devil—I beg pardon, ma'am.

JOANNA. You scarcely need to, for in a way it is true. I have seen him out there among his flowers, petting them, talking to them, coaxing them till they simply *had* to grow.

LICE [*making use perhaps of the wrong adjective*]. It is certainly a divine garden.

*They all look at the unblinking enemy.*]

MRS. COADE [*not more deceived than the others*]. How lovely it is in the moonlight! Roses, roses, all the way. [*Dreamily.*] It is like a hat I once had when I was young.

ALICE. Lob is such an amazing gardener that I believe he could even grow hats.

ADY CAROLINE [*who will catch it for this*]. He is a wonderful gardener; but is that quite nice at his age? What *is* his age, man?

MATEY [*shuffling*]. He won't tell, my lady. I think he is frightened that the police would step in if they knew how old he is. They do say in the village that they remember him seventy years ago, looking just as he does to-day.

ALICE. Absurd.

MATEY. Yes, ma'am; but there are his razors.

ADY CAROLINE. Razors?

MATEY. *You* won't know about razors, my lady, not being married—as yet—excuse me. But a married lady can tell a man's age by the number of his razors. [*A little scared.*] If you saw his razors—there is a little world of them, from patents of the present day back to implements so

horrible, you can picture him with them in his hand scra
ing his way through the ages.

LADY CAROLINE. You amuse one to an extent. Was he ev
married?

MATEY [*too lightly*]. He has quite forgotten, my lady. [*R
flecting.*] How long ago is it since Merry England?

LADY CAROLINE. Why do you ask?

MABEL. In Queen Elizabeth's time, wasn't it?

MATEY. He says he is all that is left of Merry England: th
little man.

MABEL [*who has brothers*]. Lob? I think there is a famo
cricketer called Lob.

MRS. COADE. Wasn't there a Lob in Shakespeare? No,
course I am thinking of Robin Goodfellow.

LADY CAROLINE. The names are so alike.

JOANNA. Robin Goodfellow was Puck.

MRS. COADE [*with natural elation*]. That is what was in m
head. Lob was another name for Puck.

JOANNA. Well, he is certainly rather like what Puck migh
have grown into if he had forgotten to die. And, by th
way, I remember now he does call his flowers by the ol
Elizabethan names.

MATEY. He always calls the Nightingale Philomel, miss—
that is any help.

ALICE [*who is not omniscient*]. None whatever. Tell m
this, did he specially ask you all for Midsummer week

[*They assent.*]

MATEY [*who might more judiciously have remained silent*
He would!

MRS. COADE. Now what do you mean?

MATEY. He always likes them to be here on Midsumme
night, ma'am.

ALICE. Them? Whom?

MATEY. Them who have that in common.

MABEL. What can it be?

MATEY. I don't know.

LADY CAROLINE [*suddenly introspective*]. I hope we are al
nice women? We don't know each other very well. [*Cer
tain suspicions are reborn in various breasts.*] Does any
thing startling happen at those times?

MATEY. I don't know.

JOANNA. Why, I believe this is Midsummer Eve!

MATEY. Yes, miss, it is. The villagers know it. They are all inside their houses, to-night—with the doors barred.

LADY CAROLINE. Because of—of him?

MATEY. He frightens them. There are stories.

ALICE. What alarms them? Tell us—or——[*She brandishes the telegram.*]

MATEY. I know nothing for certain, ma'am. I have never done it myself. He has wanted me to, but I wouldn't.

MABEL. Done what?

MATEY [*with fine appeal*]. Oh, ma'am, don't ask me. Be merciful to me, ma'am. I am not bad naturally. It was just going into domestic service that did for me; the accident of being flung among bad companions. It's touch and go how the poor turn out in this world; all depends on your taking the right or the wrong turning.

MRS. COADE [*the lenient*]. I daresay that is true.

MATEY [*under this touch of sun*]. When I was young, ma'am, I was offered a clerkship in the city. If I had taken it there wouldn't be a more honest man alive to-day. I would give the world to be able to begin over again.

[*He means every word of it, though the flowers would here, if they dared, burst into ironical applause.*]

MRS. COADE. It is very sad, Mrs. Dearth.

ALICE. I am sorry for him; but still——

MATEY [*his eyes turning to* LADY CAROLINE]. What do you say, my lady?

LADY CAROLINE [*briefly*]. As you ask me, I should certainly say jail.

MATEY [*desperately*]. If you will say no more about this, ma'am—I'll give you a tip that is worth it.

ALICE. Ah, now you are talking.

LADY CAROLINE. Don't listen to him.

MATEY [*lowering*]. You are the one that is hardest on me.

LADY CAROLINE. Yes, I flatter myself I am.

MATEY [*forgetting himself*]. You might take a wrong turning yourself, my lady.

LADY CAROLINE. I? How dare you, man?

[*But the flowers rather like him for this: it is possibly what gave them a certain idea.*]

JOANNA [*near the keyhole of the dining-room door*]. The men are rising.

ALICE [*hurriedly*]. Very well, Matey, we agree—if the 'tip' is good enough.

LADY CAROLINE. You will regret this.

MATEY. I think not, my lady. It's this: I wouldn't go out to-night if he asks you. Go into the garden, if you like. The garden is all right. [*He really believes this.*] I wouldn't go farther—not to-night.

MRS. COADE. But he never proposes to us to go farther. Why should he to-night?

MATEY. I don't know, ma'am, but don't any of you go— [*devilishly*] except you, my lady; I should like you to go.

LADY CAROLINE. Fellow!

[*They consider this odd warning.*]

ALICE. Shall I?

[*They nod and she tears up the telegram.*]

MATEY [*with a gulp*]. Thank you, ma'am.

LADY CAROLINE. You should have sent that telegram off.

JOANNA. You are sure you have told us all you know, Matey?

MATEY. Yes, miss. [*But at the door he is more generous.*] Above all, ladies, I wouldn't go into the wood.

MABEL. The wood? Why, there is no wood within a dozen miles of here.

MATEY. No, ma'am. But all the same I wouldn't go into it, ladies—not if I was you.

[*With this cryptic warning he leaves them, and any discussion of it is prevented by the arrival of their host.* LOB *is very small, and probably no one has ever looked so old except some newborn child. To such as watch him narrowly, as the ladies now do for the first time, he has the effect of seeming to be hollow, an attenuated piece of piping insufficiently inflated; one feels that if he were to strike against a solid object he might rebound feebly from it, which would be less disconcerting if he did not obviously know this and carefully avoid the furniture; he is so light that the subject must not be mentioned in his presence, but it is possible that, were the ladies to combine, they could blow him out of a chair. He enters portentously, his hands behind his back, as*]

*if every bit of him, from his domed head to his little feet,
were the physical expressions of the deep thoughts within
him, then suddenly he whirls round to make his guests jump.
This amuses him vastly, and he regains his gravity with
difficulty. He addresses* MR. COADE.]

LOB. [*Standing, dear lady? Pray be seated.* [*He finds a chair
for her and pulls it away as she is about to sit, or kindly
pretends to be about to do so, for he has had this quaint
conceit every evening since she arrived.*]

MRS. COADE [*who loves children*]. You naughty!

LOB [*eagerly*]. It is quite a flirtation, isn't it?

[*He rolls on a chair, kicking out his legs in an ecstasy of
satisfaction. But the ladies are not certain that he is the little
innocent they have hitherto thought him. The advent of* MR.
COADE *and* MR. PURDIE *presently adds to their misgivings.*
MR. COADE *is old, a sweet pippin of a man with a gentle smile
for all; he must have suffered much, you conclude incor-
rectly, to acquire that tolerant smile. Sometimes, as when he
sees other people at work, a wistful look takes the place of
the smile, and* MR. COADE *fidgets like one who would be
elsewhere. Then there rises before his eyes the room called
the study in his house, whose walls are lined with boxes
marked* A. B. C. *to* Z. *and* $A^2$. $B^2$. $C^2$. *to* $K^2$. *These contain dusty notes for his great work on the Feudal System,
the notes many years old, the work, strictly speaking, not
yet begun. He still speaks at times of finishing it but never of
beginning it. He knows that in more favourable circumstances, for instance if he had been a poor man instead of
pleasantly well to do, he could have flung himself avidly into
that noble undertaking; but he does not allow his secret sorrow to embitter him or darken the house. Quickly the vision
passes, and he is again his bright self. Idleness, he says in his
gay way, has its recompenses. It is charming now to see
how he at once crosses to his wife, solicitous for her comfort.
He is bearing down on her with a footstool when* MR.
PURDIE *comes from the dining-room. He is the most brilliant of our company, recently notable in debate at Oxford,
where he was runner-up for the presidentship of the Union
and only lost it because the other man was less brilliant. Since
then he has gone to the bar on Monday, married on Tuesday
and had a brief on Wednesday. Beneath his brilliance, and*

*making charming company for himself, he is aware of intel*
*lectual powers beyond his years. As we are about to see, h*
*has made one mistake in his life which he is bravely facing.*

ALICE. Is my husband still sampling the port, Mr. Purdie'

PURDIE [*with a disarming smile for the absent* DEARTH]. D
you know, I believe he is. Do the ladies like our proposal
Coade?

COADE. I have not told them of it yet. The fact is, I am afraid
that it might tire my wife too much. Do you feel equal to
a little exertion to-night, Coady, or is your foot troubling
you?

MRS. COADE [*the kind creature*]. I have been resting it,
Coady.

COADE [*propping it on the footstool*]. There! Is that more
comfortable? Presently, dear, if you are agreeable we
are all going out for a walk.

MRS. COADE [*quoting* MATEY]. The garden is all right.

PURDIE [*with jocular solemnity*]. Ah, but it is not to be the
garden. We are going farther afield. We have an adventure
for to-night. Get thick shoes and a wrap, Mrs. Dearth; all
of you.

LADY CAROLINE [*with but languid interest*]. Where do you
propose to take us?

PURDIE. To find a mysterious wood.

[*With the word 'wood' the ladies are blown upright. Their
eyes turn to* LOB, *who, however, has never looked more innocent.*]

JOANNA. Are you being funny, Mr. Purdie? You know quite
well that there are not any trees for miles around. You
have said yourself that it is the one blot on the landscape.

COADE [*almost as great a humorist as* PURDIE]. Ah, on ordinary occasions! But allow us to point out to you, Miss
Joanna, that this is Midsummer Eve.

[LOB *again comes sharply under female observation.*]

PURDIE. Tell them what you told us, Lob.

LOB [*with a pout for the credulous*]. It is all nonsense, of
course; just foolish talk of the villagers. They say that on
Midsummer Eve there is a strange wood in this part of
the country.

ALICE [*lowering*]. Where?

PURDIE. Ah, that is one of its most charming features. It is never twice in the same place apparently. It has been seen on different parts of the Downs and on More Common; once it was close to Radley village and another time about a mile from the sea. Oh, a sporting wood!

LADY CAROLINE. And Lob is anxious that we should all go and look for it?

COADE. Not he; Lob is the only sceptic in the house. Says it is all rubbish, and that we shall be sillies if we go. But we believe, eh, Purdie?

PURDIE [*waggishly*]. Rather!

LOB [*the artful*]. Just wasting the evening. Let us have a round game at cards here instead.

PURDIE [*grandly*]. No, sir, I am going to find that wood.

JOANNA. What is the good of it when it is found?

PURDIE. We shall wander in it deliciously, listening to a new sort of bird called the Philomel.

[LOB *is behaving in the most exemplary manner: making sweet little clucking sounds.*]

JOANNA [*doubtfully*]. Shall we keep together, Mr. Purdie?

PURDIE. No, we must hunt in pairs.

JOANNA [*converted*]. I think it would be rather fun. Come on, Coady, I'll lace your boots for you. I am sure your poor foot will carry you nicely.

ALICE. Miss Trout, wait a moment. Lob, has this wonderful wood any special properties?

LOB. Pooh! There's no wood.

LADY CAROLINE. You've never seen it?

LOB. Not I. I don't believe in it.

ALICE. Have any of the villagers ever been in it?

LOB [*dreamily*]. So it's said; so it's said.

ALICE. What did they say were their experiences?

LOB. That isn't known. They never came back.

JOANNA [*promptly resuming her seat*]. Never came back!

LOB. Absurd, of course. You see in the morning the wood was gone; and so they were gone, too. [*He clucks again.*]

JOANNA. I don't think I like this wood.

MRS. COADE. It certainly is Midsummer Eve.

COADE [*remembering that women are not yet civilised*]. Of course if you ladies are against it we will drop the idea. It was only a bit of fun.

ALICE [*with a malicious eye on* LOB]. Yes, better give it up—to please Lob.

PURDIE. Oh, all right, Lob. What about that round game of cards?

[*The proposal meets with approval.*]

LOB [*bursting into tears*]. I wanted you to go. I had set my heart on your going. It is the thing I wanted, and it isn't good for me not to get the thing I want. [*He creeps under the table and threatens the hands that would draw him out.*]

MRS. COADE. Good gracious, he has wanted it all the time. You wicked Lob!

ALICE. Now, you see there *is* something in it.

COADE. Nonsense, Mrs. Dearth, it was only a joke.

MABEL [*melting*]. Don't cry, Lobby.

LOB. Nobody cares for me—nobody loves me. And I need to be loved.

[*Several of them are on their knees to him*].

JOANNA. Yes, we do, we all love you. Nice, nice Lobby.

MABEL. Dear Lob, I am so fond of you.

JOANNA. Dry his eyes with my own handkerchief. [*He holds up his eyes but is otherwise inconsolable.*]

LADY CAROLINE. Don't pamper him.

LOB [*furiously*]. I need to be pampered.

MRS. COADE. You funny little man. Let us go at once and look for his wood.

[*All feel that thus alone can his tears be dried.*]

JOANNA. Boots and cloaks, hats forward. Come on, Lady Caroline, just to show you are not afraid of Matey.

[*There is a general exodus, and* LOB *left alone emerges from his temporary retirement. He clucks victoriously, but presently is on his knees again distressfully regarding some flowers that have fallen from their bowl.*]

LOB. Poor bruised one, it was I who hurt you. Lob is so sorry. Lie there! [*To another.*] Pretty, pretty, let me see where you have a pain? You fell on your head; is this the place? Now I make it better. Oh, little rascal, you are not hurt at all; you just pretend. Oh dear, oh dear! Sweetheart, don't cry, you are now prettier than ever. You were too tall. Oh, how beautifully you smell now that you are small. [*He replaces the wounded tenderly in their bowl.*] Drink, drink. Now, you are happy again. The little rascal smiles. All smile, please—nod heads—aha! aha! You love Lob—Lob loves you.

JOANNA *and* MR. PURDIE *stroll in by the window.*]

JOANNA. What were you saying to them, Lob?

LOB. I was saying 'Two's company, three's none.' [*He departs with a final cluck.*]

JOANNA. That man—he suspects!

[*This is a very different* JOANNA *from the one who has so far flitted across our scene. It is also a different* PURDIE. *In company they seldom look at each other, though when the one does so the eyes of the other magnetically respond. We have seen them trivial, almost cynical, but now we are to greet them as they know they really are, the great strong-hearted man and his natural mate, in the grip of the master passion. For the moment* LOB'S *words have unnerved* JOANNA *and it is* JOHN PURDIE'S *dear privilege to soothe her.*]

PURDIE. No one minds Lob. My dear, oh my dear.

JOANNA [*faltering*]. Yes, but he saw you kiss my hand. Jack, if Mabel were to suspect!

PURDIE [*happily*]. There is nothing for her to suspect.

JOANNA [*eagerly*]. No, there isn't, is there? [*She is desirous ever to be without a flaw.*] Jack, I am not doing anything wrong, am I?

PURDIE. You!

[*With an adorable gesture she gives him one of her hands, and manlike he takes the other also.*]

JOANNA. Mabel is your wife, Jack. I should so hate myself if I did anything that was disloyal to her.

PURDIE [*pressing her hand to her eyes as if counting them, in the strange manner of lovers*]. Those eyes could never be disloyal—my lady of the nut-brown eyes. [*He holds her from him, surveying her, and is scorched in the flame of her femininity.*] Oh, the sveldtness of you. [*Almost with reproach.*] Joanna, why are you so sveldt!

[*For his sake she would be less sveldt if she could, but she can't. She admits her failure with eyes grown still larger and he envelops her so that he may not see her. Thus men seek safety.*]

JOANNA [*while out of sight*]. All I want is to help her and you.

PURDIE. I know—how well I know—my dear brave love.

JOANNA. I am very fond of Mabel, Jack. I should like to be the best friend she has in the world.

PURDIE. You are, dearest. No woman ever had a better friend.

JOANNA. And yet I don't think she really likes me. I wonder why?

PURDIE [*who is the bigger brained of the two*]. It is just that Mabel doesn't understand. Nothing could make me say a word against my wife——

JOANNA [*sternly*]. I wouldn't listen to you if you did.

PURDIE. I love you all the more, dear, for saying that. But Mabel is a cold nature and she doesn't understand.

JOANNA [*thinking never of herself but only of him*]. She doesn't appreciate your finer qualities.

PURDIE [*ruminating*]. That's it. But of course I am difficult. I always was a strange, strange creature. I often think, Joanna, that I am rather like a flower that has never had the sun to shine on it nor the rain to water it.

JOANNA. You break my heart.

PURDIE [*with considerable enjoyment*]. I suppose there is no more lonely man than I walking the earth to-day.

JOANNA [*beating her wings*]. It is so mournful.

PURDIE. It is the thought of you that sustains me, elevates me. You shine high above me like a star.

JOANNA. No, no. I wish I was wonderful, but I am not.

PURDIE. You have made me a better man, Joanna.

JOANNA. I am so proud to think that.

PURDIE. You have made me kinder to Mabel.

JOANNA. I am sure you are always kind to her.

PURDIE. Yes, I hope so. But I think now of special little ways of giving her pleasure. That never-to-be-forgotten day when we first met, you and I!

JOANNA [*fluttering nearer to him*]. That tragic, lovely day by the weir. Oh, Jack!

PURDIE. Do you know how in gratitude I spent the rest of that day?

JOANNA [*crooning*]. Tell me.

PURDIE. I read to Mabel aloud for an hour. I did it out of kindness to her, because I had met you.

JOANNA. It was dear of you.

PURDIE. Do you remember that first time my arms—your waist—you are so fluid, Joanna. [*Passionately*.] Why are you so fluid?

JOANNA [*downcast*]. I can't help it, Jack.

PURDIE. I gave her a ruby bracelet for that.

JOANNA. It is a gem. You have given that lucky woman many lovely things.

PURDIE. It is my invariable custom to go straight off and buy Mabel something whenever you have been sympathetic to me. Those new earrings of hers—they are in memory of the first day you called me Jack. Her Paquin gown—the one with the beads—was because you let me kiss you.

JOANNA. I didn't exactly let you.

PURDIE. No, but you have such a dear way of giving in.

JOANNA. Jack, she hasn't worn that gown of late.

PURDIE. No, nor the jewels. I think she has some sort of idea now that when I give her anything nice it means that you have been nice to me. She has rather a suspicious nature, Mabel; she never used to have it, but it seems to be growing on her. I wonder why, I wonder why?

[*In this wonder which is shared by* JOANNA *their lips meet, and* MABEL, *who has been about to enter from the garden, quietly retires.*]

JOANNA. Was that any one in the garden?

PURDIE [*returning from a quest*]. There is no one there now.

JOANNA. I am sure I heard some one. If it was Mabel! [*With a perspicacity that comes of knowledge of her sex.*] Jack, if she saw us she will think you were kissing me.

[*These fears are confirmed by the rather odd bearing of* MABEL, *who now joins their select party.*]

MABEL [*apologetically*]. I am so sorry to interrupt you, Jack; but please wait a moment before you kiss her again.

Excuse me, Joanna. [*She quietly draws the curtains, thu.*
*shutting out the garden and any possible onlooker*.] I di
not want the others to see you; they might not understand
how noble you are, Jack. You can go on now.

[*Having thus passed the time of day with them she with-*
*draws by the door, leaving* JACK *bewildered and* JOANNA
*knowing all about it.*]

JOANNA. How extraordinary! Of all the—! Oh, but how
contemptible! [*She sweeps to the door and calls to* MABEL
*by name.*]

MABEL [*returning with promptitude*]. Did you call me,
Joanna?

JOANNA [*guardedly*]. I insist on an explanation. [*With*
*creditable hauteur.*] What were you doing in the garden,
Mabel?

MABEL [*who has not been so quiet all day*]. I was looking
for something I have lost.

PURDIE [*hope springing eternal*]. Anything important?

MABEL. I used to fancy it, Jack. It is my husband's love.
You don't happen to have picked it up, Joanna? If so
and you don't set great store by it I should like it back—
the pieces, I mean.

[MR. PURDIE *is about to reply to this, when* JOANNA *rather*
*wisely fills the breach.*]

JOANNA. Mabel, I—I will not be talked to in that way. To
imply that I—that your husband—oh, shame!

PURDIE [*finely*]. I must say, Mabel, that I am a little disappointed in you. I certainly understood that you had gone
up-stairs to put on your boots.

MABEL. Poor old Jack. [*She muses.*] A woman like that!

JOANNA [*changing her comment in the moment of utter-*
*ance*].—I forgive you Mabel, you will be sorry for this
afterwards.

PURDIE [*warningly, but still reluctant to think less well of*
*his wife*]. Not a word against Joanna, Mabel. If you knew
how nobly she has spoken of you.

JOANNA [*imprudently*]. She does know. She has been listening.

[*There is a moment's danger of the scene degenerating into*
*something mid-Victorian. Fortunately a chivalrous man is*

*resent to lift it to a higher plane.* JOHN PURDIE *is one to
whom subterfuge of any kind is abhorrent; if he has not
spoken out before it is because of his reluctance to give
MABEL pain. He speaks out now, and seldom probably has
he proved himself more worthy.*]

PURDIE. This is a man's business. I must be open with you
    now, Mabel: it is the manlier way. If you wish it I shall
    always be true to you in word and deed; it is your right.
    But I cannot pretend that Joanna is not the one woman in
    the world for me. If I had met her before you—it's Kismet,
    I suppose. [*He swells.*]

JOANNA [*from a chair*]. Too late, too late.

MABEL [*although the woman has seen him swell*]. I suppose
    you never knew what true love was till you met her,
    Jack?

PURDIE. You force me to say it. Joanna and I are as one
    person. We have not a thought at variance. We are one
    rather than two.

MABEL [*looking at* JOANNA]. Yes, and that's the one! [*With
    the cheapest sarcasm.*] I am so sorry to have marred your
    lives.

PURDIE. If any blame there is, it is all mine; she is as spotless
    as the driven snow. The moment I mentioned love to
    her she told me to desist.

MABEL. Not she.

JOANNA. So you *were* listening? [*The obtuseness of* MABEL
    *is very strange to her.*] Mabel, don't you see how splendid
    he is!

MABEL. Not quite, Joanna. [*She goes away. She is really a
    better woman than this, but never capable of scaling that
    higher plane to which he  has, as it were, offered her a
    hand.*]

JOANNA. How lovely of you, Jack, to take it all upon your-
    self.

PURDIE [*simply*]. It is the man's privilege.

JOANNA. Mabel has such a horrid way of seeming to put
    people in the wrong.

PURDIE. Have you noticed that? Poor Mabel, it is not an
    enviable quality.

JOANNA [*despondently*]. I don't think I care to go out now.
    She has spoilt it all. She has taken the innocence out of it,
    Jack.

PURDIE [*a rock*]. We must be brave and not mind her. Ah Joanna, if we had met in time. If only I could begin again. To be battered for ever just because I once took the wrong turning, it isn't fair.

JOANNA [*emerging from his arms*]. The wrong turning. Now, who was saying that a moment ago—about himself? Why, it was Matey.

[*A footstep is heard.*]

PURDIE [*for the first time losing patience with his wife*]. Is that her coming back again? It's too bad. [*But the intruder is* MRS. DEARTH, *and he greets her with relief.*] Ah, it is you, Mrs. Dearth.

ALICE. Yes, it is; but thank you for telling me, Mr. Purdie. I don't intrude, do I?

JOANNA [*descending to the lower plane, on which even goddesses snap*]. Why should you?

PURDIE. Rather not. We were—hoping it would be you. We want to start on the walk. I can't think what has become of the others. We have been looking for them everywhere. [*He glances vaguely round the room, as if they might so far have escaped detection.*]

ALICE [*pleasantly*]. Well, do go on looking; under that flower-pot would be a good place. It is my husband I am in search of.

PURDIE [*who likes her best when they are in different rooms*]. Shall I rout him out for you?

ALICE. How too unutterably kind of you, Mr. Purdie. I hate to trouble you, but it would be the sort of service one never forgets.

PURDIE. You know, I believe you are chaffing me.

ALICE. No, no, I am incapable of that.

PURDIE. I won't be a moment.

ALICE. Miss Trout and I will await your return with ill-concealed impatience. [*They await it across a table, the newcomer in a reverie and* JOANNA *watching her. Presently* MRS. DEARTH *looks up, and we may notice that she has an attractive screw of the mouth which denotes humour.*] Yes, I suppose you are right; I daresay I am.

JOANNA [*puzzled*]. I didn't say anything.

ALICE. I thought I heard you say 'That hateful Dearth woman, coming butting in where she is not wanted.'

[JOANNA *draws up her sveldt figure, but a screw of one mouth often calls for a similar demonstration from another, and both ladies smile. They nearly become friends.*]

JOANNA. You certainly have good ears.

ALICE [*drawling*]. Yes, they have always been rather admired.

JOANNA [*snapping*]. By the painters for whom you sat when you were an artist's model?

ALICE [*measuring her*]. So that has leaked out, has it!

JOANNA [*ashamed*]. I shouldn't have said that.

ALICE [*their brief friendship over*]. Do you think I care whether you know or not?

JOANNA [*making an effort to be good*]. I'm sure you don't. Still, it was cattish of me.

ALICE. It was.

JOANNA [*in flame*]. I don't see it.

[MRS. DEARTH *laughs and forgets her, and with the entrance of a man from the dining room* JOANNA *drifts elsewhere. Not so much a man, this newcomer, as the relic of what has been a good one; it is the most he would ever claim for himself. Sometimes, brandy in hand, he has visions of the* WILL DEARTH *he used to be, clear of eye, sees him but a field away, singing at his easel or, fishing-rod in hand, leaping a stile. Our* WILL *stares after the fellow for quite a long time, so long that the two melt into the one who finishes* LOB'S *brandy. He is scarcely intoxicated as he appears before the lady of his choice, but he is shaky and has watery eyes.* ALICE *has had a rather wild love for this man, or for that other one, and he for her, but somehow it has gone whistling down the wind. We may expect therefore to see them at their worst when in each other's company.*]

DEARTH [*who is not without a humorous outlook on his own degradation*]. I am uncommonly flattered, Alice, to hear that you have sent for me. It quite takes me aback.

ALICE [*with cold distaste*]. It isn't your company I want, Will.

DEARTH. You know, I felt that Purdie must have delivered your message wrongly.

ALICE. I want you to come with us on this mysterious walk and keep an eye on Lob.

DEARTH. On poor little Lob? Oh, surely not.

ALICE. I can't make the man out. I want you to tell me some-thing; when he invited us here, do you think it was you or me he specially wanted?

DEARTH. Oh, you. He made no bones about it; said there was something about you that made him want uncommonly to have you down here.

ALICE. Will, try to remember this: did he ask us for any particular time?

DEARTH. Yes, he was particular about its being Midsummer week.

ALICE. Ah! I thought so. Did he say what it was about me that made him want to have me here in Midsummer week?

DEARTH. No, but I presumed it must be your fascination, Alice.

ALICE. Just so. Well, I want you to come out with us to-night to watch him.

DEARTH. Crack-in-my-eye-Tommy, spy on my host! And such a harmless little chap, too. Excuse me, Alice. Besides I have an engagement.

ALICE. An engagement—with the port decanter, I presume.

DEARTH. A good guess, but wrong. The decanter is now but an empty shell. Still, how you know me! My engagement is with a quiet cigar in the garden.

ALICE. Your hand is so unsteady, you won't be able to light the match.

DEARTH. I shall just manage. [*He triumphantly proves the exact truth of his statement.*]

ALICE. A nice hand for an artist!

DEARTH. One would scarcely call me an artist now-a-days.

ALICE. Not so far as any work is concerned.

DEARTH. Not so far as having any more pretty dreams to paint is concerned. [*Grinning at himself.*] Wonder why I have become such a waster, Alice?

ALICE. I suppose it was always in you.

DEARTH [*with perhaps a glimpse of the fishing-rod*]. I sup-pose so; and yet I was rather a good sort in the days when I went courting you.

ALICE. Yes, I thought so. Unlucky days for me, as it has turned out.

DEARTH [*heartily*]. Yes, a bad job for you. [*puzzling un-steadily over himself*] I didn't know I was a wrong 'un at the time; thought quite well of myself, thought a vast deal more of you. Crack-in-my-eye-Tommy, how I used to leap out of bed at 6 A.M. all agog to be at my easel; blood ran through my veins in those days. And now I'm middle-aged and done for. Funny! Don't know how it has come about, nor what has made the music mute. [*Mildly curious*] When did you begin to despise me, Alice?

ALICE. When I got to know you really, Will; a long time ago.

DEARTH [*bleary of eye*]. Yes, I think that is true. It was a long time ago, and before I had begun to despise myself. It wasn't till I knew you had no opinion of me that I began to go down hill. You will grant that, won't you; and that I did try for a bit to fight on? If you had cared for me I wouldn't have come to this, surely?

ALICE. Well, I found I didn't care for you, and I wasn't hypocrite enough to pretend I did. That's blunt, but you used to admire my bluntness.

DEARTH. The bluntness of you, the adorable wildness of you, you untamed thing! There were never any shades in you; kiss or kill was your motto, Alice. I felt from the first moment I saw you that you would love me or knife me.

[*Memories of their shooting star flare in both of them for as long as a sheet of paper might take to burn.*]

ALICE. I didn't knife you.

DEARTH. No. I suppose that was where you made the mistake. It is hard on you, old lady. [*Becoming watery*] I suppose it's too late to try to patch things up?

ALICE. Let's be honest; it is too late, Will.

DEARTH [*whose tears would smell of brandy*]. Perhaps if we had had children— Pity!

ALICE. A blessing I should think, seeing what sort of a father they would have had.

DEARTH [*ever reasonable*]. I daresay you're right. Well, Alice, I know that somehow it's my fault. I'm sorry for you.

ALICE. I'm sorry for myself. If I hadn't married you what a different woman I should be. What a fool I was.

DEARTH. Ah! Three things they say come not back to men nor women—the spoken word, the past life and the neglected opportunity. Wonder if we should make any more of them, Alice, if they did come back to us.

ALICE. You wouldn't.

DEARTH [*avoiding a hiccup*]. I guess you're right.

ALICE. But I——

DEARTH [*sincerely*]. Yes, what a boon for you. But I hope it's not Freddy Finch-Fallowe you would put in my place; I know he is following you about again. [*He is far from threatening her, he has too beery an opinion of himself for that.*]

ALICE. He followed me about, as you put it, before I knew you. I don't know why I quarrelled with him.

DEARTH. Your heart told you that he was no good, Alice.

ALICE. My heart told me that you *were*. So it wasn't of much service to me, my heart!

DEARTH. The Honourable Freddy Finch-Fallowe is a rotter.

ALICE [*ever inflammable*]. You are certainly an authority on the subject.

DEARTH [*with the sad smile of the disillusioned*]. You have me there. After which brief, but pleasant, little connubial chat, he pursued his dishonoured way into the garden.

[*He is however prevented doing so for the moment by the return of the others. They are all still in their dinner clothes though wearing wraps. They crowd in through the door, chattering.*]

LOB. Here they are! Are you ready, dear lady?

MRS. COADE [*seeing that* DEARTH's *hand is on the window curtains*]. Are you not coming with us to find the wood, Mr. Dearth.

DEARTH. Alas, I am unavoidably detained. You will find me in the garden when you come back.

JOANNA [*whose sense of humour has been restored*]. If we ever do come back!

DEARTH. Precisely. [*With a groggy bow*] Should we never meet again, Alice, fare thee well. Purdie, if you find the tree of knowledge in the wood bring me back an apple.

PURDIE. I promise.

LOB. Come quickly. Matey mustn't see me. [*He is turning out the lights.*]

LADY CAROLINE [*pouncing*]. Matey? What difference would that make, Lob?

LOB. He would take me off to bed; it's past my time.

COADE [*not the least gay of the company*]. You know, old fellow, you make it very difficult for us to embark upon this adventure in the proper eerie spirit.

DEARTH. Well, I'm for the garden.

[*He walks to the window, and the others are going out by the door. But they do not go. There is a hitch somewhere—at the window apparently, for* DEARTH *having begun to draw the curtains apart lets them fall, like one who has had a shock. The others remember long afterwards his grave face as he came quietly back and put his cigar on the table. The room is in darkness save for the light from one lamp.*]

PURDIE [*wondering*]. How, now, Dearth?

DEARTH. What is it we get in that wood, Lob?

ALICE. Ah, he won't tell us that.

LOB [*shrinking*]. Come on!

ALICE [*impressed by the change that has come over her husband*]. Tell us first.

LOB [*forced to the disclosure*]. They say that in the wood you get what nearly everybody here is longing for—a second chance.

[*The ladies are simultaneously enlightened.*]

JOANNA [*speaking for all*]. So that is what we have in common!

COADE [*with gentle regret*]. I have often thought, Coady, that if I had a second chance I should be a useful man instead of just a nice lazy one.

ALICE [*morosely*]. A second chance!

LOB. Come on.

PURDIE [*gaily*]. Yes, to the wood—the wood!

DEARTH [*as they are going out by the door*]. Stop, why not go this way?

[*He pulls the curtains apart, and there comes a sudden in-drawing of breath from all, for no garden is there now. In its place is an endless wood of great trees; the nearest of them has come close to the window. It is a sombre wood, with splashes of moonshine and of blackness standing very still in it. The party in the drawing-room are very still also, there is scarcely a cry or a movement. It is perhaps strange that the most obviously frightened is* LOB *who calls vainly for* MATEY. *The first articulate voice is* DEARTH'S.]

DEARTH [*very quietly*]. Any one ready to risk it?

PURDIE [*after another silence*]. Of course there is nothing in it—just——

DEARTH [*grimly*]. Of course. Going out, Purdie?

[PURDIE *draws back*.]

MRS. DEARTH [*the only one who is undaunted*]. A second chance!

[*She is looking at her husband. They all look at him as if he had been a leader once*].

DEARTH [*with his sweet mournful smile*]. I shall be back in a moment—probably. [*As he passes into the wood his hands rise, as if a hammer had tapped him on the forehead. He is soon lost to view.*]

LADY CAROLINE [*after a long pause*]. He does not come back.

MRS. COADE. It's horrible.

[*She steals off by the door to her room, calling to her husband to do likewise. He takes a step after her, and stops in the grip of the last two words that holds them all. The stillness continues. At last* MRS. PURDIE *goes out into the wood, her hands raised, and is swallowed up by it.*]

PURDIE. Mabel!

ALICE [*sardonically*]. You will have to go now, Mr. Purdie.

[*He looks at* JOANNA, *and they go out together, one tap of the hammer for each.*]

LOB. *That's enough.* [*Warningly*] Don't you go, Mrs. Dearth. *You'll* catch it if you go.

ALICE. A second chance! [*She goes out unflinching.*]

LADY CAROLINE. One would like to know.

[*She goes out.* MRS. COADE'S *voice is heard from the stair, calling to her husband. He hesitates but follows* LADY CAROLINE. *To* LOB *now alone comes* MATEY *with a tray of coffee cups.*]

MATEY [*as he places his tray on the table*]. It is past your bed-time, sir. Say good-night to the ladies, and come along.

LOB. Matey, look!

[MATEY *looks*.]

MATEY [*shrinking*]. Great heavens, then it's true!

LOB. Yes, but I—I wasn't sure.

[MATEY *approaches the window cautiously to peer out, and his master gives him a sudden push that propels him into the wood.* LOB'S *back is toward us as he stands alone staring out upon the unknown. He is terrified still; yet quivers of rapture are running up and down his little frame.*]

# ACT TWO

*We are translated to the depths of the wood in the enchantment of a moonlight night. In some other glade a nightingale is singing; in this one, in proud motoring attire, recline two mortals whom we have known in different conditions; the second chance has converted them into husband and wife. The man, of gross muddy build, lies luxurious on his back exuding affluence, a prominent part of him heaving playfully, like some little wave that will not rest in a still sea. A handkerchief over his face conceals from us what Colossus he may be, but his mate is our* LADY CAROLINE. *The nightingale trills on, and* LADY CAROLINE *takes up its song.*

LADY CAROLINE. Is it not a lovely night, Jim. Listen, my own, to Philomel; he is saying that he is lately married. So are we, you ducky thing. I feel, Jim, that I am Rosalind and that you are my Orlando.

[*The handkerchief being removed* MR. MATEY *is revealed; and the nightingale seeks some farther tree.*]

MATEY. What do you say I am, Caroliny?

LADY CAROLINE [*clapping her hands*]. My own one, don't you think it would be fun if we were to write poems about each other and pin them on the tree trunks?

MATEY [*tolerantly*]. Poems? I never knew such a lass for high-flown language.

LADY CAROLINE. Your lass, dearest. Jim's lass.

MATEY [*pulling her ear*]. And don't you forget it.

LADY CAROLINE [*with the curiosity of woman*]. What would you do if I were to forget it, great bear?

MATEY. Take a stick to you.

LADY CAROLINE [*so proud of him*]. I love to hear you talk like that; it is so virile. I always knew that it was a master I needed.

[ 333 ]

MATEY. It's what you all need.

LADY CAROLINE. It is, it is, you knowing wretch.

MATEY. Listen, Caroliny. [*He touches his money pocket, which emits a crinkly sound—the squeak of angels.*] That is what gets the ladies.

LADY CAROLINE. How much have you made this week, you wonderful man?

MATEY [*blandly*]. Another two hundred or so. That's all, just two hundred or so.

LADY CAROLINE [*caressing her wedding ring*]. My dear golden fetter, listen to him. Kiss my fetter, Jim.

MATEY. Wait till I light this cigar.

LADY CAROLINE. Let me hold the darling match.

MATEY. Tidy-looking Petitey Corona, this. There was a time when one of that sort would have run away with two days of my screw.

LADY CAROLINE. How I should have loved, Jim, to know you when you were poor. Fancy your having once been a clerk.

MATEY [*remembering Napoleon and others*]. We all have our beginnings. But it wouldn't have mattered how I began, Caroliny: I should have come to the top just the same. [*Becoming a poet himself*]. I am a climber, and there are nails in my boots for the parties beneath me. Boots! I tell you if I had been a bootmaker, I should have been the first bootmaker in London.

LADY CAROLINE [*a humourist at last*]. I am sure you would, Jim; but should you have made the best boots?

MATEY [*uxoriously wishing that others could have heard this*]. Very good, Caroliny; that is the neatest thing I have heard you say. But it's late; we had best be strolling back to our Rolls-Royce.

LADY CAROLINE [*as they rise*]. I do hope the ground wasn't damp.

MATEY. Don't matter if it was; I was lying on your rug. [*Indeed we notice now that he has had all the rug, and she the bare ground.* JOANNA *reaches the glade, now an unhappy lady who has got what she wanted. She is in country dress and is unknown to them as they are to her.*] Who is the mournful party?

JOANNA [*hesitating*]. I wonder, sir, whether you happen to have seen my husband? I have lost him in the wood.

MATEY. We are strangers in these parts ourselves, missis. Have we passed any one, Caroliny?

LADY CAROLINE [*coyly*]. Should we have noticed, dear? Might it be that old gent over there? [*After the delightful manner of those happily wed she has already picked up many of her lover's favourite words and phrases.*]

JOANNA. Oh no, my husband is quite young.

[*The woodlander referred to is* MR. COADE *in gala costume; at his mouth a whistle he has made him from some friendly twig. To its ravishing music he is seen pirouetting charmingly among the trees, his new occupation.*]

MATEY [*signing to the unknown that he is wanted*]. Seems a merry old cock. Evening to you, sir. Do you happen to have seen a young gentleman in the wood lately, all by himself, and looking for his wife?

COADE [*with a flourish of his legs*]. Can't say I have.

JOANNA [*dolefully*]. He isn't necessarily by himself; and I don't know that he is looking for me. There may be a young lady with him.

[*The more happily married lady smiles, and* JOANNA *is quick to take offence.*]

JOANNA. What do you mean by that?

LADY CAROLINE [*neatly*]. Oho—if you like that better.

MATEY. Now, now, now—your manners, Caroliny.

COADE. Would he be singing or dancing?

JOANNA. Oh no—at least, I hope not.

COADE [*an artist to the tips*]. Hope not? Odd! If he is doing neither I am not likely to notice him, but if I do, what name shall I say?

JOANNA [*gloating not*]. Purdie; I am Mrs. Purdie.

COADE. I will try to keep a look-out, and if I see him . . . but I am rather occupied at present. . . . [*The reference is to his legs and a new step they are acquiring. He sways this way and that, and, whistle to lips, minuets off in the direction of Paradise.*]

JOANNA [*looking elsewhere*]. I am sorry I troubled you. I see him now.

LADY CAROLINE. Is he alone? [JOANNA *glares at her.*] Ah, I see from your face that he isn't.

MATEY [*who has his wench in training*]. Caroliny, no awk-

ward questions. Evening, missis, and I hope you will ge
him to go along with you quietly. [*Looking after* COADE
Watch the old codger dancing.

[*Light-hearted as children they dance after him, whil*
JOANNA *behind a tree awaits her lord.* PURDIE *in knicker*
*bockers approaches with misgivings to make sure that hi*
JOANNA *is not in hiding, and then he gambols joyously with a*
*charming confection whose name is* MABEL. *They chase each*
*other from tree to tree, but fortunately not round* JOANNA'
*tree.*]

MABEL [*as he catches her*]. No, and no, and no. I don't
know you nearly well enough for that. Besides, what
would your wife say! I shall begin to think you are a very
dreadful man, Mr. Purdie.

PURDIE [*whose sincerity is not to be questioned*]. Surely you
might call me Jack by this time.

MABEL [*heaving*]. Perhaps, if you are very good, Jack.

PURDIE [*of noble thoughts compact*]. If only Joanna were
more like you.

MABEL. Like me? You mean her face? It is a—well, if it is
not precisely pretty, it is a good face. [*Handsomely*] I
don't mind her face at all. I am glad you have got such a
dependable little wife, Jack.

PURDIE [*gloomily*]. Thanks.

MABEL [*seated with a moonbeam in her lap*]. What would
Joanna have said if she had seen you just now?

PURDIE. A wife should be incapable of jealousy.

MABEL. Joanna jealous? But has she any reason? Jack, tell
me, who is the woman?

PURDIE [*restraining himself by a mighty effort, for he wishes
always to be true to* JOANNA]. Shall I, Mabel, shall I?

MABEL [*faltering, yet not wholly giving up the chase*]. I
can't think who she is. Have I ever seen her?

PURDIE. Every time you look in a mirror.

MABEL [*with her head on one side*]. How odd, Jack, that
can't be; when I look in a mirror I see only myself.

PURDIE [*gloating*]. How adorably innocent you are, Mabel.
Joanna would have guessed at once.

[*Slowly his meaning comes to her, and she is appalled.*]

MABEL. Not that!
PURDIE [*aflame*]. Shall I tell you now?

MABEL [*palpitating exquisitely*]. I don't know, I am not sure. Jack, try not to say it, but if you feel you must, say it in such a way that it would not hurt the feelings of Joanna if she happened to be passing by, as she nearly always is.

[*A little moan from* JOANNA'S *tree is unnoticed.*]

PURDIE. I would rather not say it at all than that way. [*He is touchingly anxious that she should know him as he really is.*] I don't know, Mabel, whether you have noticed that I am not like other men. [*He goes deeply into the very structure of his being.*] All my life I have been a soul that has had to walk alone. Even as a child I had no hope that it would be otherwise. I distinctly remember when I was six thinking how unlike other children I was. Before I was twelve I suffered from terrible self-deprecation; I do so still. I suppose there never was a man who had a more lowly opinion of himself.

MABEL. Jack, you who are so universally admired.

PURDIE. That doesn't help; I remain my own judge. I am afraid I am a dark spirit, Mabel. Yes, yes, my dear, let me leave nothing untold however it may damage me in your eyes. Your eyes! I cannot remember a time when I did not think of Love as a great consuming passion; I visualised it, Mabel, as perhaps few have done, but always as the abounding joy that could come to others but never to me. I expected too much of women: I suppose I was touched to finer issues than most. That has been my tragedy.

MABEL. Then you met Joanna.

PURDIE. Then I met Joanna. Yes! Foolishly, as I now see, I thought she would understand that I was far too deep a nature really to mean the little things I sometimes said to her. I suppose a man was never placed in such a position before. What was I to do? Remember, I was always certain that the ideal love could never come to me. Whatever the circumstances, I was convinced that my soul must walk alone.

MABEL. Joanna, how could you?

PURDIE [*firmly*]. Not a word against her, Mabel; if blame there is the blame is mine.

MABEL. And so you married her.

PURDIE. And so I married her.

MABEL. Out of pity.

PURDIE. I felt it was a man's part. I was such a child i[n]
worldly matters that it was pleasant to me to have th[e]
right to pay a woman's bills; I enjoyed seeing her gar[-]
ments lying about on my chairs. In time that exultatio[n]
wore off. But I was not unhappy, I didn't expect much[.]
I was always so sure that no woman could ever plum[b]
the well of my emotions.

MABEL. Then you met me.

PURDIE. Then I met you.

MABEL. Too late—never—forever—forever—never. They ar[e]
the saddest words in the English tongue.

PURDIE. At the time I thought a still sadder word was Joanna[.]

MABEL. What was it you saw in me that made you love me[?]

PURDIE [plumbing the well of his emotions]. I think it wa[s]
the feeling that you are so like myself.

MABEL [with great eyes]. Have you noticed that, Jack[?]
Sometimes it has almost terrified me.

PURDIE. We think the same thoughts; we are not two, Mabel[,]
we are one. Your hair——

MABEL. Joanna knows you admire it, and for a week she di[d]
hers in the same way.

PURDIE. I never noticed.

MABEL. That was why she gave it up. And it didn't really
suit her. [Ruminating] I can't think of a good way o[f]
doing dear Joanna's hair. What is that you are mutterin[g]
to yourself, Jack? Don't keep anything from me.

PURDIE. I was repeating a poem I have written: it is in two
words, 'Mabel Purdie.' May I teach it to you, sweet: say
'Mabel Purdie' to me.

MABEL [timidly covering his mouth with her little hand].
If I were to say it, Jack, I should be false to Joanna: neve[r]
ask me to be that. Let us go on.

PURDIE [merciless in his passion]. Say it, Mabel, say it. See
I write it on the gound with your sunshade.

MABEL. If it could be! Jack, I'll whisper it to you.

[She is whispering it as they wander, not two but one, farther
into the forest, ardently believing in themselves; they are
not hypocrites. The somewhat bedraggled figure of JOANNA
follows them, and the nightingale resumes his love-song.
'That's all you know, you bird!' thinks JOANNA cynically. The
nightingale, however, is not singing for them nor for her,

*but for another pair he has espied below. They are racing, the prize to be for the one who first finds the spot where the easel was put up last night. The hobbledehoy is sure to be the winner, for she is less laden, and the father loses time by singing as he comes. Also she is all legs and she started ahead. Brambles adhere to her, one boot has been in the water and she has as many freckles as there are stars in heaven. She is as lovely as you think she is, and she is aged the moment when you like your daughter best. A hoot of triumph from her brings her father to the spot.]*

MARGARET. Daddy, Daddy. I have won. Here is the place. Crack-in-my-eye-Tommy!

*[He comes. Crack-in-my-eye-Tommy, this engaging fellow in tweeds, is MR. DEARTH, ablaze in happiness and health and a daughter. He finishes his song, picked up in the Latin Quarter.]*

DEARTH. Yes, that is the tree I stuck my easel under last night, and behold the blessed moon behaving more gorgeously than ever. I am sorry to have kept you waiting, old moon; but you ought to know by now how time passes. Now, keep still, while I hand you down to posterity.

*[The easel is erected, MARGARET helping by getting in the way.]*

MARGARET *[critical, as an artist's daughter should be]*. The moon is rather pale to-night, isn't she?
DEARTH. Comes of keeping late hours.
MARGARET *[showing off]*. Daddy, watch me, look at me. Please, sweet moon, a pleasant expression. No, no, not as if you were sitting for it; that is too professional. That is better; thank you. Now keep it. That is the sort of thing you say to them, Dad.
DEARTH *[quickly at work]*. I oughtn't to have brought you out so late; you should be tucked up in your cosy bed at home.
MARGARET *[pursuing a squirrel that isn't there]*. With the pillow anyhow.
DEARTH. Except in its proper place.
MARGARET *[wetting the other foot]*. And the sheet over my face.
DEARTH. Where it oughtn't to be.

MARGARET [*more or less upside down*]. And Daddy tiptoe
ing in to take it off.

DEARTH. Which is more than you deserve.

MARGARET [*in a tree*]. Then why does he stand so long at
the door? And before he has gone she bursts out laughing
for she has been awake all the time.

DEARTH. That's about it. What a life! But I oughtn't to have
brought you here. Best to have the sheet over you when
the moon is about; moonlight is bad for little daughters

MARGARET [*pelting him with nuts*]. I can't sleep when the
moon's at the full; she keeps calling to me to get up.
Perhaps I am *her* daughter too.

DEARTH. Gad, you look it to-night.

MARGARET. Do I? Then can't you paint me into the picture
as well as Mamma? You could call it 'A Mother and
Daughter' or simply 'Two ladies,' if the moon thinks
that calling me her daughter would make her seem too
old.

DEARTH. O matre pulchra filia pulchrior. That means, 'O
Moon—more beautiful than any twopenny-halfpenny
daughter.'

MARGARET [*emerging in an unexpected place*]. Daddy, do
you really prefer her?

DEARTH. 'Sh! She's not a patch on you; it's the sort of thing
we say to our sitters to keep them in good humour. [*He
surveys ruefully a great stain on her frock.*] I wish to
heaven, Margaret, we were not both so fond of appletart.
And what's this! [*Catching hold of her skirt.*]

MARGARET [*unnecessarily*]. It's a tear.

DEARTH. I should think it is a tear.

MARGARET. That boy at the farm did it. He kept calling
Snubs after me, but I got him down and kicked him in
the stomach. He is rather a jolly boy.

DEARTH. He sounds it. Ye Gods, what a night!

MARGARET [*considering the picture*]. And what a moon!
Dad, she is not quite so fine as that.

DEARTH. 'Sh! I have touched her up.

MARGARET. Dad, Dad—what a funny man!

[*She has seen* MR. COADE *with whistle, enlivening the wood.
He pirouettes round them and departs to add to the happiness of others.* MARGARET *gives an excellent imitation of him*

*at which her father shakes his head, then reprehensibly joins
in the dance. Her mood changes, she clings to him.*]

MARGARET. Hold me tight, Daddy, I'm frightened. I think
they want to take you away from me.

DEARTH. Who, gosling?

MARGARET. I don't know. It's too lovely, Daddy; I won't be
able to keep hold of it.

DEARTH. What is?

MARGARET. The world—everything—and you, Daddy, most
of all. Things that are too beautiful can't last.

DEARTH [*who knows it*]. Now, how did you find that out?

MARGARET [*still in his arms*]. I don't know, Daddy, am I sometimes stranger than other people's daughters?

DEARTH. More of a madcap, perhaps.

MARGARET [*solemnly*]. Do you think I am sometimes too full
of gladness?

DEARTH. My sweetheart, you do sometimes run over with it.
[*He is at his easel again.*]

MARGARET [*persisting*]. To be very gay, dearest dear, is so
near to being very sad.

DEARTH [*who knows it*]. How did you find that out, child?

MARGARET. I don't know. From something in me that's afraid.
[*Unexpectedly.*] Daddy, what is a 'might-have-been?'

DEARTH. A might-have-been? They are ghosts, Margaret. I
daresay I 'might have been' a great swell of a painter,
instead of just this uncommonly happy nobody. Or again,
I might have been a worthless idle waster of a fellow.

MARGARET [*laughing*]. You!

DEARTH. Who knows? Some little kink in me might have set
me off on the wrong road. And that poor soul I might so
easily have been might have had no Margaret. My word,
I'm sorry for him.

MARGARET. So am I. [*She conceives a funny picture.*] The
poor old Daddy, wandering about the world without me!

DEARTH. And there are other 'might-have-beens'—lovely
ones, but intangible. Shades, Margaret, made of sad folk's
thoughts.

MARGARET [*jigging about*]. I am so glad I am not a shade.
How awful it would be, Daddy, to wake up and find one
wasn't alive.

DEARTH. It would, dear.

MARGARET. Daddy, wouldn't it be awful! I think men nee
daughters.

DEARTH. They do.

MARGARET. Especially artists.

DEARTH. Yes, especially artists.

MARGARET. Especially artists.

DEARTH. Especially artists.

MARGARET [*covering herself with leaves and kicking them
off*]. Fame is not everything.

DEARTH. Fame is rot; daughters are the thing.

MARGARET. Daughters are the thing.

DEARTH. Daughters are the thing.

MARGARET. I wonder if sons would be even nicer?

DEARTH. Not a patch on daughters. The awful thing about
son is that never, never—at least, from the day he goe
to school—can you tell him that you rather like him. B
the time he is ten you can't even take him on your knee
Sons are not worth having, Margaret. Signed, W. Dearth

MARGARET. But if you were a mother, Dad, I daresay h
would let you do it.

DEARTH. Think so?

MARGARET. I mean when no one was looking. Sons are no
so bad. Signed, M. Dearth. But I'm glad you prefer daugh
ters. [*She works her way toward him on her knees, mak
ing the tear larger.*] At what age are we nicest, Daddy
[*She has constantly to repeat her questions, he is so en
gaged with his moon.*] Hie, Daddy, at what age are w
nicest? Daddy, hie, hie, at what age are we nicest?

DEARTH. Eh? That's a poser. I think you were nicest when yo
were two and knew your alphabet up to G but fell over a
H. No, you were best when you were half-past three; o
just before you struck six; or in the mumps year, whe
I asked you in the early morning how you were and yo
said solemnly "I haven't tried yet."

MARGARET [*awestruck*]. Did I?

DEARTH. Such was your answer. [*Struggling with the mo
mentous question.*] But I am not sure that chicken-pox
doesn't beat mumps. Oh Lord, I'm all wrong. The nices
time in a father's life is the year before she puts up he
hair.

MARGARET [*top-heavy with pride in herself*]. I suppose tha
is a splendid time. But there's a nicer year coming to you
Daddy, there is a nicer year coming to you.

DEARTH. Is there, darling?

MARGARET. Daddy, the year she does put up her hair!

DEARTH [*with arrested brush*]. Puts it up for ever? You
know, I am afraid that when the day for that comes I
shan't be able to stand it. It will be too exciting. My
poor heart, Margaret.

MARGARET [*rushing at him*]. No, no, it will be lucky you,
for it isn't to be a bit like that. I am to be a girl and
woman day about for the first year. You will never know
which I am till you look at my hair. And even then you
won't know, for if it is down I shall put it up, and if it is
up I shall put it down. And so my Daddy will gradually
get used to the idea.

DEARTH [*wryly*]. I see you have been thinking it out.

MARGARET [*gleaming*]. I have been doing more than that.
Shut your eyes, Dad, and I shall give you a glimpse into
the future.

DEARTH. I don't know that I want that: the present is so
good.

MARGARET. Shut your eyes, please.

DEARTH. No, Margaret.

MARGARET. Please, Daddy.

DEARTH. Oh, all right. They are shut.

MARGARET. Don't open them till I tell you. What finger is
that?

DEARTH. The dirty one.

MARGARET [*on her knees among the leaves*]. Daddy, now
I am putting up my hair. I have got such a darling of a
mirror. It is such a darling mirror I've got, Dad. Dad,
don't look. I shall tell you about it. It is a little pool of
water. I wish we could take it home and hang it up. Of
course the moment my hair is up there will be other
changes also; for instance, I shall talk quite differently.

DEARTH. Pooh. Where are my matches, dear?

MARGARET. Top pocket, waistcoat.

DEARTH [*trying to light his pipe in darkness*]. You were
meaning to frighten me just now.

MARGARET. No. I am just preparing you. You see, darling,
I can't call you Dad when my hair is up. I think I shall call
you Parent. [*He growls*]. Parent dear, do you remember
the days when your Margaret was a slip of a girl, and sat
on your knee? How foolish we were, Parent, in those distant days.

DEARTH. Shut up, Margaret.

MARGARET. Now I must be more distant to you; more like boy who could not sit on your knee any more.

DEARTH. See here, I want to go on painting. Shall I look now?

MARGARET. I am not quite sure whether I want you to. I makes such a difference. Perhaps you won't know me Even the pool is looking a little scared. [*The change i. her voice makes him open his eyes quickly. She confront. him shyly.*] What do you think? Will I do?

DEARTH. Stand still, dear, and let me look my fill. The Margaret that is to be.

MARGARET [*the change in his voice falling clammy on her*] You'll see me often enough, Daddy, like this, so you don' need to look your fill. You are looking as long as if this were to be the only time.

DEARTH [*with an odd tremor*]. Was I? Surely it isn't to be that.

MARGARET. Be gay, Dad. [*Bumping into him and round him and over him.*] You will be sick of Margaret with her hair up before you are done with her.

DEARTH. I expect so.

MARGARET. Shut up, Daddy. [*She waggles her head, and down comes her hair.*] Daddy, I know what you are thinking of. You are thinking what a handful she is going to be.

DEARTH. Well, I guess she is.

MARGARET [*surveying him from another angle*]. Now you are thinking about—about my being in love some day.

DEARTH [*with unnecessary warmth*]. Rot!

MARGARET [*reassuringly*]. I won't, you know; no, never. Oh, I have quite decided, so don't be afraid. [*Disordering his hair.*] Will you hate him at first, Daddy? Daddy, will you hate him? Will you hate him, Daddy?

DEARTH [*at work*]. Whom?

MARGARET. Well, if there was?

DEARTH. If there was what, darling?

MARGARET. You know the kind of thing I mean, quite well. Would you hate him at first?

DEARTH. I hope not. I should want to strangle him, but I wouldn't hate him.

MARGARET. I would. That is to say, if I liked him.

DEARTH. If you liked him how could you hate him?

MARGARET. For daring!

DEARTH. Daring what?

MARGARET. You know. [*Sighing*] But of course I shall have no say in the matter. You will do it all. You do everything for me.

DEARTH [*with a groan*]. I can't help it.

MARGARET. You will even write my love-letters, if I ever have any to write, which I won't.

DEARTH [*ashamed*]. Surely to goodness, Margaret, I will leave you alone to do that!

MARGARET. Not you; you will try to, but you won't be able.

DEARTH [*in a hopeless attempt at self-defence*]. I want you, you see, to do everything exquisitely. I do wish I could leave you to do things a little more for yourself. I suppose it's owing to my having had to be father and mother both. I knew nothing practically about the bringing up of children, and of course I couldn't trust you to a nurse.

MARGARET [*severely*]. Not you; so sure you could do it better yourself. That's you all over. Daddy, do you remember how you taught me to balance a biscuit on my nose, like a puppy?

DEARTH [*sadly*]. Did I?

MARGARET. You called me Rover.

DEARTH. I deny that.

MARGARET. And when you said 'snap' I caught the biscuit in my mouth.

DEARTH. Horrible!

MARGARET [*gleaming*]. Daddy, I can do it still! [*Putting a biscuit on her nose.*] Here is the last of my supper. Say 'snap,' Daddy.

DEARTH. Not I.

MARGARET. Say 'snap,' please.

DEARTH. I refuse.

MARGARET. Daddy!

DEARTH. Snap. [*She catches the biscuit in her mouth.*] Let that be the last time, Margaret.

MARGARET. Except just once more. I don't mean now, but when my hair is really up. If I should ever have a—a Margaret of my own, come in and see me, Daddy, in my white bed, and say 'snap'—and I'll have the biscuit ready.

DEARTH [*turning away his head*]. Right O.

MARGARET. Dad, if I ever should marry, not that I will but if I should—at the marriage ceremony will you let me be the one who says 'I do'?

DEARTH. I suppose I deserve this.

MARGARET [*coaxingly*]. You think I'm pretty, don't you Dad, whatever other people say?

DEARTH. Not so bad.

MARGARET. I *know* I have nice ears.

DEARTH. They are all right now, but I had to work on them for months.

MARGARET. You don't mean to say that you did my *ears*?

DEARTH. Rather!

MARGARET [*grown humble*]. My dimple is my own.

DEARTH. I am glad you think so. I wore out the point of my little finger over that dimple.

MARGARET. Even my dimple! Have I anything that is really mine? A bit of my nose or anything?

DEARTH. When you were a babe you had a laugh that was all your own.

MARGARET. Haven't I it now?

DEARTH. It's gone. [*He looks ruefully at her.*] I'll tell you how it went. We were fishing in a stream—that is to say, I was wading and you were sitting on my shoulders holding the rod. We didn't catch anything. Somehow or another—I can't think how I did it—you irritated me, and I answered you sharply.

MARGARET [*gasping*]. I can't believe that.

DEARTH. Yes, it sounds extraordinary, but I did. It gave you a shock, and, for the moment, the world no longer seemed a safe place to you; your faith in me had always made it safe till then. You were suddenly not even sure of your bread and butter, and a frightened tear came to your eyes. I was in a nice state about it I can tell you. [*He is in a nice state about it still.*]

MARGARET. Silly! [*Bewildered*] But what has that to do with my laugh, Daddy?

DEARTH. The laugh that children are born with lasts just so long as they have perfect faith. To think that it was I who robbed you of yours!

MARGARET. Don't, dear. I am sure the laugh just went off with the tear to comfort it, and they have been playing about that stream ever since. They have quite forgotten us, so why should we remember them? Cheeky little beasts! Shall I tell you my farthest back recollection [*In some awe*] I remember the first time I saw the stars. I had never seen night, and then I saw it and the stars together. Crack-in-my-eye-Tommy, it isn't every one who can boast of such a lovely, lovely recollection for their earliest, is it?

DEARTH. I was determined your earliest should be a good one.

MARGARET [*blankly*]. Do you mean to say you planned it?

DEARTH. Rather! Most people's earliest recollection is of some trivial thing; how they cut their finger, or lost a piece of string. I was resolved my Margaret's should be something bigger. I was poor, but I could give her the stars.

MARGARET [*clutching him around the legs*]. Oh, how you love me, Daddikins.

DEARTH. Yes, I do, rather.

*A vagrant woman has wandered in their direction, one whom the shrill winds of life have lashed and bled; here and there ragged graces still cling to her, and unruly passion smoulders, but she, once a dear fierce rebel with eyes of storm, is now first of all a whimperer. She and they meet as strangers.*]

MARGARET [*nicely, as becomes an artist's daughter*]. Good evening.

ALICE. Good evening, Missy; evening, Mister.

DEARTH [*seeing that her eyes search the ground*]. Lost anything?

ALICE. Sometimes when the tourists have had their sandwiches there are bits left over, and they squeeze them between the roots to keep the place tidy. I am looking for bits.

DEARTH. You don't tell me you are as hungry as that?

ALICE [*with spirit*]. Try me.

[*Strange that he should not know that once loved husky voice.*]

MARGARET [*rushing at her father and feeling all his pockets*]. Daddy, that was my last biscuit!

DEARTH. We must think of something else.

MARGARET [*taking her hand*]. Yes, wait a bit, we are sure to think of something. Daddy, think of something.

ALICE [*sharply*]. Your father doesn't like you to touch the likes of me.

MARGARET. Oh yes, he does. [*Defiantly*] And if he didn't, I'd do it all the same. This is a bit of *myself*, daddy.

DEARTH. That is all you know.

ALICE [*whining*]. You needn't be angry with her, Miste
 I'm all right.

DEARTH. I am not angry with her; I am very sorry for yo

ALICE [*flaring*]. If I had my rights, I would be as good a
 you—and better.

DEARTH. I daresay.

ALICE. I have had men-servants and a motorcar.

DEARTH. Margaret and I never rose to that.

MARGARET [*stung*]. I have been in a taxi several times, an
 Dad often gets telegrams.

DEARTH. Margaret!

MARGARET. I'm sorry I boasted.

ALICE. That's nothing. I have a town house—at least I ha
 . . . At any rate he said there was a town house.

MARGARET [*interested*]. Fancy his not knowing for certain

ALICE. The Honourable Mrs. Finch-Fallowe—that's who
 am.

MARGARET [*cordially*]. It's a lovely name.

ALICE. Curse him.

MARGARET. Don't you like him?

DEARTH. We won't go into that. I have nothing to do wit
 your past, but I wish we had some food to offer you.

ALICE. You haven't a flask?

DEARTH. No, I don't take anything myself. But let me see. . .

MARGARET [*sparkling*]. I know! You said we had five pounds
 [*To the needy one*] Would you like five pounds?

DEARTH. Darling, don't be stupid; we haven't paid our bill a
 the inn.

ALICE [*with bravado*]. All right; I never asked you for any
 thing.

DEARTH. Don't take me up in that way: I have had my up
 and downs myself. Here is ten bob and welcome. [*H
 surreptitiously slips a coin into* MARGARET'S *hand.*]

MARGARET. And I have half a crown. It is quite easy for us
 Dad will be getting another fiver any day. You can'
 think how exciting it is when the fiver comes in; w
 dance and then we run out and buy chops.

DEARTH. Margaret!

ALICE. It's kind of you. I'm richer this minute than I hav
 been for many a day.

DEARTH. It's nothing; I am sure you would do the same fo
 us.

ALICE. I wish I was as sure.

DEARTH. Of course you would. Glad to be of any help. Get some victuals as quickly as you can. Best of wishes, ma'am, and may your luck change.

ALICE. Same to you, and may yours go on.

MARGARET. Good-night.

ALICE. What is her name, Mister?

DEARTH [*who has returned to his easel*]. Margaret.

ALICE. Margaret. You drew something good out of the lucky bag when you got her, Mister.

DEARTH. Yes.

ALICE. Take care of her; they are easily lost. [*She shuffles away.*]

DEARTH. Poor soul. I expect she has had a rough time, and that some man is to blame for it—partly, at any rate. [*Restless*] That woman rather affects me, Margaret; I don't know why. Didn't you like her husky voice? [*He goes on painting.*] I say, Margaret, we lucky ones, let's swear always to be kind to people who are down on their luck, and then when we are kind let's be a little kinder.

MARGARET [*gleefully*]. Yes, let's.

DEARTH. Margaret, always feel sorry for the failures, the ones who are always failures—especially in my sort of calling. Wouldn't it be lovely, to turn them on the thirty-ninth year of failure into glittering successes?

MARGARET. Topping.

DEARTH. Topping.

MARGARET. Oh, topping. How could we do it, Dad?

DEARTH. By letter. 'To poor old Tom Broken Heart, Top Attic, Garret Chambers, S.E.—'Dear Sir,—His Majesty has been graciously pleased to purchase your superb picture of Marlow Ferry.'

MARGARET. 'P.S.—I am sending the money in a sack so as you can hear it chink.'

DEARTH. What could we do for our friend who passed just now? I can't get her out of my head.

MARGARET. You have made me forget her. [*Plaintively*] Dad, I didn't like it.

DEARTH. Didn't like what, dear?

MARGARET [*shuddering*]. I didn't like her saying that about your losing me.

DEARTH [*the one thing of which he is sure*]. I shan't lose you.

MARGARET [*hugging his arm*]. It would be hard for me if

you lost me, but it would be worse for you. I don't kno
how I know that, but I do know it. What would you c
without me?

DEARTH [almost sharply]. Don't talk like that, dear. It
wicked and stupid, and naughty. Somehow that poc
woman— I won't paint any more to-night.

MARGARET. Let's get out of the wood; it frightens me.

DEARTH. And you loved it a moment ago. Hullo! [He he
seen a distant blurred light in the wood, apparently fro
a window.] I hadn't noticed there was a house there.

MARGARET [tingling]. Daddy, I feel sure there wasn't a hous
there!

DEARTH. Goose. It is just that we didn't look: our old wa
of letting the world go hang; so interested in ourselve
Nice behaviour for people who have been boasting abo
what they would do for other people. Now I see what
ought to do.

MARGARET. Let's get out of the wood.

DEARTH. Yes, but my idea first. It is to rouse these peopl
and get food from them for the husky one.

MARGARET [clinging to him]. She is too far away now.

DEARTH. I can overtake her.

MARGARET [in a frenzy]. Don't go into that house, Daddy
I don't know why it is, but I am afraid of that house
[He waggles a reproving finger at her.]

DEARTH. There is a kiss for each moment until I come back
[She wipes them from her face.] Oh, naughty, go an
stand in the corner. [She stands against a tree but sh
stamps her foot.] Who has got a nasty temper! [She trie
hard not to smile, but she smiles and he smiles, and the
make comic faces at each other, as they have done i
similar circumstances since she first opened her eyes.]
I shall be back before you can count a hundred.

[He goes off humming his song so that she may still hea
him when he is lost to sight; all just as so often before. She
tries dutifully to count her hundred, but the wood grow
dark and soon she is afraid again. She runs from tree to tree
calling to her Daddy. We begin to lose her among the shad
ows.]

MARGARET [out of the impalpable that is carrying he
away]. Daddy, come back; I don't want to be a might
have-been.

# ACT THREE

*Lob's room has gone very dark as it sits up awaiting the possible return of the adventurers. The curtains are drawn, so that no light comes from outside. There is a tapping on the window, and anon two intruders are stealing about the floor, with muffled cries when they meet unexpectedly. They find the switch and are revealed as* PURDIE *and his* MABEL. *Something has happened to them as they emerged from the wood, but it is so superficial that neither notices it: they are again in the evening dress in which they had left the house. But they are still being led by that strange humour of the blood.*

MABEL [*looking around her curiously*]. A pretty little room; I wonder who is the owner?

PURDIE. It doesn't matter; the great thing is that we have escaped Joanna.

MABEL. Jack, look, a man!

[*The term may not be happily chosen, but the person indicated is* LOB, *curled up on his chair by a dead fire. The last look on his face before he fell asleep having been a leery one, it is still there.*]

PURDIE. He is asleep.

MABEL. Do you know him?

PURDIE. Not I. Excuse me, sir, Hi! [*No shaking, however, wakens the sleeper.*]

MABEL. Darling, how extraordinary.

PURDIE [*always considerate*]. After all, precious, have we any right to wake up a stranger, just to tell him that we are runaways hiding in his house?

MABEL [*who comes of a good family*]. I think he would expect it of us.

PURDIE [*after trying again*]. There is no budging him.

[351]

MABEL [*appeased*]. At any rate, we have done the civi
thing. [*She has now time to regard the room more a
tentively, including the tray of coffee cups which* MATE
*had left on the table in a not unimportant moment of h
history*.] There have evidently been people here, but the
haven't drunk their coffee. Ugh! cold as a deserted egg i
a bird's nest. Jack, if you were a clever detective you coul
construct those people out of their neglected coffee cups
I wonder who they are and what has spirited them away

PURDIE. Perhaps they have only gone to bed. Ought we t
knock them up?

MABEL [*after considering what her mother would hav
done*]. I think not, dear. I suppose we have run away
Jack—meaning to?

PURDIE [*with the sturdiness that weaker vessels adore*]
Irrevocably. Mabel, if the dog-like devotion of a life
time . . . [*He becomes conscious that something has hap
pened to* LOB'S *leer. It has not left his face but it ha
shifted.*] He is not shamming, do you think?

MABEL. Shake him again.

PURDIE [*after shaking him*]. It's all right. Mabel, if the dog
like devotion of a lifetime . . .

MABEL. Poor little Joanna! Still, if a woman insists on being
a pendulum round a man's neck . . .

PURDIE. Do give me a chance, Mabel. If the dog-like devotion of a lifetime . . . [JOANNA *comes through the curtains
so inopportunely that for the moment he is almost pet-
tish.*] May I say, this is just a little too much, Joanna

JOANNA [*unconscious as they of her return to her dinner
gown*]. So, sweet husband, your soul is still walking alone,
is it?

MABEL [*who hates coarseness of any kind*]. How can you
sneak about in this way, Joanna? Have you no pride?

JOANNA [*dashing away a tear*]. Please to address me as
Mrs. Purdie, madam. [*She sees* LOB.] Who is this man?

PURDIE. We don't know; and there is no waking him. You
can try, if you like.

[*Failing to rouse him* JOANNA *makes a third at table. They
are all a little inconsequential, as if there were still
some moonshine in their hair.*]

JOANNA. You were saying something about the devotion of
a lifetime; please go on.

PURDIE [*diffidently*]. I don't like to before you, Joanna.

JOANNA [*becoming coarse again*]. Oh, don't mind me.

PURDIE [*looking like a note of interrogation*]. I should certainly like to say it.

MABEL [*loftily*]. And I shall be proud to hear it.

PURDIE. I should have liked to spare you this, Joanna; you wouldn't put your hands over your ears?

JOANNA [*alas*]. No, sir.

MABEL. Fie, Joanna. Surely a wife's natural delicacy——

PURDIE [*severely*]. As you take it in that spirit, Joanna, I can proceed with a clear conscience. If the dog-like devotion of a lifetime——

[*He reels a little, staring at* LOB, *over whose face the leer has been wandering like an insect.*]

MABEL. Did he move?

PURDIE. It isn't that. I am feeling—very funny. Did one of you tap me just now on the forehead?

[*Their hands also have gone to their foreheads.*]

MABEL. I think I have been in this room before.

PURDIE [*flinching*]. There is something coming rushing back to me.

MABEL. I seem to know that coffee set. If I do, the lid of the milk jug is chipped. It is!

JOANNA. I can't remember this man's name; but I am sure it begins with L.

MABEL. Lob.

PURDIE. Lob.

JOANNA. Lob.

PURDIE. Mabel, your dress?

MABEL [*beholding it*]. How on earth . . . ?

JOANNA. My dress! [*To* PURDIE.] You were in knickerbockers in the wood.

PURDIE. And so I am now. [*He sees he is not.*] Where did I change? The wood! Let me think. The wood . . . the wood, certainly. But the wood wasn't the wood.

JOANNA [*revolving like one in pursuit*]. My head is going round.

MABEL. Lob's wood! I remember it all. We were here. We did go.

PURDIE. So we did. But how could . . . ? where was . . . ?

JOANNA. And who was . . . ?

MABEL. And what was . . . ?

PURDIE [*even in this supreme hour a man*]. Don't let go.
Hold on to what we were doing, or we shall lose grip of
ourselves. Devotion. Something about devotion. Hold on
to devotion. 'If the dog-like devotion of a lifetime . . .'
Which of you was I saying that to?

MABEL. To me.

PURDIE. Are you sure?

MABEL [*Shakily*]. I am not quite sure.

PURDIE [*anxiously*]. Joanna, what do you think? [*With a
sudden increase of uneasiness*] Which of you is my wife?

JOANNA [*without enthusiasm*]. I am. No, I am not. It is
Mabel who is your wife!

MABEL. Me?

PURDIE [*with a curious gulp*]. Why, of course you are,
Mabel!

MABEL. I believe I am!

PURDIE. And yet how can it be? I was running away with
you.

JOANNA [*solving that problem*]. You don't need to do it
now.

PURDIE. The wood. Hold on to the wood. The wood is what
explains it. Yes, I see the whole thing. [*He gazes at* LOB.]
You infernal old rascal! Let us try to think it out. Don't
any one speak for a moment. Think first. Love . . . Hold
on to love. [*He gets another tap.*] I say, I believe I am
not a deeply passionate chap at all; I believe I am just . . .
a philanderer!

MABEL. It is what you are.

JOANNA [*more magnanimous*]. Mabel, what about ourselves?

PURDIE [*to whom it is truly a nauseous draught*]. I didn't
know. Just a philanderer! [*The soul of him would like at
this instant to creep into another body.*] And if people
don't change, I suppose we shall begin all over again now.

JOANNA [*the practical*]. I daresay; but not with each other.
I may philander again, but not with you.

[*They look on themselves without approval, always a sorry
occupation. The man feels it most because he has admired
himself most, or perhaps partly for some better reason.*]

PURDIE [*saying good-bye to an old friend*]. John Purdie,
John Purdie, the fine fellow I used to think you! [*When
he is able to look them in the face again*] The wood has
taught me one thing, at any rate.

MABEL [*dismally*]. What, Jack?

PURDIE. That it isn't accident that shapes our lives.

JOANNA. No, it's Fate.

PURDIE [*the truth running through him, seeking for a
permanent home in him, willing to give him still another
chance, loth to desert him*]. It's not Fate, Joanna. Fate is
something outside us. What really plays the dickens with
us is something in ourselves. Something that makes us go
on doing the same sort of fool things, however many
chances we get.

MABEL. Something in ourselves?

PURDIE [*shivering*]. Something we are born with.

JOANNA. Can't we cut out the beastly thing?

PURDIE. Depends, I expect, on how long we have pampered
him. We can at least control him if we try hard enough.
But I have for the moment an abominably clear perception that the likes of me never really tries. Forgive me,
Joanna—no, Mabel—both of you. [*He is a shamed man.*]
It isn't very pleasant to discover that one is a rotter. I
suppose I shall get used to it.

JOANNA. I could forgive anybody anything to-night. [*Candidly*] It is so lovely not to be married to you, Jack.

PURDIE [*spiritless*]. I can understand that. I do feel small.

JOANNA [*the true friend*]. You will soon swell up again.

PURDIE [*for whom, alas, we need not weep*]. That is the
appalling thing. But at present, at any rate, I am a rag
at your feet, Joanna—no, at yours, Mabel. Are you going
to pick me up? I don't advise it.

MABEL. I don't know whether I want to, Jack. To begin with,
which of us is it your lonely soul is in search of?

JOANNA. Which of us is the fluid one, or the fluider one?

MABEL. Are you and I one? Or are you and Joanna one?
Or are the three of us two?

JOANNA. He wants you to whisper in his ear, Mabel, the
entrancing poem, 'Mabel Purdie.' Do it, Jack; there will
be nothing wrong in it now.

PURDIE. Rub it in.

MABEL. When I meet Joanna's successor——

PURDIE [*quailing*]. No, no, Mabel, none of that. At leas credit me with having my eyes open at last. There wil be no more of this. I swear it by all that is———

JOANNA [*in her excellent imitation of a sheep*]. Baa-a, he is off again.

PURDIE. Oh Lord, so I am.

MABEL. Don't, Joanna.

PURDIE [*his mind still illumined*]. She is quite right—I was In my present state of depression—which won't last—I feel there is something in me that will make me go on being the same ass, however many chances I get. I haven't the stuff in me to take warning. My whole being is corroded. Shakespeare knew what he was talking about—

'The fault, dear Brutus, is not in our stars,
But in ourselves, that we are underlings.'

JOANNA. For 'dear Brutus' we are to read 'dear audience' I suppose?

PURDIE. You have it.

JOANNA. Meaning that we have the power to shape ourselves?

PURDIE. We have the power right enough.

JOANNA. But isn't that rather splendid?

PURDIE. For those who have the grit in them, yes. [*Still seeing with a strange clearness through the chink the hammer has made*] And they are not the dismal chappies; they are the ones with the thin bright faces. [*He sits lugubriously by his wife and is sorry for the first time that she has not married a better man.*] I am afraid there is not much fight in me, Mabel, but we shall see. If you catch me at it again, have the goodness to whisper to me in passing, 'Lob's Wood.' That may cure me for the time being.

MABEL [*still certain that she loved him once but not so sure why*]. Perhaps I will . . . as long as I care to bother, Jack. It depends on you how long that is to be.

JOANNA [*to break an awkward pause*]. I feel that there is hope in that as well as a warning. Perhaps the wood may prove to have been useful after all. [*This brighter view of the situation meets with no immediate response. With her next suggestion she reaches harbour.*] You know, we are not people worth being sorrowful about—so let us laugh.

[*The ladies succeed in laughing though not prettily, but the man has been too much shaken.*]

JOANNA [*in the middle of her laugh*]. We have forgotten the others! I wonder what is happening to them?

PURDIE [*reviving*]. Yes, what about them? Have *they* changed!

MABEL. I didn't see any of them in the wood.

JOANNA. Perhaps we did see them without knowing them; we didn't know Lob.

PURDIE [*daunted*]. That's true.

JOANNA. Won't it be delicious to be here to watch them when they come back, and see them waking up—or whatever it was we did.

PURDIE. What was it we did? I think something tapped me on the forehead.

MABEL [*blanching*]. How do we know the others *will* come back?

JOANNA [*infected*]. We don't know. How awful!

MABEL. Listen!

PURDIE. I distinctly hear some one on the stairs.

MABEL. It will be Matey.

PURDIE [*the chink beginning to close*]. Be cautious both of you; don't tell him we have had any . . . odd experiences.

[*It is, however,* MRS. COADE *who comes downstairs in a dressing-gown and carrying a candle and her husband's muffler.*]

MRS. COADE. So you are back at last. A nice house, I must say. Where is Coady?

PURDIE [*taken aback*]. Coady! Did he go into the wood, too?

MRS. COADE [*placidly*]. I suppose so. I have been down several times to look for him.

MABEL. Coady, too!

JOANNA [*seeing visions*]. I wonder . . . Oh, how dreadful!

MRS. COADE. What is dreadful, Joanna?

JOANNA [*airily*]. Nothing. I was just wondering what he is doing.

MRS. COADE. Doing? What should he be doing? Did anything odd happen to you in the wood?

PURDIE [*taking command*]. No, no, nothing.

JOANNA. We just strolled about, and came back. [*That sub-*

*ject being exhausted she points to* LOB.] Have you noticed him?

MRS. COADE. Oh, yes; he has been like that all the time. A sort of stupor, I think; and sometimes the strangest grin comes over his face.

PURDIE [*wincing*]. Grin?

MRS. COADE. Just as if he were seeing amusing things in his sleep.

PURDIE [*guardedly*]. I daresay he is. Oughtn't we to get Matey to him?

MRS. COADE. Matey has gone, too.

PURDIE. Wha-at!

MRS. COADE. At all events he is not in the house.

JOANNA [*unguardedly*]. Matey! I wonder who is with him.

MRS. COADE. Must somebody be with him?

JOANNA. Oh, no, not at all.

[*They are simultaneously aware that some one outside has reached the window.*]

MRS. COADE. I hope it is Coady.

[*The other ladies are too fond of her to share this wish.*]

MABEL. Oh, I hope not.

MRS. COADE [*blissfully*]. Why, Mrs. Purdie?

JOANNA [*coaxingly*]. Dear Mrs. Coade, whoever he is, and whatever he does, I beg you not to be surprised. We feel that though we had no unusual experiences in the wood, others may not have been so fortunate.

MABEL. And be cautious, you dear, what you say to them before they come to.

MRS. COADE. 'Come to'? You puzzle me. And Coady didn't have his muffler.

[*Let it be recorded that in their distress for this old lady they forget their own misadventures.* PURDIE *takes a step toward the curtains in a vague desire to shield her;—and gets a rich reward; he has seen the coming addition to their circle.*]

PURDIE [*elated and pitiless*]. It is Matey!

[*A butler intrudes who still thinks he is wrapped in fur.*]

JOANNA [*encouragingly*]. Do come in.

MATEY. With apologies, ladies and gents . . . May I ask who is host?

PURDIE [*splashing in the temperature that suits him best*]. A very reasonable request. Third on the left.

MATEY [*advancing upon* LOB]. Merely to ask, sir, if you can direct me to my hotel? [*The sleeper's only response is a slight quiver in one leg.*] The gentleman seems to be reposing.

MRS. COADE. It is Lob.

MATEY. What is lob, ma'am?

MRS. COADE [*pleasantly curious*]. Surely you haven't forgotten?

PURDIE [*over-riding her*]. Anything we can do for you, sir? Just give it a name.

JOANNA [*in the same friendly spirit*]. I hope you are not alone: do say you have some lady friends with you.

MATEY [*with an emphasis on his leading word*]. My wife is with me.

JOANNA. His wife! . . . [*With commendation*] You *have* been quick!

MRS. COADE. I didn't know you were married.

MATEY. Why should you, madam? You talk as if you knew me.

MRS. COADE. Good gracious, do you really think I don't?

PURDIE [*indicating delicately that she is subject to a certain softening*]. Sit down, won't you, my dear sir, and make yourself comfy.

MATEY [*accustomed of late to such deferential treatment*]. Thank you. But my wife . . .

JOANNA [*hospitably*]. Yes, bring her in; we are simply dying to make her acquaintance.

MATEY. You are very good; I am much obliged.

MABEL [*as he goes out*]. Who can she be?

JOANNA [*leaping*]. Who, who, who!

MRS. COADE. But what an extraordinary wood! He doesn't seem to know who he is at all.

MABEL [*soothingly*]. Don't worry about that, Coady darling. He will know soon enough.

JOANNA [*again finding the bright side*]. And so will the little wife! By the way, whoever she is, I hope she is fond of butlers.

MABEL [*who has peeped*]. It is Lady Caroline!

JOANNA [*leaping again*]. Oh, joy, joy! And she was so sure
   she couldn't take the wrong turning!

[LADY CAROLINE *is evidently still sure of it.*]

MATEY. May I present my wife—Lady Caroline Matey.

MABEL [*glowing*]. How do you do!

PURDIE. Your servant, Lady Caroline.

MRS. COADE. Lady Caroline Matey! You?

LADY CAROLINE [*without an r in her*]. Charmed, I'm sure.

JOANNA [*neatly*]. Very pleased to meet any wife of Mr
   Matey.

PURDIE [*taking the floor*]. Allow me. The Duchess of Can
   delabra. The Ladies Helena and Matilda M'Nab. I am
   the Lord Chancellor.

MABEL. I have wanted so long to make your acquaintance

LADY CAROLINE. Charmed.

JOANNA [*gracefully*]. These informal meetings are so de
   lightful, don't you?

LADY CAROLINE. Yes, indeed.

MATEY [*the introductions being thus pleasantly concluded*]
   And your friend by the fire?

PURDIE. I will introduce you to him when you wake up—I
   mean when he wakes up.

MATEY. Perhaps I ought to have said that I am *James*
   Matey.

LADY CAROLINE [*the happy creature*]. *The* James Matey.

MATEY. A name not, perhaps, unknown in the world of
   finance.

JOANNA. Finance? Oh, so you did take that clerkship in the
   City!

MATEY [*a little stiffly*]. I began as a clerk in the City, certainly; and I am not ashamed to admit it.

MRS. COADE [*still groping*]. Fancy that, now. And did it save
   you?

MATEY. Save me, madam?

JOANNA. Excuse us—we ask odd questions in this house; we
   only mean, did that keep you honest? Or are you still a
   pilferer?

LADY CAROLINE [*an outraged swan*]. Husband mine, what
   does she mean?

JOANNA. No offence; I mean a pilferer on a large scale.

MATEY [*remembering certain newspaper jealousy*]. If you

are referring to that Labrador business—or the Working Women's Bank. . . .

PURDIE [*after the manner of one who has caught a fly*]. O-ho, got him!

JOANNA [*bowing*]. Yes, those are what I meant.

MATEY [*stoutly*]. There was nothing proved.

JOANNA [*like one calling a meeting*]. Mabel, Jack, here is another of us! You have gone just the same way again, my friend. [*Ecstatically.*] There is more in it, you see, than taking the wrong turning; you would always take the wrong turning. [*The only fitting comment*] Tra-la-la!

LADY CAROLINE. If you are casting any aspersions on my husband, allow me to say that a prouder wife than I does not to-day exist.

MRS. COADE [*who finds herself the only clearheaded one*]. My dear, do be careful.

MABEL. So long as you are satisfied, dear Lady Caroline. But I thought you shrank from all blood that was not blue.

LADY CAROLINE. You thought? Why should you think about me? I beg to assure you that I adore my Jim. [*She seeks his arm, but her JIM has encountered the tray containing coffee cups and a cake, and his hands close on it with a certain intimacy.*] Whatever are you doing, Jim?

MATEY. I don't understand it, Caroliny; but somehow I feel at home with this in my hands.

MABEL. 'Caroliny!'

MRS. COADE. Look at me well; don't you remember me?

MATEY [*musing*]. I don't remember you; but I seem to associate you with hard-boiled eggs. [*With conviction*] You like your eggs hard-boiled.

PURDIE. Hold on to hard-boiled eggs! She used to tip you especially to see to them. [MATEY'S *hand goes to his pocket.*] Yes, that was the pocket.

LADY CAROLINE [*with distaste*]. Tip!

MATEY [*without distaste*]. Tip!

PURDIE. Jolly word, isn't it?

MATEY [*raising the tray*]. It seems to set me thinking.

LADY CAROLINE [*feeling the tap of the hammer*]. Why is my work-basket in this house?

MRS. COADE. You are living here, you know.

LADY CAROLINE. That is what a person feels. But when did I come? It is very odd, but one feels one ought to say when did one go.

PURDIE. She is coming to with a wush!

MATEY [*under the hammer*]. Mr. . . . Purdie!

LADY CAROLINE. Mrs. Coade!

MATEY. The Guv'nor! My clothes!

LADY CAROLINE. One is in evening dress!

JOANNA [*charmed to explain*]. You will understand clearly in a minute, Caroliny. You didn't really take that clerkship, Jim; you went into domestic service; but in the essentials you haven't altered.

PURDIE [*pleasantly*]. I'll have my shaving water at 7.30 sharp, Matey.

MATEY [*mechanically*]. Very good, sir.

LADY CAROLINE. Sir? Midsummer Eve! The wood!

PURDIE. Yes, hold on to the wood.

MATEY. You are . . . you are . . . you are Lady Caroline Laney!

LADY CAROLINE. It is Matey, the butler!

MABEL. You seemed quite happy with him, you know, Lady Caroline.

JOANNA [*nicely*]. We won't tell.

LADY CAROLINE [*subsiding*]. Caroline Matey! And I seemed to like it! How horrible!

MRS. COADE [*expressing a general sentiment*]. It is rather difficult to see what we should do next.

MATEY [*tentatively*]. Perhaps if I were to go downstairs?

PURDIE. It would be conferring a personal favour on us all.

[*Thus encouraged,* MATEY *and his tray resume friendly relations with the pantry.*]

LADY CAROLINE [*with itching fingers as she glares at* LOB]. It is all that wretch's doing.

[*A quiver from* LOB'S *right leg acknowledges the compliment. The gay music of a pipe is heard from outside.*]

JOANNA [*peeping*]. Coady!

MRS. COADE. Coady! Why is he so happy?

JOANNA [*troubled*]. Dear, hold my hand.

MRS. COADE [*suddenly trembling*]. Won't he know me?

PURDIE [*abashed by that soft face*]. Mrs. Coade, I'm sorry. It didn't so much matter about the likes of us, but for your sake I wish Coady hadn't gone out.

MRS. COADE. We that have been happily married this thirty years.

COADE [*popping in buoyantly*]. May I intrude? My name is Coade. The fact is I was playing about in the wood on a whistle, and I saw your light.

MRS. COADE [*the only one with the nerve to answer*]. Playing about in the wood with a whistle!

COADE [*with mild dignity*]. And why not, madam?

MRS. COADE. Madam! Don't you know me?

COADE. I don't know you. . . . [*Reflecting*] But I wish I did.

MRS. COADE. Do you? Why?

COADE. If I may say so, you have a very soft, lovable face.

[*Several persons breathe again.*]

MRS. COADE [*inquisitorially*]. Who was with you, playing whistles in the wood?

[*The breathing ceases.*]

COADE. No one was with me.

[*And is resumed.*]

MRS. COADE. No . . . lady?

COADE. Certainly not. [*Then he spoils it.*] I am a bachelor.

MRS. COADE. A bachelor!

JOANNA. Don't give way, dear; it might be much worse.

MRS. COADE. A bachelor! And you are sure you never spoke to me before? Do think.

COADE. Not to my knowledge. Never . . . except in dreams.

MABEL [*taking a risk*]. What did you say to her in dreams?

COADE. I said, 'My dear.' [*This when uttered surprises him.*] Odd!

JOANNA. The darling man!

MRS. COADE [*wavering*]. How could you say such things to an old woman?

COADE [*thinking it out*]. Old? I didn't think of you as old. No, no, young—with the morning dew on your face— coming across a lawn—in a black and green dress—and carrying such a pretty parasol.

MRS. COADE [*thrilling*]. That was how he first met me! He used to love me in black and green; and it *was* a pretty parasol. Look, I am old. . . . So it can't be the same woman.

COADE [*blinking*]. Old? Yes, I suppose so. But it is the same
   soft, lovable face, and the same kind, beaming smile
   that children could warm their hands at.

MRS. COADE. He always liked my smile.

PURDIE. So do we all.

COADE [*to himself*]. Emma!

MRS. COADE. He hasn't forgotten my name!

COADE. It is sad that we didn't meet long ago. I think I have
   been waiting for you. I suppose we have met too late? You
   couldn't overlook my being an old fellow, could you, eh?

JOANNA. How lovely; he is going to propose to her again.
   Coady, you happy thing, he is wanting the same soft face
   after thirty years!

MRS. COADE [*undoubtedly hopeful*]. We mustn't be too sure,
   but I think that is it. [*Primly.*] What is it exactly that you
   want, Mr. Coade?

COADE [*under a lucky star*]. I want to have the right to
   hold the parasol over you. Won't you be my wife, my
   dear, and so give my long dream of you a happy ending?

MRS. COADE [*preening*]. Kisses are not called for at our
   age, Coady, but here is a muffler for your old neck.

COADE. My muffler; I have missed it. [*It is however to his
   forehead that his hand goes. Immediately thereafter he
   misses his sylvan attire.*] Why . . . why . . . what . . . who
   . . . how is this?

PURDIE [*nervously*]. He is coming to.

COADE [*reeling and righting himself*]. Lob! [*The leg indicates that he has got it.*] Bless me, Coady, I went into
   that wood!

MRS. COADE. And without your muffler, you that are so subject to chills. What are you feeling for in your pocket?

COADE. The whistle. It is a whistle I— Gone! of course it is.
   It's rather a pity, but . . . [*Anxious*] Have I been saying
   awful things to you?

MABEL. You have been making her so proud. It is a compliment to our whole sex. You had a second chance, and it
   is her, again!

COADE. Of course it is. [*Crestfallen*] But I see I was just
   the same nice old lazy Coady as before; and I had thought
   that if I had a second chance, I could do things. I have
   often said to you, Coady, that it was owing to my being
   cursed with a competency that I didn't write my great

book. But I had no competency this time, and I haven't
written a word.

PURDIE [*bitterly enough*]. That needn't make you feel lonely
in this house.

MRS. COADE [*in a small voice*]. You seem to have been
quite happy as an old bachelor, dear.

COADE. I am surprised at myself, Emma, but I fear I was.

MRS. COADE [*with melancholy perspicacity*]. I wonder if
what it means is that you don't especially need even me. I
wonder if it means that you are just the sort of amiable
creature that would be happy anywhere, and anyhow?

COADE. Oh dear, can it be as bad as that!

JOANNA [*a ministering angel she*]. Certainly not. It is a romance, and I won't have it looked upon as anything else.

MRS. COADE. Thank you, Joanna. You will try not to miss
that whistle, Coady?

COADE [*getting the footstool for her*]. You are all I need.

MRS. COADE. Yes; but I am not so sure as I used to be that
it is a great compliment.

JOANNA. Coady, behave.

[*There is a knock on the window.*]

PURDIE [*peeping*]. Mrs. Dearth! [*His spirits revive.*] She is
alone. Who would have expected that of *her!*

MABEL. She is a wild one, Jack, but I sometimes thought
rather a dear; I do hope she has got off cheaply.

[ALICE *comes to them in her dinner gown.*]

PURDIE [*the irrepressible*]. Pleased to see you, stranger.

ALICE [*prepared for ejection.*] I was afraid such an un-
ceremonious entry might startle you.

PURDIE. Not a bit.

ALICE [*defiant*]. I usually enter a house by the front door.

PURDIE. I have heard that such is the swagger way.

ALICE [*simpering*]. So stupid of me. I lost myself in the
wood . . . and . . .

JOANNA [*genially*]. Of course you did. But never mind that;
do tell us your name.

LADY CAROLINE [*emerging again*]. Yes, yes, your name.

ALICE. Of course, I am the Honourable Mrs. Finch-Fallowe.

LADY CAROLINE. Of course, of course!

PURDIE. I hope Mr. Finch-Fallowe is very well? We don't know him personally, but may we have the pleasure of seeing him bob up presently?

ALICE. No, I am not sure where he is.

LADY CAROLINE [*with point*]. I wonder if the dear clever police know?

ALICE [*imprudently*]. No, they don't. [*It is a very secondary matter to her. This woman of calamitous fires hears and sees her tormentors chiefly as the probable owners of the cake which is standing on that tray.*] So awkward, I gave my sandwiches to a poor girl and her father whom I met in the wood, and now . . . isn't it a nuisance—I am quite hungry. [*So far with a mincing bravado.*] May I? [*Without waiting for consent she falls to upon the cake, looking over it like one ready to fight them for it.*]

PURDIE [*sobered again*]. Poor soul.

LADY CAROLINE. We are so anxious to know whether you met a friend of ours in the wood—a Mr. Dearth. Perhaps you know him, too?

ALICE. Dearth? I don't know any Dearth.

MRS. COADE. Oh dear, what a wood!

LADY CAROLINE. He is quite a front door sort of man; knocks and rings, you know.

PURDIE. Don't worry her.

ALICE [*gnawing*]. I meet so many; you see I go out a great deal. I have visiting-cards—printed ones.

LADY CAROLINE. How very distingué. Perhaps Mr. Dearth has painted your portrait; he is an artist.

ALICE. Very likely; they all want to paint me. I daresay that is the man to whom I gave my sandwiches.

MRS. COADE. But I thought you said he had a daughter?

ALICE. Such a pretty girl; I gave her half a crown.

COADE. A daughter? That can't be Dearth.

PURDIE [*darkly*]. Don't be too sure. Was the man you speak of a rather chop-fallen, gone-to-seed sort of person.

ALICE. No, I thought him such a jolly, attractive man.

COADE. Dearth jolly, attractive! oh no. Did he say anything about his wife?

LADY CAROLINE. Yes, do try to remember if he mentioned her.

ALICE [*snapping*]. No, he didn't.

PURDIE. He was far from jolly in her time.

ALICE [*with an archness for which the cake is responsible*].
    Perhaps that was the lady's fault.

[*The last of the adventurers draws nigh, carolling a French
song as he comes.*]

COADE. Dearth's voice. He sounds quite merry!
JOANNA [*protecting*]. Alice, you poor thing.
PURDIE. This is going to be horrible.

[*A clear-eyed man of lusty gait comes in.*]

DEARTH. I am sorry to bounce in on you in this way, but
    really I have an excuse. I am a painter of sorts, and . . .
    [*He sees he has brought some strange discomfort here.*]
MRS. COADE. I must say, Mr. Dearth, I am delighted to see
    you looking so well. Like a new man, isn't he?

[*No one dares to answer.*]

DEARTH. I am certainly very well, if you care to know. But
    did I tell you my name?
JOANNA [*for some one has to speak*]. No, but—but we have
    an instinct in this house.
DEARTH. Well, it doesn't matter. Here is the situation; my
    daughter and I have just met in the wood a poor woman
    famishing for want of food. We were as happy as grigs
    ourselves, and the sight of her distress rather cut us up. Can
    you give me something for her? Why are you looking so
    startled? [*Seeing the remains of the cake.*] May I have
    this? [*A shrinking movement from one of them draws his
    attention, and he recognises in her the woman of whom he
    has been speaking. He sees her in fine clothing and he
    grows stern.*] I feel I can't be mistaken; it was you I met
    in the wood? Have you been playing some trick on me?
    [*To the others*] It was for her I wanted the food.
ALICE [*her hand guarding the place where his gift lies*].
    Have you come to take back the money you gave me?
DEARTH. Your dress! You were almost in rags when I saw
    you outside.
ALICE [*frightened as she discovers how she is now attired*].
    I don't . . . understand . . .
COADE [*gravely enough*]. For that matter, Dearth, I dare-
    say you were different in the wood, too.

[DEARTH *sees his own clothing.*]

DEARTH. What . . . !

ALICE [*frightened*]. Where am I? [*To* MRS. COADE] I seem
to know you . . . do I?

MRS. COADE [*motherly*]. Yes, you do; hold my hand, and you
will soon remember all about it.

JOANNA. I am afraid, Mr. Dearth, it is harder for you than
for the rest of us.

PURDIE [*looking away*]. I wish I could help you, but I can't;
I am a rotter.

MABEL. We are awfully sorry. Don't you remember . . . Midsummer Eve?

DEARTH [*controlling himself*]. Midsummer Eve? This room.
Yes, this room. . . . You . . . was it you? . . . were going
out to look for something . . . The tree of knowledge,
wasn't it? Somebody wanted me to go, too. . . . Who was
that? A lady, I think. . . . Why did she ask me to go?
What was I doing here? I was smoking a cigar. . . . I laid
it down, there. . . . [*He finds the cigar.*] Who was the
lady?

ALICE [*feebly*]. Something about a second chance.

MRS. COADE. Yes, you poor dear, you thought you could
make so much of it.

DEARTH. A lady who didn't like me— [*With conviction*] She
had good reasons, too—but what were they . . . ?

ALICE. A little old man! He did it. What did he do?

[*The hammer is raised.*]

DEARTH. I am . . . it is coming back—I am not the man I
thought myself.

ALICE. I am not Mrs. Finch-Fallowe. Who am I?

DEARTH [*staring at her*]. You were that lady.

ALICE. It is you—my husband! [*She is overcome.*]

MRS. CODE. My dear, you are much better off, so far as I
can see, than if you were Mrs. Finch-Fallowe.

ALICE [*with passionate knowledge*]. Yes, yes indeed! [*Gen-
erously*] But he isn't.

DEARTH. Alice! . . . I— [*He tries to smile.*] I didn't know
you when I was in the wood with Margaret. She . . . she
. . . Margaret . . . [*The hammer falls.*] O my God! [*He
buries his face in his hands.*]

ALICE. I wish—I wish—— [*She presses his shoulder fiercely and then stalks out by the door.*]

PURDIE [*to LOB, after a time*]. You old ruffian.

DEARTH. No, I am rather fond of him, our lonely, friendly little host. Lob, I thank thee for that hour.

[*The seedy-looking fellow passes from the scene.*]

COADE. Did you see that his hand is shaking again?

PURDIE. The watery eye has come back.

JOANNA. And yet they are both quite nice people.

PURDIE [*finding the tragedy of it*]. We are all quite nice people.

MABEL. If she were not such a savage!

PURDIE. I daresay there is nothing the matter with her except that she would always choose the wrong man, good man or bad man, but the wrong man for her.

COADE. We can't change.

MABEL. Jack says the brave ones can.

JOANNA. 'The ones with the thin bright faces.'

MABEL. Then there is hope for you and me, Jack.

PURDIE [*ignobly*]. I don't expect so.

JOANNA [*wandering about the room, like one renewing acquaintance with it after returning from a journey*]. Hadn't we better go to bed? It must be getting late.

PURDIE. Hold on to bed!

[*They all brighten.*]

MATEY [*entering*]. Breakfast is quite ready.

[*They exclaim.*]

LADY CAROLINE. My watch has stopped.

JOANNA. And mine. Just as well perhaps!

MABEL. There is a smell of coffee.

[*The gloom continues to lift.*]

COADE. Come along, Coady; I do hope you have not been tiring your foot.

MRS. COADE. I shall give it a good rest to-morrow, dear.

MATEY. I have given your egg six minutes, ma'am.

[*They set forth once more upon the eternal round. The curious JOANNA remains behind.*]

JOANNA. A strange experiment, Matey; does it ever have any permanent effect?

MATEY [*on whom it has had none*]. So far as I know, not often, miss; but, I believe, once in a while. [*There is hope in this for the brave ones. If we could wait long enough we might see the* DEARTHS *breasting their way into the light.*] He could tell you.

[*The elusive person thus referred to kicks responsively, meaning perhaps that none of the others will change till there is a tap from another hammer. But when* MATEY *goes to rout him from his chair he is no longer there. His disappearance is no shock to* MATEY, *who shrugs his shoulders and opens the windows to let in the glory of a summer morning. The garden has returned, and our queer little hero is busy at work among his flowers. A lark is rising.*]

THE END

# *BERNARD KOPS*

## *1926–*

BERNARD KOPS belongs to the after section of John Russel Taylor's "Anger and After" playwrights. Or perhaps it i just that Kops possesses a peculiar form of anger that leap forth looking like joy, for his plays are clearly *celebrations* in the original dramatic sense of the term.

Beginning with *The Hamlet of Stepney Green* (the firs of Kops's dramatic pieces after having tried both poetry and novel) up to the play of this volume, Kops's interest has been in a modern, vigorous, somewhat naive Jewish hero with big dreams, or—in the case of Solly Gold—schemes for his fu ture and the futures of those with whom he is involved. Kops telling their tales in a style of improvisation and spontaneity that includes dance, song, and poetry, wins the day with sheer theatrical effervescence.

But if his drama were no more than this, Kops woul hardly be of note to the serious contemporary theatre. The fact is that Kops deals in a bright, affirmative way with a universe weighed down by the bomb, and with the apparen impossibility of meaningful action in a tin can world. "Al the mountains have been climbed," says the hero of *The Dream of Peter Mann*; but he falls into a dream from which upon awakening, he has learned to participate realistically vitally, in the ordinary stuff of life, and that's a message we haven't heard for a long time.

The songs, poetry, and scenic arrangement of Kops's play suggest Brecht, and in *Enter Solly Gold* it is clear that Kops shares more than technical affinity with the German play wright. For Solly Gold is a Mother Courage type, a comic conniving con-man who succeeds in propelling a dejecte shoe magnate into some sense of significance again, into participating again in this terrible life that we live only once But garrulous Solly, the most serious of Kops's heroes to date, remains himself unchanged: he is only the catalyst that sparks the rebirth. Again, as we feel in previous Kops play it is not a big rebirth, but at least it will last for a time.

# *LETTERS  TO  A  DIRECTOR*[1]

58 Compayne Gardens,
London, N. W. 6.
17th February 1964

Lewis Palter, Esq.,
Carnegie Institute of Technology,

Dear Mr. Palter,

On the contrary, I am particularly interested in your production of *Enter Solly Gold*, chiefly because your letter both raises and answers (I believe) most of the salient points that I deem important. In other words, your letter makes very good sense and I say 'answers' because it seems to me you are already on the way forward.

Point by point; you are perfectly right about the accents. Make them your standard American yiddish in varying degrees. The play has to be pinned down to something specific, in this way it will take off, I hope, into something universal.

Identification is the main thing and I did not feel that many Americans could identify it with Golders Green, England, but they certainly would with its American equivalent which must exist. I am sure the rest of the cast who are not Jewish will get the 'message' from those eight who are.

Regarding music; we had for the Centre 42 Production a score composed by Stanley Myers, who is very talented and quite famous in this country. I had in my possession a tape of that music which is in a kind of chronological order, to marry with the action, but unfortunately on that tape there is no verbal indication and the music is often incidental.

[1] Reprinted with the permission of Mr. Lewis Palter and Mr. Bernard Kops.

You may therefore have a job finding out where exactly the music for *On The Second Sunday in December* really is, but it may be worth while digging. My agent is having the tape copied and is sending it to you. I think she will probably charge you for the cost of the copying, which won't be very much.

Now I think the music is very good, but if you want to use it I am afraid that it naturally is covered by performing rights and therefore you would have to pay something. But if you don't want to use the music it will serve to show you the mood that I feel it should follow. It could also of course indicate how you could get music out of this, and from the same source namely, a sort of swinging Mickey Katz chassidic. Anyway I am sure the tape will help you enormously.

If on the other hand you want to continue with your Christmas Carol idea, as far as I am concerned—fine—it is up to you. I wish I could be there but because I can't I take it for granted that you will do your very best for the play. I did not have the Christmas Carol idea in mind when I wrote the play, and when I write songs in plays I never have a tune in mind, so corrupt to fit if necessary.

Yes, fine, the prostitute and the policeman can both be Jewish. In England, it is just that I don't think there is a Jewish policeman and I only ever knew one Jewish prostitute, in my life, and she wasn't very good at it. Prostitution among Jewish girls in this country is virtually unknown, maybe it is because the Jews are not so much integrated into the English way of Life as they are in America. Anyway by making every character in the play Jewish you have a better opportunity in this sense of making the play more specific and therefore, more macrocosmic.

Yes, I think it is probably a good idea for Solly to do his monologues to the audience. We found in the Centre 42 Production that some of these speeches seemed to go on too long, particularly the telephone ones, and we cut down considerably. I hate standing on the dignity of words, but the technique of his talking to the audience could be quite good. I believe when Shelagh Delaney first took *A Taste of Honey* to Joan Littlewood, all the mother's speeches in the play were to herself and Joan Littlewood thought that this would never do and threw them to the audience. In this way a terrific contact was made and it worked. I personally did ot advise this method in the Centre 42 Production because he actor, to be frank, was not quite up to this means. Occaionally he did wink or make one or two statements to the udience, he could of course afford to step out of the play.

That I hope, clears up most of your problems, and I would ike to say that as I saw it, this play is not anti-religious. In act, I think it is pro-religious. If it is anti anything, it is anti-materialism, but there again I don't think it is anti in hat sense. The things I think it is anti are much too involved and complicated to go into here. I would like to think this play is for something.

Now one very important point; it is not an actor playing Solly or an actor acting Solly that should be the mainspring of the play but rather, Solly acting the rabbi and in fact, Solly being the rabbi. Because from the moment he puts he rabbi's clothing on it is almost a religious, miraculous, crazy thing that he becomes. It quite hypnotises him.

Kafka once said: 'If a leopard enters the Temple and starts drinking the sacrificial wine and repeats this often enough it soon becomes part of the ceremony.' So this is why Solly hypnotises himself before he can hypnotise others. He believes. And is this not the way Religions are born, or Philosophies, or Rituals? This is why he could swing it because he is not an actor being Solly, but Solly being a rabbi.

I think that is all I have to say because I think that what here is to say is in the play and with this I send you all a tremendous amount of thanks for your enthusiasm. To all the cast and the whole production unit and the Producer, I wish success and a happy time during the rehearsal and the run.

So with my best regards, I am
Sincerely yours,
Bernard Kops

Drama Departmen
Carnegie Institute of Technology
March 26, 196·

Mr. Bernard Kops
58 Compayne Gardens,
London, N. W. 6.

Dear Mr. Kops,

Thank you for your *Enter Solly Gold* letter. It helpe·
clear up a number of confusions on my part and served t·
excite the company and inspire the actor playing Solly. Jus
as important, it convinced him that Solly is himself hypno
tized by the role he plays—indeed becomes the Rabbi, at leas
now and again. Furthermore, we are now all convinced tha
Solly is irreparably altered by his experience at the Swartz's
If the play's main action is the conversion (and I don't mea·
to formal religion) of Morry and to a lesser extent of hi
family, the play's irony is in the conversion of Solly. As ·
matter of fact, as the actor who plays Solly and I discuss th·
play, we can't help but be intrigued with what happens t·
Solly after the curtain falls. I think of Bernard Shaw's Blanc·
Posnet. What else, if not a Rabbi?

Our composer, a very gifted composition major in th·
Department of Music, wrote a Prostitute's song, a Rabb
Solomon Goldstone song, and a Morry Swartz King of th·
Jews song. I provided the music for On the Second Sunday
I gave up the Christmas Carol idea. It didn't work. I get ·
lot of such ideas. Instead we're using a melody which wa·
sung in my grandfather's synagogue—now defunct for abou·
15 years, as are so many small Orthodox synagogues i·
N.Y. For some reason (which I like to think is significant) i·
stuck in my mind although I heard it no more than 10 or 1·
times and not for these past 15 years. Whether it was com
posed by my grandfather—a *chazan*—composer—or whethe·
it is based on traditional tunes I don't know. In any event, it'
quite beautiful and, I think, appropriate. Besides, it jumps.

We do have one problem with the music. Our composer
had to give up the project before completing an overture and
a tango for Scene 4. The tape you so kindly sent provided ·
magnificent solution. I want to use what I think is the music
for the Rabbi Solomon Goldstone song as the overture, a·

well as the tango from Mr. Myer's score. Perhaps I am way off, but although I like the overture on the tape, I think it too solemn for the opening of the play. The whole company is quite taken with Goldstone song and the tango, as am I. We will, of course be happy to pay whatever royalties you think fair.

I'm extremely nervous about the show. It's the first play I've directed whose effect on an audience I haven't been able to pretend to be able to predict. I have a feeling that it will shock, irritate, delight, and thrill people. I hope so. I keep resisting a pleasant gnawing sensation that your play will rock them. But I have counter feelings as well. Hence, my nervousness. We'll know in two weeks.

It has been a pleasure working on the play. My best wishes to you.

Sincerely yours,
Lewis Palter

# *ENTER SOLLY GOLD*

## A Comedy

## by Bernard Kops

## *1961*

# *ENTER SOLLY GOLD*[1]

## CHARACTERS

A PROSTITUTE, *35 years old*
SOLLY GOLD, *35 to 40 years old*
A POLICEMAN
TAILOR'S WIFE, *45 years old*
TAILOR, *45 years old*
AN OLD WOMAN
MORRY SWARTZ, *60 to 65 years old*
MILLIE SWARTZ, *55 to 60 years old*
ROMAINE, *28 years old*
SARAH, *23 years old*
MELVIN, *26 years old*
HERBERT FINK, *50 to 55 years old*
SADIE FINK, *50 years old*
ALAN FINK, *25 years old*

[1] Reprinted by permission of Coward-McCann, Inc. from SATAN SOCIALITES AND SOLLY GOLD by Bernard Kops. © 1961 b Bernard Kops.

*Notice:* This play is the sole property of the author and is full protected by copyright. It may not be acted by professionals or b amateurs without written consent. Public readings and radio and tele vision broadcasts are likewise forbidden. All inquiries concerning right should be addressed to the author's agent, Monica McCall, Inc., 66 Madison Ave., New York 21, N.Y.

# PROLOGUE

*Street scene. Dark stage and simple setting. A row of small houses near Aldgate in London's East End. The set is in a stylised manner and the interior can be seen as well as the exterior. When action takes place in a particular house or area that place is simply lit up. It is one o'clock in the morning; late summer. A* PROSTITUTE *stands outside her street-door and* SOLLY *enters. As she sings he sizes her up from afar.*

PROSTITUTE [*sings*].

> Yours for a short time, how about it honey?
> I'll give you five minutes, if you've got the money.
> You can have me once or have me all night.
> I'm very very versatile if the price is right.
> I can be naughty if you pay me cash,
> Now don't be so bashful, come and have a bash.
> If you want what I've got you can have it honey
> I'll give you five minutes if you've got the money.

[*She beckons* SOLLY.] Hello darling, do you want a good time with a bad girl?

SOLLY. Do you mean me?

PROSTITUTE. Why not? I'm not particular. I'll take anyone, as long as they're not jockeys or fishmongers, or Negroes.

SOLLY. What's wrong with jockeys? Some of my best friends.

PROSTITUTE. Whores are not horses, they tend to dig their heels in and treat the bed post like a winning post and fishmongers stink.

SOLLY. What's wrong with Negroes?

PROSTITUTE. You've got to draw the line somewhere. Come on, don't let's waste time.

SOLLY. Changed my mind, I thought you were fatter.

PROSTITUTE. You don't know what you want—eff off, go on.

SOLLY. But maybe I could stretch a point just this once.

PROSTITUTE. Make up your mind or it'll soon be closing time. Now come on, I want cash on delivery.

SOLLY. How much will you charge me to have a chat?

PROSTITUTE. Cut it out. What do you take me for? None of that kinky stuff for me, at least not unless you make it worth my while.

SOLLY. You mean you charge more for talking? Why?

PROSTITUTE. Cos I've heard it all before. How much do you think psychiatrists charge for listening? Five quid for five minutes, that's the fixed rate.

SOLLY. I could become Catholic for less and they'd listen for nothing.

PROSTITUTE. Take it or leave it, that's the standard charge.

SOLLY. How much do you charge ordinary rate for the ordinary thing?

PROSTITUTE. Two quid and no beating about the bush.

SOLLY. Two quid? You're a profiteer! It was only thirty bob before I left.

PROSTITUTE. You've living in the past, grand-dad, prices are rising all the time.

SOLLY. Sorry I wasted your time, fact is I've been daydreaming in the middle of the night. I'm flat broke—stoney-skint—haven't even got a bed for the night—take a look at the soles of my shoes.

PROSTITUTE. You're breaking my heart.

SOLLY. I'm hungry too, haven't eaten for days.

PROSTITUTE. Don't come the old acid with me. You might have heard of sentimental tarts with soppy hearts but yours truly is not like that—times are hard, can't even walk the streets these days. The likes of you should be shot—you've got no morals, no principles, that's your trouble.

SOLLY. Well, this is as far as I can go tonight. [He sits on his case.]

PROSTITUTE. Your mother should see you now.

SOLLY. My mother! Mum! I can just see her now. I was bad to her but she forgave me—she knew in her heart of hearts that I wanted to help her—she was a famous debutante—Martha Goldberg—I dragged her down and she died in the workhouse—I was just too late—I arrived in my Rolls to take her to the south of England.

PROSTITUTE. Poor boy— [She shakes herself.] What! You've got the spiel all right. You never had a mother. Bet you could melt the heart of a judge. Well, I'm off, I hear the Swedish Navy are pulling in tonight. I hope you don't catch cold and die of pneumonia. So long. [*She goes.*]

SOLLY. What time is it? [*A clock strikes one.*] Thank you! [*A* POLICEMAN *enters and watches* SOLLY.] My watch is stopped; wonder if I can pawn it for a few bob? [*He doesn't see the* POLICEMAN.] What can I do about kip tonight? Coo, I could kip right here and now I'm so tired—so here we are back in the old country— It's so old it's got one foot in the grave and the other foot's got ingrowing toenails. [*He takes his shoes off, and his socks, and starts cutting his toenails. The* POLICEMAN *who was just about to pounce has temporarily held off.*] What am I gonna do for cash? For the old lolly? Must think of something. But there's one thing I'm sure of—I'm not gonna work—never! Never!—never! [*He stands on the case—mocking the Hyde Park orators.*] Comrades, if you want work you can have it, as for me, work's too much like an occupation—I've committed no crimes, work is all right for workers, just the job for the working class, but for Solly Gold? There's only one thing he wants, money! And there's only one way he wants to get it—by doing nothing.

POLICEMAN. What do you think you're doing?

SOLLY [*jumping off case and quickly putting on his shoes*]. Hello, Officer—I remember you from way back. I've just returned from a world trip and do you know the world's nothing to write home about. They wouldn't let me stay in the States so I returned here—to little old England, the greatest littlest country this side of the universe.

POLICEMAN. What are you doing?

SOLLY. Isn't it obvious? I'm out here studying the stars—contemplating the infinite.

POLICEMAN. I'll contemplate your what-you-may-call-it if you don't move sharpish. What have you got in that case?

SOLLY. My worldly goods, Officer.

POLICEMAN. You're a saucy bastard, aren't you? Open up.

SOLLY [*opens it.*] One toothbrush—you know—for cleaning the teeth. [*Goes through the motions.*] One shoe brush—for brushing the shoes and one clothes brush for—

POLICEMAN. Alright, alright—what else?

SOLLY. That's the lot—I've flogged the rest. Three brushes and a brain, that's all I've got.

POLICEMAN. Where have you come from?

SOLLY. I've just landed—from Australia. Started on the bo[a]
as a dishwasher. By the time I got to Gib I was hea[d]
steward, but by the time we got to Tilbury I'd lost m[y]
position, my clothes and my money all in a card gam[e.]
That's the way it goes—up and down—everything's up an[d]
down. Ever been to Australia?

POLICEMAN. No.

SOLLY. Do yourself a favour—never go.

POLICEMAN. You said they threw you out of America, why[?]

SOLLY. Because I was a member of the blue and white shir[t]
when I was five.

POLICEMAN. What were the blue and white shirts?

SOLLY. How should I know? But I'm going to get into th[e]
States, you see. It's my spiritual home. It's dog eat do[g]
there, that's the way I like it.

POLICEMAN. Got any family here?

SOLLY. No—no family—no one. [Sings.] My mother go[t]
struck by lighting, my father crashed in a plane, my siste[r]
drowned in the Serpentine, my brother got shot down i[n]
Spain. My cousin died in a madhouse, my aunt from th[e]
sting of a bee, my uncle jumped off a skycraper— O[h]
what's gonna happen to me?

POLICEMAN. I don't believe you.

SOLLY. I don't blame you. No, chum, the things I do remem[-]
ber I try to forget and the things I try to forget, I try t[o]
forget that I'm forgetting.

POLICEMAN. You'd better hop it out of here or I'll run yo[u]
in.

SOLLY. A nice feller like you wouldn't do that to me. Wher[e]
shall I go?

POLICEMAN. Go up to the West End—another crook there[,]
more or less, won't matter—so beat it. I'm on my round[s]
now and if you're here when I come back I'll lock you up[.]

SOLLY. You've got me wrong. [POLICEMAN starts to go.] O[h]
what's the use. Thank you! Thank you! You're a very nic[e]
man—I think the English police are wonderful—

POLICEMAN. None of that moody. I'll be back in five min[-]
utes—so watch it. [He goes off muttering.] Spiv! Laz[y]
good-for-nothings—

SOLLY. I resemble that remark, I may be good for nothin[g]
but I'm not lazy. He should try living on his wits. Connin[g]
people is a full-time job—you've got to use your loaf t[o]

get through this bloody world without work and believe
me it's a damn sight harder than your union would let you
work—and I'm always on duty—twenty-eight hours a day.
[*He shouts after the* POLICEMAN, *then picks up case and
moves, but after a few feet he notices light in a window
of a tailor's shop: he knocks on the door and falls on his
face—on the doorstep. Groans*]. Oh help me—help me
—oh God—

*The tailor's wife comes to the door, opens it.*]

RITA [*calls*]. Joe! Joe! Come here, someone's in trouble.

JOE. Who isn't? [*He is busy sewing in the interior.*]

RITA. But he's on our doorstep.

JOE. So? We won't charge him any rent.

OLLY [*desperate*]. Help me—oh lady—I'm in terrible trouble.
[*He pulls on her skirt and at the same time tries to look up
her legs; she doesn't see this.*]

RITA. We've got enough of our own, son.

OLLY. If you only knew—I can't face it.

JOE. Tell him to go somewhere else—I've got this armhole to
finish.

OLLY [*loud*]. I'm so choked—I can't talk—you're a Jewish
woman, aren't you? *Sholem Alecheim.*

RITA. I don't care what your name is—what do you want?

OLLY. I'm gonna die—I'm spitting blood. Oh God, that it
should happen to me. I'm gonna die.

JOE. Tell him please not on our doorstep—bring him in.

OLLY [*as he is helped inside*]. No tongue can tell the things
I've suffered.

RITA. Just take it easy, son—try and relax. Oh the poor boy—
he's as white as a sheet.

JOE. What's he doing out this time of night?

OLLY. Oh I'm all water, my legs are just like water—I can't
go on. Take me too—kill me also. [*He collapses on the
floor.* JOE *won't leave the machine so* RITA *pulls him into a
chair.*] I'm just like water—water.

JOE. Rita, fetch him some water.

OLLY. Haven't you got something a bit stronger?

JOE. Rita, bring him some of that Palestinian wine.

OLLY. I prefer brandy if you've got it.

RITA *brings him wine.*]

JOE. I'm only a poor tailor.

SOLLY. Alright, I'll settle for this, I'm not so particular— O
no, I don't believe it—Becky—where have you gone?

RITA. He's delirious.

SOLLY. Nice wine—thank God I found you up.

RITA. You'll always find us up—he says he can't afford t
sleep.

JOE. Alright. [To SOLLY] So, what's your story?

SOLLY. I can't talk, not yet. Just let me sit here. I'll be alrigh
in a minute. Could I have another glass of wine?

JOE. Alright. Now listen, you don't feel so well, have a littl
rest, put your feet up and in two minutes you'll be as righ
as rain and be able to leave.

RITA. He drives me mad. Joe, can't you see he looks lik
death, what's the matter, 'fraid you'll lose a few stitches
Work is all he knows. Never marry a tailor [She tell
SOLLY] That's what my Aunt Sophie said. He borrows a
few hours from the next day, then a day from the nex
week and a few weeks from the next year and then he die
owing all that time. [She goes to JOE.] What's the matte
with him, Joe?

JOE. I don't like the look of him.

RITA. He's a Jewish boy, he can't be bad.

JOE. Yeah? What about Schnorrer Morry?

RITA. Can't you stop working? Can't you ever get away from
that machine?

JOE. You can grumble; did you ever go without?

RITA. Yes, without you, all my life. I'm married to a sewin
machine. [Returns to SOLLY.] You feeling better, son?

SOLLY. Oh Becky! Becky! What's the matter with you? Why
don't you jump—save the children—the children!

JOE. I don't want him having delusions on my sofa.

RITA. Oh shut up!

SOLLY. Becky, my poor wife—all burned. [Bursts into tears.

RITA. What happened to her? It's good to tell someone.

SOLLY. I'm a traveller, I only heard before. I live in Glasgow
—and my wife—oh—God rest her soul—died this morn
ing with the children.

RITA. Died? Oh, you poor feller.

JOE [leaves machine]. How?

SOLLY. Oh it was such a big fire, there were twenty engines
masks they had on. They all got burned to death, my

Becky, my little Renee, the twins, Michael and Angela—they were so beautiful. Becky had long black hair—she was a picture.

RITA. Oh, I'm so sorry.

JOE. I wish we could help you.

SOLLY. I wish I could help myself. I've been wandering in a daze, I haven't eaten.

RITA. The good die young. Don't talk no more, rest.

SOLLY. No, no, it eases me, I've cried enough. Becky tried to save them—she stood on the parapet with all the children in her arms—little Renee, she was such a lovely dancer—tap and ballet. What can I do?

RITA. Let me make you something to eat.

SOLLY. No, I couldn't, I'm all choked. Alright, if you insist, a chicken sandwich with some mustard pickle or some smoked salmon—nothing much—something light. [RITA *goes off to prepare it*.] I must go to Glasgow—now! I must give them a decent burial.

JOE. Stay here tonight, go tomorrow morning.

SOLLY. I must fly tonight—I'll have to charter a plane—

JOE. Of course, I understand.

SOLLY. I wonder if you could help me? God is good, in times of stress He sends good friends. You know your friends when you're in trouble. Listen—I need a few quid for the plane fare—the banks are closed and I must fly tonight.

JOE. How much?

SOLLY. At least twenty-five—yes, that will cover me. Oh, Becky, Becky, by my mother in the grave I'm sorry—forgive me, I tried to be a good husband.

JOE. I'm afraid I can only afford five.

SOLLY. That's no use, make it twenty then.

JOE. What about ten?

SOLLY. I'll tell you what, I'll settle with fifteen and try and manage with that.

JOE. Alright, fifteen it is! [*He gives* SOLLY *the money*.]

SOLLY. It's a deal.

JOE. Done!

[*They shake hands on it*.]

SOLLY. It's only a loan, mind. I'll send it back tomorrow morning.

JOE. There's no hurry, wait till the afternoon. I'll get it.

[SOLLY *lies back, smokes and pours himself another drink.* JOE *meets* RITA *coming in with sandwiches.*] I must be crazy, I'm lending him money.

RITA. It's good to know you've got a heart, we must all help each other. I'm pleased with you; he's the first person you've lent money to in the past twenty years.

JOE. Ah well, he's different—you can see it, it's obvious, he's a decent boy in trouble. I'm a good judge of character.

[JOE *goes off and* RITA *brings the sandwiches to* SOLLY.]

SOLLY. You're so kind—how can I repay you? [*Stuffs the sandwich into his mouth.*] You're too good. I bet no one appreciates you.

RITA. You can say that again. My husband takes me for granted.

SOLLY. When you're dead, then he'll appreciate you, just like me and Becky.

RITA. Try and look forward now, we have to get over things, life goes on.

SOLLY. You're very nice, you're an angel. Has anyone ever told you that? You've got a light in your eyes; does he ever say a kind word to you?

RITA. He hasn't got time. He's not a bad boy exactly, just got no time.

SOLLY. I'd have time for someone like you, I would—you're so nice— Oh comfort me—my Becky is dead. [*She pats him on the shoulder and puts her arms around him.*] I'm so lonely, let me cuddle you. [*He pretends to cry and soon he is completely embracing her and touching her hair.*] Oh, you're lovely, so lovely, just like my Becky.

RITA. No—no—I shouldn't—[*She tries to break away as she realises he is getting amorous.*]

SOLLY. You're lovely, you're a good woman—so big and kind. I'm in trouble, don't leave me—I need you—you're strong and fat—and oh—

RITA. Please, you'd better stop.

SOLLY. You're just my size—don't go—come closer. Can you blame me—you're so lovely, you're a friend, a real friend. You're just the right size—I'm mad about you.

[*He tries to kiss her but she breaks free and still they speak quietly, urgently.*]

RITA. How could you? With your wife just dead? How could you get fresh with me—no-one's ever done that to me. How could you?

SOLLY How should I know what I'm doing—I'm so sad and emotional. It was a sudden urge, blood is thicker than water.

RITA. With your wife just dead how could you do it?

SOLLY. Don't tell your husband, he wouldn't understand. I'll come back some other time—I'm mad for you and so unhappy.

RITA. Men! Men make me sick.

SOLLY. Me too. I was being affectionate; you're too good for your husband. I'll make it up to you somehow. Please forgive me, I'm only human and you're a beautiful woman; kiss me and tell me you forgive—for poor Becky's sake.

RITA [*wanders off and looks in a mirror.*] How could you do that to me?

[JOE *returns.*]

JOE. Here you are, fifteen quid.

SOLLY. You're a pal, how can I repay you?

JOE. With money.

SOLLY. I'll be on my way now, God bless you all, my Becky will be so pleased, I mean as she looks down on all this. Goodbye! May you live long and die happy—may you live to be a hundred and three.

JOE. Don't do me no favours.

SOLLY. You're one in a million, both of you. I must fly now.

[*He leaves the house and lingers outside, but the light goes off him for a moment.*]

JOE. Nice feller, ain't it funny how the good always suffer?

RITA. How could he do it to me? [*She rejoins her husband.*] I knew there was something fishy all along.

JOE. Well darling, I gave him the money.

RITA. Money? You bloody fool! You stupid silly sod! Didn't you see how he mauled me—he tried to rape me and you gave him money? Couldn't you see that he was just a lying thief? You gave him money? Why didn't you give me away while you were about it?

JOE. I wish I did.

RITA. Go on, back to your sewing, you silly so and so.

JOE. Why don't you go to bed? I've got a busy night ahead.

RITA. Why don't you drop dead? It's all your fault. Yes, I'm going to bed and don't wake me up whatever you do—cc the answer's no. You've had it from now on; you don' know how to treat a lady—you don't appreciate me. It' alright, I'm not so bad looking; people still think I'm at tractive. I'm not finished yet. Good night.

[*She goes to bed, the tailor continues sewing and the light i the room darkens. SOLLY is now seen again, counting th money. The PROSTITUTE comes up to him.*]

SOLLY. What happened to the Swedish Navy?

PROSTITUTE. They've got an attack of German measles o board. Bang goes another night's business. I'll have to sleep

SOLLY. Don't go, I've changed my mind, I need a room an I fancy something so I may as well kill two birds with on stone.

PROSTITUTE. No one's gonna kill this bird— My my, you've got a wad there. I'm in the wrong racket.

SOLLY. How much you charge for all night?

PROSTITUTE. Special rates for night work—time and a half.

SOLLY. Do me a favour, I want it cut price. How much?

PROSTITUTE. A fiver.

SOLLY. Come off it, I'm only a poor working man.

PROSTITUTE. Oh alright, four.

SOLLY. Make it two.

PROSTITUTE. You out of your mind? Don't you know abou the cost of living index? Three pounds ten and that's my final word.

SOLLY. Two pounds fifteen, on the nose.

PROSTITUTE. You'd auction your own mother—alright, three quid and not a penny less.

SOLLY. Right, it's a deal.

[*They shake on it.*]

PROSTITUTE. That's done. Let's go.

SOLLY. You're not as fat as I would like but you can't pick and choose all your life. [*They exit into her door and the stage darkens completely—now there is a passage of time and the stage lightens again and it is dawn—a cock i heard crowing and SOLLY comes out of the PROSTITUTE's door, yawns and does some exercises.* A cock crowing? In Whitechapel? Impossible. [*It crows again. He looks over a fence beside a third house.*] Chickens—that's handy. Come on you pretty little darlings—come and get stuffed. Oh boy, that takes me back . . . chicken soup, stuffed neck, chopped liver, giblet pie. There's one, two, three, five, eight, eleven birds in all, and one lovely rooster—beautiful bird. Looks as if you've had a heavy night like me. Never mind —I'll cut your throat and then you can have a long sleep and then I'll flog you and your girl friends down the lane. [*He is about to climb over the fence when an old lady comes out of the house with some food for the chickens.*]

WOMAN. What do you want?

[*He jumps back quickly but soon relaxes.*]

SOLLY. I want you. Good morning, my good woman, I'm the bird inspector.

WOMAN. Bird inspector? What do you want? Where are you from?

SOLLY [*more to himself*]. As a matter of fact I've been inspecting a bird all night. I'm from the Ministry of Agriculture and Poultry; I've been inspecting your birds.

WOMAN. What's wrong with my birds?

SOLLY. What's right with them? They're suffering from foot and mouth disease and they're all having a nervous breakdown. This won't do. This is a serious business.

WOMAN. Please sir, I can't help it; since my husband died I've been struggling to carry on alone.

SOLLY. Your husband dead?

WOMAN. Yes, a week ago, did you know him?

SOLLY. Of course I did, who didn't?

WOMAN. Who didn't know my Hymie? Who didn't know him and love him? He was such a wonder, he knew everyone.

SOLLY. Wonderful Hymie, with the heart of gold. As a matter of fact he owes me some money.

WOMAN. Money? He never owed anyone.

SOLLY. I mean the government. He never paid his last instalment of the Chicken Registration fee—didn't you know he owed us ten pounds?

WOMAN. Chicken Registration? No, I didn't know—he took care of everything, I'm so lost without him. I'll pay you.

SOLLY. Poor Hymie, the world won't be the same without him.

WOMAN. It's good to talk to you—I haven't spoke to a soul since he died. [*She gives him the money.*] You make me feel better—I'm glad you liked my husband so much.

SOLLY [*looking over the fence.*] The birds will have to go of course.

WOMAN. Why?

SOLLY. Neurotic birds are a menace to society—they're totally maladjusted and what's more I'll have to kill them here and now, I'm afraid. And that will be of course another six pounds disposal fee—

WOMAN. Take them, kill them. Who can be bothered feeding them anyway? Who eats eggs since Hymie died? Here, six pounds.

SOLLY. I'm letting you off light—because I like you and Hymie was a friend of mine. Actually I could report you because you didn't register the disease and then it would mean a heavy fine and even imprisonment, but Hymie was a wonderful guy, and also there will be just one further charge, two pounds ten shillings for the death entry certificate which we will send you in a matter of a few days.

WOMAN [*gives him more money*]. Take it, take it, who cares anyway.

SOLLY. I'm letting you off light.

WOMAN. Thank you, thank you—I know, you're very kind. Death is an expensive business—all I've done since my husband died is lay out, lay out.

SOLLY. I hope I'm not leaving you too short.

WOMAN. As my husband always said, you can always find money for bread and coffins.

SOLLY [*puts away money*]. Now please, I will need a sharp razor to cut their throats. [*She goes inside and he jumps over fence and inspects the birds. She returns and hands him a cut-throat razor. He sets to work though we cannot see his hands or the birds but very soon amidst a flurry of sound and feather, he emerges with a cluster of dead birds.*] We'll send you receipts.

WOMAN. One minute, do you know anyone who could use some clothes? I've got some, my husband's things, they're in marvellous condition. I can't bear to see them anymore.

SOLLY. I might be able to help you out, let's have a look.

WOMAN. Do me a favour, pull out that trunk. [*He puts the chickens down and pulls out a large suitcase.*] Only the best, as you can see—take it all.

SOLLY. A rabbi's clothes? [*He holds up some jackets and trousers and soon lifts out some rabbi's clothes.*]

WOMAN. But you knew my husband was a rabbi, didn't you?

SOLLY. Who didn't know? From Tel Aviv to Tell me the Tale he was famous—the best rabbi in the racket. It's just that I didn't think you'd part with such personal items.

WOMAN. You're right I wouldn't. Don't touch the Rabbi's clothes and his Bible. Take everything else—I can't bear to see them anymore. I must go now and sweep up. Thank you. [*She goes inside.*]

SOLLY. These clothes are not worth a light—she must be blind, they're all moth eaten; but this Rabbi's gear might come in handy—and I hear there are some very hot tales in this black book. Well, Solly boy, you're not doing too bad—last night you had sweet Fanny Adams and this morning you're worth twenty odd nicker, a dozen chickens and this odd clobber. You're in business somehow. The world owes you a living, my boy, and you've come to collect. [*He kneels down and prays.*] Oh, Rabbi Hymie— forgive me but I mean well—I'm a bad boy, but I've got my part to play, and I promise to spread love and happiness everywhere I go—cos money don't bring happiness so I'm gonna take it away from them. [*He suddenly gets an idea.*] Solly boy, you're a genius and you're in business. [*He quickly puts the Rabbi's clothes on and puts the chickens in his case.*] First I'll go from door to door, flogging these kosher chickens for charity, my charity. Thank you, Rabbi Hymie, you're a pal—I'll walk in your shoes. [*As he changes shoes*] And take the word of God—promises of redemption, love, kisses—anything they want—as long as they're happy. Watch out, world, I'm coming! Hendon! Golders Green! Hampstead Garden Suburb!—I'm knocking on your door! [*He does a little dance and some mock prayers.*]

I'm Rabbi Solomon Goldstone, I'm knocking on your door
With a new kind of religion and a brand new kind of law
If you can't get in heaven, he'll fix it in a flash
I've got the right connections, if you have got the cash.

[*He exits hurriedly.*]

THE CURTAIN FALLS

# SCENE TWO

*The next day. Interior. Living room of the house of* MORRY
SWARTZ. *Known as The Castle for obvious reasons. First because they've named it that and secondly because they've tried
to furnish it and make it appear very grand. The furniture
is in a mishmash of styles—good taste and the appalling are
side by side. A garish glassy cocktail bar, for instance, stands
next to a great Gothic-looking bookcase, without books. A
suit of armour, and animals' heads all around. A television
screen set in an antique case. Peach mirrors all around the
room. The huge ugly table is set for a wedding although it
appears the wedding feast has almost been finished. This
castle is in Golders Green. Around the table the people are
eating furiously.* SARAH SWARTZ *is dressed as a bride. She is
attractive in a slightly overblown way. Beside her is the
groom,* ALAN FINK, *a nervous slight boy, dressed in a dinner
jacket. Next to him his parents sit—*HERBERT FINK, *in a
dashy American get-up, and his intense wife. Next to them
sit* ROMAINE SWARTZ—*a buxom girl in late twenties—she
seems very hungry, as usual. And there is her brother* MELVIN
—*who wears a sports blazer and flannels—he is always
slightly aloof and seems to despise the surrounding people.
Next to him* MILLIE SWARTZ, *a rather attractive woman who
tries to look younger than her years, heavily made-up and
wearing a lot of expensive jewellery.* MORRY SWARTZ *is not at
the table but is feeding a bird in a cage—he too is dressed in
a dinner jacket but he has his slippers on. There are streamers
and balloons about. When the curtain goes up there is a
silence for a while as we just see the spectacle of people
stuffing themselves.*

MILLIE. Morry, come back to the table, we're supposed to be
celebrating.

[ 395 ]

[MORRY *takes no notice but is swaying with a champagne gla* *in his hand.*]

FINK. Come on, Alan, make a speech.

ALAN. I've already made four.

FINK. Make another one.

[*All except* MELVIN *and* MORRY *bang on the table with the* *forks.*]

ALL. Speech! Speech!

ALAN [*He pulls* SARAH *to her feet and they cuddle*]. Mum an Dad! My dear Mother- and Father-in-law, Melvin, R maine, my darling wife—I promise to be a loving husban to bring you breakfast in bed for the first three months, t look after the shop and make lots of money.

[*They all clap.*]

SARAH. I'm so happy, I could cry.

MILLIE. Don't do that, your eyeblack will run.

SARAH. I could eat him, he's so handsome.

SADIE. What a handsome couple, don't they look lovely t gether?

MILLIE. Yes, it's a good arrangement.

HERBERT. Your turn next, Romaine.

ROMAINE. Don't do me no favours. I don't trust men.

HERBERT. Alan, you've got a lovely girl there, cherish he She's a lovely well-made girl and you're a lucky well-of boy. Look, he's blushing, you naughty boy. Bet you can wait for tonight, eh? It's lovely to see young people comin together. Wish I had my time over again—that's the way used to like them—well covered.

SADIE. Herbert!

MORRY [*sings*].

Here comes the bride, short, fat and wide,
See how she wobbles from side to side.
Here comes the groom, skinny as a broom,
If it wasn't for the bride he would have more room.

[*All laugh nervously.*]

SADIE. Aren't we having a lovely time? I love a party. This i the happiest day of my life, by my life. Don't they loo lovely standing together? I could cry.

MILLLIE. Why you?

SADIE. I don't know, brides always make me cry.

HERBERT [*he is also very tipsy and holds a drink up*]. Please God by me—I'll sing a song now.

[*The others take it up.*]

ALL. For they are jolly good fellows, for they are jolly good fellows, for they are jolly good fel-el-ows.

[*At this moment* SOLLY *walks in and holds up a solitary chicken.*]

SOLLY. And so say all of us. [*They are all astonished.*] I rang the bell, but I heard singing so I came in.

MORRY. Please excuse us, we'll all upside down.

SOLLY. That's alright, my son, it's good to see people happy. What a lovely house.

HERBERT. Isn't it marvellous? What do you think of it? Do you know it cost twenty thousand to build.

SADIE. It's just like a palace, you could eat off the floor.

MORRY. Excuse us, but we're right in the middle of a wedding.

SOLLY. Carry on, it's so nice to see such a nice happy family gathering.

HERBERT. This is a nice stroke of luck, a rabbi calling on our children's wedding day. Heaven's happy with this match.

SADIE. Who wouldn't be? Look at them, they're so lovely.

MILLIE. Well, Rabbi, what can we do for you? How much money do you want?

MELVIN. Mother! You do go on—money, money, that's all you talk about.

SOLLY. Business can wait.

MORRY. Have a drink with us, please.

SADIE. Drink the health of our children.

SOLLY. Some of that Three Star brandy please. No soda.

MILLIE. What charity do you represent?

SOLLY [*holds up his glass*]. *Lechaim.*

MELVIN. Can I go now? I have a game of squash booked.

HERBERT [*points to couple*]. So have they.

MILLIE. No, you can't go. What's the matter with you? [*She pinches his cheek, he squirms.*] He's so highly strung and sensitive. Are you feeling alright, darling? Let's feel your forehead. Spit out three times and go and eat some fruit. Well, Rabbi, it's nice to see you in this house.

SADIE. Perhaps he'd like to bless the house—believe me, it'
    worth it.

MILLIE. Alright, why not? We've got everything but it can'
    do no harm.

MORRY. We've got nothing, we kid ourselves.

ROMAINE. Oh, Daddy's getting all philosophical again.

MELVIN. Dad's right and we're a load of hypocrites.

HERBERT. It's a lovely party, isn't it? And soon our dea
    children will be pushing off on their honeymoon.

MORRY. Thank God.

MILLIE. I agree, it's good at last they'll almost stand on thei
    own feet. After all, you push them out of you—into the
    world—and then it seems you have to push them righ
    through life. And now at last they're gonna push off. It's
    not fair—they leave you so suddenly—look at her, she's
    only a baby.

HERBERT. Some baby.

[SOLLY *takes another drink, walks around the couple, digs*
ALAN *in the ribs and kisses* SARAH.]

SOLLY. Have a nice time, don't be greedy—in life. Love thy
    neighbor as— [*He starts kissing all the women on the fore-
    head, lingers over* ROMAINE.] Be fruitful and drink lots of
    malt and may you have peach mirrors in your house and
    apricots on your table.

MILLIE. They're not moving out yet, we've still got them for
    a little while—until the architects have finished their house.
    Then they'll move away; they grow up and leave you.

MORRY. What do you mean? Look, Rabbi, see that building
    next door? [*Shows* SOLLY *through the window.*] That's how
    far they're moving.

MILLIE. They've got the best of everything—I've seen to that.
    It cost a fortune, but who's complaining?

MELVIN. There she goes again. Must you always mention
    money?

MILLIE. I'd like to see you manage without it.

MORRY. For once I agree with your mother. I wouldn't care if
    you worked—you're supposed to look after the shop but
    what do you do all day? You're out playing golf and in the
    Turkish baths, trying to be like an English gentleman—
    Gandhi was more of an Englishman. Something for nothing,
    that's all you want. I had to work for it.

MILLIE. He's not that bad.

MELVIN. He's almost right, but can I help it if I don't belong?

ROMAINE. There he goes again, don't belong. Go out and don't belong—just fifty years or so.

MELVIN. Shut up you, you silly fat cow.

SOLLY. Children, children, remember the Sabbath day and keep it holy.

SARAH. But this isn't the Sabbath.

SOLLY. I never said it was. You must learn to respect your parents.

MILLIE. That's what I keep on telling him, he's killing me—killing me.

MELVIN. You're a long time dying.

SOLLY. Peace, peace, my children. We must forgive and love each other.

MILLIE. Alright, Mel darling, I'll buy you your glider.

ROMAINE. I want a car.

MORRY. Two years ago she bought him a sports car and last year she bought him a yacht, and now, a glider. We've had the ground and the water and now we'll have the air. What happens when we run out of elements? I suppose next year it'll be a spaceship. Alright, let's change the subject. Rabbi, it's a great honor to have you here; tell us the purpose for your visit to our humble—big house.

SOLLY. I'm Rabbi Solly Gold, at your service. I bring the word of God, I spread love and happiness. I'm on my usual pilgrimage through Golders Green and I pass this way but once—for today of all days is the day of days.

ALAN. You said it, today's my wedding day.

HERBERT. And tonight's the night.

SARAH [*pinching* ALAN's *cheek*]. Isn't he lovely? I could eat him.

SOLLY. Apart from that, it's still a very special day.

SADIE. It's a holiday or festival or something, isn't it?

HERBERT. No, I know them all.

MELVIN. It's the Amateur Gliding championship today.

ROMAINE. It's just another Sunday.

MORRY. And I've got heartburn as usual and a splitting headache.

MILLIE. And I've got heartache, and backache and stomachache—

SOLLY. I'm ashamed of you all. All of you. Look at you! Call yourself good Jews? And you didn't even know it was rabbinical chicken Sunday? I'm disgusted.

MILLIE. Rabbinical chicken what?

MORRY. Forgive me, Rabbi, but I don't follow religion—too many hypocrites.

SOLLY. You've all heard of Mother's Day? And Father's Day? And Doomsday? Well then, you surely must know that seven years ago the American Reform Orthodox Proxy Rabbi's Association proclaimed this Chicken Sunday. In the old days it used to be a great Hasidic feast. Don't you remember? [*He dances around wildly and mumbles gibberish.*] We revived it. Five times a year it falls. Surely someone must know the famous song?

[*Sings and dances again.*]

> On the second Sunday of December,
> Don't forget to remember,
> Give, give and give some more,
> To the Rabbi at your door.
> The third Sunday that comes in May,
> That most auspicious Rabbinical Day,
> Give, give, and give your all,
> To the Rabbi who comes to call.
> On the fourth Sunday in July,
> If a Rabbi passes by,
> Give! give! Don't ask why
> It's Rabbinical Chicken Sunday.

HERBERT. Of course, now I remember, I was only reading about it the other day.

SOLLY. Then as you know, the idea is for an esteemed rabbi, like yours truly, to go humbly from door to door, giving a chicken as a symbol of life and collecting a small amount for charity.

HERBERT. Ah, charity—what a lovely word that is. I'm a Mason, Rabbi, and that's the basis of our creed. Ever thought of going on the square? I'll propose you.

MILLIE [*takes out purse*]. We always give to charity. That should be my middle name—Millie Charity Swartz. What charity this time?

SOLLY. The Rabbinical Chicken Sunday fund for the prevention of cruelty.

MILLIE. Cruelty to who? Chickens?

SOLLY. Cruelty to anyone.

HERBERT. You're a man after my own heart. Here, let me give you something. [*Hands* SOLLY *a note.*] Honestly, I give, give and never think about it. [*Turns to the others.*] Just gave him a fiver. Why not?

MILLIE. But we don't want a chicken, we've just eaten half a dozen. I'm beginning to look like a chicken.

MORRY. You always did.

SADIE. I never get tired of chicken.

SARAH. Neither do I—I love them casseroled.

ROMAINE. I prefer them fricassee with breadcrumbs.

MORRY. Take no notice of any of them. Put the bird on the table. Go on, Millie, give the Rabbi some money. As a goy named Bacon once said—

MILLIE. Please don't mention that word, this is a kosher house. What will the Rabbi think? You give him the money, you want the bird.

MORRY. Who should I make it out to? [*Takes out cheque book.*]

SOLLY. Please, please. I'm surprised with you—you must surely know that truly spiritual organisations don't believe in banks. It's unholy—it's usury, it cuts across the holy act of giving from one to the other.

MORRY. How much?

SOLLY. Shall we say ten pounds?

MILLIE. Expensive chicken!

SOLLY [*taking money from* MORRY]. Fine—wonderful. Now, let's forget all about money and get down to business, the business of blessing. [*To* SARAH *and* ALAN] What kind do you want? The special super de luxe deep significant kind, or the simple blessing of the bedchamber?

SARAH. How much do they cost?

SOLLY. Let me see— [*Takes out little book; consults it.*] The significant, cabalistic eternal marriage blessing costs enough —mind you, it's worth it—two hundred and fifty pounds.

MORRY. The man who thinks up them charges should be in charge of my business.

SOLLY. It all goes to charity mind you.

HERBERT. Our children deserve special prayers. After all, God can't be expected to be tuned in everywhere—we must have a strong transmitter. And the money goes to charity after all, don't let's stint ourselves. Mr. Swartz, you can afford it—if it was my house I'd give willingly.

SOLLY. Good, I'm glad you take that attitude. According to the law you must pay—

HERBERT. Me? Oh—

SADIE. But we—

HERBERT. How much does the cheaper blessing cost? You know, the bedchamber kind?

SOLLY. Only twenty-five pounds, and it's a pretty good blessing. For as the good book says: When the bedroom is happy every room is happy.

HERBERT. We'll have to have that one then—I haven't got the loose change here and I've left my cheque book at home—I'll owe it to you, don't forget to remind me.

SOLLY [points to MORRY]. He'll lend it to you, won't you, Mr. Swartz? Of course he will. [MORRY nods slowly and gives SOLLY more money.] That's twenty-five pounds this gentleman owes you. Now on with the blessing. Oh, what a wonderful couple they are—they take my breath away. All I can say is they deserve each other. How I envy them—wish I could get married.

MORRY. Why can't you? Rabbis can.

SOLLY. I was married once. She was beautiful. Miriam! She died in childbirth.

MILLIE. I'm so sorry.

SOLLY. That's alright—we have to get over these things. But no other girl will take her place; besides, now I've taken my vow of chastity. . . . Right, now the—let me see—the bed room all-purpose blessing. . . . [He takes up wine and starts to mumble gibberish and sways backward and forward.] May youlivelonganddiehappy.   Pleasegodbyyouyoushouldlivse longmayyougetwhatIwishyoufrompurimtoshobosnochma ohgodunitetheminmorewaysthanonewhatsdonecanneverb undonemazelmazelmazeltovmazelmazelmazeltov. [He now repeats this over and over again and claps his hands unti he virtually hypnotises himself and starts dancing sugges tively around the couple. He does this so completely and with such conviction that he has the others following him—going round and round in a circle, copying him. Seeing his power he dances around the room in conga-fashion and the others still follow him in and out of the rooms. The couple still stand where they were, completely oblivious to all this. When SOLLY stops dancing he shrugs, all the others seem rather stunned and dazed.]

HERBERT. Your Hebrew was the funniest I ever heard.

SOLLY. That's the new semantic Semitic based on the emetic

antics of the yigdal incorporating the Aztectoltec Ashkena-
zim. We're branching out.

HERBERT. Of course, I was only reading about it the other day
in the Jewish *Chronicle*.

[SOLLY *sits down at the table and eats a chicken leg with great
relish.*]

SOLLY. This is a lovely house.

SADIE. It's a palace. You could eat off the floor.

HERBERT. It's a castle. Believe me, a king could live here. And
Rabbi, come here, look at these peach mirrors—all em-
bossed—what do you think of them? I tell everyone about
them. They cost the earth.

MORRY. I hate them, they're designed to make you look better
than you are. Every day I feel lousy but the mirrors make
me look in the pink of health.

MELVIN. Mirror mirror on the wall—who is the peachiest of
us all?

HERBERT. Do you know how much this house cost?

SOLLY. You told me. But tell me, Mr. Swartz, who are you
that you can afford such opulence?

HERBERT. You mean to say you never heard of him? Didn't
you see that full page ad in the Jewish *Chronicle* last week?
This is Morry Swartz—*the* Morry Swartz—the shoe king.
He's rich, he's famous—haven't you heard the jingle on
Tele? Swartz's Shoes—Swartz's Shoes are the shoes for
You. Get some, get some, for your wife, and your children
too. My son married his daughter. His shoes are the best.

MORRY. Don't you believe it, I never wear them—they cripple
me. Don't talk about business, it's a millstone round my
neck. Let's change the subject. What synagogue are you
from?

SOLLY. Synagogue? Oh no, I'm a peripatetic rabbi—I travel.
Of course I have many synagogues under me, for between
you and me—I don't want to boast, but I'm a fully fledged
Synog. Regalia and all. You should all be ashamed of
yourselves—don't you know your own religion? [*They all
look ashamed.*] I have now renounced ceremony, severed
myself from paraphernalia and am having a Sabbatical
year, for the whole world is a place of worship. Every
house is a synagogue.

MR. FINK. I think I read about you in the *Daily Express* and the good work you are doing.

SOLLY. Of course you did, though I shun personal publicity I've just returned from the provinces where I've been making fifty conversions daily.

ROMAINE. But Jews don't go in for conversion.

SOLLY. Don't be ridiculous, I've been converting the Jews back to their own faith.

MORRY. You've got your work cut out.

SOLLY. I'm so ashamed, of all of you, everywhere I go the same story—everyone only interested in money, no thought for the spiritual.

MILLIE. What's the name of your organisation?

SOLLY. The Liberal Orthodox Hasidic Reform United Union of Peripatetics.

SARAH. Well, Mummy, it's time we started on our honeymoon.

MILLIE. Oh darling, I'll miss you.

SOLLY. Going somewhere nice? Bournemouth? Cliftonville?

ALAN. No, we're going to the Mount Royal Hotel at Marble Arch.

SOLLY. Eh?

SARAH. What's wrong with that? All sorts of interesting foreigners come and go and it's opposite the park and it's not too far away.

ROMAINE. And the food's smashing.

MILLIE. Five miles away is far enough—she's never been that far from me. Don't forget to phone me tonight, darling. If there's anything you want or want to know, I'm here at the other end of the phone. And remember I'm always here and you've always got a home here.

MORRY. Alan, look after my baby and we'll look after you.

ALAN. Don't worry, Dad, she's in safe hands.

SARAH. You ready, Alan?

ALAN. What do you think?

MELVIN. Thank God for that. Now I can get to that game— I'll drop you off in my car.

SARAH. No thanks, we're taking Daddy's Rolls. [*There is now a lot of kissing and pinching and crying by the women and back slapping by the men, then all the people talk in a group near the door as* ROMAINE *and* SARAH *exchange a few words.*] Don't worry, Romaine, it'll soon be your turn.

ROMAINE. Who's worried? Make sure you have their barbe-
cued trout—it's out of this world.

SARAH. I wish it was you who got married today, really I do.

ROMAINE. I've got no time for men. But be careful of their
horse-radish sauce.

SARAH. I know it's going to be lonely for you without me
around but maybe I'll find a nice boy there for you.

ROMAINE. Men are horrible, they only want one thing. Of
course, the speciality of the house is smoked salmon rolled
up with capers and stuffed into cold Scotch salmon.

SARAH. Oh I do wish you could get married—you've got such
lovely eyes.

ROMAINE. I told you I don't trust men. You going to cook for
Alan or employ a cook?

SARAH. I want to cook myself—I can make omelettes. Oh
look at him, he seems half-starved.

ROMAINE. What he needs is plenty of lockshen soup, gefilte
fish, apple strudel, cheesecake.

SARAH. You're so clever, you must teach me.

ROMAINE. And steaks—lots of steaks, for breakfast. It's the
latest rage—and salt beef always goes down well.

SARAH. You're so good, so good, you deserve a man.

ROMAINE. Don't do me no favours.

ALAN. Coming, darling?

MR. FINK. Well, Kinderler, be happy, tonight we'll really be
related, eh Morry? You know you haven't lost a daughter
you've gained a son.

MORRY. Looks like I've gained a family.

MRS. FINK. My boy is a good boy and she's a good girl, don't
they look lovely together?

MORRY. Alright, alright, go then—and if you need any more
money, I know that you know where to come.

MILLIE. I'm so happy, so happy for both of you.

SOLLY [blessing them]. Eat plenty of fruitcake and may all
your troubles be little ones.

MELVIN. Well, Sis, Alan, lots of splendid luck and all that
sort of rot and play the game and all that kind of thing.
[He hurries out and he is followed by SARAH and ALAN.]

MILLIE [shouts after them]. Wrap up warm—don't forget,
phone me.

MRS. FINK. Alan! Don't forget your tablets—well, they've
gone now. Suppose we'll go also.

MR. FINK. Can't we stay a little longer? Play cards or watch Tele or something, after all our families are now united? Come on, Romaine, put some records on, let's be lively

MILLIE. Alright, let's all go to the other room and play canasta—I feel funny tonight.

MRS. FINK. Believe me, Millie, I've also got the shivers—I know how you feel. My baby got married—

[*They all start for the other room but* SOLLY *and* MORRY *don't move.*]

MILLIE. Coming, Morry?

MORRY. No, I don't feel well.

MILLIE [*to the others*]. You all go, I'll be in in a moment. [*They all go in.* SOLLY *goes to the bar and drinks.*] You drive me mad you do. If you don't act a bit more sociable I'll brain you.

MORRY. I can't stand them.

MILLIE. You're ruining everything.

MORRY. Everything ruined anyway. I wanted Alan for Romaine, you married off the wrong one.

MILLIE. Well, at least we got one of them off our hands. Alan's a good boy, he's a plodder.

MORRY. Can't stand his father!

MILLIE. Well at least he's not badly off—even if he is stupid.

MORRY. He's nothing, just nothing in trousers.

MILLIE. He's a turf accountant, rolling in it.

MORRY. Turf accountant? In my day they called it bookmaker. He hasn't got two pennies to rub together. Street corner spiv.

MILLIE. He's got an office with a typewriter and two girls working for him.

MORRY. I bet!

MILLIE. Besides, he must be respectable, he's a Mason.

MORRY. That explains everything.

MILLIE. He's got marvellous connections.

MORRY. I need unconnections. I've got too many. We'll never get poor Romaine married now.

MILLIE. Why not? She's got nice eyes.

MORRY. Let's face it—she's fat and ugly and she's not a chicken. I told you to tell that marriage broker that I wanted a husband for her and not Sarah. Sarah could always find a husband.

MILLIE. She'd have got swept off her feet for a lowlife who only wanted her for her money.

MORRY. What about Alan? You think he's marrying her for love? Every time he looks at me, cash registers ring in his eyes.

MILLIE. I know, but this is different; we chose him, it's respectable this way. Anyway, who wants Romaine married? She's such a good girl around the house—no romantic-shmantic nonsense about her.

MORRY. We sold the wrong one—the wrong one. Poor Romaine, running to seed, well—hardly running—hobbling. It's all your fault.

MILLIE. Do me a favour, go to sleep—you're uncouth. A rich man with nothing. Look at him. At least I know how to treat guests, even if I don't like them.

[*She goes into the other room and we can just see them in there playing cards.* ROMAINE *is dancing rather sadly around the card table.*]

SOLLY [*giving* MORRY *a drink*]. One thing I don't understand, if you're so rich, why so few guests?

MORRY. Who do I need to impress? Anyway, I don't like anyone, not even myself. I'm surrounded by enemies, all after my money.

SOLLY. You're right, and listen, your enemies praise you but your friends tell you the truth, and I'm telling you that there's something missing in your life.

MORRY. I don't trust no one. I love my children but what's the use, they're spoilt and take no notice of me. I love my wife but we're miles apart—getting further away every minute. I'm finished.

SOLLY. They're sucking the life out of you. Bloodsuckers, that's what they all are.

MORRY. Riches? You can keep them. All my life I slaved. For what?

SOLLY. It's obvious to me you're a highly spiritually developed man. Ah well, it's time to be gone.

MORRY [*breaking away from his own thoughts*]. No, no, Rabbi! Please don't go. You give me a certain peace, when you sit beside me.

SOLLY. I've work to do, my son.

MORRY. Please spare me a little longer, I want to talk to you.

I feel I could pour it all out, you have such a beautifu
face. Please, please, just for a few minutes.

SOLLY. Oh well, if you insist, my son. [*He helps himself t*
*another drink.*] Maybe I can help you, though I do wan
you to understand that my time is valuable.

MORRY. I'll make it worth your while. It's worth anything t
me, just to get it all off my chest.

SOLLY. Alright then—just relax. Lie down. [*Using the meth-*
*od of a psychoanalyst, he makes* MORRY *lie flat on a set-*
*tee.*] Tell me everything, confide in me, God is listening t
you.

MORRY. I'm afraid of dying, I'm also afraid of living. Every
one fiddles. My accountant is a crook; so is my doctor an
my solicitor. I don't trust my wife; she tries to look to
beautiful—who for? Me? After all these years? So I hire
a private detective to watch her and now I've had to hir
another one to watch him.

SOLLY. That's right, tell me everything—unburden yourself

MORRY. Yes, I can trust you. You radiate love and kindness
I'm a humble man, Rabbi. Not very intelligent, but a bi
clever. You don't need brains to make money, you nee
knack. I don't believe in anything—what can I do? M
son is a no-good snob, my wife nags, nags, grabs, grabs
and now I'm left with Romaine on my hands. Till the da
I die I'll see her fat podgy fingers eating Turkish deligh
and marshmallow.

SOLLY. But surely anyone would marry her?

MORRY. You'd think money was good enough bait, but no
not with her—they fight shy of Romaine, and can yo
blame them?

SOLLY. But she's attractive! Lovely! A big girl, full of—

MORRY. Too bad you took that oath of chastity—still, onc
sworn, never torn—besides, as you said, you loved you
wife too much. You would have made a lovely husban
for my Romaine. Too late now.

SOLLY. So what can I do for you?

MORRY. I'm useless, not going anywhere, not getting any
where, except under the ground. I'm crippled with pain, s
Rabbi, what can I do?

SOLLY. One minute! It just dawned on me—of course, now
remember you.

MORRY. Do the synagogue boys know me then? Am I tha
well known? Have I got a good name? [*He gets up.*]

SOLLY. You started down the lane, didn't you, with a shoe stall?

MORRY. Yes, I started humble.

SOLLY. And you're still a humble man—God is pleased with you. Didn't you then start a small shoe shop in the Mile-end road?

MORRY. That's me.

SOLLY. Of course! And then you built up your shoe empire.

MORRY. Do you know, I'm shoemaker by appointment to the Queen of Tonga and the President of the U.S.A. But between you and me—I wouldn't be seen dead in my shoes.

SOLLY. My mother once brought me to your shop in Mile-end—you served me yourself, don't you remember?

MORRY. Does a prostitute remember all her customers?

SOLLY. You saw we were poor so you gave me the pair of shoes, for free. Providence has brought me to you to repay that debt—that wonderful gesture of a man with a soul, a man with such humanity—shush—don't talk—I'm trying to get in touch with the angels now. Marvellous things are going to happen to you.

MORRY. Rabbi, you're a wonderful man, I envy you. So you're an East End boy—like myself. Well, you made good, maybe there's still a chance for me.

SOLLY. I'll see what I can do. I'll put a word in.

MORRY. I know you. I know I do—as if I've known you for years. What did your father do?

SOLLY. He was a great composer and my mother was a ballerina, she used to dance at the Palaseum, didn't you ever hear of Bertha Goldskya?

MORRY. Not offhand.

SOLLY. Now, let's get down to hard facts—how much are you worth?

MORRY. Who knows? Between half a million and a million. It fluctuates. But what's the use? Has any single pound brought me a single ounce of happiness?

SOLLY. You could always give it away.

MORRY. You kidding? You're not married to my wife. Anyway, I don't really want to give it away. I mean I worked so hard for it. That's my dilemma. [*They have been drinking continuously and both are staggering around,* MORRY *more so than* SOLLY.] When I was a kid I was happy.

[SOLLY *puts his arm around him.*]

SOLLY. Tell me about it.

MORRY. Seven of us—happy kids, all sleeping in the same big bed. [*He takes some cushions and lays them on the floor.* SOLLY *does the same.*] The bedroom small, can't you see it? My father struggled and my mother worried and we played. I was rich then; caterpillars in boxes and conkers on strings and every day was an adventure. Mummeeeeeeee! Throw me down a peneneeeeeeee! And when the winter evening came we played hide-and-seek in a peasoup fog and went home to a bowl of peasoup. . . And don't you remember the pillow fights and feathers everywhere?

SOLLY. On guard!

[*He hits* MORRY *over the head with a pillow.* MORRY *is sent flying and feathers are flying everywhere.* MORRY *gets up and hits* SOLLY *over the head. Soon they are fighting and laughing with everything they've got.*]

MORRY. Hurray! Hurray! Charge! Confetti—Hiphip—Hip—Hoooray—

[MILLIE *comes into the room followed by* ROMAINE *and* MR. *and* MRS. FINK.]

MILLIE. Take no notice of him, Sadie, he never grew up. [*Pushing the others back into the room; trying to suppress her anger.*] Strange games you're teaching my husband, Rabbi.

SOLLY. I'm illustrating a theme from the Bible. We got carried away—such spirit your husband has.

MILLIE. Back inside, folks—he's a little unhinged tonight. The trouble I have with that man; never mind, there are worse fish in the sea, so they say.

MORRY. I wish you'd go fishing.

[*They all laugh as they go back into the room but* MILLIE *turns on* MORRY.]

MILLIE. You wait till I get you alone, I'll give you what-for showing me up. [*She goes in with the others.*]

MORRY. See what I mean? Who can I turn to? Child games are over. My mother and father died and everyone grew up. [*He starts to tidy the mess and* SOLLY *helps him.*] All the family have grown up and grown old— [*He groans.*]

Oh my back! It's like a knife. Everyone lives in Hendon and Hampstead Garden suburb—but there's no garden in the heart. We're all dead people in stuffy living rooms, now, but then it was paradise.

SOLLY. With my help you can become happy again.

MORRY. Come on, let's have another drink, let's eat, drink and be merry for tomorrow we die, please God. [*They drink again and* MORRY *dances and sings to the tune from* "Thieving Magpie" *by Rossini.*]

    I am a lobos, I am a lobos
    I take the shicksers to pictures on shobos.

[*He suddenly stops and becomes doubled up with pain.*] There it is—Oooooooohhhhhhh—I've overdone it. I'm finished. [*He gradually lies down*] Ohhhhhhhohohoh—I'm dying—I'm done for.

SOLLY. What can I get you?

MORRY. Stay here. Just speak to me, your voice soothes me. Will God forgive me? I'm dying. Will he forgive me, Rabbi?

SOLLY. He hasn't got much choice with me to help you. Don't speak now—you're doing alright.

MORRY. Oh my stomach, Oh my back, Oh my God.

SOLLY. Listen—I want you to stand up.

MORRY. You crazy! If I stand up I'll fall over.

SOLLY. Stand up!

MORRY. Oh go away from me. Leave me alone.

SOLLY. If you stand up you won't fall over. I have spoken.

MORRY. Leave me to die in peace.

SOLLY. Have faith in God! Stand up—He will heal you. Stand up. I promise you—you won't fall over.

MORRY. Alright, for His sake I'll chance it— Ooooooohohohooo.

[*He gradually gets to his feet*]

SOLLY. There you are—oh ye of little faith.

[*At this* MORRY *crumbles and falls over.*]

MORRY. I told you—oh let me die. I'm suffering from an incurable disease.

SOLLY. Where's the pain now?

MORRY. Where isn't it! In my toes, in my head, in my fingers, in my neck, in my back. [*He slowly crawls to his feet by holding on to the settee.*]

SOLLY. You'll be fine—I'll cure you. Nothing to worry about
Solly Gold will fix it.

[*Unintentionally* SOLLY *slaps the old man vigorously on th*
*back.* MORRY *is hurled to the floor again.*]

MORRY. Oh! You've killed me! [*He writhes and moans an*
*turns over and over in great agony but suddenly he stop*
*and stands up.*] That's it! The pain's gone! You've done it
SOLLY. Of course. What did I tell you?
MORRY. I'm cured! You don't understand—I can stand u
straight with no pain! It's a miracle. A miracle! [*He kisse*
SOLLY *resoundingly on the forehead.*] For years I've suf
fered and now I'm well, thanks to you.
SOLLY. It's the work of God, I'm just His instrument.
MORRY. It's a miracle. And to think I doubted. He sent you
to me—I can't believe it—how can I thank you? How ca
I repay you?
SOLLY. We'll find a way.
MORRY. Stay here with me—stay here for a time—for a few
days. Please be my guest.
SOLLY. I told you my time is precious—there are others who
need help . . . people starving. . . . I'm the best collecto
this side of the Thames.
MORRY. I'll make it worth your while—I'll give you mor
than you'll collect in a month. But you must stay, I nee
you. You can help me.
SOLLY. Alright, if this is the will of God, who am I to argue
I'll stay for a while. . . .
MORRY. Oh, we'll have a marvellous time, you and I to
gether! I'm young again. I'm reborn. I can move, I walk
I can dance! It's a miracle. Thank you, thank you. Watch
me dance—Kazatzka—I haven't done it for years.

[*He dances wildly to the music that comes from the othe*
*room.* SOLLY *claps his hands and they make a terrific noise*
*The family and the* FINKS *come in from the other room—*
*stand around in amazement as* MORRY *dances into the othe*
*room followed by* SOLLY *clapping. The phone rings; every*
*one rushes for it but* MILLIE *gets there first.*]

MILLIE. Hullo! Oh— It's them! They've just arrived—they'r
in the room.
MRS. FINK. What's it like?

MILLIE. What's the room like? Oh, it's all pink—and silver—overlooking the park. . . . They can see the speakers on speakers' corner . . . how thrilling—what's the weather like? Oh yes, of course.

DOMAINE. What's the food like?

MILLIE. Did you hear that? They haven't eaten yet—the waiter's just taken their order.

FINK. Tell them to behave themselves—I mean they can do what they like but tomorrow is another day.

MILLIE. Alan, your father sends his love. Wrap up warm, darling—the night's are drawing in. I'm so happy for you, you naughty girl.

MRS. FINK. Tell him to take his pills.

MILLIE. Take your pills, Alan. [MORRY *comes dancing back into the room,* SOLLY *stops clapping.*] What's that, darling? How's Dad? Morry? Morry? Did you hear that? Haven't you got a message for your daughter?

MORRY. Tell them, God is good. I'm cured at last and Rabbi Solly Gold did it. [*Carries on dancing.*]

MILLIE. How should I know, darling—he's round the bend—only more so. Says he's cured. Bye-bye—Dolly. Ring me later— Soon. If you want to know anything—I'm here all the time and don't forget. . . . Alan, look after her, and if you can't be good, be careful. . . .

*She hangs up and they all once more turn to* MORRY *who continues his dance with* SOLLY *clapping his hands once more. They stand staring in amazement as*

## THE CURTAIN FALLS

# SCENE THREE

*The next day. The curtains are drawn and the lights are on. It seems like the middle of the night but in reality it is eleven thirty A.M. SOLLY enters in a very flamboyant-looking dressing gown, goes to the cocktail cabinet and drinks, goes to the peach mirror and smiles at himself.*

SOLLY. This is the life for me, I was born for luxury.

[*He takes another drink and* ROMAINE *comes on—also in dressing gown. She touches him on the shoulder, he jumps.*]

ROMAINE. Talking to yourself, eh?
SOLLY. I was talking to God.
ROMAINE. Go away, you can't fool me. I'm not like my father.
SOLLY. Can I get you a drink?
ROMAINE. A bunny hug, please.

[*He quickly hugs her*].

SOLLY. With pleasure.
ROMAINE [*struggling free*]. A bunny hug is Advocaat and cherry brandy.
SOLLY. Oh, I'm sorry, I'll get it. You must excuse me but I want to make people happy and I thought that was what you wanted.
ROMAINE. Wait till I tell my father.
SOLLY. Well, if you don't want it, at least you need it—that's obvious.
ROMAINE. Wait till my mother comes down. [*She takes the drink and drinks it.*]
SOLLY. Your father knows what he's doing—he understands the intricacies of religion.
ROMAINE. He understands nothing, he's a fool.
SOLLY. He can't be a fool if he made a fortune.

[ 415 ]

ROMAINE. Most people who make money are mad—they'r all a bit touched.

SOLLY. My Aunt Sophie had a fortune and she was un touched.

ROMAINE. How long you staying?

SOLLY. How long do you want me? [*He pinches her cheek.* I can help you.

ROMAINE. Don't need help.

SOLLY. We all need help. Come, my daughter, think of m as a friend. [*He puts his hands on her shoulders.*]

ROMAINE. Not too close.

SOLLY. Confide in me. Tell me everything.

ROMAINE. There's nothing much to tell.

SOLLY. You're very deep, I can see it. I'm trained to searcl your inner depths. You're a restless spirit, I can see grea fires ragining in your soul. Oh, thou fairest of women—

ROMAINE. I'm starving.

SOLLY. Thine eyes are as a dove's.

ROMAINE. You been listening to Housewives' Choice?

SOLLY. Thy hair is a flock of goats.

ROMAINE. Cheek! I shampooed it last night. [*He tries to cud dle her but she keeps on retreating from him.*]

SOLLY. Thy mouth is comely and thy breasts are like two fawns—

ROMAINE. How dare you! You're a dirty old man.

SOLLY. I'm not, that's in the Bible—here read!

ROMAINE. You're still a dirty old man.

SOLLY. I'm not old.

ROMAINE. Wait till I see my father, he'll throw you out— Man of God!

SOLLY. Wishful thinking, my daughter. I have not behaved improperly. I will admit though to being human. Under this habit is the same old habit—the desire for a beautifu girl like you.

ROMAINE. Wonder what's in the frig' for breakfast? How about some steak?

SOLLY. You know how to please a man. Why is it that you're not appreciated in this house? Why do they always leave you out?

ROMAINE. How do you know?

SOLLY. God knows everything, and I've come to tell you tha you deserve better for you're the most beautiful woman I've ever seen.

ROMAINE. You trying to get round me?

SOLLY [*soft*]. That would be hard—the angels are doing their nut over you. I'm going to help you get what's coming to you, get what you deserve. Your body is a poem conceived by the love of God and my imagination.

ROMAINE. Come off it, you know I'm fat.

SOLLY. Not fat, well built, a big girl—a real woman, with everything in its place and plenty of it. A wonderful sight —paradise, the promise of bliss.

ROMAINE. Of course, I'm reducing. At least I'm trying—I'm going to cut down on potatoes tomorrow.

SOLLY. Don't! Stay as you are—you're lovely. Beauty is in the eyes of the beholder and behold thou art fantastic—colossal—a double feature—I'm here to show you how much you're wanted.

ROMAINE. Some boys whistled at me last July.

SOLLY. Oh if I wasn't a rabbi—if I hadn't taken my vow! My wife! God rest her soul, would understand, I'm crazy about you.

ROMAINE. How would you like your steak?

SOLLY. Overdone—almost burnt to a cinder.

ROMAINE. I like the opposite—very rare—

SOLLY. Go quickly before I forget that I'm a holy man. [*She smiles and goes into the kitchen. He rubs his hands and looks at reflection in mirror.*] Careful, Solly my boy. Careful, go slowly or you'll spoil everything. [*He reads the Bible.*]

ROMAINE [*calls from kitchen*]. Come and watch me cook!

SOLLY. You trying to lead me astray? [*He now fights with himself.*] Careful, boy—take it easy. Oh, what's worth more to me? A fortune or a fat girl? Nothing's ever easy, is it? Just my luck. [*He still fights with himself.*] No! Moneymoneymoneymoney! It all boils down to that in the end.

ROMAINE. Come on, come and watch me. I'm sorry I was cross with you before. I got you all wrong.

SOLLY. No, I can't come now, I'm reading.

ROMAINE. What?

SOLLY. The most stupendous, smashing, story of them all— rape, love, hate, war, sex, everything—the Bible. [*Now he flips through the book and gets really excited.*] Cooo, it's all here—everything. Now I know where everything comes from! [*Suddenly he gets wildly excited.*] This is it! Here it is! I've got it! Solly, you're marvellous! It's a cinch. A cinch, a winner! It's all here, in black and white—it can't fail.

[*He can hardly contain his pleasure. He drinks to his reflection in the mirror.* MORRY *walks in briskly.*]

MORRY. Wonderful morning.

SOLLY. How do you feel?

MORRY. On top of the world, thanks to you. [ROMAINE *comes in.*] Hello, darling. [*He kisses her.*] How are you? Isn't it a lovely day?

ROMAINE. You feeling alright?

MORRY. Alright? I'm alive at last, aware—free! Make me some breakfast.

ROMAINE. But you never eat breakfast.

MORRY. This morning I feel hungry. Just something light, there's a good girl.

ROMAINE. Bit of toast?

MORRY. No, some grapefruit juice, some cereal and to follow, some fried kidneys and eggs.

ROMAINE. Something light? Oh, I see. Daddy, you kill me.

MORRY. Don't be saucy or I'll cut you off.

ROMAINE. Cut you off! Cut you off! That's all he knows. I feel like a water supply.

MORRY. Come on, there's a good girl—let's not argue anymore. I'll buy you a pound of marzipan whirls.

ROMAINE. With almonds inside? Daddy, I don't know what's come over you, but it makes a change. [*She goes into the kitchen.*]

MORRY. I've got a good idea. Let's go to Brighton in my Rolls, lay on the sand, then maybe we'll go to the Wax Works. Oh, I forgot—no sand at Brighton! How about coming to the East End and having a salt-beef sandwich?

SOLLY. No, there's important work to do. Now that you're healthy in body we've got to consolidate our position and then make you healthy in soul.

MORRY. But I'm happy now. I feel fine, thanks to you.

SOLLY. You only think you're happy, but the spiritual inertia will creep up on you if you're not careful and you'll have more than *angst* in your pants.

MORRY. Yes.

SOLLY. I want it louder than that—an affirmation, a total acceptance. Now listen, do you trust me?—Do you—place—yourself—in my—care?

MORRY. Absolutely! For some reason I trust you with my life. I dreamed and dreamed last night—wonderful dreams—you may be a stranger but you're not so strange as my own family.

SOLLY. Good! Now! Concentrate. I'm going to make a real mench of you. First I've got a message for you.

MORRY. From the Stock Exchange?

SOLLY. Somewhere more important.

MORRY [*incredulous*]. More important than the Stock Exchange?

SOLLY. I've got a message from God—for you. He spoke to me last night.

MORRY. Go on—you're a liar.

SOLLY. Would God talk to a liar?

MORRY. I'm sorry, I didn't mean it. A message for me?

SOLLY. When I knocked on the door I had a vision. And when I saw your face I saw a purple light, and when you spoke I knew my search was over.

MORRY. Search? Purple light?

SOLLY. How can I tell him I said to myself—how? How can I prepare this humble man for the news—for his mission. The Almighty said—"Speak, speak!"

MORRY. Don't leave me up in the air—for God's sake, spit it out.

SOLLY. All night I lay awake arguing with the angels telling them that you were not ready. There I was praying and weeping. All the stars in the sky burst into the room, a great halo covered the universe, and a golden rainbow stretched from Golders Green to Stamford Hill. Then, just at dawn, amongst a choir of assembled archangels the Holy One spoke again: "Behold—I send you Elijah the Prophet—"

[ROMAINE *comes in and* SOLLY *quickly stops gesticulating.*]

ROMAINE. We haven't got any grapefruit juice.

MORRY. Grapefruit juice? What are you talking about? Go away!

ROMAINE. That's more like it. Now you're yourself again. [*She goes off.*]

SOLLY [*continues*]. "And he shall turn the heart of the fathers to the children and the heart of the children to their fathers."

MORRY. What does it all boil down to?

SOLLY. "Behold nations shall come to thy light and kings to the brightness of thy rising . . . The fires—"

MORRY. Please tell me, don't beat about the burning bush.

SOLLY. I've come to proclaim you the messiah of the world. [*He kneels before him.*]

MORRY. Me? Don't make me la— —ugh.

SOLLY. It's no laughing matter but a time for jubilation. For you and me and the whole world.

[ROMAINE *comes in to lay the table.* SOLLY *quickly gets up until she goes out again.*]

MORRY. Would it be alright if I had a cigarette? [SOLLY *nods.*] Like one?

SOLLY. What brand? [*Looks.*] Alright. [*Takes one and strikes a match.*] You'll catch the whole world alight. [*As he talks he forgets the lighted match and burns himself.*] It's hard to believe, I know, but you must believe.

MORRY. But Rabbi, you can't mean it. You're joking.

SOLLY. I never joke. Certainly not on matters like this. Would I jeopardise my immortal soul by such plasphemy?

[*He keeps his fingers crossed and offers up a silent prayer for himself.*]

MORRY. Me? The messiah? Me? Little Morry Swartz? Go on, you're having me on. Me? The messiah? [*He looks at himself in the mirror.*] I've got bloodshot eyes.

SOLLY. You should have seen Moses. Look at me—listen— I've come to help you, Morry. Look—I'm telling the truth, by my life. Tell you what I'll do—want another miracle? Alright. Will that please you? Ye of little faith, I'm surprised at you—and you already to be the messiah. Didn't I perform a miracle on you last night?

MORRY. Yes, you did—but—

SOLLY. That was the first sign—to make you stand up and believe in me.

MORRY. But why me? Why do they have to pick on me?

SOLLY. Why not you? Morry, listen. Do me a favour. Do yourself a favour. You are not the messiah yet— Oh no— not by a long chalk. Hahahah. Did you think—no, there's a long way to go and I've come to take you there—to prepare you.

MORRY. But I'm a hypocrite.

SOLLY. Who but a good man would admit that?

MORRY. When I pray my words are empty. I can't get through.

SOLLY. I've got a direct line.

MORRY. I have no real love or reverence for anything—

SOLLY. That's because you haven't been alive till now.

MORRY. Would you swear on the Bible? That what you've said is the truth, so help you God?

SOLLY. Of course I would. [*Puts his hand on the Bible while crossing the fingers of the other hand.*] I swear on the Bible that you Morry Swartz are destined to become the messiah.

MORRY. It must be true—no one would swear like that without meaning it. I feel marvellous. Know what I'm going to do?

SOLLY. What? Pray?

MORRY. No, I'm going out in the garden—something I haven't done in years. [*He goes out.*]

SOLLY. Please, God—you there? If you are there, forgive me, *feinlights*—I'm doing it for your good. You see—alright, so I'm a bad boy. To forgive is human—I'll make it up to you . . . I'll make a bit of cash and make myself happy, and if I'm happy—well, we're all sailing— So listen, do me a favour—and if you're not there—and don't exist— what am I talking for anyway?

[ROMAINE *comes in with* MORRY's *breakfast.*]

ROMAINE. Where is he?

SOLLY. In the garden.

ROMAINE [*shouts from door*]. Dad! Your breakfast is ready! [*She puts it on table then brings* SOLLY's *breakfast and* SOLLY *starts eating.* MORRY *comes back in.*] This the way you like your kidneys, Dad?

MORRY. You mad? You know I never eat a big breakfast— who feels like eating anyway at a time like this? Now leave us alone, we're having a business discussion.

ROMAINE. Suppose I'll have to eat my steak in the kitchen. Business discussion! First he wants breakfast then he doesn't. Drives you mad, he does. [*She goes back into kitchen.*]

MORRY. How we going to do this, Rabbi? How will we convince others?

SOLLY [*he furiously cuts into his meat*]. You'll convince other
not by magic but by logic, by example, by the lights tha
radiate from you—the light of wisdom, the light of knowl
edge. There, I will guide you. You'll bring people to God
by your simplicity, by being humble. No miracles. Do they
have to have miracles—disappearing tricks and rigmarole
in order to believe? Oh, ye of little faith, you will say, isn'
life a miracle?

MORRY. But why me? Surely there are others more worthy

SOLLY. It happens that way sometimes. Look at Gautama
Mohammed, and Izzy Totenspielgle. Listen, you are the
new messiah—the everyday messiah—the ordinary fellow
—the average bloke. Good common or garden messiah—
a simple, humble, kind and worthy example—a heart of
gold and an upholder of charity. This steak is tough,
change your butcher—with you being ordinary you be
come extraordinary. It is the specific, the specimen, that
makes the generalisation pointed. The microcosm proves
the macrocosm—simple! To cut a long story sideways, you
are an honest man.

MORRY. Me? Honest? How do you suppose I made a fortune?

SOLLY. Silence. I cannot tolerate your scepticism—your self-
criticism. You must learn to love yourself. It's not how
you made your money that matters anymore—it's what
you do with it! The millions you made in money we will
now make in souls. Making money was an exercise God
set you. [*He stands up and exclaims:*] The nation is ready
—the Commonwealth is linked—the world is watching and
with my help you'll come into your kingdom and heaven
will reign on earth. Cats and dogs will lick your feet—
people will be nice. God watched you from the start—He
helped you make a fortune and found a shoe empire! And
now it's no longer Morry Swartz the King of the Shoes,
but Morry Saviour Swartz the King of the Jews! [*He sits
down again and cuts more meat.*]

MORRY [*looks at mirror—gestures and poses*]. Do you think
it's possible? Why? But why not? Sure! I got a scholarship
as a kid when nobody else did.

SOLLY. You'll follow me and I'll follow you. [*He walks round
and round in a small circle and is followed by* MORRY.]
Morry Swartz the King of the Jews
Have you heard the latest news?

He saved the soles upon your feet
And now He'll save your soul—complete.
I'll help you, Morry, don't worry.

MORRY. Who'll help you?

SOLLY. God help me, I mean God'll help me. Now get on with your breakfast, you need to build up your energy for the election campaign.

MORRY. Look at me—haha—the messiah! And I'm only a small man.

SOLLY. So was Napoleon.

MORRY. Look what happened to him.

SOLLY. Well, what about my father? Look what happened to him, and he was only a small man.

MORRY. What happened to him?

SOLLY. He was the first man to swim the Atlantic, wasn't he?

MORRY. You said he was a composer.

SOLLY. Can't a crazy composer go swimming?

MORRY. Rabbi, I only hope I prove worthy of my task. This is the happiest day of my life. I want to tell everyone. At last I've got something to live for.

SOLLY. Now listen, be a diplomat—not a word to anyone, not yet. It's too soon—they're not ready yet for the shock. They're not so spiritually advanced. This must stay our secret until God says otherwise—otherwise you'll be a laughing stock. You know how people are.

[ROMAINE enters.]

ROMAINE. I've finished my breakfast. The steak was like butter.

SOLLY. Mine was like leather.

[MILLIE enters in her dressing gown, looking like death.]

MILLIE. Did the phone ring?

ROMAINE. No!

MILLIE. Why not? What's the time?

ROMAINE. Getting on for twelve.

MILLIE. What? Why didn't someone call me? Why doesn't someone draw the curtains? I feel terrible. Oh, oh, what a night I had—and I've got such a day in front of me.

SOLLY. Maybe I can help you.

MILLIE. No one can help you—you can only help yourself. I didn't sleep a wink.

SOLLY. Is it the international situation that's worrying you, my daughter?

MILLIE. International? What? What are you going on about? And stop calling me your daughter—I'm old enough to be your mother. It's the servant situation that's worrying me. Other people's worries don't keep me awake, I've got enough of my own: my baby got married, my son's driving me to the grave and my husband to the workhouse—and she's [*points at* ROMAINE] driving me to the madhouse.

SOLLY. If you go to all those places at once it should be very interesting.

ROMAINE. Would you like some breakfast, Mummy?

MILLIE. Couldn't touch a thing. I've got the shivers, and I've got daggers in my head, and my heart is pal—

ROMAINE. Made some lovely kidneys for Dad, who doesn't want them now. [*She puts the plate in front of her mother.*]

MILLIE. No, I couldn't. Do me a favour, you know I never eat break . . . [*She sniffs plate and starts eating very ravenously.*] Such a day in front of me—an appointment with the hairdresser at two, the dressmaker at three, and the chiropodist at four, and the dentist at four thirty, and I told Sandra I'd go with her to a tea dance at five, and then this evening to the theatre with Estelle to see that wonderful play about homosexual-ity, and on top of all that I've got to find a new maid.

MORRY. What's wrong with the one we've got?

MILLIE. Nothing, except we haven't got her anymore. He didn't even notice she left.

MORRY. The German girl gone? Where?

MILLIE. Back to Germany. The German girl was three girls ago—we've had French, Italian and Irish since then.

ROMAINE. I'll have to do all the washing and the washing-up now, I suppose.

MORRY. About time you did something—it's all piling up in the kitchen. You can't blame the girls for not staying in this house. Who'd want to cope with us? But I'm going to change all that. From now on we're going to be a family again—all sitting down to meals at the same time. One happy family.

[*The phone rings.* ROMAINE *and* MILLIE *dash for it.* ROMAINE *gets there first.*]

ROMAINE. Sarah! Darling, how are you?

MILLIE. Give me that phone—I'm your mother! [*She snatches it away.*] Hello, Dolly—Sweetheart. How are you darling? Did you sleep well? What? You poor girl, never mind, you'll get used to it. [*She turns to tell the others.*] He likes to sleep with the window open. Had breakfast yet? Was it nice? Bed comfy? How's Alan? Send him my love. Tell him not to worry and remember this is your honeymoon. What's that? Oh, I'm so pleased. Bye-Bye, Dolly, see you soon, then—see you— Tata—as quick as you like. Good-bye. [*She puts down the phone.*] They're coming to lunch. She misses us.

MORRY. But she's only just left.

MILLIE. It was last night. She's homesick. Blood is thicker than water.

[MELVIN *comes in dressed in blazer and white trousers.*]

MELVIN. Lovely day. Seen the papers? What's it going to do?

MORRY. We're on the brink of another war.

MELVIN. I didn't mean that. Is it going to rain? What's the forecast? [*Takes a newspaper, reads the back page.*]

MORRY. The back page—that's all he knows—and on the front page the world's doing its nut. Look at him, the English Sportsman, the Cricket Fixtures, the rugger scores—

MILLIE. You hungry, darling? Some nice fried fish in the frig'.

MORRY. I know what he needs, and I don't mean lockshen soup.

MELVIN. Think I'll have a bash in on the tennis court this morning, a nice brisk game to start the day. Has Derek phoned?

MORRY. Aren't you going to work?

MELVIN. Aren't you?

MORRY. How dare you talk to me that way—who paid for everything—who poured out his heart?

MILLIE. Melvin's not too strong, don't nag him.

MORRY. Look at him—the Sportsman. Tallyho Moishe. He's always on holiday. It's either winter sports or summer holidays. Climbing he goes, and all that horrible nonsense. What's wrong with Shoot-up Hill? All the year he's on holiday, and then he needs another year's rest to get over it.

MILLIE. How dare you chastise my child like that?

MORRY. He's a stuck-up snob, a delinquent with cash, a Teddy boy of the tennis court. Well, I'm telling you.

MELVIN. Really, this is all rather beneath me. He does go on. I'm going in the garden, can't stand the atmosphere here. [*He goes.*]

SOLLY. Morry, remember all will change by your attitude—by love and understanding—don't excite yourself, let's go for a nice drive and look at trees.

MORRY. Yes, you're right, you're so right. Melvin, forgive me.

MILLIE. Now something is really up. Morry, I'm worried about you.

MORRY. I'm in good hands.

SOLLY. As I told your husband, you must learn to love everyone—or how will you love yourself and if you don't love yourself, who will love you?

MORRY. He's so right. Well, Rabbi, what about our drive?

MILLIE [*fussing with breakfast things*]. Come on, Romaine, don't leave it all to me.

[*She and* ROMAINE *go into kitchen.*]

SOLLY. Morry, if only you could get rid of your family for a little while. They clutter up the place so—I can't concentrate.

MORRY. Now you know how I've suffered all these years.

SOLLY. Can't you send them on holiday? I must have peace to work. They inhibit me. I don't mind Melvin around—he's a fool—but the others must go.

MORRY. But how? How? If only I knew a way.

SOLLY. I'll fix it.

MORRY. You'll be lucky. She'll never leave me, never. Never let me out of her sight.

SOLLY. You leave it to me—I guarantee by tonight we'll have the place to ourselves. Let's go now and plan our campaign. [*He calls to* MILLIE.] Don't worry, Mrs. Swartz, I'm taking care of your husband.

[*He and* MORRY *leave.* MELVIN *comes back in and then* MILLIE *and* ROMAINE *follow.*]

ROMAINE. He's going mad.

MILLIE. Going? Going? He's gone. Went years ago.

ROMAINE. I don't trust that Rabbi.

MILLIE. Where was I? What was I doing? Must get a maid,

number one. There's ice cream in the frig'. Melvin, have some and be a good boy. I must get dressed. [*Doorbell rings.*] Oh, who can that be? [MELVIN *goes and voices are heard outside.*] It's them Finks again, they make me sick. [*The* FINKS *enter.*] Hello, Sadie, I was just speaking about you.

FINK. Only good I hope. You didn't mind us dropping in, did you, Millie? After all, we are related now.

MELVIN. Someone once said, "God gives us our relatives. Thank God we can choose our friends."

FINK. Heard from the children, Millie? [*He sits down, smokes one of* MORRY's *cigars and takes a lot of drink.*]

MILLIE. They just phoned me.

MRS. FINK. How are they?

MILLIE. They sounded so happy.

MRS. FINK. I know, they were the same when they phoned me an hour ago.

MILLIE. They're coming to lunch.

MRS. FINK. What a coincidence, I'm dying to see them.

MR. FINK. It will be so nice—a happy family gathering! What's nice for lunch? Eh, Romaine?

MRS. FINK. Can I help, Millie?

MILLIE. Yes, get a chicken in the pressure cooker as quickly as possible. Now you must excuse me for a few moments— I must get dressed and I've got a thousand and one things to do. [*She goes.*]

MR. FINK. Well, Romaine, it's your turn next. Who's going to be the lucky man—

ROMAINE. I'm not getting married—I like laying in bed in the morning. Anyway, men are all the same—only after one thing. . . .

FINK. Good thing, otherwise where would we be? Still, I don't know why you can't get off. Nice, well built girl like you. Wish I had my time again.

MRS. FINK. I'm sure she's going to make someone very happy; meanwhile come and help me make lunch.

ROMAINE. Lunch, lunch— We've only just had breakfast! That's all they think about in this house—food! food! [*She follows* MRS. FINK *into kitchen.*]

MR. FINK. You're a sportsman, aren't you, Melvin? Do you ever shoot any nice wild—er birds, on your travels?

MELVIN. I've bagged some grouse, and a partridge once.

FINK. You're a dark horse, you know what I mean? You're a

sport and I'm a sport—couldn't we go out together and perhaps you could show me some highlife in some low dives. Ain't that clever?

MELVIN. You're drunk.

FINK. I'm an outdoor type like you, but I love indoor sports. Anything between eighteen years and twenty-five, and female of course—

MELVIN. What do you take me for? Please, Mr. Fink, I think I've heard enough.

FINK [*digs him in the ribs*]. Come on, tell me, we're both men of the world—

MELVIN. You should be ashamed of yourself.

FINK. I'm only human, out for a bit of a skylark in the dark—

MELVIN. Have you no morals? What about your wedding vows? Play the game, for God's sake.

FINK. I was only kidding. I'm a sportsman like yourself—live only for dogs and horses. I love 'em. My wife's a girl in a million. What do you take me for? I've got a son as old as you! Never mind, Melvin—no offence, no harm meant —I won't hold it against you that you got me all wrong. I have these jokes. I understand you. Course I study a bit cycle-logy myself; what you need is a bit of this and that and one must never forget the other. Would you like to be a Mason? I'll propose you. Marvellous—the little case and the badge and the lovely apron—it's a brotherhood . . . a real brotherhood. . . . [*He almost slumps forward as he drinks and drinks.*]

[ALAN *and* SARAH *appear.*]

ALAN. Hello, Dad, been celebrating? [FINK *jumps up, kisses* SARAH *and slaps his son on the back.*]

FINK. Sadie! Sadie! They're here. Hello my boy. Yes! You've got that grown-up look.

MRS. FINK [*rushing in*]. Alan! How are you? Did you take your pills? Sarah darling, how are you?

SARAH. Ecstatic.

ROMAINE. Enjoying your honeymoon?

SARAH. Smashing! Where's Mum?

ROMAINE. Upstairs. Well, how's married life?

SARAH. Smashing. Where's Dad?

ROMAINE. Out. What's the hotel like?

SARAH. Smashing. Where's Dad gone?

ROMAINE. For a drive. What's the food like?

SARAH. Sma— Not so hot.

ALAN. She's marvellous to me, Mum—she thinks of everything. I married an angel.

SARAH. Oh isn't he lovely, I could eat him. [*Pinches his
cheek.*]

ROMAINE. Save your appetite, there's chicken for lunch.

[MILLIE *enters dressed up with lots of very expensive but
garish jewellery.*]

MILLIE. You're here! And no one told me, darling! You look
lovely.

MRS. FINK. They make such a lovely couple.

MILLIE. Taking care of her Alan? Good. Dolly, you look pale.

SARAH. I feel fabulous, Mummy. That hotel is out of this
world.

MILLIE. You're thinner.

SARAH. Mummy, I only left yesterday.

MILLIE. I don't care, I've got eyes, haven't I? I'm so happy
for you, you bad girl. It's not fair, you're only a baby. Oh
darling, you looked lovely yesterday, now your worries
will begin. I wish you every happiness. So, how do you
like married life?

SARAH. Terrific.

MILLIE. Anyone seen my silver nail varnish? Can't find a
thing in this house. Look, I'm going mad—it's in my hand
all the time. Come over here, Dolly, and tell me all about it.

[SARAH *and the other women sit on the settee chattering
quietly while* MILLIE *paints her nails.*]

FINK. Melvin, come here, have you got to know my boy yet?
I think you've got a lot in common. Have a chat—be
friends—it's nice to be happy. [*He drinks some more.*] Oh,
this is the life for me . . . I'm so sleepy. [*Dozes off.*]

MELVIN. Do you like sport?

ALAN. Who don't? Like a nice game of football, myself.

MELVIN. Cricket?

ALAN. No, it's a bit slow for me. Now football—

MELVIN. Rugger? No! Ever been yachting? Skiing?

ALAN. It's all a bit hard on the old calf muscles, ain't it? I
have a flutter on the pools each week.

MELVIN. Well, what do you play?

ALAN. I like a nice game of football, myself.

MELVIN. I loathe soccer; what about swimming?

ALAN. I'm afraid of water.

MELVIN. Do you ride?

ALAN. Sure, but only on buses, hate the underground, I like a nice game of football, myself.

MELVIN. There must be some other sport you like. What about running? Or tennis?

ALAN. I don't mind a game of ping-pong.

MELVIN. Ah! Table tennis, not a bad little game. As a matter of fact, I'm the champion player of Hampstead Garden Suburb. Care for a game?

ALAN. Well, I'm not so hot, you know—

MELVIN. Be a sport, come on—I have a table in the other room. Don't worry, I shan't play my best game.

ALAN. You'll lick me hollow.

MELVIN. It's the spirit that matters—don't worry, just relax.

[MELVIN *leads* ALAN *into the other room and now we can see them playing in there*—ALAN *wildly rushing to catch the ball with his bat and* MELVIN *being very calm.*]

ROMAINE. The chicken must be ready; come and help me, Sarah.

[*Off they go.*]

MILLIE. I wonder where that man is?

SADIE. They're all the same. I'll lay the table.

[*She and* MILLIE *start laying the table*.]

FINK [*in his sleep*]. Come on, boy—come on—Silver Flash— Silver Flash—you're there, you're almost there—come on —all my money's on you.

SADIE. Wake up, Herbert. [*She shakes him.*] Look, he's sweating. Wake up—you're dreaming.

FINK. Where am I? Where? What did you wake me up for? I had twenty-five on that dog! And he was winning—

SADIE. It was a nightmare. You look worried.

FINK. Hello, Millie, my ship was just coming in. Me worried? I never worry.

[*In the other room,* MELVIN *is now frantic and rushing around while* ALAN *is calmly lobbing the balls.* ROMAINE *and* SARAH *enter the living room with the chicken and some vege-*

*tables, and everyone sits down.* MELVIN *comes in sadly followed by the beaming* ALAN.]

MELVIN. I wasn't doing my best today, on purpose of course.

ALAN. I won, what about that, Sarah? I won. Can I join your club, Melvin?

MELVIN. I let you win, to encourage you. Who cares about stupid ping-pong anyway?

ALAN. I won! I won; since I've been married I feel like a new man. Did you see that, Dad? Did you see me win?

[MELVIN *sits down.*]

FINK. What? You won? Bravo! I'm proud of you! What did I tell you, Melvin? [*When he sees* MELVIN'S *attitude he speaks more harshly to* ALAN *but much softer in tone.*] You bloody fool! Trust you, what did you go and win for? We don't want enemies in this house—now play him again, and lose next time. [*Now they are all seated and all are eating.* MORRY *and* SOLLY *enter.* SOLLY *goes around inspecting the plates. He whistles.*] Did you have some birdseed for breakfast, Rabbi?

SOLLY. Stop! All of you. Stop eating!

[*Some are shocked and some splutter.*]

MILLIE. Oh my God—what's the matter?

SOLLY. There must be no more flesh eaten in this house.

MORRY. That's right. No more meat.

SOLLY. From now on this is a vegetarian house. [*He says a few words of gibberish—as if praying.*]

MILLIE. No more meat?

MELVIN. You gone potty?

SARAH. Mummy, what's the matter with him?

SOLLY. He has decided. No more steak, no more liver, no more fish, and no more chicken.

ROMAINE. I'll die without meat.

MILLIE. I don't mind you coming to this house—I don't even mind you hanging around for a few days—but when you tell me that I must become a vegetarian, that's the last straw.

FINK. I'm sure there's some perfectly reasonable explanation.

ROMAINE. But yesterday was Chicken Sunday, you said so yourself.

SOLLY. Don't you people realise that we're in the last equinox of the solstice? We were just sitting near Highgate Pond contemplating the nature of things when suddenly it came to us in revelation—

MORRY. Honestly, by my life, a duck swam up to me and seemed to want to communicate. The Rabbi translated.

SOLLY. It said, "The souls of innocent animals cry out in bondage. Save us from the knife; no longer must our blood be shed."

[*He and* MORRY *seem to be enjoying themselves.*]

MILLIE. A joke's a joke, but we've had enough. Eat up everyone, take no notice.

SOLLY. Don't move! This is God's word. The next one to eat flesh will be banished from this house. [MILLIE *and* ROMAINE *eat.*] Alright, you brought this on yourself.

MILLIE. Isn't it time you were going, Rabbi?

MORRY. Show them a miracle—teach them a big lesson.

SOLLY. No, why should I waste miracles upon them? Would they believe it if they saw? Clear them all out of the room —all of them—they offend my eyes.

MILLIE. Right, now I've heard enough. I must ask you to leave. Mr. Fink, please help me—Alan, Melvin!

MELVIN. Be a good chap, go quietly.

FINK. Can't we talk this over quietly?

ALAN [*hiding behind* SARAH]. Sarah, what shall I do?

MILLIE. Call yourself men? Look at you!

MORRY. I'm the boss in this house, and I'm taking over. I'm wearing the trousers from now on and the Rabbi is my guest; if you don't like it you can lump it—and Mr. Fink, please don't come so often.

MILLIE. How can you talk to our guests in this way? What's come over you?

MORRY. For once I'm saying the things I believe.

SOLLY. You've all strayed from the path of righteousness, there must be a change before God can enter.

MELVIN. Yes, it is rather stuffy in here. Toodleloo, have fun. [*He goes.*]

MILLIE. Morry, shall I send for the doctor? Do you want a rest?

MORRY. I've had a rest too long. Carry on, Rabbi—the house is yours.

SOLLY. Let's all be calm, my children, and remember the wise words of the Karma Sutra. Now I want you all to go onto your knees, and think sensuously about life—become ecstatic, at one with the pulsing beat of the throbbing universe. The fast begins tomorrow.

MILLIE. Fast?

ROMAINE. I'll die.

MILLIE. Look, what do you want? Just tell us. For charity? A bit more money? Here you are—just take it and go— [MILLIE *takes money from her purse.*]

SOLLY. You don't understand. I'm staying until the new heaven on earth is proclaimed—but don't worry, we're preparing for it right away—for Morry Swartz is to be the first acolyte.

MILLIE. Morry, listen, this is me—Millie, your wife. This will break our marriage.

MORRY. This will make our marriage.

MILLIE. This man is dangerous.

SOLLY. Of course I am. Because I'm going to wipe out pride, to drive out greed and hate, and place in its place love. And then there'll be a new heaven on earth.

MILLIE. Oh, how much will it cost us? I can't have a Rabbi in the house—what will the neighbours say?

SOLLY. Halleluiah, eventually.

MORRY. Darling, don't upset yourself—don't cry. How lucky we are to have this illustrious saint in our own living room.

MILLIE. If he doesn't leave this house right now, I will.

MORRY. You can't leave me.

MILLIE. That's what you think.

MORRY. But I need you.

MILLIE. It's him or me.

MORRY. He must stay.

MILLIE [*cries*]. I've never been so insulted in my life. Romaine, pack your bags, we'll show him. I'm going as far away as possible.

SARAH. Where to, Mum?

MILLIE. Bournemouth! He'll see, he doesn't think I'll do it! Romaine, I said pack the bags.

MORRY. Good luck to you, my love—you deserve a holiday. We both need a rest from each other.

MILLIE. What? How could you? After all these years? That settles it. Romaine! Will you go and pack those bags? [*She punches her daughter.*] It's all your fault.

ROMAINE. It always is. Mummy, don't leave them alone, who knows what will happen.

MORRY. Millie, please don't go—I need you.

MILLIE. You just said—

MORRY. I've changed my mind.

MILLIE. Well I haven't. I'm going to teach you a lesson once and for all. Come! [*She is about to stomp out and she pushes* ROMAINE.] Sarah, don't stay in this house, it may be catching. [*She goes out.*]

FINK. You're overwrought, Morry, I understand.

MORRY. Good-bye, Mr. Fink. [FINK *goes out after* MRS. FINK. MORRY *speaks to* SARAH *and* ALAN.] You going to Bournemouth with your mother?

SARAH. What, and break my honeymoon? Not on your life. We're going back to Marble Arch. Bye-bye, Daddy, I wish you better.

[*She kisses her father and leaves with* ALAN.]

SOLLY. Well, it worked. [*They shake hands.*] Am I not a great psychologist? Now we're in business.

[FINK *furtively appears as he puts on his coat.*]

FINK. Did I hear someone mention business? Can you cut me in, gentlemen? I've got connections.

SOLLY. We're going to be a very limited company.

FINK. Too bad. I want you to understand, Morry, that I sympathise with you completely. We men should demand equality. I love the way you stood up to her.

SOLLY. Good-bye, you old hypocrite.

FINK. Good-bye, Rabbi, I love your sense of humour—they need putting in their place—they need a firm hand.

MRS. FINK [*off*]. Herbert? Where are you?

FINK. Coming, love. [*He hurries out.*]

MORRY. Peace at last; all my life, for fifty years I've had screaming people around me, and you pulled it off.

SOLLY. But be careful, they'll try and turn you against me—people are afraid of purity.

MORRY. Just let them try. Oh well, I'll miss Millie, you know.

SOLLY. You won't have time. You'll be busy becoming the great messiah. Oh, I can see you now—virgins dancing around you and children, dressed in white, pelting you with rose petals.

MORRY. I don't want to show off, I want to be a quiet messiah. I don't want them to laugh at me.

SOLLY. They'll cry as you pass, cry for joy. I'll do all the talking and you do all the hand waving. [*Waves like an old queen.*] You know, just like politicians at election time—

[MILLIE *comes in having hastily packed. She is followed by* ROMAINE.]

MILLIE. Right, I'm all ready. I'll be staying at the Atlantic Hotel, Bournemouth. When you get rid of the Rabbi telephone me and I may consider coming home. You'll see, my boy, you'll learn.

MORRY. Get sunburnt and don't eat too much candy floss, and remember you're a vegetarian.

MILLIE. Right, that settles it. Good-bye! Come on, Romaine— what are you dawdling for?

[*She pulls* ROMAINE *off.*]

MORRY. This calls for a celebration. I can't believe it! [*Looks out of window.*] Yes, they're really going.

SOLLY. Now we must plan, prepare, organise.

MORRY. What can I do to help?

SOLLY. At the moment nothing but just give me a few hundred quid or so to start with, for petty cash.

MORRY. Sure. How much, exactly?

SOLLY. Eight hundred and fifty should see us through to the week-end.

MORRY. I'll get it for you. [MORRY *goes out of the room.*]

SOLLY. Here's to Morry Swartz, the saviour—certainly saved me. Give us your money, we know what to do with it. Empty your pockets. Pop goes your sadness! Oh, I'll never go hungry again—not that I ever did. But this time I've hit the jackpot. [*To the mirror.*] Well, and don't you deserve it? Ain't you working hard enough? Believe me, I like to see a Yiddisher feller getting on. You're looking well, take care of yourself. It does my heart good—so-long for now. [*He hears* MORRY *returning and returns to a pious posture.*] Give me the money. [*He snatches it and puts it away quickly.*] Shush! Don't move—hold your breath. [MORRY *obliges.*] I'm getting a message. Turn off the light—I mean, pull the curtains. [MORRY *does so.*] Ohyesohyesohyesohyes. [*He mumbles very fast some gibberish and moves backward and forward in typical Jewish praying style.*]

MORRY. What is it?

SOLLY. A revelation. Shush—go on—I can hear you.

MORRY. Is it the Lord?

SOLLY. Shush! Yes sir, I've got that clear! We will do what you say—by my mother in the grave—yes sir. I understand —whatever you say. I've got the message and I'll pass it on! [*He turns to* MORRY.] See them go? Radiant angels, look at them, what charm they have, did you ever. . . . Oh what do you think of those purple cloaks and those golden clouds like chariots—[*Sings.*] Bring me my bow of burning gold. . . . Look!—just look at their halos— Good-bye. [*He waves at space.*]

MORRY. Who are they?

SOLLY. Gabriel, Michael, and Raphael, of course. Didn't you see them?

MORRY. I'm not sure.

SOLLY. What, you didn't even see them?

MORRY. I—think I did.

SOLLY. I should think so too. Did you get the message? Surely you got the message—

MORRY. Almost—but it was a little blurred—please repeat it for me again.

SOLLY. It said that we must search for your throne—

MORRY. Yes, yes, I got that—where?

SOLLY. In the West End—it was plain enough. It once belonged to King Solomon and now it's going to be yours.

MORRY. What have I done to deserve all this? Why should I be chosen? I'm not worthy. How much will it be?

SOLLY. We must pay the earth if necessary. Don't worry, we'll beat them down. What's the matter, you worried about money all of a sudden?

MORRY. Of course not. Do you want it now? Shall we get it now?

SOLLY. No, plenty of time. We'll go tomorrow and we'll search all over Soho. That's where I'm sure it'll be, and do you know—I bet it won't cost more than three or four thousand.

MORRY. That cheap. What shall we do now?

SOLLY. Well, there's so much—lots of things, to buy—bills to get printed, clothes and everything, jewellery—ceremonial of course—but that can all wait till tomorrow. For the moment how about you and me going Morrie Bloom's and having some salt beef?

MORRY. But I thought we are vegetarians?

SOLLY. Don't be silly, that's for them, not for us. We must set the example but that doesn't mean we must follow it.

MORRY. I don't like that. I want to be pure. What's good for my Millie and everyone is good enough for me. Besides, I really feel now for the souls of little animals. It started as a joke but now I believe it.

SOLLY. Have it your own way but don't you see, how can we convert people to vegetables unless we go amongst the meat eaters? And where will we find meat eaters? Why, Bloom's, of course. And how can we go to Bloom's and not eat salt beef? Do me a favour. Use your head—don't worry—you'll lead the world, and I'll lead you.

[*He puts* MORRY'S *hat on and slaps him on the back and when* MORRY *smiles as if he understands,* SOLLY *leads him off.* MORRY *still seems slightly confused but* SOLLY'S *smiling face seems finally to convince him.*]

### THE CURTAIN FALLS

# SCENE FOUR

*A few days later. The contrast is amazing, for although it is the same room, all the furniture has been moved out. The room is completely transformed and now only contains a little table with a telephone on it, two chairs and a seductive couch. The peach mirrors remain. The interior, however, does not look bereft but rather like a throne room. MELVIN comes in, looks at himself in the mirrors, studies his nose, teeth and then starts exercising and then weight lifting. He is dressed in a swimming costume. SOLLY and MORRY enter, struggling under the weight of a grand looking throne. MELVIN doesn't notice them and carries on. SOLLY visually instructs MORRY of the exact place to centre the throne.*

SOLLY. There! Not bad for five thousand.

[*He sits on it and smokes a cigar.* MORRY *sits on the floor.*]

MORRY. Please let me smoke.

SOLLY. Please don't be so childish—you must practice frugality and economy. Self-denial is the way to sainthood.

MORRY [*peers at the throne*]. He said it was solid gold—I can't see it.

SOLLY. It's spirit gold. Can't you see the aura? It looks like wood but it has a spiritual inner tube.

MORRY. When is the coronation?

SOLLY. Be patient. Aren't you happy with the day drawing near?

MORRY. I miss Millie.

SOLLY. Look, sit down here and realise your true responsibilities.

MORRY [*sits down*]. I feel better now. It was a miracle the way you came into my life. Any message from your mother, Melvin?

[ 439 ]

MELVIN. No.

MORRY [*rising*]. I must phone her. I want her to know that
want her to be happy—that I want her to be Queen Milli

SOLLY. No, sit down. She must come to you, in her own tim

MORRY. It's the first time we've been apart.

SOLLY. Now, listen. For a few days now you've been worrie
Well, it just won't do. It's not easy being messiah. You'v
just got to grow up and stand on your own feet. You're n
allowed to worry, you've got to radiate happiness and calr

MORRY. Look, have a heart, I'm only just indentured, don
expect me to be a fully fledged graduate. You sure sh
didn't phone, Melvin?

MELVIN. Dad, leave me alone. I'm practising for the Mac
cabee games this evening.

SOLLY. I shall walk out on you if you continue like this.

MORRY. Please be patient with me. I'll be alright.

SOLLY. Now I must phone Rabbi Teitlebaum to tell him th
latest news. You go to your room and stare at the sky.
want you to study cloud formations—add up the large one
then add up the little ones and take one from the other an
take away the first number you thought of.

MORRY. Thank you. There are moments when I lost hear
Thank you for being so firm and nice to me.

[*He goes out counting on his fingers, trying to rememb
SOLLY's instructions.* SOLLY *picks up phone and dials.*]

SOLLY. Hello? International? Get me Washington, America–
Central 19684. This is Speedwell 4756. Who? [*He looks c
MELVIN and whispers.*] Joe Bloom—Yes, Joseph Bloom
What? Half an hour delay? What are you doing at the
exchange? Exchanging dirty stories? Alright, you do tha
[*He puts down phone.*] They're going to ring back. [MELVI
*is standing on his head.*] Isn't it a miracle? Do you know
you can phone anywhere? Australia! Japan! Solomon Is
lands! I used to think they belonged to me. Who do I know
in India? Good job I'm not rich, I'd spend it all on trun
calls. What are you doing standing like that? You hopin
to become the Premier of Israel? Why do you waste a
your time with muscle stuff?

MELVIN [*stands upright*]. Look, I don't tell you how to pray
So don't tell me how to play.

SOLLY. At your age you should be having a good time with girls.

MELVIN. Not interested.

SOLLY. All this sport is a cover up for the things you're really longing for.

MELVIN. Nice advice, coming from you.

SOLLY. Sex is nice, it's here to stay. You can't get away from it, it follows you everywhere. Don't swallow it, wallow in it —find yourself a nice girl, not too nice. When I was a young man I knew my onions.

MELVIN. *You?*

SOLLY. Girls were my downfall before I picked myself up. It was the fat girls—oh, fat girls were the ruin of me and the making of me. I still have a soft spot for them.

MELVIN. You surprise me.

SOLLY. Listen, a dog collar doesn't stop a man being a dirty dog. Mind you, I don't mean myself—I'm finished with all that now. [*He puts on a record. The majestic choir of "The Messiah" by Handel is heard.*] Do yourself a favour—sow your wild oats on fertile feminine ground. Throw away your discus, take up the challenge.

MELVIN. But I'm shy—how do I start?

SOLLY. If you see a skirt, follow it. You're a man now—follow your natural instincts. Forget all about games, that sort of game—and play the game of life. A woman is the prey and you are the beast—and do they love it. Follow your natural inclinations—haven't you got any? You must have. Look at yourself—all them pimples; disgusting! Put some brilliantine on your hair, a smile on your face. [*He illustrates all this for* MELVIN.] Then saunter amongst them, looking supercilious, debonaire, aggressive, like a lion, like a peacock—

MELVIN. All at the same time?

SOLLY. Like this: Inscrutable—slinky. Pout your nostril all the while and clench your jaw. [MELVIN *tries it.*] And you'll be a wow. Go amongst them boy—there are masses of waiting virgins—go and break their . . . hearts. [*He puts up the volume of the record and he leads* MELVIN *out.*] Come, I'll help you choose the right suit.

[*The music blares out.* ROMAINE *and* MILLIE *appear. They enter, gasp, and rush out of the room again after screaming.*

*Then they stealthily creep back in again and* ROMAINE *tur*
*the record off.*]

MILLIE. It must be the wrong house.

ROMAINE. No, this is my record player but not my recor
Oh, Mummy—

MILLIE. Oh, Dolly—what can we do? We're ruined! I'll ki
him—kill him— Where's everything? [*She weeps.*] I'm fi
ished, finished.

ROMAINE. Mummy, don't cry, pull yourself togeth— [*Sh*
*cries.*] Ohohohohohohohohohoho!

MILLIE. Romaine, I'm ashamed of you, always going to piece
in a crisis. Stop crying and be a big girl. [*She looks roun*
*the room.*] Oh my lovely television set—where is it? [*Sh*
*cries again and now they lean on each other and both weep*
This is the end. I'll pull my hair out, I'll scream—I'll fain
I'll kill myself. Have you got a cigarette? [ROMAINE *giv*
*her one.*] Turn your back for five minutes— I'll kill hin

ROMAINE. I told you not to go. I warned you against that rabb

MILLIE. If we didn't go you'd have been head over heels i
love with him.

ROMAINE. Me? Bloody cheek.

MILLIE. I saw you falling for that snake in the grass.

ROMAINE. *Me?* You think I'd throw myself away on that low
life?

MILLIE. That swine.

ROMAINE. A villain!

MILLIE. Crook. Rogue.

ROMAINE. Monster. Maybe it wasn't him.

MILLIE. Who else? Oh, we're ruined. My Sheraton! My cock
tail cabinet, my virginals! He's taken everything, and you
father's gone off his rocker. That's where you get it from

ROMAINE. What are we going to do?

MILLIE [*goes to phone*]. The police, that's the only thing
[*Dials.*]

ROMAINE [*stopping her*]. You out of your mind? Find out firs
who's taken the furniture. Who you going to accuse?

MILLIE. That terrible man! Don't you see, we've got to ge
him out. He's after our money.

ROMAINE. Who isn't? Listen, if you call the police, it will ge
into the papers and we'll be the laughing stock of th
neighbourhood.

MILLIE. Better a laughing stock with money than being re

spectable and broke. Your father's mad—stone bonks. I must call the police.

ROMAINE. Alright, if he's mad they'll take him away, then there'll be a whole legal rigmarole. Meanwhile we'll all be starving.

MILLIE. Sometimes you use that stupid brain of yours. You're right. But I still say you've fallen for him.

ROMAINE. Fallen? May I drop down dead on this spot if I have! Oh, I feel wobbly at the knees— [She collapses on the small settee.]

MILLIE. Darling, don't swear your life away, it's precious to me. Love is blind. You've done nothing else but talk about him since we left. I'm not a fool—you make me so mad. Feeling better, Dolly? My whole family's turning against me.

ROMAINE. Do you honestly think I'd fall for a rat like that?

MILLIE. Yes. Never mind, he's enticed you the way he has Morry. He's hypnotic—you know, like Rasputin.

ROMAINE. I never met him.

MILLIE. What have I done? Am I bad? Haven't I given to charity? Why should it happen to me?

MELVIN [breezes in]. Lo, Mum. Lo, Roroe. Back already?

MILLIE [falls on him]. Melvin! Darling! What's happening?

MELVIN [releasing himself]. You're smothering me.

MILLIE. What's happening here?

MELVIN. Oh, I don't know. Something or other. Must dash now—I'm late as it is.

ROMAINE. But where's the furniture?

MELVIN. Oh yes, it's gone, isn't it? And about time too—it was simply gasters. Now, Mummy, please—later. I'll be late for the games.

MILLIE. Where's your father?

MELVIN. Your husband is contemplating or such such thing— somewhere or other. Well, tata for now.

*She won't let him go yet.*]

MILLIE. And where's that snake of a Rabbi?

MELVIN. He's a very nice chap and I won't hear a word against him. Since he's been here the house has been tolerable.

MILLIE. What's he doing to your father?

MELVIN. I don't know and I don't care. I'm off now, please keep your fingers crossed for me. [He goes.]

MILLIE. When I see that Morry I'll kill him.

[MORRY *wanders on, looking very happy and very far away* He sees MILLIE *and kisses her*.]

MORRY. Hello, Millie—how are you darling? Two week passed already?

MILLIE [*she stifles her anger*]. I only stayed away two days Do you think I'd trust you here any longer? Look what' happened already. What have you been doing?

MORRY. Looking at the clouds. I never knew they were so beautiful. Have you ever looked at clouds, Millie? Shall we both do it together now? And there are birds in London— and trees. I've never seen them before.

MILLIE. He's gone cuckoo. Listen Morry, come to your senses

MORRY. All my senses are working overtime. I can smell and hear and see and touch.

MILLIE. This Rabbi is a phoney. Did you see his credentials?

MORRY. Do I ask for the credentials of God? He is honest and beautiful. The most trustworthy person I ever met.

MILLIE. How do you know.

MORRY. I know because I know.

MILLIE. How do you know you know?

MORRY. Because I'm happy. Really happy.

MILLIE. How do you know you're happy? You're not happy You only think you are. He's taking you for a ride—I feel it in my water.

MORRY. It's a lovely journey and at the end of it I shall be the messiah.

ROMAINE. Messiah?

MILLIE. Messiah? Romaine, shut up—don't interfere. Listen Morry—carefully—take it easy. Did you say messiah?

MORRY. Yes, very soon now I shall be ready, when I reach perfection.

MILLIE. He won't make a messiah of you, you bloody fool He'll make a mess of you. You're sinning—do you know you're sinning?

MORRY. Thought you didn't believe in God. Sinning against who?

MILLIE. Sinning against me—against you—against everything Listen, Morry, look at me—I'm your wife, your other half How can you be a messiah? You're overwrought. I under stand. There ain't no such person as God and thank God there isn't, because if He existed you'd really go to hell, and please God, soon you realise all this and come to your senses.

MORRY. All I want is for you and everyone to be happy. Don't get angry with me. I'm so happy.

MILLIE. I could ki— [*Turns to* ROMAINE *as if to show her they must bear with him for the moment.*] It's just that you're getting old, Morry, old and scared.

MORRY. I'm not old. I'm as young as the world, and happy and free. I must go now and see the new moon rise. [*He sails off.*]

ROMAINE. Poor Daddy. Isn't it funny, he's happy and we're sorry for him. Poor Daddy.

MILLIE. We'll have to humour him. I'll even become vegetarian to please him now. How could he change so quick? He wouldn't trust a fly till that Rabbi came along.

ROMAINE. Everybody believes what he wants to believe, believe me.

MILLIE. Oh shut up you! It's all your fault.

ROMAINE. But I told you I didn't trust him.

MILLIE. Now be quiet will you, and stop bickering. We've got to think of a way. To make Daddy see, somehow. But we mustn't let the Rabbi know that we suspect he's a phoney.

[*The phone rings and they both dash for it but* SOLLY *enters the room briskly and while they are struggling for the receiver he takes it from them.*]

SOLLY. If it's from America, it's for me. Would you mind, please? This call is confidential—please leave the room.

MILLIE. From America? What do you think we are—millionaires?

ROMAINE. He wouldn't be far out.

SOLLY. Now leave the room, please. You shouldn't be here anyway, but in Bournemouth. This is urgent. Rabbi Teitlebaum! [*They go but stand in the doorway. He is aware of this fact and has to modulate his conversation accordingly. Every time he looks at the door they pretend not to be there.*] 'Lo! State Department? I want Joe Cohen in the visa section. Hurry, this is costing a bomb. [*Pretends now to pray.*] I'll hold on, yes I'll hold on—oh God in heaven, give me the strength to hold on. Extension five-nine-one, so be it. Hurry up, for St. Peter's sake. Wrong testament? Sorry.

Hurry up, oh Lord— Hello! Joe? You old bastard, this is me! Who, he says! Solly Gold— Don't hang up—listen I've got money! M—o—honey— Money for a change! Listen, I need a visa urgently—I'm loaded, loaded man, and I'm all ready to blow. What's that? But I tell ya I've got loot. So make me a visa and be a sport. Who picked you up when you were on the floor? [*He sees the women coming closer.*] Do you mind? No? Not you— GOooo— — For he will bring the wicked down to the ground! I'm loaded— would I lie? What do you mean? Gone respectable? Gone straight? Don't give me that! Joe, Joe—you can't do that to me. Listen! [*Sees the women again.*] Thou shalt not covet thy neighbour's daughter nor his peach mirrors—Joe! Don't do this to me—remember the old days when we were both crooked and keep it holy. Joe, you're a lousy swine—you're my only hope! Joe! Joe! Joe. . . . [*Realises the women are there once more.*] And Joseph brought the evil report of them unto his father [*Pretends to quote from Bible—then enraged again.*] Oh, you rotten—lousy—stinking—good-for nothing. . . . [*He sees the women again.*] Bye-bye, Rabbi Teitlebaum . . . Let the wicked be no more. I'll let you know— He hung up! You can't trust no one. [*He puts the receiver down.*] Hello, my daughters, how was Bournemouth? Still kosher and godless?

MILLIE. Hello, Rabbi, glad to see you looking so well, and I'm glad to see you looked after Morry.

SOLLY. Where is he?

ROMAINE. In the garden watching the moon.

SOLLY. Good. I'll find him. Well, welcome home. Are you thoroughly cleansed and vegetarian now?

[ROMAINE *is about to protest when her mother shuts her up.*]

MILLIE. What else? It's wonderful! Nuts and raisins for breakfast, turnips and lettuce for lunch, and carrots for supper.

SOLLY. Good! Good! You've got a glow in your face. [*He goes off.*]

MILLIE. May he rot, may he burn—may he get run over and smashed—may he drown.

ROMAINE. And all at once.

[MR. *and* MRS. FINK *and* ALAN *and* SARAH *enter.*]

SARAH. Mummy! You're back.

[*They kiss.*]

ALAN. What's the matter, where's the furniture?

MILLIE. Sarah darling, we're in terrible trouble.

SARAH. I know, I've been having nightmares.

MILLIE. The Rabbi is a charlatan—what can we do?

ROMAINE. He's fleecing us—taking us for a ride.

FINK. I told you so.

MILLIE. No you didn't.

FINK. I could have told you so.

MRS. FINK. Shut up. It was a palace here, a real palace. Where's the furniture? Where?

FINK. The woodwork run away with it. [*Nobody laughs.*] Hahahahahaha! I'm only trying to cheer everyone up.

ALAN. What's it all add up to?

MILLIE. My Morry thinks he's the new messiah no less. [*She weeps.*]

ROMAINE. And that Solly Gold is getting all our money and Daddy won't hear a word against him.

FINK. I knew it. I can smell a crook a mile off.

MRS. FINK. What will the neighbours say? [*She cuddles ALAN.*] Oh my poor boy.

SARAH. To hell with the neighbours—what about us?

FINK. Open and shut case. Leave it to me, let Fink think— Simple—the police! [*Goes to phone.*]

MILLIE. What? And let my Morry be the laughing stock of all the world?

ROMAINE. They'll take him off in a strait jacket.

SARAH. And we'll be starving while the lawyers argue.

FINK. Poor Morry—what can we do?

ALAN. We must think of something.

[*MORRY wanders in.*]

MORRY. Hello everyone. Lovely evening. I just saw Sirius and Orion, and heard the music of the spheres. I'm no longer just Morry Swartz of Golders Green—I'm Morris Swartz of the Universe. I'll see you all on the great day. Toodleloo.

[*Wanders out again and the women cry and the men shake their heads.*]

SARAH. He overtaxed his brain.

MILLIE. He never had a brain—only an adding machine up there.

ALAN. Hold it—I've got an idea coming up! Shush. . . .

SARAH. Isn't he marvellous? I could eat him.

ROMAINE. Not yet, wait till he comes out with it.

ALAN. Got it! [*Claps his hands.*] That Rabbi Whatyoumaycallit must confess directly to your father, must say that he's a complete phoney, now how? How can we get him to confess? [*They all walk backward and forward thinking.*] Who would he tell the truth to? Who has he got a weakness for?

[ROMAINE *is somehow now in the centre of a circle of walking people, they all stop together, turn and stare at her.*]

ROMAINE. What's up? What have I done?

SARAH. It's not what you've done, it's what you're going to do.

ALAN. I've seen the way he stares at you. You'll have to do it.

ROMAINE. Do what? I'm getting out of here.

[*She tries to go but* MILLIE *stops her.*]

MILLIE. Dolly, do you love me? Do you love your father? Do you love luxury? Well, then you'll have to help us all.

FINK. Only you could make him confess.

ROMAINE. But I don't trust him.

MRS. FINK. This time you don't need to.

SARAH. Lead him on a little, get him hot under the collar—

ALAN. Tell him you're passionately in love with him but unfortunately you couldn't give yourself to a Rabbi—

FINK. Tell him it's against your principles, and you could make love to a layman—

ROMAINE. Are you all mad or something? What do you take me for?

MILLIE. A good girl. And when he confesses that he isn't a Rabbi, lead him on a bit more—tell him you don't like good boys—

ALAN. And when he confesses that he's a crook. . . . [*Thinks for the next move.*]

SARAH. You'll switch on Melvin's tape recorder that we'll hide under the couch.

MILLIE. And when Daddy hears the tape, we'll be rid of that worm.

ROMAINE. I won't be left alone with him.

MILLIE. You'll be alright, don't worry.

ROMAINE. Do you think I'm gonna sacrifice my purity for rotten money?

FINK. You've got to lose it sooner or later.

MRS. FINK. Herbert, shut up. Listen, Romaine, we all have to take chances—

ROMAINE. You're all against me.

ALAN. Whatever happens, we'll sympathise and understand. We're depending on you. I expect you'll pull it off.

ROMAINE. Nobody cares for my feelings [*She almost weeps*]. I'll be expecting, alright, with that snake in the grass. Mummy, look at me! I'm your daughter. Your own flesh and blood. Don't leave me alone with that monster.

MILLIE. Listen, your purity, my darling, is worth all the tea in China, all the gold in Hatton Garden. Don't worry, we won't let it go too far. If you scream we'll break the door down—but don't scream unles you can help it, they cost enough. He'll confess. After all aren't you a lovely girl? And why not, why be ashamed of what you've got?

ROMAINE. Oh go on then, go, leave me alone. What do I care? [*She does a great tragedy act and falls on the sofa.*]

MILLIE. Good luck, Dolly—a lot's at stake.

ROMAINE. Telling me!

FINK. We'll wait in there and be as quiet as little mice.

ROMAINE. Don't look through the keyholes—I'll be embarrassed. Promise?

ALL. Promise.

MILLIE. Where's the tape machine? Melvin's room?

SARAH. No, it's in here. [SARAH *gets it from the other room and brings it in and places it under the sofa.*] It's all ready. At the crucial moment just switch on, like this: [*She demonstrates and then they all troop into the other room and shut the door.*]

ROMAINE. [*overplaying*]. What do they care? Do they consider my feelings? I shall run away! [*She overweeps and then stops as she sees herself in the mirror.*] How marvellous. I looked like Anna Magnani just then. [*She smiles and poses in front of the mirror as if to make herself look enticing, then she weeps again.*] Oh, what do they care—leaving me with that shark. [*She switches off the main lighting and the indirect lighting, now makes the room look seductive. She sprays perfume upon herself and then puts on a soft tango. She settles down and starts to eat Turkish delight but changes her mind and then, fixing her dress to look more sexy, she dances to the music seductively. Then we see* SOLLY. *He comes on like a furtive fly, in quick, sharp jerking angular movements, as if drawn by an irresistible impulse. He is about to go directly to her, but goes to the adjoining door, where the family are, and locks that door on this side. When she sees this she starts to get panicky, but carries on—dancing. Suavely he pours two drinks and goes to her. As she drinks, he pinches her on the bottom.* Stop pinching me—I'll go black and blue.

SOLLY. I don't care what colour you go—I like you anyway. I don't hold with the colour bar.

ROMAINE. It's not nice, not decent, getting fresh like that.

SOLLY. I'm sorry but you see I'm homesick and my fingers twitch. Care for another drink?

ROMAINE. I'd like a bunny hug.

[*He hugs her passionately. She struggles to get free.*]

ROMAINE. I didn't mean that. I meant the drink. Cherry brandy and Advocaat. [*He pours her a vast glass full.*] Eh! When! When!

SOLLY. Anytime you want to.

ROMAINE. I didn't mean that! I meant—that's enough in the glass.

[SOLLY *gives her the drink and then takes her arms and pushes her into a dance.*]

SOLLY. May I have this dance? Do you come here often? What a smashing bit of overtime you are.

ROMAINE. I think you're crude.

SOLLY. Sorry, I get carried away by your beauty—what I mean is, God worked overtime when he created you.

ROMAINE. Never knew that Rabbis drink, and dance, and pinch girls.

SOLLY. What else? All work and no play makes Jacob a very miserable geezer. Haven't you read the Songs of Solomon? But anyway—you are so marvellous I could even leave my religious world for you. Let's sit down. I want to give you some spiritual instruction.

ROMAINE. No, no, I'm afraid.

SOLLY. Foolish lady, I'll look after you. Sit down, I'll make it worth your while.

ROMAINE. I shouldn't really. [*She sits down.*]

SOLLY. Doing what we shouldn't is one way of finding out the mysteries of creation.

[*She leans down to switch on the machine and as she does so he kisses her. First she struggles but then she subsides into his arms and while doing so, she switches off the machine again.*]

ROMAINE. You're free with your kisses. But what about your dead wife and your vow of chastity?

SOLLY. I know Sophie wouldn't mind.

ROMAINE. You said her name was Miriam.

SOLLY. Don't change the subject, I'm doing my nut over you. When the ape is king dance before him—and desire is ruling my soul right now. Shall we dance?

ROMAINE. Please come down to earth, I've got something to tell you.

SOLLY. You are as pure as the moon, as passionate as the sun, my dove.

ROMAINE. Make up your mind.

SOLLY. My undefiled one.

ROMAINE. And I intend to stay that way. Now listen! I don't know who you are or what you're after, but I'm giving you a chance to get away.

SOLLY. How beautiful are thy feet in sandals—

ROMAINE. I've got corns.

SOLLY. The joints of thy thighs are like jewels.

ROMAINE. And they're staying in the safe because you're a thief. But I like you, so I'm giving you a chance to run. Run, before you're caught.

SOLLY. What are you talking about? I've got nothing to be ashamed of.

ROMAINE. I don't know why I'm telling you, but I don't trust you, so don't try and get round me. You're a bad boy and you know it.

SOLLY. Me? I'm a—angel, a saint. Ask anyone.

ROMAINE. Listen, you can trust me. There's no time to lose.

SOLLY. Enough of this.

ROMAINE. You're no good.

SOLLY. What's good? What's bad? Relative terms, my daughter. Thy navel is like a round goblet.

ROMAINE. Cheek! How dare you, you've never seen me! Oh don't you see I'm on to your game? You're a fraud.

SOLLY. Enough of this, let's get down to something serious—
let me kiss you, let me love you!

[*He tries furiously to embrace her, but she keeps freeing herself. It's almost a chase.*]

ROMAINE. It's because I like you that I won't go along with
them—let them do their own dirty work.

SOLLY. Thy belly is like a heap of wheat.

ROMAINE. That's the last straw.

SOLLY. Forgive me, I get carried away. I was only quoting
from the Bible.

ROMAINE. Then it should be banned.

SOLLY. Nonsense, it's beautiful—have you ever read it?

ROMAINE. No, but I've seen the film. Please, listen, there's no
time to waste.

SOLLY. Alright, spit it out, what's it all about?

ROMAINE. Now he hears. Solly, my family are on to your
game, they are trying to get me to make you confess. I'm
the decoy.

SOLLY. On to my game? Confess? Confess to what?

ROMAINE. You can trust me, I'm on your side. I must be mad,
but I am.

SOLLY. Why should I trust you all of a sudden?

ROMAINE. Because here's the tape machine that I was supposed to switch on when you started confessing.

SOLLY [*as she shows him the machine*]. Tape machine? What
are you talking about? I'm a servant of the Lord.

ROMAINE. I must be mad—I'm out of my little mind. Fancy
telling you, but you've turned my head—turned it against
my own family. I'll never live it down. I'm no good.

SOLLY [*embracing her*]. We make a fine pair.

ROMAINE. So you own up that you're a crook?

SOLLY. Not on your life. I'm straight—straight up—strait as a
jacket.

ROMAINE. Solly, Solly, oh Solly boy, you can trust me. [*She
cuddles him.*]

SOLLY. Why should I?

ROMAINE. Cos I want to see you get away—I don't want them
to catch you. Because you're romantic. Take what you want
and go.

SOLLY. I want you. But why are you doing this for me? I can't
believe it.

ROMAINE. Look! They're waiting in there, waiting for me to

entice a confession out of you—I swear on my soul, on my
purity, that I'm on your side and speaking the truth. By my
Aunt Sadie's life.

SOLLY. Alright then, if that's the case I'll be on my merry
way. Good-bye, maybe we'll meet in the desert.

ROMAINE. Not so fast. Just one little thing before you go.
Please tell me everything—tell me why a nice boy like you
should be such a bad boy.

SOLLY. Why? You want to redeem me? Sorry, I pawned myself ages ago and lost the ticket.

ROMAINE. Oh Solly, what can I do? I've fallen for you, for a
tyke like you. My mum always told me I was no class.
I've fallen right down.

SOLLY. Don't believe you. [*She kisses him.*] Well, maybe I
believe you a bit—kiss me again. [*She does.*] Yeah! Oh,
Romaine—I could feel your whole heart pouring into that
kiss.

ROMAINE. I want to help you. Can't you see that? Tell me
about yourself.

SOLLY. Alright, I admit I'm not a Rabbi. I'm a liar, a lobos,
a gonif. You know—I take things from people who can
afford to do without. But I'm the best con man in the business—the world's not much to write home about is it?

ROMAINE. Maybe, but fancy doing your tricks on my father,
he's such a good man.

SOLLY. Alright, so now you know. Happy? I'm a lowlife. I'm
a thief. That lets me out. . . . [*He turns his back and is
about to go when he turns back and smiles.*] Run away
with me.

ROMAINE. Where?

SOLLY. Anywhere.

ROMAINE. Run away? No, I couldn't.

SOLLY. Why not?

ROMAINE. Why not? Why not? I love my luxury.

SOLLY. Now's your chance to really live.

ROMAINE. I couldn't run fast enough to keep up with you.
Besides I'm too selfish—I've got so much to give that I
need a lot in return . . .

MILLIE [*off*]. You alright, Dolly?

ROMAINE. Fine—fine! Hurry, hurry—Solly, Solly, time is
pressing.

SOLLY. Nobody here understands you—how deeply romantic
you are. Just like me. Chasing the stars, looking for kicks

and only getting kicked in the teeth. Look at you—you're
a child of the sun, a victim of circumstance holding on to
your chastity—saving it all for a rainy day. But why be a
pessimist? No one can love you like me. You're fat and
I love you that way.

ROMAINE. I'm not fat, I'm well built. Besides, I'm starting to
diet tomorrow.

SOLLY. No! No! No! You mustn't do that. I'm crazy about
you the way you are. I'll take you to the life of luxury you
dream about—a life of romance in the best hotels, as much
Turkish Delight as you want, we'll go to Rome, Miami,
Glasgow.

ROMAINE. But you're a liar, Solly, how can I believe you?

SOLLY. What's truth? Ask philosophers, they're all in the dark—

ROMAINE. But you've committed crimes, I know it. You're on
the run.

SOLLY. Who isn't on the run? I'm not bad darling, I'm just
good.

ROMAINE. How can I do this to my family after all they did
for me?

SOLLY. Such as?

ROMAINE. Offhand I can't remember.

SOLLY. With me you'll come first—after me. No more dull
life. I'm your man from now on and you'll hide with me.
Hiding and flying—romance on the run. Snatched hours
of passion in hotel bedrooms; different places, different
faces. Romaine, your humdrum life is almost over for
Solly Gold is taking over. Give me another kiss. [*They
kiss.*] There's plenty more in store where that came from,
and so much more—oh so much more. Why have I told
you everything? You know more than anyone now! It's
the first time I've told anyone anything. I must love you—
I must really love.

ROMAINE. That settles it. I'll get my things.

SOLLY. Don't bother, I'll buy you everything new on Broad-
way next week.

ROMAINE. With what? On peanuts and prayers?

SOLLY. With the money I've got from your father already and
the money I'm getting from him in a minute or two.

ROMAINE. Oh Solly, I was forgetting that. It's so dishonest.

SOLLY. Is it dishonest to make him happy for the first time in
years? You'll help me.

ROMAINE. I'll never forgive myself.

SOLLY. You don't have to—God will. We'll fill a suitcase full of fivers and be on our merry way.

ROMAINE. It is true, he *is* much happier. That can't be bad, can it? What about the police?

SOLLY [*he jumps*]. Please, I don't like bad language. That word makes my blood run cold. We'll go to the docks to-night and get a boat. Let's call your father now.

ROMAINE. One minute, I'm not coming with you unless you marry me.

SOLLY. Don't you relish sin? Silly girl—alright! I'll marry you, on the other side.

ROMAINE. Other side of where?

SOLLY. Tell you when we get there.

ROMAINE. Just one thing more—are you sure you're not married?

SOLLY. Absolutely, definitely not—I cross my heart, that's the truth so help me God. Come on—

ROMAINE. There's just one other thing—

SOLLY. I love the way you're so concise. What is it?

ROMAINE. Where did you get the Rabbi's clothes?

SOLLY. From an old lady in the East End.

ROMAINE. You must take them back, I'm superstitious.

SOLLY. Let me burn them, let me chuck them away.

ROMAINE. No! We'll take them back to her on our way to the docks.

SOLLY. It's too risky.

ROMAINE. If you love me you'll do it—just this once, for me.

SOLLY. I must learn the art of blackmail from you. Alright, and now I'll find your father. Wait here for me. [*He pretends to go but hides and watches* ROMAINE.]

MILLIE [*off*]. You alright, Dolly?

ROMAINE. Sure.

MILLIE [*off*]. How's it going?

ROMAINE. Perfect.

SARAH [*off*]. Got the recording yet?

ROMAINE. Not yet, be patient. [SOLLY *is obviously satisfied with her, and goes before she sees him. Now she poses herself in front of the mirror, and obviously she thinks she is stunningly beautiful.*] Oh God forgive me, but I must grab the opportunity. Why not? Eh? Oh romance, Romaine—romance at last!

[SOLLY *brings* MORRY *on.*]

SOLLY. Well Morry, the great day approacheth and verily I say unto you that a purple light surrounds you. Sit on your throne.

MORRY. How we doing, Solly? What's the score?

SOLLY. Great news. We're almost there—I saw half a dozen angels at Golders Green Station today—they're assembling and all roads converge here and now rejoice even more so, for your blessed daughter Romaine has become an acolyte. She is our very latest and brightest disciple. She has repented from her evil ways and stands before us, devoting herself to the cause.

MORRY. About time too.

ROMAINE. Daddy darling, how you feeling?

MORRY. Never felt better in my life.

ROMAINE. Solly, let's go now.

SOLLY. Yes. Now listen Morry, Romaine and I are going on a pilgrimage.

MORRY. I want to come with you.

SOLLY. I'm afraid that's impossible.

MORRY. It's so lonely becoming the messiah sometimes. Please!

SOLLY. Not tonight. We must go to sordid places to spread the word, to the docks to get love and give love. You must be unsullied—think only of higher things. And then we're going to Westcliffe-on-the-Sea where we'll distribute charities to the Jewish Society for the prevention of cruelty to dead poets and to the Sisters of Nathaniel Greenbaum. We'll need a little money for this purpose.

MORRY. How much?

SOLLY. Don't want to bother you with sordid details, tell me the combination of the safe and I'll save you the trouble.

MORRY. No, no, the secret of the combination dies with me. Not that I don't trust you. How much will you need?

SOLLY. Not too much, a few to begin with—about—erm—forty thousand?

MORRY. That's a lot of money.

SOLLY. It's to help the needy, the lonely, the sick, the lost, the sad dreamers and happy destitutes.

MORRY. Well that includes practically everyone alive. I"ll get it. You going to give all this away tonight?

SOLLY. If I can. That's why I'm taking Romaine with me.

MORRY. Good. Money must go to those who need it. As for me, what else is it but bits of metal and paper around an idea? Forty thousand. Hope I've got that much loose laying around. . . . [MORRY goes off.]

ROMAINE. I don't like it; Daddy's out of his mind.

SOLLY. We've burnt our boats now and we're in this together —sink or swim. Don't worry. [He calls out.] Morry! There'll be plaques up to you all over London "Morry Swartz, the saviour, saved our hospital"—"Morry Swartz, the messiah, got us out of a mess"—"Morry Swartz lived here"—"Morry Swartz ate here"—

[MORRY enters with some packets of money and tosses them to SOLLY.]

MOLLY. Don't want no plaques, just a plain bit of marble when I die, saying: "He tried to do good." Hope that keeps you busy. [As SOLLY stuffs it into the suitcase.]

ROMAINE. Daddy, Daddy, are you happy giving this away?

MORRY. The more that goes the happier I am.

ROMAINE. What about your life's work? You worked so hard?

MORRY. My life's work is just beginning. Listen darling, in this world you own nothing but your bones and even they let you down in the end. You come in with nothing and go out with nothing—and you're nothing unless you realise this, at least, now and again.

ROMAINE. Come on, Solly, time's getting on.

SOLLY. Rest now, Morry. Contemplate. Count the stars and lose yourself in the cosmos. Pray for us all, especially me, just in case—with all this money. We'll see you in the morning.

ROMAINE. Forgive me for everything.

MORRY. There's nothing to forgive. Go in peace. The way you both look so lovely, I could kiss you. As a matter of fact I will. [He does so.] I'm so happy because before I only thought I was rich, now I know I am. Good-bye.

ROMAINE. Good-bye, come, Solly.

SOLLY. Good-bye, Morry—you're a lucky man. I'm carrying all your worries from now on.

[He holds up the case and follows ROMAINE off. MORRY picks up the Bible that SOLLY has left behind, sits down and reads from it.]

MILLIE [*off*]. Romaine! You ready yet? Romaine? Are you there?

SARAH [*off*]. Romaine? Did you do it? Why don't she answer?

[*The door is tried and they furiously push it from the other side.*]

MILLIE [*off*]. Romaine! Stop playing about. It's locked on the other side. Romaine! You alright? Darling where are you?

FINK [*off*]. I'll have to break the door down.

[MORRY *goes to the door and unlocks it just as* FINK *has flung himself against it. They all fall into the room.* MORRY *goes from them and sits on his throne.*]

MILLIE. What are you doing?

MORRY. Isn't it obvious? Just sitting down.

SARAH. Where's Romaine?

MORRY. Gone with the Rabbi.

ALAN. Gone?

SARAH. Gone where?

MILLIE. What do you mean? Oh my poor baby.

MORRY. They've gone on a pilgrimage. She's in safe hands. Don't worry.

SARAH. Daddy, don't you realise, he's a crook! A no-good good-for-nothing. He's not a Rabbi!

FINK. I'm afraid you've been taken for a ride, Morry; it happens to the best of us.

MORRY. Don't worry about me, Fink. Go home and settle your own problems.

MILLIE. Take no notice, Herbert. Morry, you ought to be ashamed of yourself. Listen! Just listen to his confession. [*She switches on the tape recorder and "The Messiah" blares out.*]

MORRY. They're playing my music again.

[MILLIE *switches it off.*]

MILLIE. Oh, my daughter! He's carried her off.

SARAH. That would have been difficult—

MILLIE. What's going to happen to her? I knew it.

MRS. FINK. Call the police, Millie, call the police.

MILLIE. What? And have her dragged through the Sunday papers? I'll never live through it.

MORRY [*reads from the Bible*]. Praise him with the sound of trumpets, with the stringed instruments and the pipe. Praise him upon the loud cymbals—

[MILLIE crashes two metal trays together. Everyone jumps except MORRY. MILLIE also jumps.]

MILLIE. Will you shut up! He reads the Bible. Will that bring your sanity back? Don't you see? He's taken your furniture, your sanity, your money and your daughter. I suppose you won't be happy till he takes me!

MORRY. That's an interesting thought. [Returns to the Bible.]

MILLIE. I knew all along, I knew it.

SARAH. What?

MILLIE. That he was a crook and she was no good. I knew it.

FINK. I knew you knew. So did I.

MRS. FINK. What did you know?

FINK. I knew that I knew. You didn't know—but I did. I told you so.

ALAN. I knew all along—he couldn't kid me.

SARAH. I didn't know then that I knew, but now I do.

MRS. FINK. I knew. I don't say much but I see all. I could tell from his face. I knew. Mark my words, I said, he's up to no good.

MILLIE. I knew it. I knew it. Serves them right. They deserve each other. What do you think of it, eh? Your own daughter. Please God, she should be safe, the lousy bitch. I knew it. I knew it would happen. I knew it.

[MORRY sits quietly reading and they all walk around his throne. Round and around they go, talking to themselves and trying to convince each other. Then suddenly they all come into one group and carry on with the above dialogue all over again and far more quickly. It seems they are about to come to blows, when

THE CURTAIN FALLS

... begin, with the trimmed sails ... we ... set ...
... the flood tide swells ...

... back ... ... the boat in ... away. I ... a chance
... we ought to ... make it.

... will you listen ... to these folk, including this living
... past safely back. You don't ... get ... much perch in fishing.

joe. *[with sudden tender emotion]*

roman. Don't try that stuff on the Englishman, Roman.

We are Doukhobors but Rita Swere is exactly the same to the
... to us the way ...

roman. ... I'm going to tell him why we've come aboard.

joe. Go on, explain. She'll ...

roman. ... why this vessel ...

joe. *[same cold anger and wonder at these people of foreign folk]*

... will it ... the Angel's coming in to mind hands. The main ...
to the sound whatever passed as he sees it. He ...

joe. about all the talk of the Oven ... I know. Shut up. I ...

roman. But we'll come down the ... fishing and ...

joe. ... ... ...

roman. ... how ... I ... looking ... ... ...

joe. ... ... you ... ... You mean I won't get ... anything down
... nights ... they would have ... I ...

joe. She won't go up that cliff ...

roman. Well here he is ... ... ... ... ... ... I'm
sorry. You're very cruel. Look, the boat's empty. Obviously
she still trusts people ... lets go inside. He calls. Yoohoo,
—yoohoo—

*[Soon they are inside and now we cannot see them. Joe, the
sailor, jumps up and goes to a door in his house and calls his
wife.]*

joe. Rita! Rita! Get up—get up quick! Rita, for God's sake,
get up—

*[RITA wakes up in her nightclothes, she is distraught and
almost panicking.]*

rita. Joe, what is it? Is it bombs? *[She tries to dress hurriedly
and gets everything in the wrong place.]*

joe.

# SCENE FIVE

*We are back in the East End. Scene is exactly the same as in the Prologue. It is early morning. The tailor is seen working away in his house, sewing frantically; he reacts—looks up, and soon we realise he has heard something.* SOLLY *comes on followed by* ROMAINE *who carries lots of cases. She seems all in.* SOLLY *is dressed in very American-looking clothes and he carries the Rabbi's clothes in a small bundle. The tailor comes to the window and hides as soon as he sees* SOLLY *but watches them all the time.*

ROMAINE. Why did we have to get up so early?

SOLLY. The boat leaves in an hour.

ROMAINE. I'm still asleep.

SOLLY. Here's the house. I'll dump it on the doorstep.

ROMAINE. Oh no you're not. You're giving it to the lady in person and apologise.

SOLLY. She won't be up this early.

ROMAINE. We'll wake her up.

SOLLY. You're very cruel. Look, the door's open. Obviously she still trusts people . . . let's go inside. [*He calls*] Yoohoo —yoohoo—

[*Soon they are inside and now we cannot see them.* JOE, *the tailor, jumps up and goes to a door in his house and calls his wife.*]

JOE. Rita! Rita! Get up—get up quick! Rita, for God's sake get up—

[RITA *rushes in in her nightclothes, she is distraught and almost panicking.*]

RITA. Joe, what is it? Is it bombs? [*She tries to dress hurriedly and gets everything in the wrong place.*]

[ 461 ]

JOE. Shush! That blaggard who got that money from us and the lady next door has returned.

RITA. Thank the lord. I thought the world had come to an end.

JOE. And guess what?—he's got with him that missing heiress, what's her name— —Rona Swarb or something—

RITA. Missing heiress?

JOE. Wake up. The one who was in the papers. The one that reward's for. You phone her mother quickly while I keep them here. The number's in the paper.

RITA. All night he works. All night. I just want to get some sleep. I'm fed up with you and the whole business.

JOE. Do as I say. We'll make a few hundred and I'll take you on a cruise. Quick!

[*She quickly runs for the newspaper and then goes into a backroom. JOE comes out of his house and creeps towards the next house just as SOLLY comes running out with RO-MAINE; they are chased by the old woman who is throwing things at them.*]

WOMAN. A fire on you! Get out of my sight!

SOLLY. I've come to pay you back—to make it worth your while.

WOMAN. What do you take me for? Think you can buy me after what you did?

[*She hits him with a stick and he takes shelter under his coat. He brings out several pound notes and waves them about.*]

SOLLY. Truce! Truce! Is this flag the right colour?

WOMAN. Thief! Liar! Rogue! Crook—police . . . [*She suddenly stops and takes the money.*] Get out of my sight! [*She is about to go inside.*]

SOLLY [*to ROMAINE*]. See darling, anything can be bought with money, especially people. When pound notes flash, principles crash.

WOMAN. I can't afford principles. They won't buy my husband's tombstone.

[*She is about to go in and SOLLY is about to go off with ROMAINE when JOE grabs him.*]

SOLLY. Must you be so passionate?

JOE. So, you've returned to the scene of the crime?

SOLLY. Can't we talk this over like English gentlemen?

ROMAINE. Leave my Solly alone or I'll murder you.

[As JOE gets off him SOLLY gets up.]

SOLLY. I'll explain and settle everything.

JOE. Wish there was a copper about; they're never around when you want one.

SOLLY. I agree with you. And it all comes out of the tax-payer's pocket.

[RITA comes out.]

JOE. Well, what have you got to say for yourself?

SOLLY. Help.

JOE. You're a lousy rat.

SOLLY. Let me go and I'll make it worth your while.

JOE. You can't buy me.

SOLLY. I actually came to give you your money back.

RITA. There you are, Joe—I knew he was an honest feller.

SOLLY. Look, here's the money. I'll give you twice as much.

JOE. Nothing doing, I won't be bought. I demand justice.

SOLLY. You're living in the wrong world.

[The PROSTITUTE comes from her room.]

PROSTITUTE. What's all the noise? Can't a nightworker get some decent sleep? [JOE is holding SOLLY by the arm and ROMAINE is trying to pull him in the other direction. The PROSTITUTE walks around SOLLY.] Haven't we met before?

SOLLY. Perhaps in some previous incarnation.

PROSTITUTE. I've heard it called some things. Why are you holding him?

JOE. He owes me money.

SOLLY. I've offered to pay him back, twofold.

ROMAINE. It's the truth, honestly it is.

JOE. I don't want to be paid back, I want justice.

SOLLY. There he goes again, using horrible words, makes me shudder. Just think of that poor old bitch, Justice—blind, deaf, dumb, crippled, and no hands.

WOMAN. He's a thief. He got money out of me, my poor husband's clothes, and chickens.

PROSTITUTE. Come on, Joe, let the poor blighter go, the law will be around if you're not careful.

RITA. Let him go, Joe, we don't want no trouble.

SOLLY. Lady, I admire your common sense. Joe, do what your wife says.

JOE. I'm thinking about this poor girl here. He's a deceiver leading her up the garden.

SOLLY. It ain't half pretty.

JOE. Don't you see he's no good? [*To* ROMAINE] How can you fall for a type like this?

SOLLY. I'm not a type, I'm a specie.

ROMAINE. Soll's a good boy, I've changed him. Leave him alone.

RITA. Come on, Joe, let's go to bed. Poor girl, I pity her running off with a type like that.

JOE. I'm not going to let this happen. I'm going to save her.

RITA. I know what you're after—the reward.

JOE. Shush. Yesyesyes, yes. Quite, for her own good.

PROSTITUTE. Go on, let them go. You were young once.

RITA. Never. He never was young.

JOE. Will you shut up?

SOLLY [*as they argue*]. I think you're all marvellous and here's a token of my appreciation—

[*He throws a small packet of pound notes in the air. Everyone starts scrambling for them; at this* SOLLY *pulls* ROMAINE *and starts to rush off. The attaché case, however, comes undone and pound notes are flying everywhere.* SOLLY *rushes about like a madman and* ROMAINE *sits down and cries. Everyone else desperately fights each other for the money.*]

JOE. He's robbed the bank of England.

SOLLY. Have you no respect for private property?

PROSTITUTE. Someone's been working overtime.

RITA. Joe, Joe, come inside. [*As she pulls* JOE *she is stuffing pound notes into her dressing gown.*

WOMAN. Now my husband can have a marvellous memorial.

POLICEMAN [*enters*]. Hello, hello, what's all the fuss?

[*They all try to shield* SOLLY *but* POLICEMAN *walks into the centre and sees him.* SOLLY *is sitting on the pound notes now like a chicken sits on an egg.*]

SOLLY. We're discussing the political situation.

POLICEMAN. Looks like a mother's meeting—what's it all in

aid of? Eh? I remember you. Didn't I run you in? Wasn't your mug in the *Police Gazette*?

SOLLY. The only *Gazette* I was in was the London *Gazette* when I was mentioned in despatches, and the Hackney *Gazette* when I was born.

POLICEMAN. I remember you now. You're the loud-mouth spiv I spoke to last week. What are you sitting on?

SOLLY. Lettuce leaves.

[POLICEMAN *tries to drag him up.*]

ROMAINE. Leave him alone.

SOLLY [*in a gibberish codding way*]. Lettuce alone—leave us alone—they're my lettuce leaves.

POLICEMAN. Stand up.

SOLLY. Oh alright. Bloody law has to interfere.

POLICEMAN. Where did you half-inch these from? Whew! Quite a fortune—talk yourself out of this!

SOLLY. I talked myself into this. This is my personal fortune. I can explain. I won it.

POLICEMAN. What? On tiddlewinks?

SOLLY. No, on Pontoon.

WOMAN. He's a liar. He's a villain.

POLICEMAN. Alright, come along with me. We'll sort it out down at the station.

SOLLY. Come on, Romaine. Whither I goest thou must go.

ROMAINE. I've never been in a police station before.

SOLLY. Better get used to it.

JOE. One minute, Officer, may I have a word with you?

ROMAINE. Solly, tell him the truth. The fact is we're running away, we're madly in love.

POLICEMAN. Just you two wait there and don't move [*To* JOE] Now what is it?

JOE. Don't you recognise her? She's the missing heiress. Don't you read your *Express*?

POLICEMAN. What do you mean—heiress?

JOE. Listen, just keep them here for a while. Her old man's on his way to claim his daughter and to pay me the reward.

POLICEMAN [*loudly to all*]. I've got my duty to perform. There's some dirty business going on with all this money. I'm taking them into custody.

PROSTITUTE. What's the matter with you this morning,

George? Why are you so narked? Didn't you get your dropsy from the girls last night?

POLICEMAN. Now you shut up—or I'll run you in also.

SOLLY. Please, Constable—a word in your ear. [*He leads* POLICEMAN *to one side.*] This is not a bribe, it's just a present or a loan. Just turn the other way, will you? I've got a boat to catch. [SOLLY *offers him a wad.*]

POLICEMAN. Right! Bribery and corruption as well! You're for it, my lad. [*The* POLICEMAN *takes the money, puts it in his pocket and takes* SOLLY *by the scruff of his neck.*]

SOLLY. In that case give me my money back.

POLICEMAN. What money?

[MORRY. MILLIE, SARAH, ALAN, MR. *and* MRS. FINK *and* MELVIN *enter hurriedly.*]

MILLIE. Oh darling! [*She rushes to* ROMAINE.] How are you? Where have you been, you bad girl? I could murder you. You alright darling?

ROMAINE. I'm so pleased to see you, Mummy.

MORRY. Hello, Solly. How's tricks?

SOLLY. Complicated.

MILLIE. Fancy running away like that, where have you been?

ROMAINE. Lying low.

MILLIE. Naughty girl.

SOLLY. You said it.

ROMAINE [*sings*]. "Ah, sweet mystery of life, at last I found you." [*She kisses all the family on the cheek.*]

MILLIE. You'll have to marry him now. You're ruined otherwise. [*To* SOLLY] You'll have to marry her.

[SOLLY *kisses* MILLIE, *who smiles.*]

SOLLY. Who's disagreeing? Mother.

MORRY. Congratulations.

[*General back slapping.*]

ALAN. Wish you joy.

FINK. Please God, by you.

MRS. FINK. May we only meet on holidays.

SARAH. I'm so happy for both of you.

MILLIE. Isn't it wonderful?

PROSTITUTE. Here comes the bride. . . .

WOMAN. I love a wedding!

[*Everyone is joyful except the* POLICEMAN.]

SOLLY. Ladies and gentlemen: I'm delighted to announce my betrothal to Romaine and I'm going to make it all worth your while. I'm marrying a fortune—I mean I'm so fortunate. A priceless beauty. A jewel. A gem.

[*Everyone cheers and* JOE *brings out some drinks and everyone drinks.*]

POLICEMAN. Hold on! What is all this? Is all that money his legal property? Didn't he steal it from you?

MORRY. Steal from me? He'd have a hard job.

POLICEMAN. There's something fishy here.

SOLLY. Probably your socks.

POLICEMAN. I'm not letting you get away with this. There's some conspiracy somewhere—abduction, seduction, larceny— Come on, I'll get to the bottom of this if it kills me.

SOLLY. Now listen, what have you got against me?

POLICEMAN. You're guilty. You're a common crook. Society ain't safe with you around.

SOLLY. We'll hear what society has to say. Nobody has anything against me. Now listen folks. [*He addresses the people around him.*] You judge me dispassionately. I'll make it worth your while. You stick by me and I'll stick by you. Be my tribunal. Roll up, roll up one and all—am I guilty or not guilty?

WOMAN. Not guilty—a nice boy. Look at his eyes, so kind.

RITA. Not guilty. I hope you'll come and visit us sometime.

JOE. Not guilty. I'll make you a nice suit. Saville Row cut—Mile-end Road cost.

FINK. Not guilty. A potential Mason of the highest order—an influential custodian of property.

MRS. FINK. Not guilty—a nice boy. Thoughtful.

ALAN. Not guilty. Blood is thicker than water.

SARAH. Not guilty. He makes my sister happy.

MELVIN. Not guilty. He's a sportsman.

MILLIE. Not guilty. How could he be? He's my future son-in-law.

MORRY. Not guilty. Officer, you haven't a leg to stand on.

SOLLY. You're wasting your time, Constable. Back to your beat now, my good man.

POLICEMAN. Alright, but I'm keeping my eye on you.

[*He goes off and everyone cheers.*]

SOLLY. Whenever you want to get the better of them call them Constable or my good man. [*To* MORRY] How can you forgive me?

MORRY. You showed me the way.

SOLLY. But I must confess to you now, I'm not a rabbi.

MORRY. I've known that for days now.

SOLLY. You know?

MORRY. Suddenly I came to my senses but in such a way that I see more clearly now than ever before.

SOLLY. But you did believe that I was a rabbi, admit it. I'm a bloody marvellous actor.

MORRY. Yes, I believed. You see, I'm a simple man and you swore on the Bible.

SOLLY. Aren't you disappointed that you're not the messiah?

MORRY. In a way; I just wanted to make people happy. But now maybe I can be a saviour in another way. I was bored with life until you came, but now I can feel a miracle working inside me. I'm going to travel and relax from now on and try and do some good with my money.

SOLLY. And what about my money? This money?

MORRY. It's yours. Call it my dowry for Romaine. Besides, you earned it. You cured my backache. Hundreds of doctors treated me for years and fleeced me blind and still I suffered. You worked a miracle.

SARAH. It was an accident.

MORRY. Call it what you like. The point is the pain is gone.

SOLLY. But I must admit, Morry—I've been a bad boy. Can you forgive me for my past?

MORRY. Easily. What about my financial advisers? My solicitor and accountant? And my branch managers? They've been diddling me for years. You're an amateur compared to them.

SOLLY. I'm not an amateur—I won't have you say that.

MILLIE. Relax, Solly, let's all be friends. You're one of the family now.

[*She kisses him.*]

SOLLY. I'm so glad you like me now. You had me worried at first.

MILLIE. No, I admit that I didn't understand you but I feel so much better since you came into our lives. I'm a vegetarian now—on your advice, and it's working wonders. I've lost two pounds in three days—I look so young, don't I? Besides you've got such a big dowry from Morry, we must keep it in the family—so welcome.

SOLLY. Mother! At last I've got a Mum of my own. My Mum took one look at me and run away.

MILLIE. No more lies now. We want you to look after the business—to take complete charge.

SOLLY. What?

MORRY. It's true. If you can't lick them, make them join you. With you in the business nothing can stop us.

SOLLY. You said it. You're very smart. I'll make it the greatest shoe concern in the universe! I can sell anything, even your shoes. "Swartz's everlasting immortal soles." I can sell binoculars to a blind man, roller skates to a cripple. Romaine, Romaine, I'm the happiest guy in the world. [*He cuddles her but she doesn't react.*]

SARAH. Solly, you're as good as gold.

[*Everyone slaps him on the back.*]

MELVIN. I would like to thank you, Solly, for helping me so much.

SOLLY. You as well? I'm so glad I helped. But tell me how?

MELVIN. I took your advice. The other evening at the Maccabee games I took the plunge and spoke to a girl, and now we're mad about each other. We're going to Israel next week—going to get married. And then we're going to start a new Kibbutz—devoted entirely to the propagation of sports and English sportsmanship. You know, cricket, polo, and badminton. She's lovely. What a figure, and can she throw the discus!

MORRY. Come on then, let's all go home and prepare for more weddings.

SOLLY. I feel like dancing. [*He dances with* MILLIE *and soon everyone is dancing round and round as* JOE *plays the mouth organ.*] Come on Romaine, back to Golders Green, back to a life of luxury and love. [*She was the only one not dancing.*]

ROMAINE. I'm not going back.

[SOLLY *leaves* MILLIE. *He wonders if he heard right. Meanwhile the rest of the cast dances around—in and out of the houses—where they drink and eat.*]

SOLLY. What do you mean, not going back?

ROMAINE. I love you, Solly. I want to go forward with you.

SOLLY. But everything's arranged, everything's marvellous. Your family approve of me.

ROMAINE. Well, I don't approve of them. I want us to start afresh—without their lousy money. For you and I to go off into the world with nothing except our love.

SOLLY. Oh God, you've been reading *True Romances*.

ROMAINE. Darling, I want us to start from scratch.

SOLLY. I've been scratching all my life. Sweetheart, I want us to have a little money to start with.

ROMAINE. I want you to work for me—to prove you love me.

SOLLY. Work? That's something I've done without for thirty years and I'm damned if I'm going to start now. You're mad. I agree let's not go back with them—we'll just go as we are—take the money and ourselves, that's all.

ROMAINE. It's the money or me.

SOLLY. Why do you see everything in black or white?

ROMAINE. What do you want—the money or me?

SOLLY. I want both. Don't you see I was born for luxury?

ROMAINE. Well I've had enough of it.

SOLLY. Come on, darling, I love you, you know I do.

ROMAINE. You work so hard at not working, you may as well work and have a holiday. It's good-bye then.

SOLLY. Good-bye? What? What about last night and the night before? What about the things you whispered in the Three Nuns Hotel?

ROMAINE. No! No! No! I don't trust you—I never should. I should have listened to my Mum.

SOLLY. Alright darling, come with me, now.

ROMAINE. No, it's too late, you're hoping to get that money later on. I don't want you any more.

SOLLY. Alright then, I'll take the money.

[*The family have now stopped dancing.*]

ROMAINE. I'm not going with him.

SOLLY. She's mad.

ROMAINE. He doesn't love me for myself.

MILLIE. Oh darling, you sure?

ROMAINE. Oh Mummy, I don't want a life of poverty, I want to come home with you— [*She weeps.*] He just wanted, that was all—after he ruined me.

MILLIE. I don't like my Dolly unhappy, and on such a happy day.

SOLLY. But it's all crazy. I do want her! Morry, please try and persuade her—

MORRY. Do you want him, Romaine? Make up your mind.

ROMAINE. No! I never want to see him again. I don't want him or any man—you can't trust them.

SOLLY. Morry, as her father it's your duty to make her see sense. You know I'm right for her.

MORRY. Sorry, my boy. She must make her own decisions— I'm not going to interfere. I learned from you how to be tolerant. Thanks.

SOLLY. Alright then, I'll go—I'll take my money and go.

MILLIE. Oh no you don't! That's my money—Romaine's money, for her dowry, and as she's not getting married, I'll keep it for her.

ROMAINE. I don't want it.

SOLLY. Well I do. I earned it, you said so.

MILLIE. Well, it's mine now.

SOLLY. But I made you all so happy—you said so.

MORRY. I know, but women—what can you do with them? Tell you what I'll do—to save any arguments—I'll send it to Israel when Melvin goes, and with it, maybe they'll plant avenues of orange trees. I might even live to see them grow —the way they work out there. Well, that's that. Goodbye, my boy—thanks for everything. If you're ever passing, drop in for a chat.

SOLLY. A chat! A chat! I say, can you lend me a fiver?

MORRY. Sorry, I don't keep any loose change on me. Come on, everyone. Come on, Fink.

[*They start to move off.*]

FINK. I told you, Morry, never to trust that man.

MRS. FINK. Herbert, shut up.

MILLIE. Feeling better, darling?

ROMAINE. Smashing; what's for lunch?

SARAH. Chicken, casseroled, and Neopolitan ice cream to follow.

MELVIN. Goodbye, Solly. If you ever want to become a pioneer—and play hockey in the Holy Land, look me up.

MORRY. Come on, everyone—liven up. Goodbye, Solly—all the best. . . .

[*They are gone and now the other people go in.*]

SOLLY [*forlorn. Looks around, picks up a cigar butt*]. I made them all happy and I didn't earn a bean and I let a fortune and a fat girl slip through my fingers at the same time. What am I going to do for cash? There you are, you try and help and that's the thanks you get. What a life. The world's nothing to write home about. Believe me, if we can't help ourselves how are we going to help others? One thing I'm sure of, I'm not going to work. No, work's too much like an occupation—work's alright for the working class, but for me—it's got to be something better. I must think of something—something really spectacular this time. . . . I've got it! No, no [*He walks around the stage.*] One minute— No. I'm bloody fed up. You can't con an honest coin these days. . . . [*He sits down, picks up some fag ends, rolls a cigarette and becomes deep in thought as*

**THE CURTAIN FALLS**

# THE WRITERS AND THEIR PLAYS

WILDE, OSCAR FINGALL O'FLAHERTIE WILLS—1856–1900 (publication dates)

*Vera, or The Nihilists, a Drama, in a Prologue and Four Acts*, 1880 (privately printed); *The Duchess of Padua, a Tragedy of the XVI Century, Written in Paris in the XIX Century*, 1883 (privately printed); *Lady Windemere's Fan, a Play About a Good Woman*, 1893; *A Woman of No Importance*, 1894; *An Ideal Husband*, 1899; *The Importance of Being Earnest, a Trivial Comedy for Serious People*, 1899; *Salomé*, 1894; *A Florentine Tragedy*, 1908; *For Love of the King*, 1922.

SHAW, GEORGE BERNARD—1856–1950 (completion dates)

*Widowers' Houses*, 1892; *The Philanderer*, 1893; *Mrs. Warren's Profession*, 1893; *Arms and the Man*, 1894; *Candida*, 1894; *The Man of Destiny*, 1895; *You Never Can Tell*, 1896; *The Devil's Disciple*, 1896; *Caesar and Cleopatra*, 1898; *Captain Brassbound's Conversion*, 1899; *The Admirable Bashville*, 1901; *Man and Superman*, 1903; *John Bull's Other Island*, 1904; *How He Lied to Her Husband*, 1904; *Major Barbara*, 1907; *Passion, Poison, and Petrifaction, or The Fatal Gazogene*, 1905; *The Doctor's Dilemma*, 1906; *The Interlude at the Playhouse*, 1907; *Getting Married*, 1908; *The Shewing-up of Blanco Posnet*, 1909; *Press Cuttings*, 1909; *The Fascinating Foundling*, 1909; *The Glimpse of Reality*, 1909; *Misalliance*, 1910; *The Dark Lady of the Sonnets*, 1910; *Fanny's First Play*, 1911; *Androcles and the Lion*, 1912; *Overruled*, 1912; *Pygmalion*, 1912; *Great Catherine*, 1913; *The Music Cure*, 1914; *O'Flaherty, V.C.*, 1915; *The Inca of Perusalem*, 1916; *Augustus Does His Bit*, 1916; *Annajanska, the Bolshevik Empress*, 1916; *Heartbreak House*, 1919; *Back to Methuselah*, 1920; *Jitta's Atonement*, 1922; *Saint Joan*, 1923; *The Apple Cart*, 1929; *Too True to Be Good*, 1931; *Village Wooing*, 1933; *On the Rocks*, 1933; *The Simpleton of the Unexpected Isles*, 1934; *The Six of Calais*, 1934; *The Millionairess*, 1935; *Cymbeline Refinished*, 1937;

*Geneva*, 1938; *In Good King Charles's Golden Days*, 1939; *Buoy ant Billions*, 1948; *Shakes Versus Shav* (puppet play), 1949; *Far fetched Fables*, 1950; *Why She Would Not*, 1950 (unfinished).

## GALSWORTHY, JOHN—1867–1933 (publication dates)

*The Silver Box*, 1906; *Joy*, 1907; *Strife*, 1909; *Justice*, 1910; *The Little Dream*, 1911; *The Pigeon*, 1912; *The Eldest Son*, 1912 *The Fugitive*, 1913; *The Mob*, 1914; *Hallmarked*, 1914; *A Bit o Love*, 1915; *The Little Man*, 1915; *The Foundations*, 1917; *The Skin Game*, 1920; *Defeat*, 1920; *The First and the Last*, 1921 *Punch and Go*, 1921; *A Family Man*, 1921; *The Sun*, 1921 *Windows*, 1922; *Loyalties*, 1922; *The Forest*, 1924; *Old English* 1924; *The Show*, 1925; *Escape*, 1926; *Exiled*, 1929; *The Roof* 1929.

## BARRIE, SIR JAMES MATTHEW—1860–1937 (publi cation dates)

*Richard Savage, a Play in Four Acts* (with H. B. Marriott Wat son), 1891 (privately printed); *The Little Minister*, 1898 (pri vately printed); *The Wedding Guest, a Play in Four Acts*, 1900 *Walker, London, a Farcical Comedy in Three Acts*, 1907; *Quality Street, a Comedy in Four Acts*, 1913; *The Admirable Crichton* 1914; *Der Tag*, 1914; *Half Hours: Pantaloon, Rosalind, The Twelve-Pound Look, The Will*, 1914; *Shakespeare's Legacy*, 1916 (privately printed); *Who was Sarah Findlay?*, 1917 (privately printed); *Barbara's Wedding*, 1918; *The New Word*, 1918; *The Old Lady Shows Her Medals*, 1918; *A Well-Remembered Voice* 1918; *What Every Woman Knows*, 1918; *Alice-Sit-By-The-Fire* 1919; *A Kiss For Cinderella*, 1920; *Dear Brutus*, 1923; *Mary Rose*, 1924; *Shall We Join the Ladies?*, 1927; *Peter Pan, or The Boy Who Would Not Grow Up*, 1928; *Seven Women*, 1930; *The Boy David*, 1938.

## KOPS, BERNARD—1926– (publication dates)

*The Hamlet of Stepney Green*, 1959; *The Dream of Peter Mann* 1960; *Enter Solly Gold*, 1961; *Home Sweet Honeycomb*, 1964 *The Lemmings*, 1964.

THE WRITERS AND THEIR PLAYS

# SELECTED BIBLIOGRAPHY

## General

ALLSOP, KENNETH, *The Angry Decade*, London, 1958
BEERBOHM, MAX, *Around Theatres*, New York, 1954
DOWNER, ALAN S., *The British Drama*, New York, 1950
GASSNER, JOHN, *The Theatre in Our Times*, New York, 1954
HUDSON, LYNTON, *The English Stage, 1850–1950*, London, 1951
KNIGHT, G. WILSON, *The Golden Labyrinth*, London, 1961
NICOLL, ALLARDYCE, *British Drama*, rev. ed., London, 1947
TYNAN, KENNETH, *Curtains*, New York, 1961

## Oscar Wilde

BENTLEY, ERIC, *The Playwright As Thinker*, rev. ed., New York, 1955
GIDE, ANDRÉ, *Oscar Wilde: a Study*, trans. by S. Mason, New York, 1905
McCARTHY, MARY, *Sights and Spectacles: Theatre Chronicles 1937–1956*, New York, 1957
POPKIN, HENRY, "Introduction," *The Importance of Being Earnest*, Chandler Editions in Drama, San Francisco, 1961

## George Bernard Shaw

BENTLEY, ERIC, *Bernard Shaw*, rev. ed., New York, 1957
BRUSTEIN, ROBERT, *The Theatre of Revolt*, New York, 1964
GASSNER, JOHN, *The Theatre in Our Times*, New York, 1954
HENDERSON, ARCHIBALD, *George Bernard Shaw: Man of the Century*, New York, 1956
KRONENBERGER, LOUIS, ed., *George Bernard Shaw, a Critical Survey*, Cleveland and New York, 1953

## John Galsworthy

COATS, ROBERT, *John Galsworthy As a Dramatic Artist*, New York, 1926
LAMM, MARTIN, *Modern Drama*, Oxford, 1952

MARROT, H. V., *Life and Letters of John Galsworthy*, New York
   1936
OULD, HERMAN, *John Galsworthy*, London, 1934
SCHOLIT, LEON, *John Galsworthy: a Survey*, New York, 1929

*James Barrie*

DARLINGTON, WILLIAM A., *J. M. Barrie*, London, 1938
MACKAIL, DENNIS G., *Barrie: the Story of J.M.B.*, London, 1941
PHELPS, WILLIAM LYON, *Essays on Modern Dramatists*, New
   York, 1921
WALKLEY, ARTHUR B., *Drama and Life*, London, 1907

*Bernard Kops*

JONES, MERVYN, "Introduction," *The Dream of Peter Mann*, Lon-
   don, 1960
KITCHIN, LAWRENCE, *Mid-Century Drama*, London, 1960
POPKIN, HENRY, ed., *The New British Drama*, New York, 1964
TAYLOR, JOHN RUSSELL, *The Angry Theatre*, New York, 1962

*D-12461
5-05

FR
1272
C82m

Corrigan, Robert Willoughby, 1927-      comp.
    Masterpieces of the modern English theatre.
Edited by Robert W. Corrigan.   New York,
Collier Books [1967]
    476p.   18cm.   (Masterpieces of the modern
theatre)

    Bibliography: p.475-476.

1.English drama-20th cent.   I.Title.

317006